Docufictions

Docufictions

Essays on the Intersection of Documentary and Fictional Filmmaking

Edited by GARY D. RHODES
and JOHN PARRIS SPRINGER

McFarland & Company, Inc., Publishers
Jefferson, North Carolina, and London

ALSO BY GARY D. RHODES
AND FROM MCFARLAND

Horror at the Drive-In:
Essays in Popular Americana (2003)

White Zombie: Anatomy of a Horror Film (2001)

Lugosi: His Life in Films, on Stage,
and in the Hearts of Horror Lovers (1997)

LIBRARY OF CONGRESS CATALOGUING-IN-PUBLICATION DATA

Docufictions : essays on the intersection of
documentary and fictional filmmaking /
edited by Gary D. Rhodes and John Parris Springer
p.   cm.
Includes bibliographical references and index.

ISBN-13: 978-0-7864-2184-8
ISBN-10: 0-7864-2184-3
(softcover : 50# alkaline paper) ∞

1. Documentary-style films—History and criticism.
I. Rhodes, Gary Don, 1972–   II. Springer, John Parris, 1955–
PN1995.9.D62D63   2006   070.1'8 — dc22   2005012767

British Library cataloguing data are available

Cover images (clockwise from upper left): The Great Train Robbery (1903),
Aleita, Queen of Mars (1924), A Sea of Fragrant Snow (1934),
The Osbournes television series (2002–2004)

Manufactured in the United States of America

McFarland & Company, Inc., Publishers
Box 611, Jefferson, North Carolina 28640
www.mcfarlandpub.com

In memory of Alan Hoyt

Acknowledgments

I would like to thank Prof. Tom Lutz of the University of Iowa, who provided valuable feedback on early drafts of my contribution to this volume. I would also like to thank my co-editor Gary Rhodes, with whom I share scholarly interests and obsessions too numerous to list, for his friendship, insight, and generosity. Many friends and colleagues at the University of Central Oklahoma provided useful suggestions and support when I presented segments of my research at the Annual Liberal Arts Faculty Colloquium in 2003. As always, my deepest debt of gratitude goes to my wife, Laura, and our children, Justin, Clare, Elliot, and Nora. In different ways they have all shared the burden of my research and have helped to make the work worth doing.

John Parris Springer

I extend many thanks to Michael Lee, who provided much inspiration at the onset of this book. I hope he continues to shed light on the otherwise quite cinematically dim University of Oklahoma. I'd also like to thank longterm friends and traveling companions Tom Weaver and Alex Webb for assistance in finding various still images that appear herein. To John Parris Springer, I have a hard time expressing my joy at being able to work closely with such a dear friend and mentor. And of course, heartfelt appreciation goes to Marina McDonnell, love of my life.

Gary D. Rhodes

Contents

Introduction

During the 1920s, the turbulent political and intellectual environment of the newly formed Soviet Union gave rise to a burst of critical and theoretical discussion concerning the role of the cinema in the cultural life of the new country. Filmmaking in Russia had followed the aesthetic path of the American industry in its emphasis on narrative, producing a cinema dependent upon literary and theatrical models of representation. But would such a traditional approach to the new medium, one with stylistic and ideological roots in such bourgeois forms of representation as the "well-made play" and the 19th-century realist novel, be adequate to convey the new ideas and energies of a revolutionary society? Such concerns led filmmakers and theorists to search for alternative approaches to film that could challenge the dominant narrative paradigm.

The most important figure in these debates was the avant-garde filmmaker and pioneer documentarian Dziga Vertov, whose *Kino Pravda* (*Cinema Truth*) series provided one of the first indications of a creative new path for Soviet film. This was to be a cinema of the recorded fact, of life unscripted, and Vertov rejected any attempt to introduce fictional or narrative elements as rearguard. "Three-fourths of the human race is stupefied by the opium of bourgeois film-dramas," he wrote, and the alternative to such fictionalized mediations of the real world was to be found in documentary film practice.[1] For Vertov, the cinema rose to its full potentials as a medium only when it "was built on the organization of documentary footage recorded by the camera." Narrative cinema, which was "founded upon the organization of acted footage recorded by the camera," could only be considered "a phenomenon of a *secondary, theatrical* nature."[2]

Such debates ultimately came to influence the cultural policies of the Soviet government, which, following the interest in film expressed by the Soviet leader V.I. Lenin, subsidized film production and created state film schools to train personnel for the new industry. Lenin himself preferred the educational content found in newsreels and documentaries, and argued for the establishment of a "fixed ratio between entertainment pictures and scientific [documentary] ones." He added: "If you have good newsreels, serious educational films, then it doesn't matter if some useless film, of the more or less usual sort, is shown to attract an audience."[3] What came to be known as the "Leninist Ratio" was a call to balance the production of fictional nar-

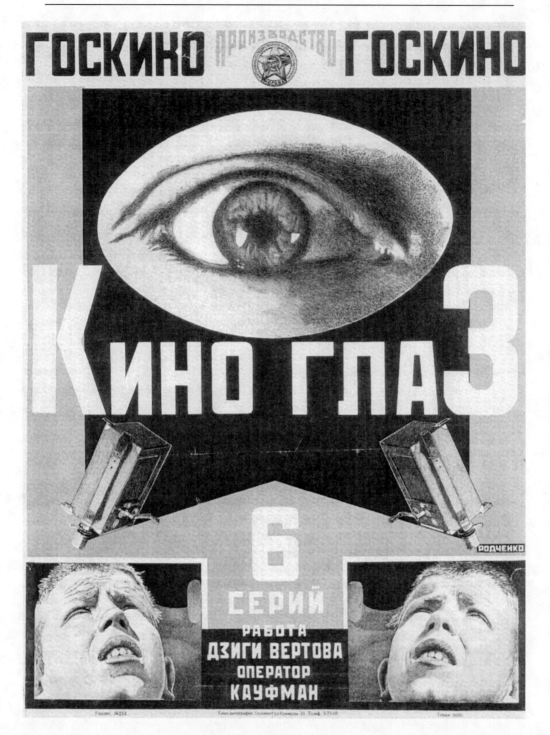

For Vertov, the cinema reaches its full potential as a medium only when built "on the organization of documentary footage recorded by the camera." *Kino-Glaz* movie poster, 1924.

ratives with an equal or greater production of documentary films in the Soviet Union. However, Soviet audiences proved as enamored of their movie stars and film dramas as Americans and Europeans, and Vertov's call for a revolutionary documentary cinema went largely ignored at the time.

Arguably "nonfiction" film had dominance over "fiction" in the cinema of the 1890s, at least in terms of numbers, but that privileged position quickly eroded, more quickly indeed than many early filmmakers foresaw. Cinematic production shifted towards the fictional narratives of, say, a Méliès and away from the "actualities" of Lumière. The distinction between the fictional narrative film and the documentary was vigorously maintained throughout most of the twentieth century by filmmakers, critics, and viewers alike. The "documentary tradition" developed side by side but in the shadow of the more commercially successful "feature film" industry, exemplified by classical Hollywood cinema. Following its early appearance, the predominantly nonfiction cinema faded and would not return in the United States or indeed any other nation.

As a result, twentieth-century critical theories of cinema developed around the given of narrative — the dominance of fiction films that are scripted, staged, and performed — rather than a notion of the cinema as a record of the unscripted social "fact." Such emphases in critical thinking, however, inevitably produce certain blind spots. For instance, traditional histories of film tended to ignore the frequent intermingling of documentary and fictional devices in narrative films which constitutes a persistent tendency in the cinema from its very beginning. As a visual medium based upon a photographic representation of the world, the cinema has always been uniquely suited to such ambiguities regarding the fictional and factual status of its representations. During the 1970s and 1980s, when academic film studies was establishing itself as a discipline, the dichotomy between narrative and documentary uses of film was generally preserved by the leading theoretical perspectives of neo–Formalism, post–Structuralism, and psychoanalysis. It was not until the last quarter of the twentieth century, under the influence of television and other new media, that filmmakers (and then critics and theorists) began questioning the old dichotomies that had held narrative and documentary film apart for so long. The rise of the docudrama, the self-reflexive documentary, and the mockumentary, each of which is chronicled in this volume, all signaled the breakdown of the stable critical dichotomy which had for so long kept fictional narrative and documentary film in separate analytical boxes. Yet this is hardly a critical point that has been resolved and put to rest for all time.

From a variety of perspectives, the essays which comprise *Docufictions* are all involved in an ongoing cultural project. Roughly analogous to the "Leninist Ratio," that project seeks to redress a crucial critical oversight by recognizing the multiple ways in which documentary concerns and techniques have influenced and been taken up by mainstream, narrative cinema; indeed, how on some level all film and media texts function as both records (of what is placed in front of the camera) and representations (of the "real"). Vertov's belief in the political and ideological superiority of documentary, no less than Hollywood's commitment to a particular kind of narrative cinema, inevitably meant that documentary and fictional narrative film would be seen as cultural opposites whose essential differences defined irreconcilable stylistic and rhetorical ends. But in true dialectical fashion, late twentieth-century film culture has given rise to a rich corpus of hybrid texts which show, in increasingly self-conscious, even *generic* ways, the creative merging and synthesis of documentary and fictional narrative cinema. What the essays in *Docufictions* persuasively demonstrate is that the segregation of documentary and narrative, which held sway for so long as critical orthodoxy, is unsupported by either the historical record or close textual analysis of particular films.

This collection of essays examines the multiple intersections between documentary uses of cinema, which aim at an objective recording of the world, and fictional uses of cinema, which rely on the forms and devices of narrative to construct a representation of the "real." To map the various permutations of this highly complex network of cinematic forms and techniques, rhetorical strategies and aesthetic choices, we offer a structural definition based on a distinction between documentary and fictional narrative cinema and their respective forms and contents.

On the one hand there is documentary form (style), which includes historically specific devices such as the authoritative voiceover narration found in newsreels such as the *March of Time*; the use of on-camera interviews; forms of evidence such as archival photographs, diagrams, maps, and charts; and such visual characteristics as handheld camera, the hallmark of a particular movement in documentary film history—*cinéma vérité*. On the level of content, documentaries can be said to be films about *real* people, places, and events, and their stated aim is to record or document a segment of the real world.

Fictional narratives, on the other hand, employ their own historically determined forms and devices of representation derived from literature and the theater, including a more conscious attention to emplotment and characterization and a concern for the thematic or ideological significance of these elements organized through narrative structures and conventions of genre. On the level of content, fictional narratives involve the use of *invented* people, places, and events, even when such people and events are depicted as belonging to the real world (Realism).

A structural mapping of the interrelationships between documentary and fictional narrative film involves an interplay among four basic categories: documentary form, documentary content, fictional form, and fictional content. The relations among these categories can be diagrammed as follows:

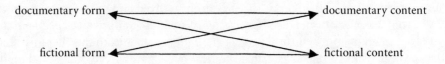

Such a model helps us to define the subject matter of this book through a series of combinations:

documentary form + documentary content = documentary
documentary form + fictional content = mockumentary
fictional form + documentary content = docudrama
fictional form + fictional content = fiction

The essays in this volume focus on the two middle forms—the mockumentary and the docudrama—in which documentary and fictional materials are intentionally combined, merged, and synthesized, leading to hybrid forms which, we would argue, constitute a diverse but pervasive strand in film history and practice. And given the prevalence of such hybrid forms in contemporary media culture—the increasing tendency to foreground such syntheses as a self-conscious aesthetic strategy— we are proposing a new term, *docufictions*, as a way of naming an insufficiently analyzed tendency in film practice that has produced an increasingly large and varied canon of texts.

The initial impetus for this collection came from what seems to us be a cultural phenomenon of great interest and importance: the rise of the "mockumentary" as a film and televisual form. At first glance the genre of the mockumentary would seem to be the postmodern cinematic form *par excellence*, based as it is on rhetorical modes of parody, pastiche, and self-referential irony. In practice, the category of the mockumentary has been quite varied and diverse, encompassing such works as the genre-defining *This Is Spinal Tap!* (1984), episodes of the TV series *M.A.S.H.*, the independently produced, cult horror film *The Blair Witch Project* (1999), and MTV's *The Real World* and E! Entertainment Television's *Hollywood's Mysteries and Scandals*, to name a few. Such reality-based programs utilize the devices of documentary (voiceover narrations, on-camera interviews, reenactments) to lend the appearance of documentary authenticity to events that are actually staged and scripted in ways that barely conceal the marketing and programming concerns that motivate their production. Such fundamental variations in the generic field of the "mockumentary" suggest that there is much work to be done simply defining basic terms and conventions before we can proceed to a general analysis and history of the docufiction genre (see Lipkin, Paget, and Roscoe's essay "Docudrama and Mock-Documentary: Defining Terms, Proposing Canons").

Perhaps the dominant notion of a "mockumentary" involves a recognition by the viewer that the standard conventions of documentary film are being placed in the service of a satirical or ironic examination of a fictional subject (e.g., the heavy metal band "Spinal Tap"). Such films are profoundly intertextual on several levels. To be read correctly, *Spinal Tap* relies upon the viewer's knowledge of both the tradition of documentary filmmaking and the social attitudes and lifestyles of the heavy metal music scene. To fully understand the film (and grasp its humor) the viewer must be able to recognize and keep both of these areas of culture discourse in mind in order to appreciate how skillfully the film serves as a metacommentary on them. According to our mapping of critical terms, the film presents a fictionalized subject in the style of a documentary, making it a classical example of the mockumentary.

But a second type of synthesis between fiction and fact is possible, one that has a much longer history in film practice and in film culture. This is the idea of a film as a dramatization or reenactment—the docudrama—a fabricated *recreation* of actual people or events. Such an approach usually does not imply an ironic or satirical attitude towards the subject; on the contrary, such knowing irony would destroy the illusion of facts being "documented" and "truths" being told. Moreover, such a knowing, self-conscious perspective would undercut the often heavy-handed ideological messages of such films. In these texts the devices of fictional narrative are used to render more vivid the conflict and drama of the "real" subject. The docudrama represents an attempt to present factual material through the organizing aesthetics of fiction and narrative, and inevitably it utilizes certain forms of narrative patterning and visual composition that facilitate audience identification with the "characters"— even when these characters are well-known historical figures. Docudramas thus move away from the presumed objectivity of documentary and closer towards the techniques of narrative fiction.

The essays in *Docufictions* all attempt to examine the insufficiently theorized relationships between narrative fiction and documentary filmmaking, and in so doing they offer some significant rethinking of film history and criticism. For the authors in this collection, these intersections begin literally at the beginning of the cinema, blurring the lines between fact and fiction. *Blacksmith Scene* (1893), Edison and Dickson's first publicly exhibited film, purports to show exactly that: three blacksmiths working and enjoying a beer. But of course the men captured on film were not professional blacksmiths but Edison employees, and the film was staged and shot at the Edison laboratory. Examples of such fabrications continue famously through a series of the then-popular Spanish-American War films that used miniatures sets and model ships to recreate sea battles, which were vigorously marketed as authentic depictions.[4]

This willingness to stage and recreate events for the documentary and newsreel camera continued through the silent and sound era: Much of Robert Flaherty's *Nanook of the North*, for example, was staged for the camera (see Jared Green's essay in this volume); Depression-era newsreels recreated the robberies and getaways of famous outlaws; MGM even produced a series of phony newsreels in 1934 reporting that California was being invaded by the nation's destitute and poor in order to defeat the socialist Upton Sinclair who was running for governor of the state.[5] Such fakery was so well known that it could be openly lampooned in the 1938 MGM film *Too Hot to Handle*, in which Clark Gable played a newsreel cameraman who routinely stages the stories he reports. The very act of cinematic observation

An early use of reenactment featuring miniatures can be seen in this Edison film record of the *Bombardment of the Taku Forts, by the Allied Fleets* (1900).

involves an inevitable encounter with Heisenberg's "uncertainty principle"—the idea that the presence of the observer always alters the behavior of the observed. Filmmakers had long known that the motion picture camera could inspire less-than-authentic behavior. See, for example, Charlie Chaplin as the tramp desperately trying to "act" for the newsreel cameraman in *Kid Auto Races at Venice* (1912), or the moment when Bela Lugosi as General Petronovich alters his demeanor dramatically when filmed by a newsreel cameraman in the W.C. Fields movie *International House* (1933). In moments like this, we see fictional cinema foregrounding the inadequacies of the "nonfiction" camera decades before a term like mockumentary emerges.

The connections between the two worlds of fiction and nonfiction film proceeded on another front as well, as commercial narrative films increasingly incorporated the forms and techniques of nonfiction filmmaking. This occurs most famously in *Citizen Kane*, which can lay some claim to being the first mockumentary film—not only because of the "News on the March" segment, but because the whole apparatus of the off-screen interviewer is closely akin to documentary. However, the film's subject, Charles Foster Kane, is an invention of Orson Welles and Herman Mankiewicz, loosely based on the historical figure of William Randolph Hearst.

The fictional film foregrounds the inadequacies of the "nonfiction camera" in this example of Bela Lugosi (far left) in ***International House*** (1933).

This creative blurring of the distinctions between fiction and nonfiction can be detected in such later films as the voiceover in Stanley Kubrick's *Dr. Strangelove* (1964), the intertitle dates of boxing matches in Martin Scorsese's *Raging Bull* (1980), and the use of on-camera interviews in Warren Beatty's *Reds* (1981). In numerous ways *Citizen Kane* predicts the transfer of documentary aesthetics to fiction film that will become increasingly commonplace. The use of different film stocks, the scratches and aging added to images in the "News on the March" sequence, and the placement of the fictional Kane with actual historical figures like Hitler are devices subsequently used in the films of Woody Allen, Oliver Stone, Roger Zemeckis, and many others.

More clearly than anywhere else, perhaps, this synthesis between fiction and nonfiction crystallizes in a single shot in *Citizen Kane* when the elderly newspaper magnate, now wheelchair bound, is photographed over a fence with a handheld camera. The liberation of the camera from the tripod in the world of documentary had hardly begun and would not fully manifest itself until the 1960s. But here we have a single, very prophetic shot that in some ways signals the beginning of a contemporary dialogue between nonfiction and fictional cinema. This dialogue flowers in the films of later decades in which the presence of handheld camera becomes a signifier of a "real" moment captured on film, even when that moment has been completely staged and scripted.

And it was the increasing use of what could be "false" signifiers of reality, like handheld camera, that allowed filmmakers to extend the vocabulary of film language by encompassing the use of mixed media and video to suggest in the format of film what is "more real" than film itself. Oliver Stone's use of 8mm film stocks, for instance, in which larger grain character seems suggestive of larger ties to reality, suggests that nonfiction is tethered to specific types of visual representation. Even HBO's *Larry Sanders Show* photographed its fictional late-night talk show host in video stock for his "on air" look and film stock for his "off air" time. The imbrication of nonfiction and fictional elements in contemporary film and media extends from genres and character types (such as the fictional talk-show host played by Martin Mull on the 1970s series *Fernwood 2night*) to sophisticated manipulations of image technology tied to cultural codes of verisimilitude.

The synthesis between fiction and nonfiction crystalizes in this handheld shot from *Citizen Kane* (1941).

The expanded vocabulary of film language brought about through the cross-fertilization of fiction and nonfiction has not only made films more nuanced and varied in their approaches to depicting the "real," it has also made audiences more sophisticated. And so—despite the fact that some viewers of *This Is Spinal Tap!* or *The Blair Witch Project* were led to believe in the authenticity of those films, just as some viewers believed in the miniatures of Spanish-American War films—audiences are, in some respects, growing in their understanding of these techniques and can appreciate the levels of self-reference and manipulation at play in their use. It is not necessarily unexpected when a university professor writes a book on the problems inherent in the Abraham Zapruder footage of the JFK assassination.[6] But when newspapers and journalists (and, consequently, many viewers) discuss *ad infinitum* the "realism" of a fictional film like *The Passion of the Christ* (2004) or argue over the political "distortions" in a nonfiction film like *Fahrenheit 911* (2004), we can see that this overlap between fiction and nonfiction in the cinema, now more than 100 years old, has only continued to grow in complexion and complexity.

Docufictions stand, then, at the blurred boundary between fiction and documentary, questioning the possibility of a clear distinction, let alone a specific ratio—Leninist or otherwise—between the codified but increasingly outmoded idea of a stable division between fiction and nonfiction in film and media. Given the sheer magnitude of film production since the 1890s, as well as the increasing awareness on the part of filmmakers and audiences about these issues, *Docufiction* begins what will doubtless be an ongoing critical dialogue over this emerging genre which, paradoxically, is as old as the cinema itself.

John Parris Springer
Gary D. Rhodes

1. Dziga Vertov, "Kinoglaz" from *Kino-Eye: The Writings of Dziga Vertov*, ed. by Annette Michelson, Berkeley: University of California Press, 1984, p. 39.
2. "Replies to Questions," *ibid.*, p. 103.
3. Quoted by Vertov in "Kinopravda and Radiopravda (By Way of Proposal)," *ibid.* p. 54.
4. See Kirk J. Kekatos' "Edward H. Amet and the Spanish-American War Film," *Film History*, Volume 14, Issue 3/4, 2002: 405–418.
5. See Greg Mitchell's *The Campaign of the Century: Upton Sinclair's Race for the Governor of California and the Birth of Media Politics*, New York: Random House, 1992, p. 369.
6. Fetzer, James H. *The Great Zapruder Film Hoax: Deceit and Deception in the Death of JFK*. New York: Catfeet Press, 2003.

1

Docudrama and Mock-Documentary: Defining Terms, Proposing Canons

by Steven N. Lipkin, Derek Paget *and* Jane Roscoe

A collection such as this, that aims to map the multiple uses made of documentary film practices in narrative/fiction cinema, must inevitably address the *docudrama* and its close relative the *mock-documentary*. The status of these two forms has been and still is a matter of debate because, by their very nature, they break boundaries. Or rather, both forms break *documentary* boundaries in rather confusing ways. For documentary theorist Bill Nichols, for example, docudrama exists in an "essentially fictional domain." Logically, this should be true for mock-documentary too, for this form has no documentary *content* whatsoever, and yet Nichols accommodates mock-documentary within the mode of "reflexive documentary."[1]

The writers of this chapter have explored the problematic nature of docudrama and mock-documentary in monographs listed in the Notes. In our view it is significant that book-length studies did not appear until the millennial period. We do not say that there were no important interventions before this—far from it. But it is the case that industrial practices were highly developed well in advance of the academy's willingness to take them seriously. We will argue that both forms only entered the eye of critical storms after filmmakers had been using them in sophisticated ways for many years. These forms burgeoned in film and television, and suffered critically, from the fact that they were and are *popular* forms.

To some extent ongoing arguments about docudrama and mock-documentary are directly related to three wider, period-defining academic debates. At the end of the twentieth century, anglophone (and other) cultures became variously animated by debates about: the mass media and its effects; the distinction between "high art" and "low art"; and the furore that has increasingly condensed around notions of the "fake" and the "authentic." Weakening confidence in the benign effects of the media and the value of artistic expression, and questioning of the correspondence of the image to "reality" (however defined) has characterized debates in late twentieth-century developed societies troubled about the nature of representation and the influence of representation on perception.

Documentary is the primary form from which both docudrama and mock-documentary have developed and to which both continue to allude — the dramatic is important but in most cases should be seen as servicing the documentary. Once documentary was prized as unproblematically worthy and truth-telling — benign in intention, beneficial in effect, and demonstrably *real*. When compared to the fiction film, tainted with the structures and economics of Hollywood, the documentary film had — still has in some ways — a certain cultural *cachet* and a claim to artistic purity. All that changed with the advent of television's power as a mass medium, and the continued convergence between two formerly separate industries has added fuel to the fire.

Differences/synergies between film and television must always be considered when docudrama and mock-documentary are under discussion. Both forms have distinctively televisual as well as cinematic roots and branches. Historically the moral superiority of independent documentary film put it at odds with both television's and with mass-produced cinema's commercial imperatives. In the last years of the twentieth century the mandate to deliver audiences to advertisers and profits to shareholders clashed with documentary's earlier, between-the-wars, public service social ethic. Docudrama's, and to a lesser extent mock-documentary's, positions within critical debate are partly due to such complex issues.

In the present chapter we try to do three things:

- to think again about our earlier definitions of the key terms *docudrama* and *mock-documentary* — and to mount a defense of the forms against common accusations of "poor art" and "dubious ethics"
- to facilitate further consideration not only of what might constitute a *canon* for such works, but also to consider the ramifications of offering "canons" in the first place, leading to
- an engagement in further thoughts on the place in contemporary culture of what has been termed "post-documentary" forms — with their tentacular reach into twenty-first century popular culture.[2]

Canons, Key Texts and Samples

The docudrama is ubiquitous in both television and cinema. Cinema used "true stories" from very early in its history and from 1945, when the first national television services in the UK and the USA began to develop, docudramas have been an important part of production in both documentary and drama departments of television networks and production companies. The once separate industries of Film and Television grew closer together from the moment that film companies first sold their back catalogues to television in the 1950s. Digitalization has resulted in even closer convergence. As the processes of production, distribution and exhibition have accommodated to the forces of late capitalism so the boundaries between the two media have become ever more porous.

Critical opinion has tended to divide docudrama production output into "high" and "low concept" examples. The former, treating subjects most commentators accept as 'serious," are sometimes controversial at the level of "fidelity" to an idealized historical truth. The "low concept" docudrama, a sub-genre of the "TV Movie of the Week," is often perceived as "tabloid," but it can be just as controversial as its more prestigious sibling.[3] In contrast, the mock-documentary existed until quite recently at the margins of culture in "art-house" cinema. Today it flourishes in both television and cinema. Its move from "high culture" to "low culture" has brought with it both greater acceptance and greater suspicion.

Films fitting into these categories, we shall argue, perform the useful function of ventilating issues of concern in current affairs and drawing attention to the nature of media representation. Large assumptions about the extent to which they "dumb down" (that is, sensationalize, destabilize, and simplify) issues have often been made in commentary both journalistic and academic. There have been worries, too, about the extent to which such forms might "mislead" their audience. We try here to indicate key works that have contributed to understandings of docudrama and mock-documentary and to the histories of the forms' production and reception. As we review these understandings and analyze the histories, we do not see ourselves as proposing a canon. Canons must depend on at least two critically dubious factors: the ideological intentions of the "canon makers," and the availability of the texts being canonized. What values, it is necessary to ask, are being asserted and valorized in any canon and what are the means of valorization? Without available texts, how can works even be canonized at all? Television is especially problematical in this regard, given that preservation of texts has only recently become an issue of importance.

We prefer to read examples from all periods for significant features of production and reception rather than as works to be celebrated for any iconic potential. At present, when not only television docudrama but also mainstream cinema production is producing large numbers of films and even series using docudramatic and mock-documentary modes, we prefer to link the idea of "sampling" to "key works." Key works acknowledge texts that have formal and/or historical significance. Sampling resists elevating individual works to a universal significance but acknowledges their importance *within a specific timeframe and context*. Sampling can be single-text based, or can look at a range of films in order to take the temperature of the times. For example, in his 1998 book, Derek Paget singles out a briefly controversial US/UK co-production docudrama about the Beirut hostages (*Hostages* 1992) in order to illustrate the form's interface with a historical reality it is attempting to represent. This might be termed paradigmatic sampling. In Steven Lipkin's 2002 monograph, by contrast, he discusses a series of television and cinema works from the 1990s with a view to illustrating their rhetorical purchase, their ethical structuring and their political significance within US culture — a syntagmatic sampling. Jane Roscoe and Craig

Hight in their 2001 account of mock-documentary work in a similar way with the particular and the general in order to demonstrate the form's re-inflection of an originary documentary perception.

Faced as we are today with such a proliferation of material these approaches seem more promising than the nomination of "great works"—particularly since the "low culture" nature of much docudramatic and mock-documentary production inherently resists such canon-making. There is an additional problem with the notion of a canon. Importantly it also assumes the genres under scrutiny to be unproblematic fixed categories rather than fluid discourses that encompass a range of styles and agendas and which alter over time.

Functions, Definitions, Codes and Conventions

Docudrama and mock-documentary can both be defined in part in terms of their *function*. In the case of docudrama:

- such films/TV programs re-tell events from national/international histories, either reviewing or celebrating these events;
- they re-present the careers of significant national/international figures, for broadly similar purposes as the above;
- they portray issues of concern to national/international communities, in order to provoke discussion about them.

In more recent times, they have:

- increasingly focused upon "ordinary citizens," thrust into the news through special (and often traumatic) experiences.

Mock-documentary's functions are more clearly intertextual and more directly subversive:

- they appropriate documentary aesthetics to create a fictional world thereby severing the direct relationship between the image and the referent;
- they take as their object of parody both documentary as a screen form, documentary practitioners, and cultural, social and political icons;
- they seek to develop a relationship with a knowing audience who through being in on the joke can appreciate both the humor and the inherent critical reflexivity of the form.

Finally, docudrama and mock-documentary share a common function. They have provoked and continue to provoke:

- questions about *form*—specifically, about the permissibility, usefulness and even danger of mixing the functions of documentary and drama.

Because of cultural convergence in the late twentieth century, it is more convenient to classify all documentary/drama mixes (those, at any rate, that cannot be categorized as "mock-documentary") as docudrama. This short-circuits the welter of terms available (routinely mixed up in common usage). However, it is still worth separating out the main categories that have emerged over fifty years of film and TV program making because demonstrating provenance illustrates history. The main terms are:

DRAMA-DOCUMENTARY

It is useful to see "drama" here as an adjective modifying a noun — so, literally, this is a "drama-styled," "dramatized," or "dramatic" documentary. This type of TV program/film comes from traditions of investigative journalism. It uses the sequence of events from a real historical occurrence or situation, and the identities of its principal protagonists, to underpin a film script intended to provoke debate about the significance of the events/occurrence. The resultant film usually follows a cinematic narrative structure and employs the standard naturalist/realist performance techniques of screen drama. If documentary material is directly presented at all, it is used in a way calculated to minimize disruption to the realist narrative. A classic example of a drama-documentary is ABC's 1974 *The Missiles of October*, dramatizing the 1962 Cuban Missile Crisis.

DOCUMENTARY DRAMA

Again, "documentary" is an adjective, and could be described as a "documentary-style" drama (this construction is sometimes found in the case of American and British propaganda films from World War Two). By contrast to (1), this type of TV program/film uses a wholly invented sequence of events, and fictional protagonists, in order to illustrate the salient features of actual occurrences or situations. The film script may or may not conform to a classic narrative structure; if it does not, documentary elements may be non-naturalistically presented and may actively disrupt the narrative (for example, direct address *interview* material may be cut into the film, statistical information presented through *graphics*). But "documentary" in this form is just as likely to refer to style as to content, and to be about the "look" and 'sound" of documentary proper which is directly referenced by imitation. In this case, the structures of film naturalism may once more obtain in terms of performance. It should be said that the documentary "look" most imitated is that of "Direct Cinema." A classic documentary drama is Peter Watkins" *The War Game*. This film imagined the scenario of a nuclear strike over southern England following a Cold War superpower confrontation over the then-divided Berlin. It should have been screened by the BBC in 1965, but was controversially withdrawn from the schedules.[4]

FACTION

Faction is a term less frequently used than once was the case. A faction is a TV program/film using a real world template of events and characters to create a fiction that runs in parallel to a set of known occurrences. Factions rely on their audiences to connect with the parallel "out of story" factual template in reception — nothing is done within the film directly to effect this connection. Such films rely far more than the other types of docudrama on an *intertextual connection* with news and current affairs and documentary inserts of any kind are conspicuous by their absence. Film naturalism is, almost inevitably, the staple dramatic means of representation. The best example of a faction is still *Washington Behind Closed Doors* (1977). Here, the facts of Watergate were replicated in an imaginary Presidency. Nonetheless, the TV film did present a powerful implicit commentary on the corruption of the Nixon period. It is impossible to imagine this series being repeated for a new audience without quite a complex historical gloss.

DRAMADOC AND DOCUDRAMA

These are contemporary shortened terms describing television programs and films that mainly follow the drama-documentary methodology as defined above. The desire to shorten complicated terms is endemic in sophisticated societies. The two words are now used virtually interchangeably — and, for most people, confusingly. But "docudrama" wins on any usage test. "Dramadoc" more accurately refers to a British tradition more journalism-led, more "fact rich"; the term is more often used in the UK. The "docudrama" tends towards person-centered "biopics" and 'social dramas"— individual stories illustrative of particular issues— popularized by the American film industry.[5] "Docudrama" is used on both sides of the Atlantic, but would be recognized by most Americans as the key term. The two traditions began to merge as the film and television industries began to synergize. Home Box Office's co-production agreements with British TV companies in particular re-focused high concept docudrama in the 1990s.[6]

MOCK-DOCUMENTARY

Mock-documentary is entirely fictional yet, unlike most docudrama, appropriates the look of documentary much more closely. Jane Roscoe and Craig Hight argue that mock-documentary's "genealogy" can be described as operating through "three degrees" of distance from "documentary proper": through *parody, critique* and *deconstruction*. The *parody* mock-documentary is comparatively muted in its critique of the documentary project. Documentary aesthetics are appropriated mostly for stylistic reasons and to emphasize the humor. In examples such as *The Rutles* (1978) or *This Is Spinal Tap!* (1984) documentary's "classic objective argument" is used as a prop against which the absurdity of the parody is contrasted. Often nostalgic, the parody frequently comments on easy targets— particularly cultural icons whose currency is exhausted and ripe for mocking. Documentary, like history, could be said to be returning as farce. In contrast, *critique* mock-documentaries engage more critically in the form's inherent reflexivity towards factual discourse, and raise questions about both the documentary form and wider factual media practices. Films/programs such as *Bob Roberts* (1992) or the 1997 series première episode of *ER* also developed the

Bob Roberts (1992) develops the satirical possibilities of the mock-documentary form. Here, Tim Robbins as Bob Roberts appears in a music video.

satirical possibilities of the form. In the former example a critique was made of modern political processes and a parallel satirical swipe was taken at the factual media (as was the case with the *ER* episode — see below). But it is the *deconstruction* mock-documentary that brings to the fore an explicit critique of documentary form. Texts such as *David Holzman's Diary* (1967) and *Man Bites Dog* (1992) demonstrated a rather hostile appropriation of documentary codes and conventions and utilized them in order to undermine and deconstruct the very foundations of the documentary project. Humor is often underplayed in favor of representations that seek to create "ethical unease" that will lead to critique. This latter quality is very much part of the post-documentary cultural moment.[7]

Mock-documentary talks to a "knowing" audience even more directly than the docudrama. It is assumed that audiences will be able to distinguish between fact and fiction in media representation and thereby to participate in the inherent playfulness of the form. What marks the mock-documentary out from the "hoax" or "fake" is this *contract* set up between producer and audience. It requires the audience to watch as if at a documentary presentation, but in the full knowledge of an actual fictional status. Audiences have to be in on the joke to be able to access and participate first in the humor, then in the cultural and political critique on offer.

Codes and conventions in the docudrama and mock-documentary can be usefully sub-divided into those with a documentary and those with a drama provenance. In the former, factual input can be measured directly in terms of the screen time given to: *captions, voiceover* commentary, *newsreel footage* (sometimes cut to make it appear that actors have talked to real historical individuals), *graphics, direct address* of the camera and one-on-one *interviews* with actual historical protagonists. All such documentary codes, and the conventions through which they are presented, are *subverted* in the mock-documentary — they *appear* to be documentary but have been convincingly faked.

From documentary, too, comes the concept of *research*, the tradition of citing of *sources* and providing *disclaimers* that partially account for the documentary element — the latter signals also a very different *legal* requirement than that needed for fiction filming. The mock-documentary routinely appropriates such markers of documentary in order to spoof and to critique them.

As regards their audience, filmmakers hope to trigger a level of *belief* (borrowed from the documentary) in the events unfolding in the docudrama — again, to encourage questioning of that belief. Such questioning is at a higher level in the mock-documentary since the means by which belief itself is generated are under review.

In films with a drama provenance, codes and conventions comprise those to do with performance —*script, direction, acting style, set design, costume, lighting*. In most productions these conform to concepts of the *believable in performance. Characters* are established in the writing and acting and reinforced in the direction, *plots* tend towards positively Aristotelian structures of climax and anti-climax. Docudramas in general obey the rules of the fictional film if they are to convince an audience: *continuity editing, realist mise-en-scène* and *naturalistic acting*— all the paraphernalia of the realist movie —combine to persuade an audience to *suspend its disbelief*. In the case of the mock-documentary — where, despite appearances, everything is actually dramatic fiction — realist techniques and the conventions of documentary presentation try to persuade audiences to accept what is presented as a genuine pro-filmic reality.

Jane Feuer has characterized much movie-of-the-week docudrama production as "trauma drama."[8] Docudrama presents its actual subject matter, the real-life people and events it tells us about, through the prism of classical Hollywood realist narrative. If some of the central components of classical Hollywood narrative are character, conflict, and closure, these are fused in docudrama with subjects that configure as victims and witnesses. The notion of trauma drama underlines how much the "drama" in docudrama necessarily becomes *melodrama*. The lens of melodrama lends a moral clarity to the issues present — though some would claim that clarity is bought at the expense of complexity.

"Persuasive Practice"

Such dramatized accounts of the real have always held a "persuasive power" that rests ultimately on their *proximity* to the real. Robert Flaherty's 1920 *Nanook of the North*, often touted as the first feature documentary film, was almost wholly invented action. From its inception in 1935, the famous US film newsreel series *The March of Time* used actors to recreate occurrences at which cameras had not been actually present. Pare Lorentz in *The Plow That Broke the Plains* (1936) and *The River* (1937) unhesitatingly utilized footage from Hollywood feature films. The 1938 Orson Welles radio broadcast of *War of the Worlds* offers an early example of a media hoax, and one which can be regarded as an early precursor of the mock-documentary form. In all cases the "drama" was convincingly "real" and authentic enough to allow these representations to go unchallenged and to be believed.[9]

During World War Two, British and American filmmakers embellished their propaganda documentaries with dramatic codes. William Wyler's original *Memphis Belle* in 1943 presented an aircrew metonymically representative of (white) America. At the time, as Erik Barnouw has noted, "There was little public discussion about the validity of such techniques."[10] This was equally true for postwar television: throughout the 1950s, US anthology drama series "Armstrong Circle Theatre" could mix drama and documentary unproblematically.[11] In the same period BBC TV documentaries, too, would re-enact for illustrative purposes without provoking adverse comment. Wherever technical deficiencies were evident, whether in pre-war film or in the new post-war television services in the UK and the US, "reconstruction" routinely took place and did not need to be labeled as such.

In postwar cinema, the 1946–49 20th Century–Fox "Hathaway Trilogy" (*The House on 92nd Street*, 1945; *13 Rue Madeleine*, 1946; *Call Northside 777*, 1948) built on the cycle of Warner's 'social problem films" in the early 1930s (for example: *I Am a Fugitive from a Chain Gang*, 1932). As these films used their documentary base to *warrant* their claims about actuality, 20th Century–Fox's cycle of post-war "semi-documentaries" provided a precedent for the persuasive strategies characteristic of contemporary film and TV docudramas. As docudramas employ rhetorical strategies based on the closeness of actuality and re-creation, they argue that it is both logical and emotionally valid to associate cinematic proximity with moral truth. The use of a documentary base as warrant defines a tradition that continues in contemporary TV and film (*Quiz Show* in 1994, for example, worked in a similar way).

Early modes of docudrama, predicated like documentary itself upon John Grierson's classic 1933 formulation that documentary was "the creative treatment of actuality," were radically re-inflected by European *cinéma vérité* and US "Direct Cinema" practices of the late 1950s and 1960s.[12] The new camera and microphone technology offered more flexibility and an *apparent* access to the real. The burgeoning of docudramatic activity that took place from the late 1960s occurred for two principal reasons:

- Filmmakers began to tackle social issues via the film grammar of the Direct Cinema documentary,
- Hollywood studios began to supply television with movies, giving rise to the "Movie-of-the-Week" from the early 1970s. Hollywood had always had an inclination toward films based on true stories, but the volume of TV production ensured that the "ready-made" plots of the docudrama would become a staple.

In the 1960s, and continuing as shooting film for TV transmission became standard practice, questions began for the first time to be asked about the kinds of recreation involved in the UK "dramadoc" and US "docudrama" traditions. British television's more journalistic, investigative, tradition is best exemplified by Ken Loach's 1966 film *Cathy Come Home* (about the UK's post-war housing crisis). On both sides of the Atlantic in the 1970s and 1980s, subjects both important and trivial were treated through docudramas. In the USA miniseries such as *Roots* (1977) and *Holocaust: The Story of the Family Weiss* (1978) addressed major questions of American and international history. *The Day After* (1983) explored in detail the major Cold War concern with the nuclear arms race. Saudi-Arabian/British diplomatic relations were briefly suspended as a result of a 1980 UK docudrama, *Death of a Princess*, a film that seems in the light of current Mid-East problems oddly prophetic in its tale of mutually misunderstanding and misrepresenting cultures. Many of these examples can be matched in later filmmaking that pursued similar subjects of continuing major import (matching, for example, 1993's *Schindler's List* with the *Holocaust* miniseries; 1997's *Amistad* with *Roots*).

A useful example of a docudramatic attempt to raise social awareness within a specific historical context was the 1993 *And the Band Played On*. This dramatization of the discovery and social and cultural effects of the AIDS virus could be easily conflated with trauma drama, but this film continues and maintains a US tradition that began with *Brian's Song* in 1971. It presents a forensic examination of the actual events through which AIDS was acknowledged as a significant "new" disease with social ramifications. There was a series of films in the 1990s—co-productions between HBO and British companies—about international terrorism. Post-9/11 these still seem impressive in their ambition and willingness to tackle subjects of demonstrable import. They include *Investigation: Inside a Terrorist Bomb*ing (1990 — about the IRA's bombing of Birmingham in 1974 and the trial of the "Birmingham 6") and *The Tragedy of Flight 103* (1990 — about the 1987 Lockerbie disaster in which a Pan-Am jet was destroyed over Scotland by Libyan terrorist action).

Nor should apparently trivial examples of the format be ignored; as well as constituting staple examples of "movie of the week" docudrama, there are demonstrable levels of persuasive practice going on in these films too. In the 1993 *Victim of Love: The Shannon Mohr Story*, an argument about moral issues involving parental (and societal) responsibilities was developed in dealing with a murder case that first surfaced on the *Unsolved Mysteries* television program. The most egregious "movie of the week" docudrama was possibly the so-called "Long Island Lolita" trilogy of 1992/93. Three films, made by the three oldest networks in the USA, were made about a tabloid adultery saga in New York. The films (ABC's *The Amy Fisher Story*, NBC's *Lethal Lolita*, CBS's *Casualties of Love*) epitomize Rod Carveth's notion (1993: 121) of the "headline docudrama" primarily dependent on checkbook journalism.[13]

Docudramatic rhetoric uses three basic kinds of warrants to connect its presentations of its subjects to the claims the narratives forward.[14] First, works construct models of the people, places, and events that make up their stories. Models bear directly motivated resemblances to their subject. Modeling warrants are as evident in the casting of principal parts (Anthony Hopkins as Nixon; Denzel Washington as Malcolm X in the 1995 and 1992 films) as they are in the re-creation of key locations (Mogadishu in 2001's *Black Hawk Down*, or the Warsaw ghetto in *The Pianist*). Sec-

The Hollywood docudrama and the representation of history: Anthony Hopkins in *Nixon* (1995) and Denzel Washington in *Malcolm X* (1992).

ond, docudramas will sequence the real and what it must re-create, that is, alternate between re-created and actual footage, so that the modeled material benefits from its literal closeness to documentary imagery. The interviews with Easy Company veterans that open each episode of the HBO miniseries *Band of Brothers* (2001) set up this strategy. For better or worse, Oliver Stone used sequencing throughout *JFK* (1991) as a means to augment the authenticity of the claims the film would forward.

A third warranting strategy, interaction, places actual and re-created elements within the *mise-en-scène*, so that real-life principals move through scenes with actors (the real Jim Garrison in *JFK*), or actors move through the actual locations where the re-created events originally occurred (the Illinois State Penitentiary in the 1948 *Call Northside 777*; the town hall with its memorial wall in 2000's *Perfect Storm*). Proximity strategies both warrant the arguments the films would forward about their subjects, and create potential ethical issues when the degree of proximity becomes questionable. While the cases of *JFK*, *Mississippi Burning* (1988) and *The People vs. Larry Flynt* (1996) have been notorious in the matter of the closeness of their re-creations to the known actuality they reference, there have also been concerns raised on the same basis about *The Insider*, *The Hurricane* (both 1999) and *A Beautiful Mind*.[15] By contrast, *The Positively True Adventures of the Alleged Texas Cheerleader Murdering Mom* suggests, in its ironic reflexivity, the maturity of a form now very well known in terms of codes and conventions to its audience. The persuasive discourse of this film entails not only discussion of the moral implications of its immediate subject matter but also about its own nature as dramatized document. In some ways the docudrama and mock-documentary forms meet in this 1992 HBO film. [Editor's note: See Harvey O'Brien's essay "That's Really the Title?" elsewhere in this volume.]

Mock-documentary did not emerge as a distinct form until the 1960s. Just as the technological project to bring documentary closer to the real seemed to be making significant headway, so awareness of the roles of the documentary camera and crew in inflecting representation became part of the debate. The mock-documentaries made at this point were concerned with these very issues. The black and white film *David Holzman's Diary*, made by Jim McBride in 1967, featured a young filmmaker inspired by Godard's claims that "film is truth 24 times a second." He attempts to discover the truth of his own life by recording it all on film. After eight days of filming he becomes frustrated by the lack of revelations provided by the camera. This is a commentary on the relationship between film and reality and the claims that documentary can both access and reveal the "truth."

In 1978 Eric Idle (*Monty Python's Flying Circus*) and Gary Weiss (*Saturday Night Live*) collaborated on *The Rutles*. This indicates a shift in the mock-documentary form away from a direct critical engagement with the apparatus of film or documentary, to a commentary on popular cultural icons. The group in *The Rutles* is a playful and knowing parody of The Beatles. It appropriates the rational and serious expositional form and juxtaposes this with the irrationality and absurdity of a content recognizable to an audience as "close to" truths about The Beatles. An openly fictional text, it both critiques documentary and uses the form both to celebrate and to poke fun at a hugely successful group. In a similar vein *This Is Spinal Tap!* (1984) provided a critical commentary on the hyper-masculinity of the heavy metal rock scene. The film is a brilliant parody of the "rockumentary" of the 1960s (films like D. A. Pennebaker's 1967 Dylan vehicle *Don't Look Back*). It became the benchmark film for those attempting to produce mock-documentary texts.

Recent Developments

The last decade has seen docudrama maintain a prominent niche in both feature film and movie-of-the-week production. The ongoing importance of docudrama as a mode of representation is evident in recent Academy Awards, where winners in important categories such as Best Picture have included *A Beautiful Mind* (2002), with Roman Polanski winning Best Director for *The Pianist* (2003).[16] Mock-documentary, too, has achieved new levels of cultural visibility. *This Is Spinal Tap!* director Christopher Guest made *Best in Show* (2002) and *A Mighty Wind* (2003) in a similar style. *The Blair Witch Project* (1999) provided a commentary on the camcorder culture and made impressive use of the internet in building its audience and reputation. *Waiting for Guffman* (1996) appropriated and critiqued the televisual form docu-soap; and *Series 7* (2000) commented directly on the rise of the reality TV game show. The form has expanded a repertoire that now includes responses to even broader shifts within media culture.

Continued resonance for audiences stems from several sources that seem on the face of it unlikely to diminish in the future. Works based on true stories and works affecting the discourse of "true stories" do not simply represent their subjects and forms, but offer arguments about ways to perceive those subjects and forms. To do this, they draw on powerful elements of both narrative and rhetorical modes of presentation. The fusion of documentary premises and feature film narrative structure contributes to the appeal of docudramatic and mock-documentary argument in both film and television. The "mantra" that "movie of the week" docudrama producers recite, that their offerings must be "rootable, relatable and promotable" to their viewers, applies to a wide range of topics, and indicates how such diverse works constitute responses to the larger social and political constraints affecting their audiences.[17] In the commonest forms of the docudrama and mock-documentary an *argument by analogy* is conducted.

Docudrama asserts that what it re-presents occurred *much like* what we see unfold on the screen; mock-documentary asserts that what it presents is *much like* what we conventionally see in documentary. Both forms present us a mixture of presentational modes. Docudramas indicate their roots in actuality when they are "based on" or "inspired by" "true stories." The prior text of mock-documentary is documentary itself. However, these works indicate equally to their audiences the need to receive them as entertainment products and enter the market place as feature films. Their dominant codes and conventions are dramatic and melodramatic, documentary and non-fictional. In semiotic terms, hybridity depends upon indexical icons, re-creations that bear close, motivated resemblances to the real and to representations of the real.

Evidence of the timeliness of the rhetoric of American movie-of-the-week docudrama is in the frequency of production during sweeps periods. A brief profile of the

May 2003 sweeps illustrates this. During the May sweeps American networks programmed no less than seven "movie of the week" docudramas, including a two-night miniseries, *Hitler: The Rise of Evil*. Of the seven titles, three centered on war or war-related stories (*Hitler: Out of the Ashes*; and *Daughter from Da Nang*). Three others gave the "inside" stories of famous subjects (*Lucy: Behind the Camera; 3's Company: The Unauthorized Story; Martha Inc.*). Two of the "movie of the week" docudramas coat-tailed prominent news events (*Martha Inc.; Ice Bound*). This typology has been typical of network "movie of the week" production for more than a decade. The sampling's emphasis on war subjects has been characteristic of sweeps docudrama programming since 2000.[18] This factor can be attributed to many things, but notably to a post–September 11 audience's awareness of being in a quasi-war situation. Successive military interventions by American foreign policy into overseas conflicts followed by the September 11 attack have reactivated a Pearl Harbor mindset in the United States and led to a perceived need for effective leadership and rescue in an atmosphere of victimization. Not surprisingly, then, traditional war docudramas like *Band of Brothers* fit appropriately the culture of conflict encouraged by the Bush administration.

Television producers and network executives believe that docudrama subjects offer stories that a significant percentage of their target audience will find personally significant. The target audience remains women between the ages of 18 and 49. Consequently working mothers, for example, will find something exemplary in the struggles for survival and success facing Martha Stewart or Lucille Ball. The same will be true of Jerri Nielson's self-diagnosis and treatment of her breast cancer in *Ice Bound*. Favoring story subjects that have been in the public's awareness, such as Pennsylvania miners trapped in a cave-in, establishes the movie-of-the-week as a narrative in contemporary reality, warranting the initial claims the film would forward, that what happened was important, worth knowing more about, and happened in much the way that audiences see. For similar reasons networks favor docudrama subjects because they are simple and efficient to promote. Sweeps periods limit the scope of possible publicity and advertising. It becomes easier and more cost effective to promote a known subject in this limited amount of time. The network executives, producers, and writers who make "movie of the week" docudrama all use the same terms—all seek the "rootable, relatable, and promotable," all acknowledge that docudrama offers cost-effective product that can be marketed directly to consumers.

If the docudrama is a something of a staple product for film and television, in recent years there has been something of an explosion in television mock-documentary production (especially in the UK). There has certainly been a growth in audience appetite for a sophisticated form that has exploited the current success of "Reality TV." The UK's *The Office* notably attracted good-sized audiences and critical acclaim. A series such as this was a site for social and cultural commentary. As Frederic Jameson amongst others has noted, the actual intent of parody is critical comment, although in many examples the critical edge is muted or left implicit.[19] What is absolutely central is the relationship set up between the audience and the text. The audience must be a "knowing" audience that recognizes the object of the parody to be able to access the critiques on offer.

Mock-documentary has been quick to use parody and satire to reflect on the rapidly changing nature of factual screen forms, especially the proliferation in "reality" formats. As these formats have reshaped the prime-time schedules across the globe, a space in those schedules has also been found for a critique of them. An early example of this new trend was the 1997 series premiere of *ER* mentioned earlier. The episode, entitled "Ambush," presented as a mock reality show with the narrative structured around the visit to the ER ward by an observational documentary crew there to document the behind the scenes activities of the hospital and staff. Shot to look as if it were a reality show, it was actually performed live. While reinforcing the sense of a "documentary look" it harked back to the earliest days of "anthology TV drama" at the same time it critiqued the modern tendency towards "cops and docs" reality shows. As the episode unfolded, issues were raised about the ethics of the crew and a critical commentary was developed about new "bastardized" forms of documentary.

A similar critique was on offer in the BBC's series *The Office* (2001–3 — a hit when shown on PBS). It provided an examination of work-place politics and psychology, but more importantly a commentary on the "docu-soap." This form's obsession with the mundane and banal was satirized, as was the process through which ordinary people are turned into TV stars by performing themselves. Creator Ricky Gervais played the lead character, David Brent, and performed this role of docu-soap star so well it was by turns hilarious and painful to watch. A mixture of cruel satire and playful parody, *The Office* was a fine example of the mock-documentary disrupting normal and serious communication to ask its audience to question both the form and content of television documentary formats.

By the early 2000s hybrid fact-fictional forms were no longer on the margins, but at the very centre of media production. As audiences and producers became more comfortable with and interested in the play-off between fact and fiction, so new forms explicitly worked with this tension in order to exploit the fact that their time had come. It is not only a case of documentary borrowing and appropriating dramatic codes and conventions, drama has also be enlivened by its appropriation of documentary and factual codes. Recent inventive hybridizing developments would include:

- The use of non-actors in Michael Winterbottom's 2002 *In This World* and Khoa Do's 2003 *The Finished People*,
- Hand-held/naturalistic camera work and sound in *Morvan Callor* (2002),
- New developments in "faction" as defined earlier in the chapter (the intertextuality between Gus Van Sant's 2003 *Elephant* and Michael Moore's 2003 *Bowling for Columbine*, for example),
- Provocative appearances of real-life originals in "biopic" docudrama (Robert Crumb in the 2003 *American Splendor*),
- Use of opera and musical styles in the UK (*When She Died ...* a 2002 docu-opera based on Princess Diana's death; docu-musicals such as Brian Hill's 2002 *Feltham Sings* and his 2003 *Pornography: the Musical*).

The latest round of popular factual entertainment TV programs make no pretense about utilizing both dramatic codes and those documentary codes that connect their narratives to the real. In fact, much of this television output relies on producers, participants and audiences being engaged by this tension between what is staged and what is real. The performances in examples such as *Big Brother* or *Survivor* or the many derivatives of such programs are framed through those competing discourses. Docudrama and mock-documentary have played a significant role in familiarizing audiences with the aesthetics and ethics of forms that mix factual and fictional material. Docudrama and mock-documentary continue to have a role beyond their formal adoption and subversion of documentary and its codes and conventions. To the extent to which they are cultural and social commentators, the forms draw very close to the original aims and intentions of documentary "proper." Adding popular reach to formal grasp as they do enables some films and programs, at certain times, to punch significantly above their apparent weight.

1. Bill Nichols, *Representing Reality: Issues and Concepts in Documentary* (Bloomington: Indiana University Press, 1991) 160.

2. See John Corner, "What Do We Know About Documentary?," *Media Culture and Society* 22 (2000) 5.

3. See Gary Edgerton, "High Concept, Small Screen: Reperceiving the Industrial and Stylistic Origins of the American Made-for-TV Movie," *Journal of Popular Film and Television*, 19: 3, 114–27.

4. Widely screened over the years at film festivals and in cinema clubs, *The War Game* was eventually transmitted by the BBC in 1985.

5. See George F. Custen, *Bio/Pics: How Hollywood Constructed Public History* (New Brunswick, New Jersey: Rutgers University Press, 1992).

6. For further details on definitions, see Derek Paget, *No Other Way To Tell It: Dramadoc/docudrama on Television* (Manchester and New York: Manchester University Press, 1998) 81–3; and Steven N. Lipkin, *Real Emotional Logic: Film and Television Docudrama as Persuasive Practice* (Carbondale and Edwardsville: Southern Illinois University Press, 2002) 1–11.

7. For further details see Jane Roscoe and Craig Hight, *Faking It: Mock-documentary and the Subversion of Factuality* (Manchester and New York: Manchester University Press, 2001) 68–74.

8. See Jane Feuer, *Seeing Through the Eighties: Television and Reaganism* (Durham: Duke University Press, 1995).

9. See Brian Winston, *Claiming the Real: The Documentary Film Revisited* (London: British Film Institute, 1995) 99–103.

10. Erik Barnouw, *Tube of Plenty: The Evolution of American Television* (New York and Oxford: Oxford University Press, 1975) 131.

11. For more details, see A. William Bluem, *Documentary in American Television: Form, Function, Method* (New York, Hastings House, 1965) 180ff.

12. John Grierson, "The Documentary Producer," *Cinema Quarterly* 2: 1, p. 8.

13. Rod Carveth, "Amy Fisher and the Ethics of "Headline" Docudramas," *Journal of Popular Film and Television* 21: 3, 121–7.

14. See Lipkin 13, 23–27.

15. On *The Insider*, see www.brillscontent.com/features/Real —1— 0899.html; on *A Beautiful Mind*, see *The New York Times* 21 December 2002: "From Math to Madness, and Back"; on *The Hurricane*, see http://www.suntimes.com/ebert/ebert_reviews/2000/01/010705.html.

16. Other recent Academy Award winners: *Erin Brockovich*, *Monster* (Julia Roberts: Best Actress 2001; Charlize Theron: Best Actress 2004); *Black Hawk Down* (Best Editing and Best Sound in 2002).

17. See Lipkin 55–75.

18. Other war-related works of note aired in the UK and USA in the period since May 2000 include: *Submerged*; *Haven*; *Nuremberg*; *Uprising*; *Gathering Storm*; *One Night in Baghdad*; *Daughter from Da Nang*; *Out of the Ashes*; *Saving Jessica Lynch*; and *Dunkirk*.

19. See Frederic Jameson, *Postmodernism, or The Cultural Logic of Late Capitalism* (London: Verso, 1991). On p. 17, he discusses his notion of "blank parody."

2

The Newspaper Meets the Dime Novel: Docudrama in Early Cinema

by John Parris Springer

During the period of cinema's emergence in the late nineteenth century it was not at all clear what motion pictures would become. The ability of the motion picture camera to make a moving record of that segment of the world placed in front of it possessed a tremendous potential for both science and the arts, though initially the artistic applications of the new technology were not immediately obvious. The appeal of the earliest one-shot films resided in such simple records of movement as waves crashing on the shore or a train pulling into a station. Such films aimed not at documenting the crashing waves or the train's arrival but rather the arrival of the latest technological wonder — moving pictures; scientific progress was the real star of the show. Soon the subjects for motion pictures broadened to include vaudeville turns, athletic exhibitions, and "actualities," filmed records of actual happenings. Now the cinema was being utilized as a tool to document particular individuals and events, and the "scientific wonder" of motion pictures began to be upstaged by the subjects the new medium could place in front of the viewer. Yet cinematic representations were still not divided into clearly demarcated categories of fiction and non-fiction simply because photographic literalness in motion remained the point of its display. This is the moment in film history when the cinema is a purely iconic medium and objects on the screen mean only what they are in the world — a wave is a wave and a train is a train. But, according to some historical accounts, gradually audiences lost interest in such records of a performance or an event, and filmmakers turned to fictional narratives as a way of maintaining the public's interest.[1] By placing film within the purview of narrative a purely iconic cinema was partially abandoned in favor of a visual discourse that encouraged a certain connotative looseness in regards to the image. Within narrative cinema waves and trains could have additional, thematic and cultural meanings beyond their iconic value, and thus the introduction of narrative revealed a fundamental ambiguity implicit in the cinema: The tension between the photographic literalness of its mode of representation and the fabricated, invented, and often conventionalized view of the world found in its fictional elements and devices.

The turn towards narrative in the cinema was not an aesthetic inevitability but a calculated strategy by filmmakers to enhance the profitability of filmmaking.[2] The rapid spread of nickelodeon and store front theaters after 1905 created a growing demand for films by exhibitors and led production companies to standardize production practices. Increasingly filmmaking was subjected to a process of business rationalization that aimed at increasing production and maximizing profits, and the simple fact was that filmed narratives were easier to budget and pre-plan and could be supplied more reliably and with a greater assurance of audience interest than films based upon the recording of people and events. Motion pictures gradually became a narrative art form for commercial rather than artistic reasons, a fact which must be considered in order to fully understand film as either a form of art or commerce.

Arguably all films are both records (of what is placed in front of the camera) and representations (a selection and arrangement of textual elements and devices). But at a certain point in the development of film as a commodity it became advantageous to acknowledge, even promote the fact that motion pictures provided much more than a mere recording of objects and events placed in front of the camera. To become an art, film had to renounce its origins in the proto-documentary, iconic cinema of the first films and move in the direction of the illusionist narrative aesthetic of Classical Hollywood cinema. Yet, even though such a film aesthetic received institutional sanction within the Hollywood studio system, the ability of cinema as a medium to function as both record and representation — that is, as a document of what is placed in front of the camera as well as a constructed fiction — has been an ongoing dialectic in the history of film textuality. The interplay and exchange between the "documentary tradition" in its various modes and narrative filmmaking with its forms and devices has certainly been pervasive within commercial filmmaking. While the fusion and blurring of documentary devices and fictional narrative elements might at first seem a contemporary, even postmodern cultural phenomenon, arguably such docufictional synthesis was at its height during the period of Early Cinema (1893–1905), precisely because film's critical identity as a vehicle for fictional narrative was not yet fixed and taken for granted by either filmmakers or audiences. The period of Early Cinema represents a moment in film history when the conventional distinctions between narrative and non-narrative film were not as clearly drawn, nor as ideologically important, as they are today. Early Cinema was, as Tom Gunning has characterized it, "a cinema of attractions,"[3] based upon the display of visual spectacles for an audience less inclined to make the kinds of generic distinctions between documentary and non-documentary filmmaking that later film viewers would routinely make.

In fact, during the period of Early Cinema the production of actualities and other proto-documentary films comprised the majority of U.S. film production.[4] According to Tom Gunning, "until about 1905 the bulk of American production was non-fiction films, but these have not received the investigation that reflects their importance in this period."[5] No doubt this is in part because of the uncertain generic status of early films *vis-à-vis* classical Hollywood forms. Early films were defined by their photographic literalness and ability to record movement rather than their ability to tell different types of stories.[6] Short films of dancing girls, locomotives, and weight lifters were screened alongside with "actualities" that often served a journalistic impulse to depict contemporary events such as the Spanish American war. However, because dramatic news events rarely occurred within sight of a movie camera these early "newsreels," not infrequently, were staged reenactments and often delivered heavy-handed political and patriotic messages.[7] Comic vignettes and vaudeville turns were also common, and many early films were records of simple comic sight-gags based on physical exaggeration and action. Films built around special effects and visual tricks, of the sort pioneered by Georges Méliès in France and J. Stuart Blackton in the U.S., were popular with audiences and made startling use of the camera as a tool for altering the viewer's perception of the world through simple techniques such as stop-motion and double exposure. But finally, by the turn of the 20th century, an emerging genre of "story film" appeared that often relied on plots derived from fairy tales and popular fiction, along with familiar current events, in order to insure the comprehensibility of their narratives and sustain audience interest. As film production companies increasingly turned towards narrative, the initial appeal of the cinema as a recording device began to give way to an emerging conception of cinema as a form of narrative representation, and many films were produced that attempted to dramatize social life through the visual recreation and narrativization (as in the staging and scripting) of actual social situations and events. However, until the rise of the "story film," with the system of genres it inherited from popular literature, motion pictures comprised a heterogeneous set of subjects whose principal appeal was photographic likeness in motion.

　　To explore this period of transition from an iconic cinema to a cinema based on the staging of fictional narratives I will focus on two films which I take to be indicative of the fluid relationship between documentary and narrative in early film: Edwin S. Porter's *Life of an American Fireman* (1902) and *The Great Train Robbery* (1903). These are hybrid texts, operating in both the narrative and the documentary film registers, and they exemplify the continuance of the cinema's iconic beginnings into the new narrative paradigm. Both of these films were tremendously popular and commercially successful in their day. According to many accounts these two films had a tremendous impact on audiences of 1903, and they should be considered among the most important films of this period.[8] Both films have also played an important role in histories of early American cinema and in discussions of the development of film narrative. Their significance to several generations of film historians resided in the belief that they were the first "story films," the earliest films to construct narratives out of technical devices which were uniquely cinematic: Essentially, a continuity of action constructed out of the arrangement of shots or scenes.[9]

　　The work of more recent film historians has challenged the received wisdom concerning these films by arguing that they were certainly not the first to tell stories, and such revisionist accounts have significantly expanded our understanding of early film.[10] In addition, it is possible to explain the popularity and commercial success of these two films in other ways as well. I would argue that their significance for early cinema audiences was based not merely upon their use of narrative, but upon their depiction of events which were familiar facts of contemporary life — the devastation of urban fire and the chronic social problem of banditry — which are given an ideological coherence through their depiction in narrative. While neither of these films would be called a "documentary" according to contemporary usage, they establish a reportorial/documentary stance towards their social subjects and are more properly considered early docudramas — staged reenactments of events which could provoke profound social anxieties for their original audiences.

The question of the origin of the "story film" cannot be satisfactorily addressed without confronting the issue of what constitutes a properly filmic narrative. Terry Ramsaye, for example, in his early study of the American film industry *A Million and One Nights* (1926), excludes work by Georges Méliès from his discussion of the "story film" because it was based on the device of "artificially arranged scenes" (396), and not on the arrangement of shots and scenes to achieve a continuity of action. Méliès' films are certainly narrative, but the "story" is advanced through a series of discontinuous tableaus rather than a series of shots comprising scenes and achieving a continuity of action. Both Porter's *Life of an American Fireman* and *The Great Train Robbery* link a continuous series of narrative events through a series of one-shot scenes. These quite different approaches to storytelling suggest the extent to which the cinema in 1903 was a developing artistic medium whose aesthetic norms and conventions were provisional and unstable. In exploring cinema's narrative potentials, early filmmakers utilized, as John Fell has observed, a "conventional narrative code" derived from a variety of cultural sources.[11] Different approaches to visual storytelling coexisted (even within the same film) along with the impulse to document and record the world in front of the camera, and the result was the production of scores of docufictional texts. The key point to keep in mind is that in the period of early film "commercial cinema was dominated by the documentary impulse of the actuality film and variants on it,"[12] and that in the transition to narrative many films retained a large measure of that "documentary impulse."

Coming at a time when public interest in short, one-shot films was apparently in decline,[13] *The Life of an American Fireman* and *The Great Train Robbery* were longer than other films which allowed them to construct more complex narratives, with more scenes and characters. But more importantly, these films essentially brought together two genres — the "actuality" and the "story film" — and in so doing created a new dramatic form for documenting social reality — the motion picture docudrama. In hybrid films such as these, the representation of reality achieved through the photographic literalness of the cinematic image functioned alongside the conventional literary devices of narrative emplotment, theme, and (in a rudimentary sense) character, while the thematic and connotative potential of narrativity that the story film introduced to cinema provided an ideological and cultural framework which could explain and interpret images of "real" events. The result was a cinema that exploited the photographic verisimilitude of the medium to dramatize the social fact and framed the social fact within the narrative conventions of late 19th century fiction.

The first film historians were right about these two films in one crucial respect: *Life of an American Fireman* and *The Great Train Robbery* were highly influential films in their day. But their influence lies not solely in the fact that they told stories, but that they told certain kinds of stories that involved audiences in ways and to an extent that earlier films had not succeeded in doing. What was most innovative about these films was that they anticipated a new relationship between the audience and the events on the screen — encouraging the viewer's rapt identification with the narrative and thereby contributing to a reconstitution of the relationship between film viewer and film text.[14] They achieved this heightened sense of vicarious involvement and identification through a combination of formal and thematic elements. That is, part of their rhetorical ability to move and excite audiences, surely rested on the technical features for which these two films are justifiably well-known (their length, editing, camera placement and movement). But an equally important component of both films' success with audiences lies on the level of content; in the socially defined characters and situations they present and the cultural issues they evoke, which the films attempt to both document and render ideologically coherent through narrativization. Both films, operating within an iconic, referential style associated with *realism*, dramatize a threat to the stability of the social order, a narrative pattern associated with *melodrama*. As texts, *Life of an American Fireman* and *The Great Train Robbery* are structured by the intersecting goals of realism and melodrama; the first convinces us of the authenticity of the events we see on the screen, the second instructs us how to respond to these events. However, as complex, cultural artifacts, these films function as sites of intersection for opposed, contradictory social and aesthetic discourses. Thus, while on a denotative level *Life of an American Fireman* and *The Great Train Robbery* can be seen to celebrate a restoration of social order that valorizes conservative social values, on a connotative level, the issues of gender and class which they raise can be seen to undermine their putative ideological message and suggest contradictory social and political tensions at work in these films, the product of a narrative excess symptomatic of late 19th-century social tensions.

Realism and Melodrama

Two powerful aesthetic paradigms can be seen to shape the cultural work performed by these two films: *realism* and *melodrama*. The realism of these films can be understood in several different ways. As photographic records of the physical world all films are composed of iconic images that refer us to reality, even when that reality is entirely fabricated and artificial. The development of film technology was part of the immense cultural and scientific project of recording the physical world which had given rise to photography and precipitated movements in painting and the graphic arts during the nineteenth-century. The initial fascination in film derived precisely from its ability to achieve photographic likeness in motion and in so doing to document a *real* event.[15] One of the chief appeals of films such as *The Life of an American Fireman* and *The Great Train Robbery* derived precisely from their promise to present visual images of burning houses and train robberies. Yet even in the technological sense of photographic realism it is necessary to be aware of the cultural and ideological saturation of the photographic image and resist naïve notions of photographic "truth."[16] The images that compose early films are replete with cultural and historical meanings that require careful contextualization and informed analysis.

Another way of framing the notion of realism in early film is to see it as part of the aesthetic strategy of modern storytelling. The elaboration of logical spatio-temporal continuities in the creation of a fictional world through cross-cutting and match cuts, so important to the development of classical narrative, were, as Janet Staiger has argued, "already aspects of a standard of verisimilitude," as was the "matching of character actions and mise-en-scène to ideologically determined conceptions of reality."[17] In constructing narratives and delineating character and setting, early filmmakers had a rich heritage of literary and theatrical models of realistic representation to draw on and adapt to their own purposes.

Finally there is a journalistic notion of realism at work in early film "actualities" which claim to be authentic depictions of real events. Actualities such as *The Seventy-First Infantry Embarking* (1898) for Cuba during the Spanish-American war, *Searching Ruins on Broadway, Galveston, for Dead Bodies* (1900) in the aftermath of a hurricane, or *Sky Scrapers of New York City from North River* (1903) are indicative of the vast majority of films made up until around 1905, when the number of filmed narratives began to dominate production. Clearly, film's capacity to record the historical or socially significant movement was apparent from the start, as was its ability to shape and influence our response to that moment. Indeed, as already noted, the popularity of actualities led enterprising film-makers to blur the distinctions between document and fiction by creating staged reenactments of events the cameras had inconveniently missed. Both *Life of an American Fireman* and *The Great Train Robbery* participate in this mode of film realism insofar as they were seen as plausible, fictional versions of real social events. They must be read, therefore, within a kind of pseudo-journalistic cultural discourse about the events that they depict. That Porter's films occupied an unspecified generic space between narrative and actuality is evident in the advertising strategies used to sell these films to exhibitors, as these excerpts from the Edison catalogue show.

The Life of an American Fireman (1903)

In giving this description to the public we unhesitatingly claim for it the strongest motion picture attraction ever attempted in this length of film. It will be difficult for the exhibitor to conceive the amount of work involved and the number of rehearsals necessary to turn out a film of this kind. We were compelled to enlist the services of the fire departments of four different cities, New York, Newark, Orange, and East Orange, N.J., and about 300 firemen appear in the various scenes of this film.

From the first conception of this wonderful series of pictures it has been our aim to portray *Life of an American Fireman* without exaggeration, at the same time embodying the dramatic situations and spectacular effects which so greatly enhance a motion picture performance....

This film faithfully and accurately depicts his thrilling and dangerous life, emphasizing the perils he subjects himself to when human life is at stake.

The Great Train Robbery (1903)

This sensational and highly tragic subject will certainly make a decided "hit" whenever shown. In every respect we consider it absolutely the superior motion picture ever made. It has been posed and acted in faithful duplication of the genuine "Hold Ups" made famous by various outlaw bands in the far West, and only recently the East has been shocked by several crimes of the frontier order, which will increase the popular interest in this great *Headline Attraction.*

SCENE 14 — REALISM. A life size picture of Barnes, leader of the outlaw band, taking aim and firing point blank at each individual in the audience.... The resulting excitement is great.[18]

Clearly the rhetoric of the advertising copy goes to some length to make what appear to be contradictory claims for the realism of these films. On the one hand they are "faithful," "accurate" depictions told without "exaggeration" and which "duplicate" "genuine" events. On the other hand they are "dramatic," "spectacular" representations which emphasize the "thrilling" and "sensational" qualities of their narratives. The explicit tension between these aesthetic aims indicates a conflict of mimetic codes at work in these films; a conflict, particularly apparent in their *mise-en-scène*, between documentary realism and fictional artifice. For instance, scenes 5 and 6 in *Life of an American Fireman*[19] are shots of real fire engines racing down a city street. Porter incorporated these documentary images into his own invented story, and they stand in obvious contrast to the more theatrically staged scenes of the fire station, house façade, and burning bedroom. In *The Great Train Robbery*, the artificiality of interior sets such as the Dancehall — with a stove painted on a flat backdrop — contrasts sharply with the actual train and real horses which appear in the exterior scenes. In both films, interior shots are staged and photographed theatrically, that is with a single, static, medium long shot against a painted flat, while exterior shots, utilizing pans and limited camera movement, create a more dynamic and open sense of space. Similarly, there is a range of acting codes represented in these films from the hysterics of the woman in the burning room and the exaggerated death of the train passenger during the robbery, to the more natural performances of the fireman and the bandits. The uneasy coordination of these distinct mimetic standards suggests something of the ideological and aesthetic tensions at work in these films, as two quite different modes of representation overlap yet fail to meet.

Both *Life of an American Fireman* and *The Great Train Robbery*, as the advertising copy indicates, were intended to be depictions of real and, we can assume, familiar social events. Their effort to both document and dramatize the social facts of fire and crime reveal the docufictional address of these two films. *Life of an American Fireman* capitalized on the "popular appeal"[20] and interest in firemen and the work of fire departments, as evidenced by a number of films that predate it.[21] Likewise, part of the interest and excitement generated by *The Great Train Robbery* stemmed from the chronic problem of lawlessness on the American frontier.[22] Of course, the treatment of banditry in a western setting had an important cultural precedent in the popular dime novels of the late 19th century. Even further, the narrative

treatment of social events such as fire and crime were subject to relatively circum-
scribed cultural codes derived largely from melodrama.[23]

The aims of realism and melodrama might appear opposed to one another at
first glance. Melodrama relies on highly conventionalized codes of characterization
and narrative emplotment. It generally involves a threat to some valorized cultural
idea (honesty, virtue, law and order), institution (the family, marriage, private property), or character type (a child, young woman or widow), which is sustained through
narrative devices that are designed to delay resolution and create suspense until an
extraordinary and heroic intervention neutralizes the threat and restores social and
moral order. Ostensibly realism resists such rigid narrative patterning, character
typology, and overt moral didacticism in favor of a more objective, comparatively
open depiction of the real. Yet, as I have suggested, realism is itself as culturally coded
and ideologically laden as melodrama, perhaps more so because so often its representational strategies and ideological agendas are naturalized through both institutional practice and widespread cultural acceptance, and thus rendered "invisible."
But realism and melodrama are not entirely antagonistic: the effects of melodrama
require a distinct diegetic presence, a recognizable world with tangible threats and
dangers.[24] To be effective, melodrama requires a strong realistic premise.

An important contribution to the impact these two films had on audiences rests
on their deployment of melodramatic narrative patterns that create suspense and
apprehension in the audience. The heightening of emotional tension through the
application of traditional melodramatic devices such as "the chase" and "the last-
minute rescue" from peril serves to both intensify the audience's involvement with
the events of the narrative and to render more acute the social crisis that they depict.
The synthesis of realism and melodrama in these two films creates a measure of
uncertainty concerning their outcomes. Will the mother and child die a fiery death?
Will the bandits escape the law and flee with their ill-gotten loot? The possibility of
these "realistic" endings suggests the profound cultural anxieties raised by these subjects. More to my point, they reveal the extent to which documentary and fiction
could be fluidly merged in the telling of a dramatically compelling yet socially authentic narrative.

The Life of an American Fireman

From its title one could assume that this is a film about work; specifically the
job of being an *American* fireman, the nationalism of the title providing an explicit
political frame for its depiction. But from the start this film announces a somewhat
different social agenda. Scene 1 establishes a relationship between the brooding, conscientious fire chief and the idealized image of the mother and child that appears
within the dream balloon, a device for representing the subjective thoughts of the
fire chief derived from newspaper comic strips. This juxtaposition announces the
central ideological project of the film: The domestic sphere, with its narrowly cir-
cumscribed construction of the feminine, is to be rescued by the masculine values
of the fireman — his strength, his work ethic, and professional skill. As conventional

figures of sentimental representation, the mother and child are objects of a kind of occupational male gaze in scene 1, which appropriates them by assuming responsibility for their safety and protection. Thus, issues of gender are raised from the start and the central cultural concerns of this film can be seen to emerge from its sexual politics. An important aspect of this film's ideological work lies in its efforts to articulate and support dominant notions of feminine helplessness and masculine strength and resourcefulness.

The real threat of urban fire gets melodramatic treatment in Edwin S. Porter's *Life of an American Fireman* (1902).

As a cultural topos, the domestic ideal is a tremendously powerful idea. As Alan Trachtenberg has observed, "the domestic sphere, with its hearth, its parlor table, its warm kitchen, and loyal wife-mother, served as the centerpiece of a cluster of images representing the norm of American life."[25] Trachtenberg's comment helps us understand what was at stake in this film: The consuming element of fire, with its sexual implications resonant, threatens nothing less than fundamental social and sexual norms. Through a dramatic enactment that places the domestic sphere in peril, *The Life of an American Fireman* evoked deep social anxieties for its audiences, vicariously involving them in its scenes of peril and heroic rescue.

The second shot in the film is one of the most interesting historically, in that it documents a rapidly developing technology of urban fire prevention; an anonymous hand opens a New York fire-alarm box and activates the alarm. This shot signals the mobilization of formidable technological and social forces in defense of the domestic sphere. Technology is an explicit theme here: From the instantaneous alert, electronically transmitted to the fire station to the deployment of the apparatus and equipment of urban fire fighting, *The Life of an American Fireman* celebrates technology and enlists its aid in a battle to defend the domestic sphere. There is an almost military quality to the mobilization of firemen and the organization of their activities (shots 3 and 4). Martial elements are maintained in shots 5, 6, and 7, as the fireman and their equipment race through city streets to the scene of the fire. As a uniformed representative of municipal authority, the fireman is a particularly salient embodiment of state power. The cultural image of the fireman evokes the authority of government in the defense of the mother and child, and it marshals the coordinated energies of society in its efforts to protect the dominant socio-sexual norms represented by the domestic sphere. At the same time, shots 2 through 7 seem specifically intended to serve the "documentary impulse" to record real events (the fire engines' race through city streets as actuality footage) and such ideological meanings as I have suggested here are the products of the imbrication of these images within a narrative structure organized by a melodramatic social logic.

The cultural topos of the domestic ideal is based upon two fundamental dichotomies: Socially constructed notions of masculinity and femininity on the one hand, and a rigid socio-economic division between home and work on the other. The final two shots (scenes 8 and 9) vividly dramatize these divisions. In scene 8 we see the mother awake suddenly in the burning room, go to the window and then frantically run about the room before fainting on the bed. At this point a fireman breaks down the door, smashes out the window, and carries the woman through the window and down a ladder, returning a moment later for the child. As Jackson Lears has observed concerning the role of the domestic sphere: "Under urban conditions of life, 'work' became radically separated from 'home' and that separation reinforced another: between productive adult males and nonproductive women and children."[26] The abject helplessness of the mother and child in this scene is emblematic of the "nonproductivity" attached to women, and of their objectification within the ideology of the domestic ideal. They are depicted, finally, as little more than dead weights to be moved and carried. The narrative of *Life of an American Fireman* is constructed on these ideologically charged notions of male and female, work and home. At the moment of crisis the categories of masculine activity and feminine passivity stand out in sharp contrast to each other, while the social spaces of work and home momentarily collide as the fireman battles the blaze consuming the bedroom. Much of the impact of this scene can be attributed to the violent penetration of the feminine domestic space of the bedroom by the masculine world of the fireman's work.

In contrast to the clear temporal continuity of action achieved in classical Hollywood narration, the ninth shot temporally overlaps the eighth, as we see a repetition of the same actions but from a position outside the burning house.[27] In this shot we see the fireman enter the burning house while another places a ladder at the upstairs window. A moment later the window is smashed out and the fireman carries the woman down the ladder. The woman quickly revives and pleads with the fireman to rescue her child. The fireman climbs the ladder once more and rescues the baby. The final, tableau-like image in the film is an emotional reuniting of mother and child as the firemen tend to business. Clearly, this ending performs a particularly forceful narrative closure: with the mother and child rescued the social crisis is averted and the dominant socio-sexual norms are upheld. By providing the audience with both a documentary-like, photographically "realistic" view of events and a reassuring sense of narrational coherence and ideological closure, *Life of an American Fireman* presents itself as a hybrid text, on the cusp of two competing notions of what the cinema could be.

The Great Train Robbery

The social phenomenon of banditry, as Eric Hobsbawm[28] has observed, develops and flourishes during periods of "social tension and upheaval," and often the bandit appears as "a figure of social protest and rebellion," particularly within popular culture. Such a political reading of banditry helps us to understand the cultural conflicts at work in *The Great Train Robbery*. The subversive image of the bandit dominates this film, eroding its putative social message — "crime does not pay." This warning provides a kind of moral veneer, an ideological screen, for a narrative which, in fact, provides its audience with the vicarious thrill of crime itself, realized in documentary-like detail. In shots 1 through 7 it is the robbery which holds the viewer's attention, appealing to an interest in the stratagems and techniques of the criminal act. The detail with which the robbery is depicted satisfies the requirements of realistic verisimilitude and the audience's curiosity, implicating as well as informing them through its meticulous depiction. And we see the collision of mimetic

Direct address to the audience: The bandit leader (George Barnes) fires point-blank into the camera in *The Great Train Robbery* (1903).

codes that we have already identified as a characteristic element in films of this period of transition from iconic to narrative cinema. In scene 4 we witness a realistic struggle between the bandits and the train's engineer shot from on top of the moving coal car. However, just as the bandit prepares to throw the engineer's unconscious body off the train a dummy is substituted. In this moment two different standards of verisimilitude — one documentary and journalistic, the other narrative and melodramatic — overlap in the film.

One of the ways in which *The Great Train Robbery* unconsciously aligns our sympathies with the bandits is through the juxtaposition of contrasting mimetic codes mentioned above. The *mise-en-scène* of the telegraph office, the express car, and the dancehall — the sites of social, economic, and political authority in the film — are flat, one-dimensional, limited by an artificial theatricality which underscores the fabricated and inauthentic nature of these representations. The cinematic spaces occupied by the bandits, in contrast, are actual locations and are thus more dynamic and open. In shot 8, for instance, the camera pans to follow the bandits as they escape down a steep slope and into the woods, and shot 9 follows the bandits as they cross a stream to retrieve their horses. The use of outdoor locations in these scenes and a more mobile use of the camera produce an effect of exhilaration in contrast to the static theatricality of the interior scenes. In other words, the bandits' scenes are more interesting to watch

The representation of a familiar social occurrence can be seen in this image from *The Great Train Robbery* (1903).

because of the way they are staged and shot; their style marks them as, in some sense, privileged moments in the narrative.

In contrast to the bandits, the other characters—the telegraph operator, the engineer, the railroad employee guarding the safe—are all weak and ineffectual as defenders of law and order. The passengers who are robbed at gunpoint in scene 6, figures of middle class affluence, cringe before the bandits until one of them panics and attempts to flee, only to be gunned down by one of the bandits. The train itself can be read as a symbol of a triumphant industrial order, emblematic of an economic and technological transformation of American society in the late 19th century that resulted in a consolidation of political control by class interests hostile to those elements of society—radically individualistic and loosely working class—that were most likely to challenge its authority through criminality. Beneath the surface of its dime novel narrative, *The Great Train Robbery* evokes a clash of class interests which subvert its overt ideological intentions.

Scene 11 in the dancehall provides a counterpoint to the robbery that functions as a display of frontier community and social cohesion, yet several elements in the scene complicate such a reading. Most significant is the appearance of the "tenderfoot," a dandified visitor from the city. He is taunted by the men in the dancehall who force him to dance by firing shots at his feet. Such an incident evokes an underlying social tension between the country and the city, and suggests the uneasy relations between urban centers and the frontier margins of society. But perhaps even more importantly, it calls into question the behavioral codes that govern "Western" society. The men in the Dancehall go from a somewhat dangerous intimidation of the "tenderfoot" to the formation of an armed posse, presumably in the service of law and order. *The Great Train Robbery* shows that the difference between the bandits and the posse is one of degree and not of kind; that the categories of social morality and authority on the one hand, and social deviance and disruption on the other, are permeable and contingent on the frontier of American society, and that this represents an essential social "fact" about the west.

This idea is rendered even more explicit in scene 13. While we watch the bandits divide the loot the posse approaches unobserved and ambushes them from behind. In the shootout the bandits are all killed and the posse begins to collect the money. In the absence of individualizing close-ups and that iconography of character type that would eventually help us distinguish the "good guys" from the "bad guys," in the western (e.g. white hats or a marshal's star), the posse is physically indistinguishable from the bandits. One way of understanding this failure to differentiate characters is to recognize that the film is attempting to synthesize a documentary-like reenactment *and* tell a dramatically compelling and ideologically coherent story.

Shot 14, the final image of the film, is a medium close-up of the bandit leader firing his pistol point blank at the audience. Noel Burch has written of this famous "emblematic" shot that it introduces "the dimension of individual presence" into a film composed largely of anonymous identities, and that it represents an "attempt to encapsulate the 'essence' of the film."[29] Clearly it gives the last word, so to speak, to the bandits, an enviable rhetorical position which once again serves to undermine the social ideology which superficially the film is concerned with valorizing and upholding. In one sense, this shot repeats the temporal overlap that occurs in the final shot of *The Life of an American Fireman* by showing us the bandit leader after he is supposed to be dead and granting him a larger-than-life status as image (he is shown in a framing that is somewhat larger than a medium close-up). But above all, this final image addresses the audience in regards to the narrative and thematic content of the film, positioning them directly in the path of its social and class conflicts, and inviting their identification with the socially transgressive figure of the bandit.

Conclusion: The Newspaper Meets the Dime Novel

The Life of an American Fireman and *The Great Train Robbery* were important films in their day because they dramatized social content that was important to their first audiences. They are of interest today because they exemplify the as yet fully theorized capacity of cinema to function simultaneously as both record and representation.[30] I mean to suggest more than that Porter's films were important to their first audiences because they appealed to that audience's taste for topicality and sensation. Rather, I would argue that they appealed to the audience's expectation for seeing something "real"—socially significant events rendered in photographic detail—an expectation bred in the iconic cinema of the earliest films. *Life of an American Fireman* and *The Great Train Robbery* essentially synthesized the topical concerns of the contemporary newspaper with the melodramatic appeals of the dime novel. Out of such an imbrication of cultural influences in early cinema the dramatic form of visual storytelling and reportage eventually known as "docudrama" first appeared.

1. The transition from preclassical early cinema to classical "Hollywood" cinema has long been conceived of as a transition from a use of cinema as a recording device to a use of cinema as an instrument of narrative storytelling, but the precise determinants of this transition have been the subject of much debate among film historians. In opposition to the idea that the transition to narrative signaled a reflection of the early audiences' increasing lack of interest in actualities and other types of filmed records, others have argued that film producers began to increase their output of filmed stories because they were easier to budget and preplan, and therefore served the industry's desire to rationalize the production process. Important arguments in this debate can be found in Charles Musser, *Before the Nickelodeon: Edward S. Porter and the Edison Manufacturing Company*, (Berkeley: University of California Press), 229–230; Musser, *The Emergence of Cinema: The American Screen to 1907*, Chapter 11: "The Transition to Story Films: 1903–1904" (New York: Charles Scribner's Sons, 1990) 337–369; Robert Allen, "Film history: the narrow discourse," in *Film: Historical-Theoretical Speculations: The 1977 Film Studies Annual (Part Two)*, eds. Ben Lawton and Janet Staiger (Pleasantville, New York: Redgrave Publishing Co., 1977) 9–17.

2. See David Bordwell, Janet Staiger, and Kristin Thompson, *The Classical Hollywood Cinema: Film Style and Mode of Production to 1960* (New York: Columbia University Press, 1985), 113–116.

3. See Tom Gunning, "The Cinema of Attractions: Early Film, its Spectator and the Avant Garde" in *Early Cinema: Space, Frame, Narrative*, ed. by Thomas Elsaesser (London: BFI Publishing, 1990); 56–62.

4. See Allen, "Film history," 12–13.

5. Tom Gunning, "Early American Film" in *American Cinema and Hollywood: Critical Approaches*, ed. by John Hill and Pamela Church Gibson (New York, Oxford University Press, 2000); 42.

6. For a discussion of genre in Early Cinema see Robert C. Allen's "Contra the Chaser Theory" in *Film Before Griffith* (Berkeley: University of California Press, 1983) 105–115.

7. Staged reenactments of military actions began as early as 1898 with such Edison films as *Battle of San Juan Hill* and *Charges of the Rough Riders at El Caney*, both made in 1898. See Charles Musser, *Before the Nickelodeon: Edwin S. Porter and the Edison Manufacturing Company*, 146. Perhaps the apothosis of such fakery was J. Stuart Blackton's film *The Sinking of the Maine*, which was shot in a bathtub.

8. According to Terry Ramsaye in *A Million and One Nights* (New York: Simon & Schuster, 1926), "The Life of an American Fireman" was considered a "gripping masterpiece"(416) by its first audiences. Edward Wagenknecht in *The Movies in the Age of Innocence* (Norman: University of Oklahoma Press, 1962) described "'The Great Train Robbery' as *The Birth of a Nation* of early film days" (38).

9. Terry Ramsaye, a committed exponent of Edison's importance in the history of the motion picture, dismisses earlier film narratives by Cecil Hepworth in England and J. Stuart Blackton and Albert E. Smith in this country as "tiny, trivial efforts"(414). It was from the Edison studios, "where the art of the film was born"—according to Ramsaye—that the "emergence of the narrative idea" first occurred. Similarly, Paul Rotha, in his survey of world cinema *The Film Till Now* (Feltham: Hamlyn House, 1930), asserts that "...it was not until 1903 that the first real attempt to tell a story by moving pictures was made. The event was achieved by Edwin S. Porter's "The Great Train Robbery..." (70). In *The Rise of the American Film* (New York: Harcourt Brace and Company, 1939), Lewis Jacobs refers to Porter as "the father of the story film" (20). A. Nicholas Vardac, in his important study of the relationship between theater and film, notes: "The photoplay, a series of situations pictorially developed not only to tell a story but so interlaced that this story became cinematically dramatic, had not found significant expression prior to 1902. It came in that year with E.S. Porter's "The Life of an American Fireman" (180). *Stage to Screen: Theatrical Method from Garrick to Griffith* (Cambridge: Harvard University Press, 1949).

10. "Standard accounts of the history of the cinema state that the [motion picture] business was stymied until the motion picture grew out of its 'primitive' stage to attain a certain length, around one thousand feet, fifteen minutes of screen time. This length allowed filmmakers to tell an effective story with a beginning, middle, and end. "The Great Train Robbery," directed by Edwin S. Porter in 1903, paved the way.... This 'narrative structure' theory can be found in the histories of Terry Ramsaye, Benjamin Hampton, Lewis Jacobs, and others, but in light of recent research by young scholars such as Robert Allen, Janet Staiger, and Charles Musser a revision of our understanding of this entire period is in order." Tino Balio, "A Novelty Spawns Small Businesses, 1894–1908" in *The American Film Industry* (Madison: University of Wisconsin Press, 1985) pp. 21–22. Charles Musser, in his article "The Early Cinema of Edwin Porter," (*Cinema Journal*, Vol. XIX, No. 1, Fall 1979) concludes that "Porter was hardly the father of the story film" (34). "No inventor of film editing existed. Directors [like Porter] developed or adopted certain specific editorial strategies, often to abandon or modify them sometime later" (34). Arguing that the editorial principles used by Porter to construct his story films have a history significantly older than cinema itself in literature, theater, and 19th century lantern shows, Musser locates the development of the story film in a transference of editorial control from exhibitors to producer/cameramen. The short one and two minute films that were the staple of early filmmaking were arranged into programs by exhibitors who also often supplied a narrator and musical accompaniment in order to achieve a "unified program." This arrangement, as Musser notes, gave the exhibitor "a major creative role" (5). The development of continuity editing as an instrument of film narrative was based on the "creation of a fictional world with spatial and temporal relationships between scenes" (24) which were not subject to the editorial intervention of the exhibitor. The "story film" was the product of this "decisive shift in editorial control from exhibitor to cameraman"(34). Tied to both technical and commercial considerations, this new balance of creative power was meant to insure "a standardized product that could be marketed like other commercial items"(35). As Philip Rosen has most recently pointed out, the emergence of narrative cinema required two fundamental transitions: The first was the transition from an iconic cinema that served a documentary interest in the real to a "deliberate, explicit narrative" (163) cinema governed by the conventions of popular fiction. The second transition was from short, one and two reel films to features, a development that led directly to those narrative and stylistic features that we now identify as Classical Hollywood cinema. See Chapter 4, "Detail, Document, and Diegesis in Mainstream Film," *Change Mummified: Cinema, Historicity, Theory* (Minneapolis: University of Minnesota Press, 2001) 147–199.

11. John Fell, *Film and the Narrative Tradition* (Norman: University of Oklahoma Press, 1974). Fell's study examines "the very nonuniqueness of the movies' techniques. They are reflected in media as seemingly different from one another as the nineteenth-century novel, early comics, magazine illustration, the Cubists and Impressionists, the most pop of popular literature, and entertainments of the theater, fairground, and parlor" (XII). Taken together these disparate cultural sources constitute a "common narrative direction" which culminates in early film.

12. Rosen, *Change Mummified*, 162–163.

13. Citing as historical support Edison's monopoly on film production between the end of July and the end of March 1902, Charles Musser has argued: "Histories of early cinema often refer to a decline in the popularity of moving pictures around the turn-of-the-century. The decline has customarily been attributed to a jaded audience tired of actuality scenes and news footage, only to be reversed by the appearance of the story film. Unsubstantiated, it always seemed to be one of those vague myths that pass for the history of those 'early years.' An Eastman Kodak report on motion picture film sales, however, indicates that a decline in sales did take place in 1901 and 1902, coinciding with Edison's control of the industry. Edison's monopoly was a significant blow to American film culture, not only to Edison's competitors but to exhibitors and audiences as well" "The Early Cinema of Edwin Porter," 20–21.

14. The following critical assessment appeared in a *New York Times* article entitled "Creative Path of Soviet Films," March 1, 1931 A: "It is believed that with the filming of "The Great Train Robbery" the motion picture camera first began legitimately to photograph adventure scenes not from the outside, as a coward peeking at them, but as a conscientious, energetic participant in the events—a participant who hurries to aid and who himself joins the battle for right and justice. Having become the twin of each of the *dramatic personae*, the motion picture camera gave the spectator an opportunity to see upon the screen all the scenes in a form which could be felt by participants only. And, following the camera, the spectators ceased being indifferent witnesses and turned into participants of the events. What took place here, intrinsically, is just what happened to modern literature. Its renaissance was aided by the evolution of the 'journalistic' printing press into the modern machine. Here, the freshness of newspaper material, its proximity to life and the reality of the subject, played the role of the motion picture camera, the penetrating and deft chronicler. The newspaper created a more active reader, just as the American method of filming transformed the lover of picture-gazing into an active spectator." Significantly, as this passage suggests but comes just short of saying, it was a kind of social content in "The Great Train Robbery," its "proximity to life and the reality of the subject," that brought about a new participatory involvement with the film text. Such an assessment of the film points to the processes of identification mobilized by any narrative but perfected within the conventions of Classical Hollywood narration.

15. Perhaps the defining moment for early cinema was Eadward Muybridge's use of the pre-cinematic technology of still photography to document the fact that all four of a horse's hoofs leave the ground in full-gallop, the occurrence of which was in dispute until Muybridge provided irrefutable photographic evidence that such was the case.

16. "Photography is not merely the camera apparatus. It is also the entire system of picture-making practices: the subjects chosen; the photographer's aims, commercial or artistic; and the modes of representation such as the code of perspective, which governs two-dimensional imitation of deep space. By the 1890s, this cultural process had infiltrated the entire society, establishing itself as perhaps the prime arbiter of 'reality.'" Alan Trachtenberg, "Photography/ Cinematography" in *Before Hollywood: Turn-of-the-Century American Film* (New York: Hudson Hills Press, 1987) 74.

17. Janet Staiger, "Blueprints for Feature Films" in *The American Film Industry*, ed. by Tino Balio, (Madison: University of Wisconsin Press, 1985) 181.

18. These are reproduced from *The Classical Hollywood Cinema: Film Style and Mode of Production to 1960* by David Bordwell, Janet Staiger, and Kristin Thompson (New York: Columbia University Press, 1985), 98.

19. Reference to specific scenes are based on the shot-by-shot descriptions of these films in the Edison Catalogue. These are reproduced in A.R. Fulton's *Motion Pictures: The Development of an Art From Silent Films to the Age of Television* (Norman: University of Oklahoma Press, 1960) 47–49, 52–54. They also appear in Lewis Jacobs' *The Rise of the American Film*, 38–41, 43–46.

20. Jacobs, 37.

21. These include a popular twelve slide lantern show entitled *Bob the Fireman* that is discussed

by Musser, as well as *Fire Rescue* (1894), *A Morning Alarm*, *Starting for the Fire*, and *Fighting a Fire* (all 1896) produced by the Edison Company. Musser notes that in "the Edison Catalogue of September 1902, ten fire films were grouped under a single heading while others on the same subject were scattered throughout its 120 pages" (26). Musser also suggests that a British film by James Williamson, *Fire!* (1901), was a possible inspiration for *Life of an American Fireman*.

22. "[T]rain robberies were being reported in the newspapers almost daily." Jacobs, 42.

23. An important discussion of melodrama and its role in early film narrative appears in John Fell's *Film and the Narrative Tradition*. He notes: "Melodrama was the product of an industrial society — the urban working class — and the topical excitements of its period — crime, military adventure, wilderness explorations. It developed out of morality plays and sentimental plays as well as from the Gothic novel.... Audience participation was strong. The people who attended this theater, and later its filmed equivalent, shared a desire to see dramatized allegories of human experience.... Speech, behavior, and settings were coded for instant recognition. Justice prevailed — as inevitable consequence of the struggle and torment. Thus melodrama guised fantasy in the costume of naturalism.... It presented a world of problems and characters made fraudulently comprehensible, then costumed with palatable thrills, climaxed in reassuring resolutions. The narrative form developed to guarantee unflagging interest by omitting the 'dead spots' of other drama, enlisting identifications with the performers and refining resources of suspense" (14).

24. "To create a strong identification between the screen and the audience — pretending to the reality of the action, facilitating a strong emotion on the part of the spectator, making the suspense plausible, increasing the efficiency of the close-up — a consistent universe had to be shaped. This was an essential condition. The last-minute rescue, as a basic structure for the construction of a narrative, required it." Andre Gaudreault, "Temporality and Narrativity in Early Cinema, 1895–1908," in *Film Before Griffith*, 327.

25. Alan Trachtenberg, *The Incorporation of America: Culture and Society in the Gilded Age*, (New York: Hill and Wang, 1982), 129.

26. Jackson Lears, *No Place of Grace: Antimodernism and the Transformation of American Culture 1880–1920*, (New York: Pantheon Books, 1981), 15.

27. *Life of an American Fireman* exists in two versions, Porter's original cut of the film that contains the temporal overlap in which the same actions are repeated but from two different spatial view points, and a "cross-cut" version that was circulated by the Museum of Modern Art for several years, in which the last two shots are intercut to achieve something like the continuity of action we associate with Classical Hollywood narration. See Charles Musser, "The Early Cinema of Edwin Porter," *Cinema Journal*, Vol. XIX, No. 1, Fall 1979, 29–31.

28. Eric Hobsbawm, *Bandits*, (New York: Pantheon Books, 1981), 18.

29. Noel Burch, "Primitivism and the Avant Gardes: A Dialectical Approach," in *Narrative, Apparatus, Ideology: A Film theory Reader* (New York: Columbia University Press), 492.

30. An important step in this theoretical project has been made by Philip Rosen in *Change Mummified* (2001), along with the work of the contributors to this volume of essays.

3

On the Edges of Fiction: Silent Actualités, *City Symphonies and Early SF Movies*

by Mark Bould

Beginning at the End, or, a Slightly Wayward Introduction

Consider these two scenes. The first is from "Bodies Without Minds," chapter nine of the *Buck Rogers* (Beebe, Goodkind 1939) movie serial. Following the cliffhanger conclusion of the previous episode, everyone thinks Buck (Larry "Buster" Crabbe) and Wilma Deering (Constance Moore) are dead, killed in a mid-air collision with one of the evil dictator Killer Kane's (Anthony Warde) spaceships—everyone, that is, but Buddy (Jackie Moran), Buck's relentlessly chirpy juvenile sidekick.[1] Having witnessed the collision and crash-landing and the nearby landing of several of Kane's other spaceships over the televisor, and having heard Captain Rankin (Jack Mulhall) report the failure to recover any bodies from the twisted, melted wreckage, Buddy suggests that maybe Buck and Wilma did survive and were taken captive. Dr. Huer (C. Montague Shaw) points out that if this were the case, then their deaths would be every bit as certain and terrible.

"But Kane wouldn't kill them, sir," Buddy protests. "I know. I was with them on Saturn. I ... Dr. Huer, could your pastoscope bring back a scene that happened on another planet?"

"Why, yes, I believe we could pick it up if it happened recently."

"Then please try to bring back the scene where Kane's men captured Buck on Saturn. I am sure it would prove to you, sir, why Buck is so much more valuable to Kane alive than he is dead."

"Very well. But it will only be an experiment. We may not be able to recreate a scene that happened on another planet." Dr. Huer and Buddy cross to a device that resembles the offspring of a coin-operated telescope and a futuristic machine gun. "Of course, the first thing to do is blot out the present from our vision. The next is to coordinate the time with the distance to Saturn..." — the shot cuts to a viewscreen filled with a swirling image — "...and if we can find the exact point of convergence...."

The swirling is replaced by a shot, taken from a previous episode, of Buck, Wilma, and Buddy crossing the desert landscape of Saturn. "That's it," Buddy cries, "It's right near where our ship was forced down."

There follows a two-and-a-half minute, 32-shot sequence lifted straight from the earlier episode,[2] framed by the viewscreen's TV-like casing, in which our heroes first capture two of Kane's men and are then in turn captured by another pair of Kane's men.

"There," Buddy exclaims as this interpolated footage comes to an end. "You see what I mean, sir?"

"That still doesn't give us reason to believe Buck and Wilma escaped from the ship, Buddy," replies the sceptical Dr. Huer.

"Oh, I don't care what any of you say. I know Buck is still alive. I just know it." And with that, Buddy stomps sulkily out of the room.

The second scene is from "Beneath the Earth," chapter five of *The Phantom Empire* (Brower, Eason 1935). Gene Autry (playing "himself") has been captured by the inhabitants of Murania, a subterranean city of superscience located 25,000 feet beneath Radio Ranch. Determined to demonstrate the superiority of Murania to the surface world, Queen Tika (Dorothy Christie) escorts Gene to an antechamber in which is located a viewing device.

"You have referred to your sunlight and planes. Now let me prove that they are not all that is worthwhile," she says, nodding to a minion to activate the device, a large circular surface into which they look from above. A spiral graphic rotates rapidly on the surface, accompanied by a sound like a washing machine, and then the surface displays a vista of Murania's spectacular skyline.

"Radium resistance elevation," says Tika as the view shifts to one of a futuristic elevator car racing up a clear cylinder to the roof of the vast cavern Murania occupies. "Do you have that in your surface world?"

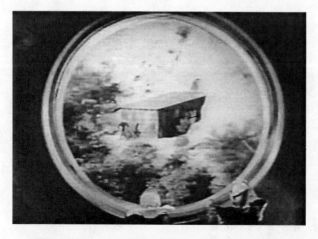

The televisor screen in Chapter Five of the serial *The Phantom Empire* (1935).

The spiral graphic spins. "In Murania we have mechanical men for all our labour." The viewscreen pans along a line of four utterly ludicrous robots as they hammer — very slowly — on anvils. "My subjects devote their time to thought," Tika boasts, "to advancing their minds."

The spiral spins again, giving way to a shot of a dishevelled man, sitting on stone steps, his cap held out to passers-by, begging. "Feast your eyes. He is from your world. We have none of that here."

The spiral spins yet again.

Gene's young friends, Frankie (Frankie Darro) and Betsy (Betsy King Ross), decide to ride back to Radio Ranch. "These are friends of yours," Tika intones. "They may become beggars." Gene calls their names out loud, and Tika, amused by his failure to understand the technology, says, "That's right, speak to them."

On Tika's nodded command, the spiral spins one last time to reveal a room containing massive electrical devices from which lightning bolts of energy burst. "The death chamber," she explains. "That's where you'll be in five minutes."

Although worthy of remark, these scenes are, in another sense, unremarkable — in part at least because such screens-within-the-screen are a familiar sight in SF movies; as Garrett Stewart has persuasively argued, science fiction or "SF" film repeatedly demonstrates a self-reflexive dimension through its invocation and embedding of such technologies of the image.[3] In *Buck Rogers*, we have a device which displays images of the past (that is, although set in the 25th century, they occupy the past of narrative chronology); and these images not only usurp the diegetic future's present from its inhabitants' vision but also make some claim, diegetically, to depict the reality of that future's past. One of the tensions in the depiction of this device is that it is clearly not an extrapolation of how such surveillance technologies might operate, were it possible to look into the past; or, rather, because audiences are now familiar with surveillance footage and the conventions that pseudo-surveillance footage observes and by which it (mis)identifies itself,[4] the unaltered re-use of an earlier sequence utilising the conventions of continuity editing nowadays, at least, makes the ambiguous status of the footage (diegetically, it is supposed to be actuality footage, while extra-diegetically it clearly is not) rather pronounced.[5] In *The Phantom Empire*, the viewing technology is initially used to display the technological wonders of the age of superscience before revealing the underbelly of the less-modern contemporary world and the uncertainties it holds. Again, the status of this footage is ambiguous. Diegetically, it all claims to be actuality footage; and the four shots of Murania, whether the model shots of the skyline and the ascending radium repulsion elevator or the scenes of the robots and the death chamber, could, with sufficient suspension of disbelief, be taken for surveillance footage from wall-mounted cameras. The shots of the beggar and of Frankie and Betsy differ. Whereas the exchange between the juvenile sidekicks was obviously shot for the movie serial, the provenance of the footage of the beggar is less clear. It does not appear to be actuality footage, but, partly because of its urban setting, it does look like it was borrowed from another movie.[6] However, the shots of the beggar and of Frankie and Betsy — not unlike the footage replayed on Dr. Huer's pastoscope — seem to do away with the diegetic camera in favour of some disembodied and invisible eye capable of unrestricted movement.

In the coda to his *Critical Theory and Science Fiction*, Carl Freedman succinctly demolishes attempts to distinguish between modernism and postmodernism on aesthetic grounds, and insists that they can only be understood within their general historical situation. Classical modernism corresponds to the collapse of entrepreneurial capitalism and the birth of monopoly capitalism, and is characterized by a particularly intense struggle between modern and premodern forms, whereas the postmodern emerges after World War II, alongside the multinationalization of capital, and is perhaps better understood as the period of pure modernity, when battles with premodern forms are no longer so prevalent and "capitalist modernization is so thoroughly triumphant that, owing to the lack of contrast on which visibility depends, it becomes somewhat difficult to see."[7] Although this argument runs the risk of constructing an image of the late-capitalist world as a totally reified and integrated monolith, it nonetheless provides a valuable framework within which, I would argue, SF, both filmic and literary, offers a privileged site for witnessing the conflicts between the premodern and the modern — one need only consider religious subtexts and the pseudo-classical and pseudo-feudalist — not to mention racist, patriarchal and heterosexist — social structures that continue to haunt SF's visions. As I have argued elsewhere[8] — and this is evident in both Murania and the various worlds of *Buck Rogers*'s 25th century — the most common site of such collisions and conflicts is in the very *mise-en-scène* of the constructed/depicted world.

Alongside SF, early documentary film, from Lumière shorts to city symphonies, seem to share this fascination with modernity and the conflicts of which it is constituted, as well as a recurring sense — and interrogation — of the camera as an unrestricted invisible eye. The remainder of this chapter is divided into two parts. The first is concerned with mapping out the epistemologically ambiguous status of actuality footage suggested above, but here taking as its object a number of Lumière's *actualités*. The second part turns to the film poem and city symphony film — *La Tour* (aka *The Tower*; Clair 1928) and *Chelovek s kineapparatom* (aka *The Man with the Movie Camera*; Vertov 1929), respectively — and returns to the use of actuality and actuality-like footage in a pair of rather more prestigious early SF movies, *Paris qui dort* (aka *The Crazy Ray*; Clair 1923) and *Aelita* (Protazonov 1924).[9]

Spectacle, Narrative and Epistemological Ambiguities in Silent Actualités

In a paper delivered in 1985, André Gaudreault and Tom Gunning introduced the term "cinema of attractions" to describe the filmic output of cinema's first decade. Since then, and following Gunning's elaborations upon the concept in a number of articles and his book on D.W. Griffith there has developed a new orthodoxy in the Anglophone study of early film. Traditionally, early film was divided into the alternative possibilities offered by the realist and documentary impulses represented by Louis and Auguste Lumière's *actualités* and the fantastic and narrative impulses represented by Georges Méliès's *féerie* films. Following the interventions of Gaudreault and Gunning, it has now become something of a critical commonplace that, until the emergence of a properly narrative cinema (variously dated at some point during cinema's second decade between 1904–1914), filmmaking was primarily concerned with the presentation of spectacle, whether Méliès's trickery or the Lumières' observations of landscapes, locations, and incidents. Gunning writes

> Such apparently different approaches as the trick film and actuality filmmaking unite in using cinema to present a series of views to audiences, views fascinating because of their illusory power [from the realistic illusion

of motion offered to the first audiences by Lumière, to the magical illusions concocted by Méliès] and exoticism. The cinema of attractions, rather than telling stories, bases itself on film's ability to show something. Contrasted to the voyeuristic aspect of later narrative cinema analyzed by Metz, this is an exhibitionist cinema, a cinema that displays its visibility, willing to rupture a self-enclosed fictional world to solicit the attention of its spectator.[10]

Discussing the "directness of ... display" of the cinema of attractions, Gunning argues that, in contrast to "psychological narrative, [it] does not allow for elaborate development; only a limited amount of delay is really possible.... This is a cinema of instants, rather than developing situations."[11] Although largely concurring with Gunning's argument, the first part of this essay is concerned with identifying the narrative elements to be found in the cinema of attractions, focusing on a number of Lumière *actualités*.

Gunning himself acknowledges the possibility of narrative emerging in the exhibition context of such films. Not unlike Murania's Queen Tika, J. Stuart Blackton, on exhibition tours with his *The Black Diamond Express*—"a one-shot film of a locomotive rushing towards the camera"—would present the film to his audience with a dramatic spoken introduction:

> Ladies and gentlemen you are now gazing upon a photograph of the famous Black Diamond Express. In just a moment, a cataclysmic moment, my friends, a moment without equal in the history of our times, you will see this train take life in a marvellous and most astounding manner. It will rush towards you, belching smoke and fire from its monstrous iron throat.[12]

Gunning sensibly questions the reliability of the author's memory, but nonetheless concedes that such an oral address "captures the address of the first film shows."[13] However, in comparing Blackton to a "fairground barker, ... build[ing] an atmosphere of expectation,"[14] and in emphasizing exhibition and display, Gunning overlooks another aspect of such an introduction. Stood in front of a projected frame, Blackton identifies his protagonist, the train, and offers a proleptic flashforward to catastrophe — effectively extending the instant both backward and forward in time into a developing situation stretching beyond the duration of his brief film — before returning to the moment of animation as the film begins to run through the projector.

Gunning argues that the "showman rather than the films themselves gives the program an overarching structure, and the key role of the exhibitor showman underscores the act of monstration that founds the cinema of attractions."[15] However, following the same logic as Gunning, if one can identify in the exhibitor showman's words not only a drive towards spectacular display but also one towards expanding the instant of the individual film or the instants of the program of films into developing situations— expanding the attractions into narratives, however perfunctory — then one must return to the films themselves to examine them for narrative elements.

In this context, it is a pleasing irony to turn to Gunning's discussion of film's narrative discourse in order to begin to explore the dialectic of attraction and narrative in the cinema of attractions. He writes,

> Describing the narrative discourse of film must involve cutting up the filmic text so that its dynamic forces are exposed. Of course, a narrative text functions as a whole, and analysis only untangles the synthesis that makes it work. I believe film's narrative discourse can best be described as the interrelation of three different levels that interrelate and express narrative information: the pro-filmic, the enframed image, and the process of editing. I do not claim that they function in isolation, nor do I construct a hierarchy of importance.[16]

In an endnote to this passage, he acknowledges that his "schema does not deal with the important issue of sound in film" as he is only concerned in this context with silent movies, but adds that it "would have to be approached as a fourth level, itself in need of subdividing."[17] In turn, as the first part of this essay will only be considering silent, one-shot movies, its focus will be exclusively on the pro-filmic and the enframed image.

The pro-filmic "refers to everything placed in front of the camera to be filmed."[18] Initially, in terms of actuality films one might suggest that Gunning's phrasing should be reversed: i.e., the pro-filmic refers to everything in front of which the camera is placed. However, as I will demonstrate, the relationship between the camera and the pro-filmic in actuality films is a rather more complex interplay of these alternatives. Gunning notes that,

> Strictly speaking, pro-filmic elements do not appear on the screen except through the next level of discourse, their capture on film as enframed images. However film viewers see the images on the screen as images of things, and the selection of the things that make up the image plays an extremely important role in conveying narrative information. Every film makes a selection of elements based on a preexisting set of possibilities.... Therefore, as narrative discourse the pro-filmic embodies a series of choices and reveals a narrative intention behind the choices. The viewer receives the results of these choices and makes inferences based on them.[19]

At the level of the enframed image, filmic discourse transforms the pro-filmic

> from preexistent events and objects into images on celluloid. The process is far from neutral. Placing an image within a frame entails arranging composition and spatial relations. The act of filming transforms the pro-filmic into a two-dimensional image, filmed from a particular point of view, framed within the camera aperture that geometrically defines the borders of the image. The whole host of formal devices that derive from the effects of perspective, selection of camera distance and angle, framing for composition, and effects of movement within a frame determine specific choices available within this level of discourse. Whether on a conscious or preconscious level the viewer recognizes this construction of the image as a powerful narrative cue.[20]

Other critics have argued for the status of various Lumière *actualités* as narrative films, most notably Marshall Deutelbaum, who contends that rather than being "recording[s] of unadjusted, unarranged, untampered reality"[21] utterly devoid of plot many of the more familiar *actualités* are in fact highly structured artefacts. Gaudreault's discussion of narrative in Lumière films draws on the work of narratologists Claude Brémond to establish a minimal definition of a narrative which nonetheless describes even the most basic of the Lumière *actualités*. Brémond writes, "The message should place a subject (either animate or inanimate) at a time *t*, then a time *t+n*, and what becomes of the subject at the moment *t+n* should follow from the predicates characterising it at the moment *t*."[22] Gaudreault considers three examples from 1895. In *La sortie des usines Lumière* (aka *Leaving the Factory*),[23] factory gates open, the workers leave, the factory gates close, fulfilling the minimal conditions of a narrative. In *L'Arrivée d'un train en gare de la Ciotat* (aka *Arrival of a Train at La Ciotat*), a train approaches the platform, stops, passengers disembark, other passengers board the train; again this fulfils minimal narrative conditions, although as it lacks the same sense of closure or completion as the first example it is an even more minimal narrative. To these two *actualités* Gaudreault contrasts *L'Arroseur arrosé* (aka *The Sprinkler Sprinkled*) in which a boy treads on a hose pipe being used by a gardener; when the gardener looks down the hose to see what is causing the blockage, the youth lifts his foot, soaking the gardener; the youth tries to flee but is captured and spanked by the gardener. Unlike the other examples, *L'Arroseur arrosé* not only fulfils the conditions of a minimal narrative but also constitutes a "minimal complete plot"[24] which, in Tzvetan Todorov's sense, involves the transition from equilibrium through disequilibrium to a fresh equilibrium.

If Gaudreault arranges these three films in terms of how narrative they are, it is worth noting that the extent of their narrative seems to depend upon the extent to which the events they depict were staged for the camera. *L'Arrivée d'un train* observes the actual arrival of a train, whereas the whole sequence of actions in *L'Arroseur*, which despite its verisimilitude is not to be considered an *actualité*, is clearly performed before and because of the camera (indeed, at one point, the boy is struggling so much that the gardener, dragging him back to be spanked, appears anxious about completing the action before the film in the camera runs out). *La sortie* falls somewhere between the two, and the degree of deliberate staging involved can be tentatively ascertained by comparing the version Gaudreault describes, *La sortie des usines Lumière (pas de chevaux/no horses)*, with two earlier versions, *La sortie des usines Lumière (un cheval/one horse)* and *La sortie des usines Lumière (deux chevaux/ two horses)*. All three were shot at different times of year; each subsequent version was shot from closer to the gate and slightly further to the left; and each version contains more or less the same action. However, there is a significant difference between them. As the first two versions start, the gates are already open, and when they end the gates remain open. Thus they lack the sense of completion, of closure, that the third version possesses; but the very precise timing of the third version makes it suspect as an unstaged *actualité*: how likely is it that all the workers would be positioned directly behind the gate in order to leave as soon as it opened, and to be out of shot 50 seconds later?

This version of *La sortie* should be contrasted with the similarly well-structured *Attelage d'un camion (Hitched to a Truck/The Stonecarver's Team)*, in which a stonecarver's cart, pulled by a team of ten horses enters the frame from behind the left of the camera, passes diagonally away in front of it, and exits the right of the frame almost exactly 50 seconds later. Despite being so clearly delineated, with such a pronounced start and finish, it seems unlikely that this moment could have been deliberately staged beyond an agreed starting point; in contrast to the third *La sortie*, the very precision of its ending seems coincidental.

There are a number of Lumière *actualités* which are less narrative than *L'Arrivée d'un train* because they do not even feature such a minimally completed action. *Panorama de l'arrivée en gare de Perrache pris du train (Arrival of a Train in Perrache)*, *Venise: Panorama du Grand Canal pris d'un bateau (Venice: View of the Grand Canal from a Boat)*, and *Constantinople: Panorama de la Come d'Or (Constantinople: View of the Come d'Or)* consist of tracking shots of passing landscapes taken from moving vehicles—respectively, a train as it passes through Lyons, a boat as it travels along Venice's Grand Canal, a ship as it leaves the harbour at Constantinople—and in each case the selection of the moment at which to start the camera running appears to be completely arbitrary and, consequently, so is the moment at which the film runs out (a similar arbitrariness can be seen in the 1903 American film *Skyscrapers of New York City from North River*, even though its title very specifically identifies its object). In addition to these lateral panoramas, there is *Indochine: Le village de Nama, Panorama pris d'un chaise à porteur (Indochina: Namo Village, Panorama Taken from a Rickshaw)* in which the camera is positioned facing out of the rear of a rickshaw and begins shooting as it is pulled away from the village of the title, pursued by children and other villagers. Again, there is little in the way of narrative although it is a deliberately staged event inasmuch as the movement of the camera is planned and instigated by the cameraman.

One of the Lumière *actualités* which has least claim to be a narrative film is *Vue prise d'une baleinière en marche (View from a Whaling Boat)*. The camera is situated in a whaling boat, facing the crew as they row; the shore is visible in the distance, but despite their persistent, rhythmic efforts they make no discernible headway. The film begins and ends arbitrarily, and throughout its brief duration its subjects repeat the same set of movements over

A staged moment from Méliès' "nonfiction" *Attelage d'un camion (Hitched to a Truck/The Stonecarver's Team)*.

and again. As in the other panoramas, the camera is observing activity without transforming it into a discrete incident. This is, in part, a consequence of the incident being the movement of the camera itself; in contrast to many *actualités*, the camera is moving rather than framing a world which moves past it. Whereas the static frame encourages us to observe the subject, the moving frame of the panoramas seems to endow the camera itself with subjectivity — although this is less the case in *Vue prise d'une baleinière*, where the moving frame hardly seems to move in relation to the world.

The failure to transform activity into an incident does not necessarily arise from the moving frame. For example, in *Football*, shot with a static camera and intended to show part of a game of soccer, the ball is almost immediately kicked out of the frame and does not return, leaving a view of the players milling about rather pointlessly. If the camera had been able to move so as to keep the ball in shot, then the activity might have been transformed into an incident.

If the transformation of activity into incident can occur at the filmic level, either through the judicious selection of when to start filming, or by the decision to move or not move the camera, it can also occur on the pro-filmic level. Lumière *actualités* manipulate the pro-filmic in at least three different ways in order to effect such transformations. Possibly inspired by the presence of uncoached subjects who notice the camera and either return its gaze, as with the uniformed figure in the middle of the frame of *Russia: Moscow, rue Tverskaïa* (*Russa: Moscow, Tverskaïa Street*), or play up to the presence of the camera in numerous crowd shots, the first kind of transformative manipulation of the pro-filmic is the insertion of a character to comment on the events, such as the jovial waiter serving the three card-players in *Partie d'écarté* (*Card Game*), the laughing onlooker who finds the events of *Saut à la couverture* (*Blanket Toss*) so hilarious, and, albeit in a somewhat different vein, the cameraman being filmed while he films the parade in *Fête de Paris: Concours d'automobiles fleuries* (*Festival of Paris, 1899: Parade of Flowered Cars*). (This kind of figure provided Charlie Chaplin with his first short masterpiece in only his second short movie, *Kid Auto Races at Venice* (1914).

The second technique, the artificial temporal extension of the pro-filmic, usually takes the form of a variant on the first technique. In *Partie de boules* (*Game of Balls*), the game of boules proceeds with utter disregard for the rules so as to provide action of sufficient duration. In *Water-To-Bogant* (*Water Toboggan*), the action — a toboggan slides down a ramp, crosses a pool, the passengers disembark onto a jetty and exit the frame — terminates while the film is still running, so one of the passengers reenters the frame, points at something in the water, and is joined by several other figures looking at whatever it is he is indicating. In *La petite fille et son chat* (*The Little Girl and Her Cat*), a young girl in a high chair feeds titbits to a cat until it loses interest and exits the frame, but from the speed and angle of the cat's return moments later it is not unreasonable to suppose that it was thrown back into shot because the camera was still running.

The third technique, of which *Partie d'écarté*, *Saut à la couverture*, *Partie de boules*, and *La petite fille et son chat* can all also, to an extent, be seen as examples, is the event staged for the camera presented as if it were an event which would have occurred anyway. The clearest example of this is *Alger: Prière du Muezzin (Algeria: The Muezzin's Prayer)*, in which a putative muslim engages in a bogus ritual prayer. One of the more curious aspects of this little orientalist fantasy is its uncharacteristically poor framing. Every time the muezzin kneels and bows, his head goes out of shot, leaving one to wonder whether at some level this indicates a consciousness of the bad faith involved in trying to pass off this fictional, staged event as actuality, or even whether it was a deliberate attempt to lend the film a greater sense of authenticity through the simulation of arbitrariness.

The arbitrariness of the pro-filmic world itself can also, on occasion, transform activity into incident. Probably the best example of this is to be found in *Mexique: Baignade de chevaux (Mexico: Bathing the Horses)*, in which the intention of the film was almost certainly to record footage of horses as they were driven through a pool of water in order to be cleaned. However, there are a number of waterfowl swimming on the pool and they do not take kindly to being disturbed by the horses. Panicked by the birds' protests, the horses retreat in disarray, transforming footage fulfilling the minimal conditions of narrative into a completed action hinging on a comic reversal. (It is worth noting that it was precisely this sense of the spontaneity of the filmed world that Méliès, a guest at the Lumières' first Paris performance, found so thrilling, making "particular mention of the rustling of leaves in the background of *Le Déjeuner de bébé* [aka *Repas de bébé/A Baby's Meal*]." Dai Vaughan suggests that for an audience accustomed to the theatre, with its "painted backdrops," the motions of "photographed people were accepted ... because they were perceived as performance, as simply a new mode of self-projection; but that the inanimate should participate in self-projection was astonishing.")[25]

Comic reversals became important to the Lumières, of course, when, as the story goes, *Démolition d'un mur (Demolition of a Wall)* was accidentally projected while the film was being rewound: the wall which was demolished when the film was first projected leapt back up from the mound of rubble it had become. The practice of projecting a film first forwards and then in reverse became fairly common, lending even the most unstructured of films the potential for narrative completion and closure as well as the possibility of a generic shift from *actualité* to comedy.[26] A fine example of this is provided by *Charcuterie mécanique (Mechanical Butcher Shop*, 1895), in which a pig is hauled into a large box attached to a primitive motor; moments later various cuts of pork are extracted from the other end of the machine and placed on a table for display. This gag or trick film prompted numerous imitators, including the British *Making Sausages* (Smith, 1897) and the American *Fun in a Butcher Shop* (Porter, 1901), both of which run for less than a minute. In 1904 Porter made the four minute-long *Dog Factory* in which the machinery was used to transform different strings of sausages selected by customers back into different kinds of dogs. It is highly probable, however, that audiences were already familiar with such effects from the practice of projecting films as they were being rewound. The facility with which the *actualité* could be transformed into the overtly narrative short is, at the very least, suggestive of the extent to which it was not innocent of narrative components and tendencies; and, self-evidently, the notion of the *actualité* as somehow revealing the world through its spectacular display is rendered profoundly problematic by the epistemological ambiguities which arise when the structuration, both narrative and compositional, of so-called actuality footage is acknowledged.

The Film Poem, the City Symphony and the Machine-Age Urban SF Movie

The Lumières' *Charcuterie mécanique* works as a gag film — in both senses: a trick film and a comic film — because of the extremely naturalistic behaviour of the men operating the mechanical butcher. Square on to the camera, they make no pretence that they are doing anything other than demonstrating the operation of their marvellous device to an observer, but their manner is casual and undemonstrative, as if they are not acting at all. This grounding in *actualité* convention is in stark contrast to the style that Méliès would develop in his trick films, and thus makes the "punchline" of the gag both unexpected and effective even today.

Although *Charcuterie mécanique* and its imitators are, at least retrospectively, comedies, they are all also science fiction movies.[27] This is not a spurious connection: as Brooks Landon has argued, SF cinema is perhaps best understood as a cinema of attractions.[28] However, it is the contention of this essay that SF and *actualités* are related not just by their concern with spectacle.[29] Situating SF as a variety of paraliterature, Samuel R. Delany argues that:

> For the last hundred years, the interpretative conventions of all the literary reading codes have been organized, tyrannized even, by ... "the priority of the subject." Everything is taken to be about mind, about psychology. And, in literature, the odder or more fantastical or surreal it is, the *more* it's assumed to be about mind or psychology.
>
> SF, developing in the statistically much wider field of paraliterature..., has to some extent been able to escape this tyranny....
>
> At the level where the distinction between it and paraliterature is meaningful, literature is a representation of, among other things, a complex codic system by which the codic system we call the "subject" [with which, in any given culture, literature must overlap] can be richly criticized. By virtue of the same distinction, SF is a representation of, among other things, a complex codic system by which the codic system we call the "object" [which, in those cultures that have SF, SF must ditto] can be richly criticized — unto its overlap with the subject.[30]

A more succinct statement of this position can be found in Delany's description of SF as "a critique of the object rather than a critique of the subject — or of the subject in terms of the object."[31] These characterisations of SF seem equally applicable to actuality films, and the remainder of this chapter will seek to develop this comparison between urban actuality films and the machine-age SF movie.[32]

As a genre, the city symphony is said to originate with *Manhatta* (Sheeler, Strand 1921), a movie concerned to demonstrate the sheer scale of Lower Manhattan's modernist architecture, dominating the minuscule and frequently undifferentiable humans who work there. More or less ignored in the US, its progeny were mainly

European—*Rien que les heures/Nothing but the Hours* (Cavalcanti 1926), *Berlin, die Symphonie einer Grosstadt/Berlin: Symphony of a City* (Ruttman 1927), *Moskva/Moscow* (Kaufman 1927), *Berliner Stilleben/Berlin Still Life* (Moholy-Nagy 1929), *Chelovek s kinoapparatom, À propos de Nice/About Nice* (Vigo 1930) and *Images d'Ostende/Images of Ostende* (Storck 1930), as well as related film poems like *De brug/The Bridge* (Ivens 1928), *La Tour*, and *Regen/Rain* (Ivens 1929)—although late US examples include *A Bronx Morning* (Leyda 1931) and *City of Contrasts* (Browning 1931). As the silent period drew to a close, the city symphony was transformed in a number of ways before effectively disappearing. For example, the British avant-garde agitprop short *Every Day* (Richter 1929) charted a day in the life of the city, repeating it several times in increasingly truncated and thus accelerated form so as to capture the everyday and every day nature of capitalist oppression while, like Walter Benjamin's angel of history,[33] suggesting a headlong rush to disaster; and the German "semi-documentary" drama *Menschen am Sonntag/People on Sunday* (Siodmak and Ulmer 1929) established its setting through city symphony-like montages of Berlin, and contained footage which, in situating actors in long shot in the bustling streets, further problematized the distinction between location shooting and actuality footage already confounded by the inclusion of "characters" to comment upon the action in Lumière *actualités*. However, the remainder of this essay is concerned with some of the ways in which the representation of the modern city is developed in machine-age actuality films and SF movies so as to produce epistemological and ontological uncertainties, pairing *La Tour* with *Paris qui dort*, and *Chelovek s kinoapparatom* with *Aelita*.[34]

La Tour *and* Paris qui dort

After quoting a passage from Karl Gutzkow's *Briefe aus Paris* (1842) in which a "bolt of lightning flashes over the Pont d'Austerlitz," Walter Benjamin notes that the "Austerlitz Bridge was one of the first iron structures in Paris. With the lightning flash above it, it becomes an emblem of the dawning technological age."[35] This combination of elements would still provide a popular image of technology's cutting edge around the time Benjamin was writing. For example, in the April 1928 issue of *Amazing Stories*, the first US SF pulp magazine, editor Hugo Gernsback launched a competition to design a symbol for what he was still calling "scientifiction." In the September issue he announced the winners and unveiled his own symbol, which combined elements of the three winning entries: the struts of the cog in the centre of his design are shaped like lightning bolts; the cogs interlocking with the central one are fixed to a framework of structural steel whose girders frame the design.[36]

An iron structure—the Eiffel Tower—dominates *La Tour*, René Clair's exhilarating short film which explores and celebrates its complex construction, its "twelve thousand metal fittings, ... two and a half million rivets, ... machined to the millimeter."[37] In addition to recording criticisms of the kitsch, ugly, aesthetically bankrupt, barbarous design of this "useless and monstrous"[38] "knickknack"[39] by which "[a]ll our monuments are debased, our architecture diminished,"[40] Benjamin traces the development of iron construction from railway tracks, silos, hangars, arcades, exhibition halls, and train stations via such showcase attractions-*cum*-monuments as the Eiffel Tower to the mass delights, distractions and *divertissements* of amusement park rides.[41] Equally importantly, Benjamin captures something of the same celebratory tone of *La Tour*,[42] its sense of the inspirational qualities of the tower and iron construction more generally:

> the plastic shaping power abdicates here in favor of a colossal span of spiritual energy, which channels the inorganic material energy into the smallest, most efficient forms and conjoins these forms in the most effective manner.... On this work site, one hears no chisel-blow liberating form from stone; here thought reigns over muscle power, which it transmits via cranes and secure scaffolding.... Around 1878, it was thought that salvation lay in iron construction. Its "yearning for verticality" ..., the predominance of empty spaces over filled spaces, and the lightness of its visible frame raised hopes that a style was emerging in which the essence of the Gothic genius would be revived and rejuvenated by a new spirit and new materials.[43]

For Clair, *La Tour* represents a return to the Eiffel Tower. Five years previously he had made *Paris qui dort*, an SF-comedy in which a scientist uses a ray to send all of Paris—possibly all of the world—to sleep, except for the nightwatchman who resides in the Eiffel Tower and five people in an aeroplane which subsequently lands in Paris. The earlier movie shares *La Tour*'s celebration of structure, space and verticality, repeatedly delighting in the complexity of the tower's construction, clear skies, and the distance above the city made possible by its sheer altitude.

Paris qui dort opens with magnificent aerial views of the Seine and Paris's urban sprawl. These views are significant inasmuch as they continue the project of the actuality film. As Benjamin wrote, "[i]t must be kept in mind that the magnificent urban views opened up by new constructions in iron ... for a long time were evident only to workers and engineers.... For in those days who besides the engineer and the proletarian had climbed the steps that alone made it possible to recognize what was new and decisive about these structures: the feeling of space?"[44]

The platform onto which the tower's nightwatchman emerges to have a smoke is surrounded by a railing, on top of which are mounted a pair of

This shot introduces the idea of observation in René Clair's *Paris qui dort* (*The Crazy Ray*) of 1925.

telescopes. The presence of these instruments introduces the theme of observation, of interrogating the object. This epistemological imperative is emphasized when he looks over the railing: there is a cut to what appears to be a point-of-view shot as the camera tilts down so as to take in the view of the formal gardens at the base of the tower; that this is not a point-of-view shot becomes clear when the nightwatchman's head appears in the bottom of the frame. Clair plays a number of similar tricks—for example, as the nightwatchmen wanders the dormant city, we see a number of what appear to be still frames, into one of which he, after a moment, strolls; as the people from the aeroplane drive into the city, we see a figure sitting on the kerb, head bowed, apparently frozen like the rest of the city's inhabitants, but as the car approaches he (for it is the nightwatchman) suddenly leaps up — each of which prompts the viewer to question what he or she sees. This interrogation of the image, or, more properly, this revelation of the partiality of the image's meaning, raises important epistemological issues: it not only questions the authority of the image but of the visual field more generally. There is, of course, a tension here as the nature of Clair's gags are such that the authority of the image is, in some sense, sustained by the fact that in each case a subsequent image reframes the meaning of the previous image and reveals the truth of the situation; however, simultaneously, there is produced a sense that the second, reframing image might itself be subject to subsequent reframings. This is made evident by a further gag in which one of the men appears to commit suicide by jumping off the tower; in the next shot he is shown hanging from a bar, from which he then climbs to safety. What is significant about this sequence is the way in which it differs from the earlier gags: it is a diegetic trick played by one character on the others as well as an extra-diegetic trick played by Clair on the viewer. Such metaleptic shenanigans[45] suggest the possibility of an infinite regress of ontological levels and consequently the possibility of further reframings.[46]

In order to extend the movie's "critique of the object"—i.e., the fundamental partiality and therefore untrustworthiness of the visual—to a critique "of the subject in terms of the object," it is necessary to consider the sequences which combine actuality footage with science-fictional spectacle as the Professor freezes and unfreezes the dormant inhabitants of Paris. These moments are achieved simply through halting motion with a still frame and animating still frames into motion. This process achieves a mechanical equivalence between humans and machines as they are all subjected to the ray/camera. As Benjamin writes, the problem of how to build with glass and iron "has long since been solved by hangars and silos. Now, it is the same with the human material on the inside of the arcades as with the materials of their construction. Pimps are the iron bearings of this street, and its glass breakables are the whores."[47] Benjamin, however, is generally critical of such equivalizations as are made in the new capitalist marketplace of which he writes, arguing that within the *divertissements* offered by world exhibitions "the individual abandons himself in the framework of the entertainment industry," becoming "an element of a compact mass" who is "thus led to that state of subjection which propaganda, industrial as well as political, relies on"[48]; and further that the man in the crowd has become convinced of his ability to accurately classify the passer-by, to see "straight through to the innermost recesses of his soul — all on the basis of his external appearance."[49]

Paris qui dort not only enacts such equivalizations and subjections, but also suggests the link with capitalism made by Benjamin. As the five male characters inhabiting the tower become overwhelmed with ennui and recognise the uselessness of the stolen money they have hoarded, they suddenly decide that the one thing worth having is the female character. In a comical moment, they all start to try to pay court to her, to compete for her; and Clair briefly interpolates a heart-shaped iris around her face. This wonderfully ironic moment — with one possible exception, none of the men feels anything for her beyond acquisitiveness — emphasizes the reducibility of the individual to the kind of equivalence with which capital imbues commodities.

Chelovek s kinoapparatom *and* Aelita

Metaleptic play and gags are also an important element in *Chelovek s kinoapparatom*, most famously in the way in which it constructs what appears to be a single city from footage shot in Moscow, Odessa, Kiev, and elsewhere. The movie's prologue shows the cameraman (Mikhail Kaufman)[50] entering the deserted movie theater in which the film itself is to be screened, and the projectionist loading *Chelovek s kinoapparatom* into the projector. This disruption of ontological levels and the strange loop[51] it generates — the film we are about to watch is the film within the film we are about to watch — is followed by a gag: we see a rope being pulled and expect it to open the curtains in front of the screen; instead, it lowers the hinged cinema seats. Such playfulness dominates the movie, exploring the relationship between "real" reality, observed reality, and constructed reality; and questioning whether unmediated observed reality, observed reality mediated through such technologies as the camera, or the reality constructed through the full apparatus of the cinema is more capable of conveying "real" reality.

In various manifestos and polemics, Vertov claimed that the camera, conceived of as a mechanical eye (a "kino-eye"), was more capable of seeing the world accurately than the human eye.[52] This proposition is seemingly reiterated throughout the movie by the positioning of the cameraman. If not exactly a disembodied and invisible eye capable of unrestricted movement, he nonetheless seems to enjoy access to all areas — this sense is probably strongest towards the end of the movie when the cameraman looks down the barrel of a gun at airplanes in flight, only for the footage he is apparently "shooting" to appear, apparently unmediated, immediately on the screen in the theater from the prologue — while the camera which films the cameraman does seem to function as this kind of universal surveillance system. However, as the presence of the cameraman within the shot points to the existence of another cameraman behind the camera filming the cameraman, the greater objectivity of the kino-eye is simultaneously undercut by exactly the same footage that asserts it. It is further destabilized by the very image — the superimposition of a human eye (usually Vertov's own) over the camera lens — intended to capture the notion of the kino-eye; rather than merely functioning as a visual equivalent of the semantic unit "kino-eye," it also insists upon the presence of the human, suggesting that the camera is a cyborg technology containing elements of both the mechanical/objective and the organic/subjective. The kino-eye's putative objectivity is also undermined by a sequence which takes us into the editing suite where Elizaveta Svilova, the editor of the movie, is shown editing the movie. In addition to producing the same kind of strange loop as the projectionist in the prologue, Svilova's role also emphasizes that even if the kino-eye sees the world accurately, for the viewer that "seeing" is always mediated through the construction of the movie from film fragments. One of the sequences in which this constructed mediation is most clearly articulated comes early in the film, when the cameraman, thanks to some self-consciously flamboyant editing, seems to be in danger of being hit by a train — precisely the kind of thrilling scenario Vertov would have loathed in narrative cinema — before it is all revealed as trickery.

As with *Paris qui dort*, but rather more systematically, *Chelovek s kinoapparatom* indicates the prevalent equivalization of humans and artefacts/commodities, the parallels between the human eye and the camera lens suggested by the image of the kino-eye being only the most obvious. (On one occasion this image creates a strange loop, as the eye is superimposed over a lens which reflects the cameraman cranking his camera as he shoots the lens.) This equivalization is captured by a number of visual echoes. For example, a newborn baby is held between its mother's legs, and then the shape and position of her legs are "repeated" by shots of buildings, of trams. An extended series of equivalences and visual echoes occurs in the opening reel: during the cameraman's early morning journey across the city, we see the poster for a German film called *The Awakening of a Woman*; his journey is intercut with shots of a sleeping woman (is he part of her dream?); the woman wakes up just as the city is coming to life; the streets are hosed down as she washes her face; she dries her face and opens her eyes, the blinds on her windows open, a camera lens is adjusted into focus. These conscious echoes are clearly artefactual, but do they point to arbitrary and coincidental similarities, or to some essential quality shared by the various elements? are they collocations or juxtapositions?

Just prior to this sequence, there are a number of shots of shop window mannequins who appear, particularly to anyone familiar with shot/reverse-shot conventions, to be watching the empty streets. Initially, this seems to suggest the continuity of a world without observers, but as the subsequent series of self-conscious visual echoes is based upon edited-together fragments the artefactual and mediated nature of this world-continuity is indicated. And if this is the case for the mannequins, whose ability to observe is purely a product of the camera and the editing suite, to what extent is it also the case for human observers?

Such epistemological and ontological uncertainties can also be found in *Aelita*. The movie opens with the reception of a three-word radio signal, with a pair of scenes set in stereotypically oriental and arabic locations before we witness it being received in Moscow.[53] This celebration of the distance-defying possibilities of radio technology (compare with the sequence about radio toward the end of *Chelovek s kineapparatom*) and, more generally, communications technology (Engineer Los (Nikolai Tseretell) is soon interrupted in his efforts to decipher the cryptic message by a telephone call from his wife, Natasha (Vera Kuindzhi), with whom he is clearly very much in love), is complicated by the problem it poses: what does "Anta Odeli Uta" mean? Los, who along with his colleague Spiridonov (Nikolai Tseretell) has long dreamed of travelling to Mars, decides that the message must have been broadcast from the red planet. Meanwhile, on Mars, Aelita (Yuliya Solntseva) seduces Gor (Yuri Zavadsky) in order to gain access to the device he has invented which will permit her to examine life on other worlds. When she turns this machine onto the Earth she is treated to actuality footage of various urban centres and a non-actuality view of arabs in a desert. She then discovers Los, waiting for Natasha, and watches as they passionately embrace. Although the look of this location footage distinguishes it from the interpolated actuality footage, more significant is the cut to a slightly-irised close-up as the couple kiss. This transition neatly poses the old question, typically cast as a debate between André Bazin and Jean Mitry, as to whether the frame should be thought of as a window which opens onto a world extending into offscreen space or as a border[54]; although important distinctions can be made between actuality and location footage, in both there is a very real sense of the world continuing out of shot, but the cut to a close-up emphasizes the composition within the frame as the primary determinant of meaning. Moreover, whereas the stereotypically oriental and arabic shots are paralleled by the actuality footage, suggesting a similar subject position for the viewer and Aelita, this shot collapses the distinction between these subject positions and thus the distinction between Metz's voyeuristic and Gunning's exhibitionist cinema.

This rough equation of the viewer's position with Aelita's is rendered increasingly problematic as the film proceeds, perhaps most notably in a sequence which complicates this complex of gazes and subjectivities by showing Los, looking longingly out of a window, and imagining Aelita on Mars watching him. At times, the viewer seems to occupy a position of privileged knowledge akin to that of Aelita. For example, when the greedy, lecherous Erlich (Pavel Pol) hosts a dinner party, various of his guests recall pre-revolutionary times, but in each flashback to what is remembered as a better time an ironic distance is opened permitting the viewer to witness the oppression upon which this former privilege was built; similarly, when Los becomes convinced that he is being cuckolded by Erlich, the viewer is disinclined to accept Los's interpretation of what he sees.

Issues of appearance, perception, and interpretation are returned to at various point in the movie. For example, when the spaceship is launched on its jour-

Should the iris frame in Protazonov's *Aelita* (*Aleita, Queen of Mars*) of 1924 be thought of as a window which opens onto a world extending into offscreen space, or as a border?

ney to Mars, it is crewed by the would-be police spy Kravtsev (Igor Ilyinsky), Los, who is disguised as Spiridonov, and Gusev (Nikolai Batalov), who is dressed in women's clothes because his wife has hidden all of his in an effort to prevent his departure. A moment more evocative of the cinematic apparatus and the interpretive role it demands of the viewer comes when Los, returning home from a six-month self-imposed exile from his wife, sees cast on the wall what appear to be the shadows of Natasha and Erlich as they embrace and shut themselves in his room. This prompts Los to shoot Natasha, construct the spaceship and flee to Mars. There, he and Aelita requite their passion for each other, but at a couple of key moments—and, importantly, these are not his point-of-view shots—Aelita is replaced by Natasha.

Following Aelita's betrayal of the Martian revolution, Los wakes up. One of the curious features of *Aelita* is that, despite most of the Martian sequences being preceded by an intertitle indicating Los's tendency to daydream about the red planet, it is not until this depiction of him waking up that the possibility of Mars being something other than just a dream is finally closed down. The dénouement sees Los return home to find Natasha alive. Again, there is a shadowplay on the wall, and although its status is unclear, it does prompt Natasha to offer an explanation, which Los turns down. This rejection of a concrete explanation repositions the viewer. Throughout Los's dream of Mars, there has been the option of reading the preceding intertitles literally rather than as a mere bridge between the events on the two planets. The viewer has always had the chance of knowing more than the characters. However, with Los's refusal of Natasha's offer of an explanation, that privileged position of knowledge — which has already been undermined by the revelation that Aelita, who seemed to occupy a similar position, was merely a figment of a character's imagination — disappears for good.

In combination, the interrogation of the object undertaken by *Aelita*'s generic blend of actuality and (science-) fictional footage raises some profound epistemological and ontological questions which concern the possibility of distinguishing between subject and object: not only, how are we to understand and interpret the image? but also, what is the status of the image in relation to the world it depicts? what is our status in relation to the image? what is our status in relation to the world? And, regardless of genre, the same is true of each of the movies discussed in this essay, even *Buck Rogers* and *The Phantom Empire*.

1. And except for the audience, who have just witnessed their survival, capture, and enslavement to Kane in the opening minutes of the chapter.

2. The serial was originally intended to have 13 episodes, with a seventh episode composed almost entirely of such recapped material. Universal discarded the episode, releasing *Buck Rogers* as a 12-part serial, but made the extra episode "available to theaters caring to exhibit it and expand the serial's run by an extra week" (Roy Kinnard, *Science Fiction Serials*. Jefferson: McFarland, 1999, p. 76).

3. See Garrett Stewart, "The 'Videology' of Science Fiction Film" in George Slusser and Eric S. Rabkin, eds, *Shadows of the Magic Lamp* (Carbondale: Southern Illinois University Press, 1985), pp.159–207, and Garrett Stewart, *Between Film and Screen: Modernism's Photo Synthesis* (Chicago: The University of Chicago Press, 1999), especially chapter 5.

4. One of the most interesting versions of this tension between the identification and misidentification of the status of film footage comes in *The Blair Witch Project* (Myrick and Sanchez

1999), in which, adopting a technique more familiar in prose form, a fiction film purports to be constructed of found footage. However, to the extent that the idiosyncratic mode by which much of the film was reportedly shot — abandoning the cast in the woods to film themselves being terrorized and terrified — is true, then some of the movie presumably can be regarded as being composed of actuality footage.

5. This is not to say that the original and subsequent audiences would not note some version of this tension, but rather this particular description of it could presumably only be made after surveillance and pseudo-surveillance (rather than, say, documentary and pseudo-documentary, footage) become common.

6. The use of borrowed footage was, of course, not uncommon. For example, despite a budget at least three times that of the average movie serial, *Flash Gordon* (Stephani 1936), in addition to reusing sets, props, miniatures and music from *Just Imagine* (Butler 1930), *The Mummy* (Freund 1932), *The Invisible Man* (Whale 1933), *The Black Cat* (Ulmer 1934), *Bride of Frankenstein* (Whale 1935), *Werewolf of London* (Walker 1935), and *Dracula's Daughter* (Hillyer 1936), also reused footage from *Just Imagine* and the lost movie *The Midnight Sun* (Dimitri Buckowetzki 1926). For more details, see Kinnard, *Science Fiction Serials*, pp. 30–40.

7. Carl Freedman, *Critical Theory and Science Fiction* (Hanover: Wesleyan University Press/University Press of New England, 2000), p. 188.

8. Mark Bould, "Science Fiction Film and Television" in Edward James and Farah Mendlesohn, eds, *The Cambridge Companion to Science Fiction* (Cambridge: Cambridge University Press, 2003).

9. Where possible, English translations of titles are taken from the titles given them on their original release. In other instances, direct translations are given.

10. Tom Gunning, *D.W. Griffith and the Origins of American Narrative Film: The Early Years at Biograph* (Urbana and Chicago: University of Illinois Press, 1994), p. 41.

11. Tom Gunning, "An Aesthetic of Astonishment: Early Film and the (In)credulous Spectator" in Leo Braudy and Marshall Cohen, eds, *Film Theory and Criticism: Introductory Readings — Fifth Edition* (Oxford: Oxford University Press, 1999), pp. 818–832, p. 824.

12. Gunning, "An Aesthetic of Astonishment...," p. 824. The oration he is quoting is taken from Albert E. Smith and Phil A. Koury, *Two Reels and a Crank* (Garden City: Doubleday, 1952), p.39. Gunning expands upon his discussion of this movie in "'Now You See It, Now You Don't': The Temporality of the Cinema of Attractions," *The Velvet Light Trap*, 32 (1993), pp. 3–12.

13. *Ibid*, p. 824.

14. *Ibid*.

15. *Ibid*, p. 826.

16. Gunning, *D.W. Griffith...*, p. 18.

17. *Ibid*, p. 29, n.30. It is unfortunate that Gunning does not here take the opportunity to reflect on the importance of the exhibitor's extra-diegetic monstrating voice with early silent film.

18. *Ibid*, p. 19.

19. *Ibid*, p. 19.

20. *Ibid*, p. 19.

21. Marshall Deutelbaum, "Structural Patterning in the Lumière Films," *Wide Angle*, 3.1 (1979), p. 30.

22. Brémond, quoted in André Gaudreault, "Film, Narrative, Narration: The Cinema of the Lumière Brothers' in Thomas Elsaesser with Adam Barker, ed., *Early Cinema: Space, Frame, Narrative* (London: BFI, 1990), pp. 68–75, p. 68.

23. All of the Lumière films mentioned in this essay can be found on the DVD *The Lumière Brothers' First Films*, which contains 85 of their short films shot — not necessarily by the Lumière brothers themselves — between 1895 and 1900; I have, with a couple of minor exceptions, used the French titles given in this collection. The other actuality shorts to which I refer can be found on the DVD *Landmarks of Early Film*, which also includes fifteen Lumière films.

24. Todorov, quoted in Gaudreault, "Film, Narrative, Narration...," p. 69.

25. Dai Vaughan, "Let There Be Lumière" in Elsaesser, ed., *Early Cinema*, pp. 63–67, p. 65.

26. This "accident" has a literary precedent in Camille Flammarion's *Lumen* (1872), in which such a reversal transforms tragedy into comedy. This early visionary sf novel, consisting of five dialogues between the youthful Quaerens and the eponymous departed soul, is obsessed with questions of sight, vision and perspective. In the second dialogue, Lumen describes his departure from

the Earth at faster than the speed of light which enables him to see human history played out in reverse. In a remarkable passage he describes the Battle of Waterloo: "It was really Waterloo, but a Waterloo of the afterlife, for the combatants were being raised from the dead.... The longer they fought, the more the number of combatants increased; each gap made in the serried ranks by the cannon was immediately filled up by a group of the resuscitated dead. When the belligerents had spent the whole day tearing one another to pieces with cannon, grapeshot, and bullets, bayonets, sabres, and swords—when the great battle was over—not a single person had been killed. No one was even wounded. Even uniforms that had been torn and disordered before were now in good condition. The men were safe and sound and the ranks in correct formation. The two armies slowly withdrew from one another, as if the heat of the battle and all its fury had had no other objective than the restoration to life, amid the combat, of the two hundred thousand corpses that had lain on the field a few hours earlier. What an exemplary and desirable battle it was! ... The moral aspect of it far surpassed the physical when I found that this battle resulted not in the defeat of Napoleon but in placing him upon the throne. Instead of losing the battle, it was the emperor who won it; instead of a prisoner, he became a sovereign." (Camille Flammarion, *Lumen*. Translated by Brian Stableford. Middletown: Wesleyan University Press, 2002. pp. 49–50.) Towards the end of the fifth dialogue, Flammarion describes in effect both slow-motion and time-lapse photography (pp. 114–116), although the paragraph describing the latter was added in 1897.

27. For example, they all receive entries in Phil Hardy, ed., *The Aurum Film Encyclopedia: Science Fiction* (London: Aurum, 1995), on which I have relied for the above information about the imitators which I have been unable to see.

28. See Brooks Landon, *The Aesthetics of Ambivalence: Rethinking Science Fiction Film in the Age of Electronic (Re)Production* (Westport: Greenwood, 1992); also see Scott Bukatman, "The Artificial Infinite: On Special Effects and the Sublime" in Annette Kuhn, ed., *Alien Zone II: The Spaces of Science Fiction Cinema* (London: Verso, 1999), pp. 249–275.

29. Although, it is worth noting that in the first great flourishing of sf movies in the 1950s, much of their spectacular nature depended on actuality footage—usually stock footage of the US military in action, poorly-matched to the footage of whatever alien threat they were being called upon to tackle.

30. Samuel R. Delany, *Silent Interviews: On Language, Race, Sex, Science Fiction, and Some Comics—A Collection of Written Interviews* (Hanover: Wesleyan University Press/The University Press of New England, 1994), pp. 32–33. The interview from which this passage is taken originally appeared as "The Semiology of Silence" in *Science-Fiction Studies*, 42 (14.2) (July 1987), pp. 134–164.

31. Samuel R. Delany, "Teaching to Learn," *Locus*, 361 (February 1991), pp. 5 and 74–75; p. 74.

32. On the machine-age sf movie, see J.P. Telotte, *A Distant Technology: Science Fiction Film and the Machine Age* (Hanover: Wesleyan University Press/The University Press of New England, 1999).

33. See thesis IX in Walter Benjamin, "Theses on the Philosophy of History" in Hannah Arendt, ed., *Illuminations* (London: Fontana, 1992), pp. 245–255, p. 249. Translated by Harry Zohn. *EveryDay* is available on the video *History of the Avant Garde: Britain in the Twenties*.

34. A parallel project beyond the scope of this essay would balance this focus on urban films with an examination of non-urban "ethnographic" movies. Central to the transformation of the "ethnographic" documentary, such as Robert Flaherty's *Nanook of the North* (1922) and *Moana* (1926), into the more fully narrativized adventure documentary are Ernest B. Schoedsack and Merian C. Cooper's *Grass* (1925) and *Chang: A Drama of the Wilderness* (1927). Such documentaries have much in common with non-urban "ethnographic" horror/sf/adventure movies like *Trader Horn* (Van Dyke 1932), *The Most Dangerous Game* (Schoedsack, Pichel 1932), *Tarzan, the Ape Man* (Van Dyke 1932), *White Zombie* (Halperin 1932), *Island of Lost Souls* (Kenton 1933), *Tarzan and His Mate* (Gibbons, Conway 1933), *I Walked with a Zombie* (Tourneur 1943), and, of course, *King Kong* (Cooper, Schoedsack 1933), in which its co-directors not only appropriated and adapted the techniques of their earlier documentaries but also narrativized this appropriation and adaptation. Preliminary work on the documentary and generic traditions behind *King Kong* can be found in Cynthia Erb, *Tracking King Kong: A Hollywood Icon in World Culture* (Detroit: Wayne State University Press, 1998).

35. Walter Benjamin, *The Arcades Project*. Translated by Howard Eiland and Kevin McLaughlin. (Cambridge: The Belknap Press of Harvard University Press, 1999), p. 151 [F1, 5].

36. For a full and illustrated account of this competition, see Gary Westfahl, "Wanted: A Symbol for Science Fiction" in *Science-Fiction Studies*, 65 (22.1) (March 1995), pp. 1–21. Gernsback's design is reproduced on p.4 and also on the cover of Gary Westfahl, *The Mechanics of Wonder: The Creation of the Idea of Science Fiction* (Liverpool: Liverpool University Press, 1998).

37. Quoted in Benjamin, *The Arcades Project*, p.161.

38. *Ibid*, p. 168.

39. *Ibid*, p. 163.

40. *Ibid*, p. 168.

41. See, for example, Benjamin, *The Arcades Project*, pp. 4, 18, 154, 155.

42. The celebration of the modern one finds in *La Tour* is also evident to an extent in those *actualités* which Deutelbaum describes as depicting "operational processes" (cited in Thomas Elsaesser, "Introduction" in Elsaesser with Barker, eds, *Early Cinema*, pp. 11–30, p. 15). A similar fascination, albeit with fictional operational processes, is evident in a number of sf movies (e.g., the complex procedurals followed by the crew of the *Nostromo* as they wake and are despatched to investigate the alien signal in *Alien* (Scott 1979). Space does not permit a detailed consideration of the operational processes displayed in, for example, *Berlin, die Symphonie einer Grosstadt* and *Chelovek s kinoapparatom* alongside the operation of the machines in *Metropolis* (Lang 1926) and the construction of the new Everytown in *Things to Come* (Menzies 1936).

43. Quoted in Benjamin, *The Arcades Project*, pp. 160–161.

44. Benjamin, *The Arcades Project*, p. 156.

45. On metalepsis, see Brian McHale, *Postmodernist Fiction* (London: Routledge, 1989), especially pp. 119–121 and 222–227. References to this volume for descriptions and examples of textual techniques should not be interpreted as claiming these early films for postmodernism; if anything, it should operate as a rebuke to postmodernism's colonial tendency of claiming a wide range of techniques and then implying that anything using those techniques is therefore postmodernist (something McHale tries to avoid).

46. Gaudreault, drawing on Christian Metz, argues that the filmic macro-narrative is "formed not by the micro-narratives being added together but by their being systematically disregarded as such" ("Film, Narrative...," p. 73). Such a gag highlights this process as the gag only works by adding the second shot to the first, thus altering the meaning of the first, but in terms of the movie's whole narrative the meaning of the whole sequence supersedes the meaning of individual shots.

47. Benjamin, *The Arcades Project*, p. 155.

48. *Ibid*, p.18.

49. *Ibid*, p.21.

50. Kaufman and Vertov were brothers; coincidentally, their other brother, Boris Kaufman, shot Vigo's city symphony, *À propos de Nice*.

51. On loops, see McHale, *Postmodernist Fiction*, pp. 108–111.

52. See Annette Michelson, ed., *Kino-Eye: The Writings of Dziga Vertov*. Translated by Kevin O'Brien. (Berkeley: University of California Press, 1984).

53. For more detailed treatments of *Aelita*, see Ian Christie, "Down to Earth: *Aelita* Relocated" in Richard Taylor and Ian Christie, eds, *Inside the Film Factory: New Approaches to Russian and Soviet Cinema* (London: Routledge, 1994), pp. 80–102, and Telotte, *A Distant Technology*, pp. 28–46.

54. For their respective positions, see André Bazin, "Theater and Cinema, Part Two" in *What is Cinema? Volume One* (Berkeley: University of California Press, 1967), pp. 95–124, and Jean Mitry, *The Aesthetics and Psychology of the Cinema* (London: Athlone, 1998), pp. 72–80.

4

This Reality Which Is Not One: Flaherty, Buñuel and the Irrealism of Documentary Cinema

by Jared F. Green

"There is no such thing as documentary."—Trinh T. Minh-ha

"Less than ever does the mere reflection of reality reveal anything about reality ... something must in fact be built up, something artificial, posed."—Bertolt Brecht

Documentary cinema, along with the complex paradoxes that the term implies for the practice and theory of the representation of actuality, begins with the *mise-en-abîme* of the "first contact" narrative. In *The Odyssey of a Film-Maker: Robert Flaherty's Story*, Francis Hubbard Flaherty's hybrid of memoir and hagiography of her husband, Robert, the first screening of the climactic walrus-hunting scene from *Nanook of the North* (1922) to the Inuit subjects of the film is recounted as an epochal instance of the "primitive" encounter with what Jean-Louis Comolli calls the "machines of the visible"[1]:

> The projector light shone out. There was complete silence in the hut. They saw Nanook. But Nanook was there in the hut with them, and they couldn't understand. Then they saw the walrus, and then, said Bob [Flaherty], pandemonium broke loose. "Hold him!" they screamed. "Hold him!" and they scrambled over the chairs and each other to get to the screen and help Nanook hold that walrus![2]

The reflexivity here is itself twofold, itself a sort of *mise-en-abîme*: on the one hand, there is the mimetic slippage between the on-screen image of Nanook and the historical man who portrayed him, watching his own projected and fictionalized image. This moment of duplication is registered (albeit with purported noncomprehension) by the spectators in Flaherty's Hudson Bay cabin, who we are asked to believe have not yet grasped that their transition into modernity has been signaled by their trans-formation into images. More important, this utter confusion of categories between the materially real and the represented real is literalized in the pandemonium of par-ticipatory spectatorship that misrecognizes the filmic sign for its referent in much the same way that Nanook famously tests a phonograph record by biting it to deter-mine "how the white man cans his voice."

The status of Francis Flaherty's recollection becomes particularly problematic when considered in light of the well-documented artifice of *Nanook of the North*, as well as the fact that the Inuit were active participants in their own cinematic represen-tation and were thus as familiar with the cinematic image as they were with the gramo-phone (which had been introduced to the Hudson Bay region well before Flaherty's arrival). Moreover, what to do with Francis Flaherty's second-hand reportage regard-ing Inuit confusion about the apparent doubling of Nanook when Nanook was, in fact, not a real person but a carefully crafted composite character — at once unfamiliar ethno-graphic object and Other-as-everyman — portrayed by the historical Inuit subject who went by the name of Allakariallak? In a further complication of this apparently simple encounter, it will not escape notice that the narrative of Inuit reaction to Flaherty's screening bears more than a passing resemblance to the widely circulated and persist-ent myth of audience panic at the screening of *L'Arrivée d'un train dans la gare de la ciotat* at the first Lumière projection at the Grand Café's Salon Indien in 1895. The homology between these two accounts, wherein the Lumières' latent first contact fan-tasy is made patent in Flaherty's anecdote, is richly suggestive of how documentary cinema imagined itself as a further perfection of the early (i.e. pre-narrative) cinema's virtual reality. Just as the early cinema propagated its mode of spectacle by inventing a primitive spectator agog before the industrial magic of motion pictures, Flaherty lit-eralizes this ethnographic discourse by restaging the Other's first encounter with his own image as an epochal moment that challenged prior perceptions and initiated a new form of visuality uncannily continuous with lived experience.

Witnessed in this claim to a historically unprecedented mode of representation is, as Fatimah Tobing Rony puts it, "the creation of a myth that Flaherty had pro-duced for the first time a form of cinema paralleling participant observation."[3] Jane Gaines, referring to Rony's reading of *Nanook* as a "cinema of taxidermy" anchored by a relationship of similitude and duplicitously offered as "more true to the posited original,"[4] suggests a somewhat more nuanced view of the film by placing it within its historical circulation as an attraction that also serves as a "route to knowledge."[5] The knowledge that Gaines places in view here is not, as Rony would have it, reduced to a falsifying knowledge of the Other as object of epistemophilia, but of the oper-ations of cinema itself. Citing the Paramount press books' promotional advertising for the 1921 exhibitions of *Nanook*, Gaines insists that we consider

> the audiences who rushed to "see," as encouraged by [the promotional press]: "See Nanook spear the seal, fight to get it and then eat the raw flesh"; "You'll not even wink your eyes"; "So much interest, so much heart-throb, so many pulse-quickening sensations, you'll sit as if hypnotized." Here audiences are attracted by the hoax and *by* the very success of the hoax — by the ability of the maker to produce a perfect illusionistic imitation.[6]

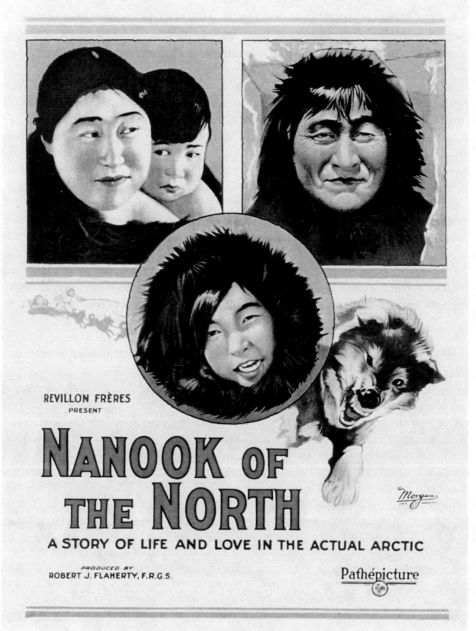

The one-sheet poster for *Nanook of the North* (1922).

To Gaines' reading of these advertisements, I would add that the status of *Nanook* as fiction, announced throughout as a "Story of the Snowlands," providing "rare drama, great story," and "the most dramatic story you ever read, saw or heard about," is clearly integral to the marketing of the film's visual and thematic novelty ("It's newer than new"). We might go further to note that the tagline of this promotional copy, "You'll see it twice," can be understood as an unwitting acknowledgment of the double experience offered by documentary film: to literally see twice, first as resemblance to the real and second as difference from the real. It is in this sense that Gaines challenges Rony's reductive interpretation by insisting that "[T]he cinema of taxidermy, a cinema of fascination with resemblances, has its connotations of prurient looking (looking to see Nanook embalmed), but there is a danger that these negative connotations may overshadow any possibility of seeing cinematic realism as an invitation to knowledge."[7]

Gaines, remarking that her own critique offers interpretive implications "[I]n direct contradiction to the critique of realism that holds that realism is incapable of delivering analytic knowledge,"[8] articulates a reading of documentary film that I wish to take up here in order to volatilize the fiction/nonfiction and representation/reality binarisms. In so doing, it is my intention to suggest an analytical framework for pursuing questions of documentary representation that simultaneously acknowledges the historical significance of what I will call the "documentary effect" (that is, the semiotic process by which the real is produced as a symptom of its transformation into image) while unlinking documentary film from any claim to objectivity.

To this end, I will regard *Nanook* as far less valuable for its contribution to anthropological knowledge about the Quebec Itivimuit circa 1922 than for what it tells us about Western visuality and the complex negotiation of multiple fictions that constitute cinematic realism. The fact that *Nanook* has acquired a reputation as the originary moment of both documentary and ethnographic cinema suggests at once the potent set of creation myths surrounding the film as well as the salient linkage between anthropological practice and documentary cinema.[9] In arguing for this parallelism in the mythic accounts that bind narratives of the Western spectator's first sight of the cinematic image with those of the non–Western spectator's "first contact," it is not my intention to challenge their veracity but rather to propose that this myth participates in the invention of the codes of cinematic realism that would lead to both the Hollywood mode of fiction film and the development of its ostensible discursive other, the documentary mode of nonfiction. It might be more accurate to say, then, that documentary cinema as both (sub)genre and practice begins *as a mise-en-abîme*, a feedback loop between the verisimilitude of the recorded image and the empirically real object to which it refers.

In film theory, the hermeneutic problem that is commonly thought to divide nonfiction from fiction film is almost invariably traced back to early French cinema's aesthetic and conceptual scission between the Lumière brothers and Georges Méliès. This ostensible divide may be extended a bit further to allow a more accurate sense of the reciprocal relationship between cinematic artifice and realism as an *effet retour*: the Lumières' attention to scenes of "everyday life" did indeed formulate cinema's realist conventions, but it took the elaborately fantastical films of Méliès to train spectators to regard the Lumières' films as "real."[10] It has become a commonplace of literary studies of the nineteenth century to note that gothic or fantastic narratives serve to reify the "reality" of the literary realism that they appear to violate. The same might be said of how the stagecraft and stylized illusionism of Méliès consolidated and foregrounded the spectacular vocabulary of cinematic trickery against which the authentic and objective eye of *actualité* could be clearly defined (even when so-called "realist" films achieved their mimetic effects by applying all of the tricks in the Méliès arsenal). But in what sense have documentaries ever been "real" or "actual?" It is well known that the term "documentary" as it applies to cinema came into usage in 1926, with John Grierson's review of Robert Flaherty's film, *Moana,* for the *New York Sun.* In the *Sun* review, Grierson praised the film's "documentary value," by which he meant the film's authentic representation — couched as it was within romantic narrative — of Samoan life. Documentary value for Grierson was something of a symptom of the film rather than its aim, and the less often quoted part of the review goes on to attest that this documentary value was "secondary to its value as a soft breath from a sunlit island."[11] Subsequent to the 1926 review, Grierson further elaborated his idea of documentary in "First Principles of Documentary" (1932–1934) in order to define as "documentary" the cinematic practice that could be understood as the "creative treatment of actuality."[12] In *Claiming the Real*, Brian Winston seizes upon what he finds to be the contradictory signification of the Griersonian formula and suggests, after Paul Rotha, that Grierson "thereby created a problem.... The supposition that any 'actuality' is left after 'creative treatment' can now be seen as being at best naive and at worst a mark of duplicity."[13] Winston's tone is indicative of the somewhat hyperbolic alarmism that suffuses *Claiming the Real* with a not altogether persuasive exigency, as though the claim must be staked before the land is seized by the malign forces of artifice. Yet the idea of documentary as a deliberate shaping of the world rather than an objective recording is already contained within the etymological root of the word "documentary" itself, which the OED traces to the Latin *docere*, to teach, as well as *documentum*, a warning or lesson. Documentaries, in short, never simply gaze and present what is seen; documentaries *do something* to the world upon which this gaze is cast. The notion that documentary film might counteract its own transformative powers is an invention of direct cinema (the American correlative of cinéma vérité) as the set of highly stylized "purifying," de-differentiating techniques devised by Richard Leacock, Fred Wiseman, and D.A. Pennebaker, among others, to manufacture an "as-it-happens" relationship to historical events and social actors that props up the conceit of a non-rhetorical institutional discourse. As I will examine shortly, this set of twentieth-century approaches to the recording of reality is in fact a form of atavism, a reanimation of nineteenth-century theories of the mimetic power of the photographic image. Far from resolving the purported problems that critics of Flaherty and Grierson associate with documentary film's formal, narrative patterns, direct cinema's suppression of questions of constructedness seems particularly duplicitous.[14]

According to Grierson, the narrative patterning that defines both scientific discourse and literature finds a point of contact in documentary film, which he believes affords its observers a means for recognizing and conducting the complex process of acquiring knowledge about the world: "Even so complex a world as ours could be patterned for all to appreciate if only we got away from the servile accumulation of fact and struck for the story which held the facts in living organic relationship together." For Grierson, then, cinema is a sort of colloidal form in which the underlying truths of carefully shaped, recorded moments, only become apperceptible *as truth* when held in suspension by narrative.[15] When it comes to the cinematic image, then, the relationship between "truth" and "the real" is perhaps best regarded as metaphoric rather than metonymic, since the only indexical truth of the photographic image prior to digital technology (still or motion) is the fact of the impression of light on photosensitive film. All else is the property of iconicity — or "lookalikeness"[16] — transformed into discourse by the subjective eye behind the camera, the hand in the editing room, and the institutional framework according to which the film is received by its spectators.[17] Iconicity, however, has little to do with the meaning and power of "documentary" as Grierson understood it: that is, as a form that can reveal the truth of mediation — that is, the truth that images *are other than* the world they represent and that the fact of mediation always asserts a copresence alongside the object of the camera's gaze. The most important nuance of Grierson's deliberate ambivalence in articulating documentary as the "creative treatment of actuality" is that it sought to liberate the documentary film and its as-yet untested narrative, aesthetic and epistemological possibilities from nineteenth-century claims about the indexicality of the photographic and cinematic image as the guaranteed and automatic result of the mechanical apparatuses. The insight is Grierson's rather than Flaherty's, although it is Flaherty whose films teach Grierson the specific mode of *looking* that the latter sought to define in "First Principles of Documentary."

Taking a cue from what Gilles Deleuze celebrates as cinema's "powers of the false,"[18] I wish to reexamine the implications of the Griersonian account in pursuit of a notion of visuality that separates documentary *looking* from the regime of ocularcentric power/knowledge relationships and liberates the documentary image from the limitations of mere resemblance. To this end, I will place Flaherty's *Nanook of the North* and John Grierson's conceptualization of documentary into conversation with Luis Buñuel's *Tierra sin pan* (*Land Without Bread*) in order to argue for what I see as resonant, if significantly divergent, means of approaching the relationship between the mediated gaze and its object of inquiry. Of course, in so saying, I will presume, at least for the duration of this article, that such a problem does indeed exist, if nowhere else, then demonstrably so in theoretical works on documentary film that have inflected documentary practice and yielded scholarly-critical attempts to distinguish between documentary modes.[19]

Since the poststructural "critique of realism" mounted in the 1970s, arguments privileging the cinematic sign for its verisimilitude or "reality effect" have largely fallen into scholarly disfavor. In fact, cinema's complex and shifting status as both indexical and iconic sign-system has been the flashpoint of poststructural aesthetic and philosophical reconsiderations for nearly three decades now. In this arena of theoretical conflict, proponents of filmic illusionism, such as André Bazin, have often been trotted out as "straw men" by critics whose antipathy to the interpellative power of film demands a naïve interpreter of cinematic realism against whom to argue. Yet

Jane Gaines dismisses such misconstruals of Bazin by reminding her readers that Bazin is "capable of employing several notions of 'realism' and 'reality' at once" and that he is "one of the more adept negotiators of these concepts, simultaneously able to give the impression that realism is both achieved through artifice and unproblematically expressed, and to create the sense that 'reality' is found as well as constructed."[20] Appropriately, Bazin includes Robert Flaherty among the pantheon of filmmakers cited in *What Is Cinema?*, in particular for the famous long take during which Nanook struggles to spear and retrieve a seal in "real time."

Bazin's rationale here is of a piece with his vigorous valorization of the long take as the technique that allows reality to find its way into the projected image. What Bazin does not explicitly consider, however, is that our concept of "real time" — itself a symptom of the time-collapsing technology of cinema — must surely become *other* than real when the action filmed in the entirety of its duration is, in fact, inauthentic. Once it has been acknowledged that the entire seal-hunting sequence was a carefully staged dramatic set piece involving an already-harpooned seal (a fact of which Bazin was undoubtedly aware but which passes without comment), must we then judge Flaherty's documentary as having failed the test of realism, that is, having failed to honor the documentary film's implicit promise of authenticity? Is it not possible instead to use this instance of friction between the actual, the profilmic event and the represented real to see how documentary film permits us to query categories of representation and relations between the phenomenal and the ontological?

In contemporary documentary, the last refuge of the Griersonian ideal is in the comparatively marginalized categories of the "reflexive" and "performative" modes of documentary (which, for the purposes of my argument, I will treat as a single category defined by a self-conscious relationship to documentary discursivity) and the emergent field of inquiry into mock-documentary or, as it is more popularly known, "mockumentary." Yet as the title *Blurred Boundaries*, Nichols' 1994 study of documentary modes indicates, such categories are so unstable and mutually permeable as to be barely useful as classificatory terms for identifying fixed subgenres. Nichols' definition of performative documentary as a mode that "stress[es] subjective aspects of a classically objective discourse"[21] does little to distinguish this model of documentary from the reflexive, particularly since both modes occasion Nichols' discomfort with what he believes to be the inverse proportion between a documentary's self-awareness and its ability to adequately represent its ostensible subject.[22] At the same time, Nichols is adamant in his insistence that objectivity in documentary film is impossible, which raises an apparent paradox for documentary practice that prevails in most contemporary treatments of documentary cinema. But this is paradoxical only insofar as one imagines that the documentary does and ought to strive to not only capture the real world but to actually *be* the real world. Any insistence on documentary realism as a privileged link to the unmediated world requires some belief that the apparatus can guarantee objectivity, an anachronistic retention of nineteenth-century positivist notions that have all but vanished from accounts of other technologically mediated representational modes such as photography, phonography, and the novel.

This is not to say that the interrogation of representational "authenticity" requires one to adopt the iconophobia of poststructuralist accounts of the image that derive from the Frankfurt School. Film theories that insist on "unmasking" the deleterious effects of the image, as well as those which attempt to imagine a documentary mode that can do away with intervention and subjectivity and give rise to absolute "authenticity," invariably come to one of two hermeneutic dead ends: either that cinematic representation fails in its adequation to the real or that no trace of the real can survive mediation. Documentary studies have thus become beset by false arguments that misconstrue the production and reception of the "documentary" text and needlessly delimit the ways in which documentary cinema can provide a space in which the relationship between signifier and signified, sign and referent, can be thought through.[23] But let us not be overly hasty in tossing out the term "documentary" or the concept of creative re-presentation to which this term clings. In fact, it might benefit any analysis of documentary to ask when and how a certain set of visual codes acquired the authority to make statements for and about the unmediated world and how these codes derive not from fiction film, as Bill Nichols contends, but rather from the necessity to distinguish films that aimed to present non-fiction from the fictional narrative films that had, by 1905, fully absorbed the visual language that early cinema had developed for the representation of actuality.

It is my contention that it will prove more useful to retain "documentary" in lieu of the equally problematic and necessarily binarized term, "non-fiction," as a means of defining films about the social or historical world that operate according to a set of codes that can either mask or interrogate the means of their own production. Linda Williams' suggestion that "some form of 'truth' is always the receding goal of documentary film"[24] is a useful point of departure from which to investigate documentary as a process for placing the cinematic image in dynamic tension with its referent and with referentiality more generally. Similarly, Stella Bruzzi's more recent attempt to redirect theoretical discourse on the documentary, *New Documentary: A Critical Introduction*, begins with her determination to "initiate an analysis of documentary as a perpetual negotiation between the real event and its representation (that is, to propose that the two remain distinct but interactive)."[25] In short, Bruzzi wishes to bring to a close what she calls the "Bazin vs Baudrillard tussle,"[26] since she is equally bothered by claims for objectivity and authenticity as she is by arguments that insist that the image inevitably degrades or invalidates reality. Notably, Bruzzi points out how often contemporary documentary theorists such as Michael Renov and Bill Nichols feel compelled to place terms such as reality and truth in inverted commas, "as if the real can never be authentically represented and that any film, whether documentary or fiction, attempting to capture it will inevitably fail."[27] While the contemporary spectator may regard the Frankfurt School's link between mass art, advertising and fascist propaganda as hysteria or at least hyperbole, in an era of government-produced video news releases, docusoaps, docu-dramas and reality TV with spy-thriller twists, it is not inverted commas but inverted reality that warrants constant vigilance. As it happens, however, documentary film itself has, from its inception, allowed spectators to develop a keen understanding of the cinematic image's *difference* from the real. In this respect, documentary's salient truth is that it can en-*vision* the very means by which the human perceptual-cognitive apparatus grasps aspects of the real through its manifold apparatuses (mechanical, linguistic, symbolic) of representation. Bruzzi's desire to lay to rest unproductive and often meretricious debates over documentary success or failure in binding its images to concrete referents in the real world is meant to clear some theoretical space, to suggest lucidly and simply that "a documentary will never be reality nor will it erase or invalidate that reality by being representational. Furthermore, the spectator is not in need of signposts and inverted commas to understand that a documentary is a negotiation between reality on the one hand and image, interpretation and bias on the other."[28] In other words, documentary in all but its most malign and deliberately deceptive modes of propaganda, is a form of metatext, an irreal superposition that operates, to use Elizabeth Cowie's suggestively paradoxical phrasing, as a "spectacle of actuality"[29] that allows us to observe the world and the mediation of the world at once.

Such arguments in favor of reflexive documentary are hardly new; in fact, as I have attempted to sketch out here, they are as old as documentary itself. Bruzzi suggests as much, commenting that "[M]any theorists view ... reflexivity as breaking with documentary tradition — but this is only valid if one takes as representative of the documentary 'canon' films that seek to hide the modes of production."[30] To Bruzzi's caveat, I will add that such an account is only valid if one forgets that the notion of reflexivity as a break with documentary tradition is an *invention* not of the genre itself but of that caste of theorists whose insistence on mimesis obscures the fact that reflexivity is wholly *within* the tradition of documentary as adumbrated by its founding practitioners, Flaherty and Grierson. The radicalism of *Land Without Bread*, then, lies not in its break from Flaherty and Grierson but in its ability to tease out the auto-critical and irrealist dimension already present within these prior texts.

Of course, Flaherty and Grierson have their antecedents and while it is commonly understood that they derived their representational practices from the cinema of the Lumières, the full scope of this precedence tends to subordinate ideological homologies in favor of arguments that trace aesthetic influences. If we are to understand why it would be possible to maintain that any particular cinematic genre would be able to codify the means by which the moving picture could be construed as objective visible evidence, it is necessary to examine when and how the filmic image itself acquired such epistemological and classificatory power. The belief that the filmic image could claim a privileged relationship to the real is, of course, grounded in the prior network of relations (technological, social, aesthetic and juridical) that relied upon the nineteenth-century conceptualization of photography's indexicality as the paradigm of visual evidence.[31] As John Tagg puts it, "That a photograph can come to stand as *evidence* ... rests not on a natural or existential fact, but on a social, semiotic process, though this is not to suggest that evidential value is embedded in the print, in an abstract apparatus, or in a particular signifying strategy."[32] Demythologizing the aura that Barthes associates with the photographic image in *Camera Lucida*, Tagg argues that "evidential force" can only be understood as a "complex historical outcome ... exercised by photographs only within certain institutional practices and within particular historical relations."[33] Following Tagg, I posit that the late-nineteenth century popularization of imperialism as commodity culture in the form of anthropological photography, ethnographic exhibition and the early "cinema of attractions"[34] constituted the matrix of "particular historical relations" that allowed the cinema to elaborate its documentary effect and thus its claim on the real.

It would be incorrect to suggest that nineteenth-century British and Continental culture is reducible to the techniques and ideological operations of what could be considered a unitary "Realism." Rather, of the *multiple* realisms propagated by nineteenth-century popular entertainment. It is what historian of anthropology George Stocking calls the "anthropological idea of culture"[35] that is most useful as a heuristic for examining the documentary effect as an outgrowth of the practices of ethnographic exhibition that transvaluated anthropological science into commodity spectacle in the form of photography, *cartes-de-visites*, exhibition halls and the midways of the World's Fairs. Given that the anthropological idea of culture was propped on the semiotic logic according to which exterior signifiers (in this case, biotypes, anthropometrically measured) are thought to point toward fixed interior signifieds, it is unsurprising, that late-nineteenth century ethnography would have taken up the claims of the iconic and indexical fidelity of the cinematic image as quickly as it had adopted the still photographic image as a tool for the transparent recording of empirical truths—or, as Charles Read so effusively put it, for "dealing with facts about which there can be no question."[36]

Anthropological photography, as I will understand it here, has little to do with the bourgeois codes of portraiture, the tradition of the picturesque in landscape photography or the aesthetic aims of such early promulgators as Henry Fox Talbot. Rather, the photograph pressed into the service of anthropological science is both a mechanical technology and a representational medium that captures, collates and exhibits data and, as such, participates in what Allan Sekula designates as a "larger ensemble: a bureaucratic-clerical-statistical system of 'intelligence.'"[37] What Sekula chooses to emphasize is the systemic, archival aspect of photography in the nineteenth century, and I wish to take up his assertion that the "central artifact of this system is not the camera but the filing cabinet."[38] It is this concept of the visual archivability of the world that survives well into the twentieth century, and which surfaces as a key figure (*les archives filmées*) in Jean Rouch's link between the anti-illusionist ethos of cinéma vérité and the illusory realism of the Lumières:

> This century's filmed archives began with its first primitive films. Was the cinema going to be the objective instrument capable of capturing human behavior from life? The marvelous ingenuity of *La sortie des usine*, *le déjeuner de bébé*, of *La pêche à la crevette*, allowed us to believe that it would be.[39]

The very idea of the archive as a project of social control, a project in which photography played an integral part in producing a somatic poetics by which the human body could be measured, classified, and assigned a place in the world (or exiled to the margins of it), is symptomatic of what Jean-Louis Comolli calls the "ideology of the visible" that would give rise to cinematic visuality as a moving archive by which the world assembled itself for display.[40]

Instrumental to this ideological dimension of cinematic visuality was the cinematograph's unique ability to add the element of duration to its representational arsenal.[41] One of the Lumières' principal cameramen, Boleslaw Matuszewski, extolled the ability of the moving image to capture time as well as motion and thus promoted the ethnographic (and auto-ethnographic) uses of the cinema in what many consider to be the first true film manifesto, *Une nouvelle source de l'histoire* (1898). Here and in a subsequent publication, *La photographie animée*, Matuszewski argues for the importance of establishing an archive of historical film and praises the virtues of the cinema as the ideal medium for science, education and citizenship. Matuszewski's encomia are representative of the competing fantasies of the cinematograph's future, fantasies which circulated around the idea of the cinema's imagined capacity to capture and reproduce all of the elements of contemporary life; to be, in effect, the archive of all archives and thus the summa of nineteenth-century technologies of classification.

As with photography, there were many initial proponents of the potential applications of film as an ethnographic tool. Chief among these was French anthropologist Félix Regnault, who sought to use the moving image to produce a comparative archive of human motion, cataloging "manières de marcher, de s'accroupir, de grimper" [manners of walking, crouching, climbing] around the world.[42] In 1900, Regnault conceived of combining the cinematograph with Edison's gramophone to produce an audio-visual ethnographic museum in which the image, supplemented by motion and sound could — spectacularly — exceed all other modes of representing culture:

> Ethnographic museums must incorporate chronophotography into their collections. It does not suffice to have knowledge of a loom, a pottery wheel, spears ... one must know how such things are used; now we cannot know this precisely except through the medium of chronophotography.[43]

Regnault's project was never realized, but his enthusiasm for the indexical power of the cinematograph is indicative of how the early motion pictures were first received in the ethnographic community. Such exhortations notwithstanding, it would not be until the nineteen-twenties, when Robert Flaherty's films developed the narrative structure, and in particular, the visual codes that continue to constitute documentary authenticity, that "ethnographic" cinema would emerge as anything more than a moving counterpart to the ethnographic photograph.

As the cinema rapidly evolved from an attraction in which mere motion and the apparatus that produced it were sufficient to draw crowds, content became increasingly important to its continued appeal, and as a result, "early cinema categorised the visible world as a series of discrete attractions, and the catalogues of the first production companies present a nearly encyclopedic survey of this new hypervisible topology."[44] This privileging of the cinema's ability to render all things visible is clearly the organizing principle of the late-nineteenth century cinematograph program. Comprised as it was of single-shot shorts that drew by turns upon sensational and mundane subject matter, early cinematic programs were oriented toward producing a sensory experience; a succession of moments of shock, of tension and release, and therefore spectatorial pleasure, that required no distinction between fiction, reconstructed historical events and nonfiction. Instead, cinema as an institution borrowed from both the music hall and the exhibition hall, the former providing the mutually entailing structures of showmanship and spectatorship and the latter providing the discursive logic that transformed otherwise incoherent series of image-sequences into a legible cultural practice.[45] As I have insisted above, the drive toward visual mastery of the world bears the mark of an ethnographic dispensation that is always on display in the early cinema, whether the scenes projected were of "exotic" peoples and locales or of the equally anthropological documentation of the everyday life and labor of the same populations of the major urban centers who comprised the audiences of these exhibitions.[46] A quick glance at the composition of typical Lumière, Paul, and Edison programs[47] is sufficient to demonstrate that it is the power to render visible that is on display and that pre-narrative cinema binds its individual representations together in an overarching imperialist-positivist narrative — what Trinh T. Minh-ha criticizes as the "totalizing quest of meaning."[48]

In this light, *Nanook of the North* might best be understood as an archive not only of the Inuit cultural practices that it places on display, but also of the cinematic forms that preceded it. As Rony so aptly puts it, "[T]he 'archive' thus manifested itself in popular cinema as the desire to prospect the world as tourist-explorer."[49] *Nanook*, then, is literally a consummate entertainment, a single film that has absorbed within its narrative structure and techniques of representation elements from the entire spectrum of the Lumière, Edison and Pathé programs. Thus Flaherty's film is the "frenzy of the visible" tamed and subordinated to (but by no means eclipsed by) narrative, an admixture of the travelogue/*vue*, the *actualité*, the ethnographic film and even carefully staged gags (such as the Nanook biting the phonograph record or the sequence in which Nanook, Allee, Nyla and her infant ("Rainbow"), Cunayou, and the puppy, Comock, all emerge from Nanook's one-man kayak, a comedic moment that Richard Barsam has likened to circus clowns emerging from a tiny car). It is arguably the radical otherness of the Arctic and its seemingly unimaginable human subjects— eclipsing British and Continental imperialism's more "familiar" racial others in their degree of alterity — that liberated Flaherty to develop a representational idiom that could incorporate the various modes of early cinema into one continuous and internally coherent spectacle. That Flaherty did so by burying beneath the documentary effect all traces of the machinic, cultural and institutional apparatuses that brought him to the Hudson Bay Area in the first place cannot be overlooked, nor can the paradoxes of ethnographic vision that always undermine "salvage ethnography" with the inescapable irony that the one who wields the camera is complicit with the forces that imperil the "authenticity" of the culture to be preserved on film. If Flaherty elided such paradoxes by creating a thoroughgoing veneer of fiction that re-presented Nanook's generation as a nostalgic fantasy and transcribed Inuit culture into a living museum of its own ancestry, it is worthwhile to note that his method for doing so closely resembles (if in a somewhat unrefined manner) the contemporary anthropological practice of participatory observation. Jay Ruby goes so far as to laud the collaborative nature of Flaherty's reconstructions:

> The Inuit performed in front of the camera, reviewed and criticized their
> performance, and were able to offer suggestions for additional scenes in the

film — a way of making films that, when tried today, is thought to be 'innovative and original' and confounds the naïve assumption that ethnographic films are merely a record of what happens in front of the camera.[50]

As noted above, the many liberties taken by Flaherty in his quest for the sentimental power of his romantic fable have been thoroughly documented[51] and his fidelity or misrepresentation can and will continue to be debated. Yet given that the film's subtitle is "A *Story* of Life and Love in the *Actual* Arctic" (my italics), exactly whose assumptions of authenticity do the critiques of Flaherty's film destabilize? Flaherty himself suggested without circumlocution: "Sometimes you have to lie. One often has to distort a thing to catch its true spirit."[52] Leaving aside the obviously contentious point as to the inevitably subjective evaluation of a thing's "true spirit," it is in Flaherty's assertion that I find the direction of contemporary documentary theory — including Bruzzi — already articulated. The only thing that the film directly claims as actual is the only thing that can be framed but not constructed — the Arctic — while the representation of Inuit life elicits (but cannot legitimately be said to impose) spectatorial complicity in order to be accepted as actual.

Rony's reconceptualization of *Nanook* as a "kind of taxidermic display"[53] explicitly situates the film's spectatorial pleasure as "preceded by a historical fascination for Inuit performers in exhibitions, zoos, fairs, museums, and early cinema [and] represents a paradigm for a mode of representing indigenous peoples which parallels the romantic primitivism of modern anthropology."[54] Rony's term, "taxidermy," refers in particular to modern anthropology's tendency to romanticize the imperiled "native" as the sign of authenticity, such that the representation of indigenous culture is often a tissue of fictions, a reconstruction of an earlier generation's lifeways as opposed to an accurate depiction of the conditions that constitute the present habits, rites and structures of the object of inquiry. Indeed, Nanook comes to us, as is the case with any subject coded as "primitive" by the ethnographic gaze, without the means to self-represent. Lacking the "civilized" coordinates of history, technology and language (Flaherty limits Nanook's mode of communication to gesture and facial expression), Nanook is a sign on a metonymic chain that proffers his image as a generalizable artifact of all peoples of the Canadian Arctic, and by extension, of Otherness itself and *in extremis*.

Once again, it is Félix Regnault who is Flaherty's precursor here, as witnessed by the comment in "*Le langage par geste*" (1898) that "all savage peoples make recourse to gesture to express themselves; their language is so poor it does not suffice to make them understood."[55] Regnault's sense of the photographic image as a tool for "speaking for" those who cannot linguistically represent themselves is echoed in Flaherty's belief that cinema is "well-suited to portraying the lives of primitive people whose lives are simply lived and who feel strongly, but whose activities are external and dramatic rather than internal and complicated."[56] In the case of *Nanook*, Flaherty's 'taxidermic impulse" is manifested in the variety of misrepresentations of Inuit life, most of which stem from his insistence that his subjects perform their otherness by adopting the clothing and hunting techniques of past generations. In addition, certain elements of Inuit life presented as actual, were in fact, constructed (sometimes literally, as in the case of the igloo that Nanook builds, which was an enlarged yet partial structure that allowed both light and the camera crew into the space) in order to accommodate the particular demands of filming.

Of these cultural manipulations, the most egregious elisions have to do with the institutional background of the film, which was sponsored by the Revillon Frères fur company and is therefore, inescapably, a film that promoted the interests of the fur industry and burnished the public image of Revillon Frères in particular.[57] While there are few, if any, mainstream films that include a disclosure of corporate funding within their discourse, the status of the Revillon Frères is especially noteworthy since Flaherty's connection to their exploitation of Inuit labor makes him and his film direct harbingers of the threat to the very authenticity that he strives to capture. In this respect, the sequence at the trading post, identified as if through Nanook's perspective as the "white man's big igloo," is represented unproblematically as a beacon of Western beneficence. At no point does Flaherty allow the camera to pause in its narrative world-making to register the disparity between the plenitude of the "trader's precious store," where "pelts of fox and polar bear [are] bartered for knives and beads and bright colored candy"[58] and the exigencies of Inuit life. This enormous structure, bedecked with countless fox pelts in a staggering display of accumulation, is the arena in which cultural conflict will be played out as gentle comedy and frictionless coexistence. It is here that Nanook acts out the fantasy of primitive first contact with the phonograph record and where Allegoo is treated with castor oil after "banqueting" to excess on the trader's sea biscuits and lard, but nowhere in this brief, utopian pause in the struggle for subsistence are we encouraged to contemplate that the trading post is evidence of an imposed shift toward a market-based economy for which Nanook and his followers are ill-equipped.

Concealed in plain sight, in other words, are the material relations that render *Nanook*'s romantic revisionism uncomfortably cannibalistic. It is essential to keep in mind, however, that Flaherty was unapologetic about this approach, stating outright that "I am not going to make films about what the white man has made of primitive peoples.... What I want to show is the former majesty and character of these people, while it is still possible — before the white man has destroyed not only their character, but the people as well."[59] Of course, I do not mean that Flaherty's intentions make *Nanook of the North* beyond critique. Indeed, the chief problem with *Nanook* is that Flaherty's acknowledgment of the difference between representation and the real is more readily in evidence in his production notes and recollections than it is on the screen. Lost in the film's series of exchanges between actuality and artifice is the spectatorial distance that maintains an active interrogation of how Flaherty substitutes visual pleasure for veridical statements.

The elaboration of a directly related but alternative model for representing the real would have to wait for ten years after *Nanook of the North*, with the 1932 release of Luis Buñuel's *Land without Bread* (*Tierra sin pan*, a.k.a. *Las Hurdes*). William Rothman has noted a certain homology between the struggles of *Nanook's* Inuits to survive in their inhospitable Arctic terrain and *Land without Bread*'s subject, the desperately impoverished, malnourished and technologically backward Hurdanos. Separated geographically from the rest of Spain by their mountainous terrain and, it would seem, separated historically as well from the modernization programs of the Franco regime, the Hurdanos as represented by Buñuel share with *Nanook's* Inuits the status of the imperiled object of ethnographic knowledge. Indeed, surface similarities between the two films abound: both begin with a contemplation of a map of the region in which the film's subjects will be "discovered" and filmed, a convention that metonymically links land and inhabitant and places us fully within the twinned idioms of both exploration narratives and anthropological science.

Much as Flaherty's film begins with a title card rhapsodizing about the Arctic as "The mysterious Barren Lands—desolate, boulder strewn, wind-swept— illimitable spaces which top the world—,"[60] Buñuel's narrator claims that "Nowhere does man need to wage a more desperate fight against the hostile forces of nature." Whereas Flaherty's film, in a manner typical of what James Clifford calls "ethnographic allegory," romanticizes and fetishizes the heroism of its imperiled primitive object of scrutiny, *Land without Bread* produces the abjection of the utterly hapless Hurdanos by observing merciless ironies that render peasant life in the "Unpromised Land"[61] as horrific absurdist comedy. For instance, an image of local flora is accompanied by a narratorial gloss that claims "this harmless looking plant" is "a haunt of the deadly adder. The peasants are frequently bitten. This is seldom fatal in itself. But the Hurdanos generally infect the wound by their unhygienic efforts to cure it." Similarly, the narrator notes that the inadequate water supply that remains in the summers that scorch this arid and uncultivable land must be used "despite the disgusting filth it carries." Herein lies a formula—the "cure" that is more deadly than the disease, the "relief" that brings only renewed suffering—that Buñuel adopts throughout much of the film in order to portray the Hurdanos themselves as symptoms of industrial modernization. No such critique is to be found in *Nanook of the North*, which imagine similar hardship (via intertitle) as cause for wonder and an opportunity for paternalistic admiration: "The sterility of the soil and the rigor of the climate no other race could survive; yet here, utterly dependent upon animal life, which is their sole source of food, live the most cheerful people in all the world—the fearless, lovable, happy-go-lucky Eskimo."[62]

There is no room in Buñuel's film for rendering his "human geography" with such rhapsodic mythologizing. Unlike *Nanook*, in which the intertitles serve as the "voice" of the documentary to lend both narrative structure and dramatic heft to the visual track, Buñuel's film deliberately creates moments of disjuncture between image and soundtrack. Exemplary of this technique are two notably rhymed instances of misrepresentation: the first an image of a clearly elderly woman afflicted with goiter, identified by the narrator as "only thirty-two years old" and the second, conversely, a shot of an obviously preadolescent girl who is noted as being of advanced age. At several junctures in the film, the narrator appears to drop all pretense of both objectivity and sympathy and indulges instead in outright mockery, as when the narrator refers to several villagers as "dwarves and morons," announces the image of a Hurdanos man with the comment "here is another type of idiot" or sardonically entreats the spectator to "[N]ote the efforts at interior decorating" as the camera observes a bare home punctuated by a handful of functional objects.[63]

A telling difference between *Land Without Bread* and *Nanook of the North* occurs in two resonant moments that also constitute the most striking point of overlap between the two films. One of the sharpest critiques of the ethics of Flaherty's documentary reconstruction concerns his insistence on outmoded hunting practices (i.e. harpoons instead of rifles) as authentic representations of contemporary Inuit life, a decision that very nearly changed the outcome of *Nanook*'s infamous walrus-hunting scene.[64] Along with the seal-hunting scene, Nanook's struggle to kill and retrieve a walrus stands out as one of the most dramatic and memorable scenes in *Nanook of the North* but as Rony recounts the profilmic event, "[M]aking this particular scene, Flaherty said, was a difficult struggle requiring subterfuge: the men were afraid that they would be pulled out to sea and kept calling on Flaherty to shoot the walrus with his rifle, but Flaherty pretended not to hear them."[65] If the subjects of *Nanook* were indeed "on the thin edge of starvation," goes the critique, then Flaherty's subordination of human need to narrative — and in the name of "authenticity," no less — is surely inexcusable.

Buñuel, however, takes a startlingly different tack: In one particularly remarkable sequence, the camera tracks a mountain goat as it negotiates the peaks of a mountain. The narrator proclaims that "[T]he goat is the only animal able to survive in this parched region. Goat milk is saved for the sickest members of the community. A rare treat is a crust of bread moistened with a few precious drops."[66] What immediately follows is a magnificent bit of cinematic and rhetorical sleight-of-hand. Since the image track and sound track have been carefully aligned here to produce the impression of the goats having been recorded in real time, the sequence achieves a moment of shock when, as the narrator continues, "Goat meat is eaten only when *this* happens..." the goat, in a medium shot, takes a leap and is then shown, in a long shot, plummeting down the mountain, followed by an overhead shot of the fall. The rhetorical suggestion is that of cause-and-effect, yet the obvious impossibility of this being a spontaneous record of the profilmic event brings the constructedness of continuity editing fully within view and casts the basic premises of observational documentary into further doubt. Moreover, and in direct contrast to Flaherty's refusal to bring a rifle to the aid of Nanook and his men, a careful examination of this sequence reveals a telltale puff of smoke from an off-screen firearm at the moment of the goat's precipitous fall.[67] This degree of manipulation, by turns subtle and overt, is indicative of Buñuel's appropriation and ultimate subversion of the techniques of visual anthropology and documentary cinema. Although *Land Without Bread* might seem to be the antithesis of Flaherty's romanticism and "salvage ethnography," both films are expressions of the same impulse with one key difference: Flaherty borrows from the visual vocabulary of the Lumières in order to render his fiction realistic while Buñuel makes documentary irrealism an insistent presence within — and pressure on — the discourse of his film.

In contradistinction to Flaherty's tendency toward mawkish sentimentalism, Buñuel's sardonic paternalism has no interest in portraying the Hurdanos as noble savages or as imperiled innocents not-yet encroached-upon by the civilized world. In this respect, we might be inclined to regard Buñuel's elaborate and often brutal artifice as yielding the more "honest" text. Moreover, the frequent disjunctures between image and voiceover and between "voice" and tone challenge the spectator in such a way that the pleasurable spectacle afforded by Flaherty is repeatedly revealed as a grotesque and pornographic impulse to penetrate the other visually and episte-mologically. Perhaps the most potent example of Buñuel's foregrounding of the twin violations of the ethnographic gaze and the distorting ethnological gloss is the dis-turbing sequence in which the narrator happens upon a sickly young girl lying pros-trate in the street. In an arrestingly grotesque satire of the penetrative gaze of Western anthropological and medical science as well as the cinematic apparatus' will to knowl-edge/power,[68] Buñuel's camera centers on the lower half of the girl's face while an off-screen assistant opens her mouth for inspection. Although Flaherty's camera pays a great deal of attention to the smile of Nanook and to orality as an expression of Inuit contact with the world (Nanook eating raw meat, biting the phonograph record, licking blood from his knife; Nyla chewing Nanook's boots to soften the material — all of these points of oral contact meant to metonymically reveal an interiority at once connected to but alien from that of the spectator), only Buñuel's camera goes literally further, entering the girl's mouth to examine her body on the inside. It is a testament to the complexity of Buñuel's film and its "invitation to knowledge" about cinematic discourse itself that the work of this sequence is complete only when we recognize that, despite its invasion of the girl's body, the camera reveals no visually interpretable information, even when the narrator pronounces that what we see is evidence of the girl's disease, a disease which leads to the equally unverifiable report that "two days later they told us that the child had died." Whereas the introductory titles of *Nanook of the North*, in announcing that Nanook had died of starvation after the completion of the film, serve to ennoble and sentimentalize both Nanook and his struggle to survive as well as the film itself as a form of "salvage ethnography," the young girl's reported death in *Land without Bread* either forces the spectator into a position of discomfiting complicity or demands a recognition of the narrator's unreliability. In either case, Buñuel activates the spectator in ways that Flaherty's film ultimately circumscribes.

While the focal point of *Land without Bread* remains the misery of Hurdanos life, against which the hypocrisies of the wealthy Church and the Spanish fascists' claim to triumphant modernization are thrown into stark relief, Buñuel eschews political didacticism and instead makes his argument by rupturing the surface of the film and violating the discursive strategies of documentary "objectivity" to such a degree that he systematically presses a vertiginous secondary subject onto the spec-tator: that of filmmaking itself. As Rothman notes, "the narrator's study of the Hur-danos, its aspiration to scientific objectivity and detachment, is no less an object of Buñuel's "study" than are the Hurdanos themselves."[69] It seems reasonable, then, to regard *Land Without Bread* as the first truly reflexive documentary (Rothman even calls it a "mock documentary"[70]), one which vehemently repudiates the possibility of documentary objectivity and goes so far as to indict the ethnographic gaze of doc-umentary film as complicit in a cultural and political modernity that might senti-mentalize the Hurdanos but produce only narratives that are powerless to alleviate their abject misery. The fundamental paradoxes of the kind of paternalistic, moral-izing that would render a "social documentary" about the Hurdanos indistinguish-able from the Spanish government's ludicrous efforts to modernize the Hurdanos via

a standardized education that ensures they "receive exactly the same primary education as children all over the world." That this education inculcates the capitalist ideology of private property to people who cannot manage to raise crops much less
accumulate capital is an irony that Buñuel proffers with particular savagery and it is
not coincidental that he does so by developing a rhetorical method for which irony
is the sole ideal modality.

Nichols finds in Buñuel's destabilizing of documentary discourse a *clin d'oeil* to
the spectator, "hinting to us that this is *not* a factual representation of Hurdanos life
as he found it or an unthinkingly offensive judgment of it but a *criticism* or exposé
of the forms of representation common to the depiction of traditional peoples."[71]
Herein lies the most significant institutional difference between Flaherty's and
Buñuel's films as well as what is perhaps *Land Without Bread*'s most pointed critique
of discursive orthodoxy. Accepting cinematic representation as truth, Buñuel's film
appears to suggest, would be tantamount to accepting the triumphalist propaganda
of the fascist government. The insistence with which the film dismantles its own
authoritative relationship to its filmed subjects, however, constitutes the training of
a form of spectatorship that includes the critical faculties to interrogate all forms of
information as necessarily mediated and therefore suspect if not outright meretricious.

It might be best, at this point, to dispense entirely with questions of the truth
quotient of documentary films that are propped on misleading binarisms such as
fiction/non-fiction, realism/fantasy, true/false. As Derrida suggests in "Le facteur de
la vérité," his examination of Lacan's inquiry into the relationship between truth and
fiction, the "opposition [truth/reality], which is as orthodox as can be, facilitates the
passage of the truth through fiction: common sense always will have made the division between reality and fiction."[72] Fiction, according to Lacan, is a "passage" through
which truth is midwifed, or as Lacan puts it in the "Seminar on 'The Purloined Letter,'" fiction is a habitation for truth, a proposition that leads Derrida to open up a
set of questions that are equally valuable to an analysis of documentary cinema: "To
inhabit fiction: is this, for the truth, to make fiction true or truth fictive? Is this an
alternative? A true or fictive one?"[73] For Lacan, insists Derrida, fiction is "permeated
by truth as something spoken, and therefore as something non-real."[74] In short, Derrida is predictably troubled by Lacan's yoking of truth to the power of speech and to
the operations of "adequation" and "unveiling," both of which insist on the voice as
validating "presence" (and for Lacan, the voice of the analyst as "the master of
truth"[75]). In response to this "massive co-implication ... of truth and speech," Derrida offers an uncharacteristically direct formulation: "What is neither true nor false
is reality."[76]

Given that all filmed material is by definition mediated and therefore re-presents reality, in lieu of generic distinctions between fiction and nonfiction and the sci-
entistic criteria of objectivity and subjectivity, we might well substitute the categories
of the "mediated" as opposed to the "unmediated," in the sense that Derrida uses the
term to designate the fantasy of "unmediated presence" that inheres in Western traditions of representation. In this sense, all documentary cinema is a mediated real,
and as such, it will perhaps further our investigation to animate Nelson Goodman's

still under-utilized term, "irrealism," to define the productive dimension of documentary's construction of the real. For Goodman, "irrealism" opens a negotiatory
space between realism and anti-realism, a space in which the world enters experience only by way of representational practices. Moreover, in *Languages of Art*, Goodman forwards a theory of representation that is dedicated to the elimination of the
privileged status of realist representations predicated on resemblance and referentiality in favor of an irrealist, non-hierarchical pluralism in which "the choice among
systems is free."[77]

Of the many things that Buñuel's self-conscious irrealism allows us to see — or
invites us to *know*— one is *Nanook of the North*, not simply as historical precursor
and intertext, but as the root grammatical structure of documentary's difference
from the real. Flaherty's impulse to entertain and to bind the spectator in a "family
of man" relationship with the ethnic Other may have come to dominate our reception of the film since the early twentieth century, but this should not eclipse its ability to demonstrate that documentary as a form of irrealist imagination has been with
us from the very beginning. In *Nanook Revisited*, Charles Nayoumealuk, whose father
had personally known Allakariallak, methodically dismisses much of Flaherty's
(mis)representational choices as constructions intended to please white audiences.
Of note, however, is Nayoumealuk's comment that the iconic smile that has been traditionally read as a sign of "Nanook's" childlike simplicity, was in fact Allakariallak's
bemused commentary on the way in which he was being represented:

> Each time a scene was shot, as soon as the camera was starting to shoot, he
> would burst out laughing. He couldn't help it. Flaherty would tell him —
> "Be serious." He couldn't do it. He laughed each time.[78]

In this anecdote lies a particularly felicitous example of how the real can indeed
inhabit fiction, for Allakariallak's smile may be seen as the joyous irruption of the
historical subject, the trace of a consciousness subtly in tension with the expropri-
ation of the body as it becomes image. In as much as the surrealist laughter of Buñuel
refers us to documentary's irreference, to the necessary fictions of mediation, the
silent laughter of Allakariallak is an invitation to share the subject's *real* enjoyment
of the irrealism of Nanook. To deny Allakariallak his last laugh is not only to deny
him the power to express himself but also to disallow his image from inviting us, ten
years before Buñuel, to the knowledge of how to see in film the vast and plural
world — the "illimitable spaces" that enter experience — by asserting the distance
between the real and its avatars.

1. Jean-Louis Comolli, "Machines of the Visible," *The Cinematic Apparatus*, ed. Teresa de
Lauretis and Stephen Heath, (New York: St. Martin's, 1980).
2. Francis Hubbard Flaherty, *The Odyssey of a Film-Maker: Robert Flaherty's Story* (New York:
Arno Press and the New York Times, 1972), p. 18.
3. Fatimah Tobing Rony, *The Third Eye: Race, Cinema and Ethnographic Spectacle* (Durham:
Duke University Press, 1996), p. 109.
4. Rony 102, also quoted in Jane M. Gaines, "Introduction: 'The Real Returns,'" *Collecting
Visible Evidence*, ed. Jane M. Gaines and Michael Renov (Minneapolis: University of Minnesota
Press, 1999) 17.

5. Gaines, p. 8.

6. *Ibid*, p. 7–8.

7. *Ibid*, p. 8.

8. *Ibid*.

9. Although *Nanook of the North* is cited by many film theorists (e.g. Bazin, Leprohon) as the first ethnographic film, it hardly fits any contemporary definition of ethnographic cinema unless this category is conceived so broadly, as Jay Ruby critiques, to indicate "any documentary film about non–Western culture" [Jay Ruby, *Picturing Culture*, Chicago: University of Chicago Press, 2000), p. 7]. Ruby refuses to label as ethnographic any film not "produced by competent ethnographers and explicitly designed to be ethnographies" (Ruby 28), and I will not argue with his intention to return ethnography to its precise disciplinary parameters, nor with his observation that most contemporary film theorists tend to reflexively regard all "anthropologically intended" (Ruby, p. 28) film as mired in nineteenth-century positivist illusions. Nonetheless, I find that Ruby's argument minimizes the value of exploring the generalized ethnographic impulse that made cinema's claim on the real historically — if no longer *logically* — possible. Disciplinary frictions aside, it seems to me that such analysis is thoroughly compatible with Ruby's contention that 'Once it is acknowledged that no one can speak for or represent a culture but only his or her relationship to it, then a multiplicity of viewpoints is possible and welcome — some from within and others from without and all the marvelously gray areas in between' (Ruby, p. 31).

10. One could argue that the subgenre of the mock-documentary or "mockumentary," that is, films marked by the appropriation of documentary style in the service of fictional narratives serve a similar function in contemporary cinema. The profusion of fiction films that satirize, parody or otherwise replicate the signature visual vocabulary of the non-fiction film (a category that includes films as diverse in scope, aim and effect as Abbas Kiarostami's *Close Up*, Jim McBride's *David Holzman's Diary*, Mitchell Block's *No Lies*, Woody Allen's *Zelig*, Rob Reiner's *This Is Spinal Tap!*, Christopher Guest's *Best in Show*, Peter Jackson's *Forgotten Silver,* and Eduardo Sánchez and Daniel Myrick's *The Blair Witch Project*) might well be analyzed symptomatically as a consolidation of the documentary film's claim on the real. In short, although it is beyond the parameters of this article, an argument might well be made that mock-documentary, in its hyperbolic and carnivalesque subversion of non-fiction film techniques, reinforces the perception that those films that discursively define themselves as somberly dedicated to the purpose of edification are indeed authoritatively linked to actuality.

11. John Grierson, *Grierson on the Movies*, ed. Forsyth Hardy (London: Faber, 1981), p. 24.

12. Grierson, qtd. in Brian Winston, *Claiming the Real: The Documentary Film Revisited* (London: BFI, 1995), p. 6.

13. Winston, p. 11.

14. It is for this reason that Errol Morris provocatively argues that "cinéma vérité set back documentary filmmaking twenty or thirty years. It sees documentary as a sub-species of journalism. There's no reason why documentaries can't be as personal as fiction filmmaking and bear the imprint of those who made them. Truth isn't guaranteed by style or expression. It isn't guaranteed by anything" (Errol Morris, "Truth Not Guaranteed: An Interview With Errol Morris," *Cineaste* 17 [1989]: 16–17).

In a remarkable anticipation of Morris' assessment, Jim McBride's seminal 1967 pseudo-documentary, *David Holzman's Diary*, formulates a critique of direct cinema — *in situ*, as it were — by employing its signature stylistic affectation while revealing the limitations of the idea that the documentary could possibly gain a purchase on the unmediated real. In this sense, the mock-documentary serves a valuable function insofar as it can remind its spectators that all film is fundamentally shot through with subjective interpretations, perspectival distortions and outright fictions — or, as "David Holzman" notes, "[A]s soon as you start filming something, what happens in front of the camera is not reality anymore ... it becomes a movie."

15. A rather less sanguine version of this dialectic between fiction and the real is that voiced by Hayden White, who suggests that "every mimesis can be shown to be distorted and can serve, therefore, as an occasion for yet another description of the same phenomenon.... All discourse *constitutes* the objects which it pretends only to describe realistically and to analyze objectively." To pursue the matter further, we might rework the persistent notion, inherited from the Western tradition of pictorialism, that confounds seeing with knowing, or as Heidegger puts it in *Being and Time*, "the tradition of philosophy has been oriented from the beginning primarily towards 'seeing' (*sehen*) as the mode of access to beings *and to being*."

16. Gaines, p. 5.

17. From the very outset of cinema, the discursive practices of fiction and non-fiction film have crystallized around particular techniques for concealing cinematic apparatuses, including the institutional structure that has produced the film. In fiction film, the apparatuses that produce the effect of suture must be utterly invisible lest the spectator be jarred out of the pleasant illusionism of the cinema's virtual reality. In non-fiction film, the opposite effect is sought, yet its reality is no less virtual and what is concealed is not necessarily the camera (a great deal of documentary cinema from Vertov to Rouch does, in fact, insist on a spectatorial awareness of the mechanical apparatuses of filmmaking) just as the institutional relationship between the filmmaker and his/her subject also determines the justification for the act of filming. In all documentary cinema that places its apparatuses within view — a practice that culminates in direct cinema and its problematic and hyperbolic insistence on objectivity, spontaneity and non-mediation — what is suppressed is the *influence* of the camera on that which is observed and how the entirely unusual circumstance of being filmed engenders in the recorded subject an awareness of becoming an image for the purposes of future examination. It is only in this sense that *Nanook* instantiates a problem that subsequent documentary up to and including direct cinema attempts to resolve by "real-izing" its techniques, that is, by insisting on "realness" by foregrounding the presence of the camera, the voice of the interviewer, the use of available light and live sound to signify non-constructedness.

18. Gilles Deleuze, *Cinema 2: The Time-Image*, trans. Hugh Tomlinson and Robert Galeta (Minneapolis: U of Minnesota P, 1989): 126–156.

19. Bill Nichols insists on the existence of a "documentary family tree" (in "evolutionary" order: the poetic, the expository, the observational, the interactive, the reflexive and the performative). Before I proceed, and in anticipation of objections to the terminology that I will use here, a brief word on my decision to speak of only two documentary modes may be necessary. Although Bill Nichols' classification of documentary cinema has had a great deal of influence on documentary theory's insistence on thinking in terms of the distinct, if often overlapping, categories of expository, observational, interactive, reflexive and performative documentary, I tend to agree with Bruzzi's objection to such taxonomy: "Documentary has not developed along such rigid lines and it is unhelpful to suggest that it has. [...If different modes overlap and interact], then what is the point of constructing genealogical tables?" (Bruzzi, p. 2). It may well be that Nichols' work is far more interesting and heuristically utile for the ways in which it *blurs* boundaries rather than for the ways in which it attempts to clarify and restore them. Nichols' will to blur produces an even more suggestive conflation in *Introduction to Documentary* in which he calls fiction films "documentaries of wish-fulfillment" in order to define them in relation to the "documentary of social representation" that he nominates as his blanket term for non-fiction film (Nichols 2001, p. 1). In an attempt to simplify my terminology, documentary practice I will understand it throughout this analysis can be construed as belonging to either the expository-observational mode or the reflexive mode. Expository-observational documentary, whether naturalistic in its representational form and spectatorial address, as with *Harlan County, USA* (Kopple), *Chronique d'un été* (Rouch and Morin) and *High School* (Wiseman) or inflected by dramatic (re)constructions, such as *Nanook of the North* and *Moana*, refers to any film orientated toward the claim to have achieved a direct link to "some form of truth." By contrast, reflexive documentary, such as *Land Without Bread*, *Night and Fog* (Resnais), *Sherman's March* (McElwee), *Reassemblage* (Trinh) and *The Thin Blue Line* (Morris), to name but a few, destabilizes the techniques that naturalize documentary observation in order to incorporate an awareness (shared between filmmakers and spectators) of the "receding goal" of truth — that is, the *recession* itself — as an essential aspect of its discursive operations.

20. Gaines, p. 3–4.

21. Bill Nichols, *Blurred Boundaries: Questions of Meaning in Contemporary Culture*, (Bloomington: Indiana University Press, 1994), p. 95.

22. Nichols, *Blurred Boundaries*, p. 97

23. For contemporary documentarians such as Jill Godmilow, the yoking of the definition of documentary to empiricism is not simply a paradox but a form of artistic and conceptual paralysis. Speaking in a 1997 interview with historian Ann-Louise Shapiro, Godmilow reflects on the production of her film, *Far from Poland* (1984), a non-fiction film on the Polish Solidarity movement that relies primarily on reconstructions (it was filmed in the US) while largely foregoing actuality footage: "[In the process of making *Far from Poland*] I began to address the limits of the genre, and to understand what the presence of that validating, authenticating footage was all about. I began

to understand that the claim to, and reliance on, 'the real' strangled ideas, originality, and truth in documentary filmmaking." [Jill Godmilow, "How Real is the Reality in Documentary Film,"1997, 3 April 2002, www.nd.edu/jgodmilo/reality.html].

24. Linda Williams, "Mirror Without Memories: Truth, History, and the New Documentary," *Film Quarterly* 46.3 (1993): 20.

25. Stella Bruzzi, *New Documentary: A Critical Introduction* (London: Routledge, 2000) 9.

26. Bruzzi, p. 4.

27. *Ibid*, p. 2.

28. *Ibid*, p. 5. In the interest of interrogating the realist presuppositions that cling to documentary theory, Bruzzi sets out to rethink the "performative" documentary in positive terms, that is, along the lines of the Judith Butler's account of performativity (following J.L. Austin) as any "speech act" that simultaneously describes and enacts that which is described. For Bruzzi, reflexive and performative documentary — she deliberately collapses the distinction to argue for a tradition that includes Dziga Vertov, Jean Rouch, Nick Broomfield, Michael Moore and Jennie Livingston, among others — heralds the necessary overthrow of the dogged allegiance to cinematic realism that I have indicated above.

29. Elizabeth Cowie, "The Spectacle of Actuality," *Collecting Visible Evidence*, ed. Jane M. Gaines and Michael Renov (Minneapolis: University of Minnesota Press, 1999): 19.

30. Bruzzi, p. 154.

31. See Nancy Armstrong, *Fiction in the Age of Photography: The Legacy of British Realism* (Cambridge, MA: Harvard University Press, 1999), Elizabeth Edwards, ed., *Anthropology and Photography*. (New Haven: Yale University Press, 1992), John Tagg, *The Burden of Representation* (Minneapolis: University of Minnesota Press, 1992), Allan Sekula, "The Body and the Archive," *October* 39 (1986): 3–64.

32. Tagg, p. 4.

33. *Ibid*.

34. Tom Gunning, "The Cinema of Attractions: Early Film, Its Spectator and the Avant-Garde," *Early Cinema: Space, Plane, Narrative*, ed. Thomas Elsaesser (London: BFI, 1990): 56–67.

35. George W. Stocking, *Victorian Anthropology* (New York: The Free Press, 1987) *passim*.

36. Charles H. Read, *Notes and Queries on Anthropology, for the Use of Travellers and Residents in Uncivilized Lands*, ed. George Garson, Charles H. Read (London: Anthropological Institute, 1899). In his introduction to the 1892 edition, Read emphasizes the function of photographic data collection, "for by these means the traveller is dealing with facts about which there can be no question and the record thus obtained may be elucidated by subsequent inquirers. Read's implicit message emerges clearly: the evidential force of the photograph is such it that can maintain its fidelity to the recorded moment, a perfected ethnographer's eye capturing the "authenticity" of uncivilized lands for exploration by subsequent interpreters.

37. Sekula, p. 16.

38. *Ibid*.

39. "Les archives filmées de ce siècle commencent avec ses premières réalisations naïves. Le cinéma allait-il être l'instrument objectif capable de saisir sur le vif le comportement de l'homme? La merveilleuse ingénuité de *La sortie des usines, Le déjeuner de bébé*, de *La pêche à la crevette*, permettait de le croire." Jean Rouch, "La caméra et les hommes." *Pour une anthropologie visuelle*. ed. Claudine de France (Paris: Mouton Éditeur, 1979), 55. My translation.

40. Comolli suggests that this "ideology of the visible" defines: "[t]he second half of the nineteenth century [which] lives in a sort of frenzy of the visible. It is, of course, the effect of the social multiplication of images: ever wider distribution of illustrated papers, waves of prints, caricatures, etc. The effect also, however, of something of a geographical extension of the field of the visible and the representable: by journeys, explorations, colonisations, the whole world becomes visible at the same time that it becomes appropriatable" [Comolli, p. 122–123].

41. R.H. Mere, writing in *Pearson's Magazine* trumpeted exactly this quality above all others as the miracle of cinematic documentation: "Posterity will have good cause to bless the nineteenth-century geniuses who were responsible for the invention of the Biograph ... an instrument for taking in rapid succession a series of photographs of any living, moving scene, and of bringing these photographs before the eye so quickly that one is enabled to see the entire scene reproduced as in actual life.... It brings the past to the present and it enables the present to be handed down to the future. Already we look back and witness, as they occurred in life, events of the last two or three

years which might never have been faithfully preserved without the Biograph's help. For example, we may watch each incident in the Queen's triumphal procession through the streets of London on the day of her Diamond Jubilee. Provided the films are still in existence, our descendants a thousand years hence may do likewise." R. H. Mere, "The Wonders of the Biograph." *Pearson's Magazine* (February 1899).

42. Claudine de France, ed. *Pour une anthropologie visuelle: recueil d'articles* (Paris: Mouton, 1979): 55.

43. Les musées d'ethnographie devraient annexer à leurs collections des chronophotographies. Il ne suffit pas de posséder un métier, un tour, des javelots ... il faut encore savoir la manière de s'en servir; or, on ne peut la connaître d'une manière précise qu'au moyen de la chronophotographie." Félix Regnault, "La chronophotographie dans l'ethnographie," *Bulletins et Mémoires de la Société d'Anthropologie de Paris* 1 (1900): 172–178 . My translation.

44. Tom Gunning, "An Aesthetic of Astonishment," *Art and Text* 34 (Spring 1989): 34.

45. With regard to concerns of genre, however, it is essential to note here that while I am interested in how the "anthropological idea of culture" (Stocking) shaped the early cinema and its spectator, it would be erroneous to assume a uniform continuity between "views/*vues*," domestic "realities/*actualités*" and what can properly be called ethnographic film. For a more comprehensive account of differences in early cinema's genres, see Renov 1999, Elsaesser 1990, Musser 1990. In a similar vein, Jay Ruby devotes the entire volume of *Picturing Culture* to limning the distinction between the actual theories and practices of visual anthropology and what he believes to be the misuse of the category of the "ethnographic" in poststructural and postcolonial cinema studies.

46. Auguste Lumière often filmed his own workers for the express purpose of projecting the film to the workers themselves, creating a self-perpetuating circuit between their labor and their entertainment. This practice was one adopted by numerous itinerant film exhibitors who would move from town to town, inviting local residents to be filmed and then inducing them to attend the cinema in order to see screenings of their own image [Colin Harding and Simon Popple, *In the Kingdom of Shadows: A Companion to Early Cinema* (London: Cygnus Arts, 1996): 20].

47. An advertisement announcing the arrival at Hull of the exhibit from the Royal Agricultural Hall and Victorian Era Exhibition, Earl's Court, London lists the program (a mixture of Lumière, Pathé, and probably Paul or Edison films, among others) as: "The Village Blacksmith; Mme Louis Fuller in a most beautiful Serpentine dance; the teetotaller that got drunk roars with laughter; the old gardener watering the plants, very humorous; the express train coming into the station, people coming in and out of the train very realistic; the sea waves; prize fight between Fitzsimmons and Corbett, a young woman taking a morning bath, wrestling match for the Championship of the World; Grand March past of the Royal Blues; the unfaithful wife; the good wife; on the beaches in the parz; bathing at Blackpool; a snow storm; and last but not least the Queen's Diamond Jubilee Procession" (*Hull Daily Mail*, 12 October 1897).

48. Trinh T. Minh-ha, "The Totalizing Quest of Meaning," *Theorizing Documentary*, ed. Michael Renov (London: Routledge, 1993): 90–107.

49. Rony, p. 82–83.

50. Ruby, p. 88–89.

51. Along with the substantial body of scholarship that queries Flaherty's authenticity (e.g. Rony, Barnouw, Rothman, Huhndorf, Nichols, and Grace), see Claude Massot's 1990 documentary, *Nanook Revisited*, in which contemporary Inuits of the Inukjiak and the Belcher Islands recall Flaherty and the making of *Nanook* and reflect on the disconnect between Inuit life in the 1920s and the film's representation thereof.

52. Robert Flaherty, qtd. in Richard Corliss, "Robert Flaherty: The Man in the Iron Myth," *Nonfiction Film Theory and Criticism*, ed. Richard Barsam (New York: E.P. Dutton, 1973), 234.

53. Rony, p. 100.

54. *Ibid.*

55. Félix Regnault, qtd. in Rony, p. 48.

56. Robert Flaherty, qtd. in Rony, p. 104.

57. Flaherty's earlier expedition into the Hudson Bay region in 1910 — which produced preliminary travelogue footage that would eventually lead to *Nanook*— was conducted at the behest of Sir William Mackenzie in order to prospect for mineral potential and railway feasibility

58. *Nanook of the North*, dir. Robert Flaherty, Les Frères Revillon/Pathé, 1922.

59. Robert Flaherty, quoted in Erik Barnouw, *Documentary*, (New York: Oxford University Press, 1993): 45.

60. *Nanook*

61. *Land Without Bread*, dir. Luis Buñuel, Ramón Acín, 1932.

62. *Nanook*

63. *Land Without Bread*

64. Postcolonial critiques such as Rony's have made a great deal out of the imperialist imposition of power that is arguably on display in this sequence. Although it is undeniable that Flaherty's subordination of actuality to drama is particularly problematic in this instance, it must not be forgotten that this decision to film a hunt conducted in the manner of the prior generation was arrived at in collaboration with Allakariallak. As Flaherty recounts in his 'An Early Account of the Film': "'Suppose we go,' said I 'do you know that you and your men may have to give up making a kill, if it interferes with my film? Will you remember that it is the picture of you hunting the ivuik [walrus] that I want and not their meat?' 'Yes, yes, the aggie [movie] will come first,' earnestly [Allakariallak] assured me. 'Not a man will stir, not a harpoon will be thrown until you give the sign. It is my word' We shook hands and agreed to start the next day" (Robert Flaherty, quoted in Jay Ruby 67).

65. Rony, p. 114.

66. Buñuel *Land without Bread*

67. Nichols *Introduction*, p. 8.

68. Linda Williams, *Hard Core: Power, Pleasure, and the "Frenzy of the Visible"* (Berkeley: University of California Press, 1999) *passim*.

69. William Rothman, *Documentary Film Classics* (Cambridge: Cambridge University Press, 1997) 25.

70. Rothman, p. 32.

71. Nichols *Introduction*, p. 8.

72. Jacques Derrida, "Le Facteur de la vérité," *The Postcard: From Socrates to Freud and Beyond*. trans. Alan Bass (Chicago: University of Chicago Press, 1987) 468.

73. Derrida, p. 421.

74. *Ibid*, p. 469.

75. Jacques Lacan, quoted in Derrida, p. 469.

76. Derrida, p. 469. Michael Renov picks up on this same pronouncement in the introduction to *Theorizing Documentary*, in which he applies Derrida's analysis of Lacan to documentary film in order to offer a nuanced account of the paradoxes of documentary form: "Every documentary representation depends upon its own detour from the real, through the defiles of the audiovisual signifier (via choices of language, lens, proximity, and sound environment).... What differs [between fictional and non-fictional representations] is the extent to which the referent of the documentary sign may be considered as a piece of the world plucked from its everyday context rather than fabricated for the screen" (Renov *Theorizing Documentary*, 7).

77. Nelson Goodman, *Languages of Art: An Approach to a Theory of Symbols* (Indianapolis: Hackett, 1976) 40.

78. *Nanook Revisited*, dir. Claude Massot, IMA Productions/La SEPT, 1990.

5

Reconstructing Reality:
The Industrial Film as
Faux Documentary

by Donald Levin

There is no nonrepresentational
unmediated access to "reality"; reality is a
construct of our sign systems. — James Paul Gee[1]

On first consideration, industrial films would seem to have little in common with either documentaries or mockumentaries. No one who has sat through, say, a video on the features and values of a new minivan in an automobile dealer's showroom would mistake what they are seeing for a "truthful and accurate portrayal of the social world," which is one attempt Roscoe and Hight make at defining the unstable term *documentary* in *Faking It: Mock-documentary and the Subversion of Factuality.*[2] Even the Academy of Motion Picture Arts and Sciences definition of documentary film specifically excludes non-theatrical motion pictures or, more recently, video and DVD programs, produced by businesses for promotional, technical, or instructional purposes.[3] And certainly no one would confuse the urgent blandishments of such productions, with their clear and commercial rhetorical purposes, for the postmodern parody or critique of the mockumentarian.

Yet film historians like Erik Barnouw have noted important, long-standing connections between industrial films and documentaries. Barnouw points out that industrial sponsors had funded some early documentaries (underwriting from the fur trading company Revillon Frères, for example, made possible *Nanook of the North*),[4] and he refers to the production of promotional films for business and industry as documentary's "most prolific sub-genre."[5] While the social world that industrial films represent may not suggest what James Paul Gee called the kind of "unmediated access to 'reality'" that many believe to be a defining characteristic of the documentary, industrials do in fact use the same codes and conventions of both the serious documentarian and the playful mockumentarian to accomplish their specific rhetorical ends. This chapter will suggest the ways in which a sampling of industrial films used those codes and conventions as strategies to help legitimate a particular kind of social reality, that is, helped to construct for their audiences specific attitudes toward products, objects, and technical processes, as well as toward larger and more diffuse social and economic institutions.

Specifically the codes and conventions this chapter will use in its analysis include the following:

- the presence of authoritative commentaries as Roscoe and Hight suggest not only to guide the reader through the experience but to shape the film's thematic structures;
- the presence of authentic appearing settings and activities, represented through naturalistic sound and lighting;
- the presence of eyewitnesses who provide viewers with a specific link to the event, or experts who rely on the authority of legitimizing discourses (of science, medicine, and the law, for example) for their credibility; and
- the presence of a visual intertextuality, the purposeful use of photographic stills or film footage "to authenticate a story ... contextualise events and issues ... and provide essential material."[6]

These codes and conventions have developed since the early days of cinema to support the look of an unmediated reality that positions the documentary as "a mere recorder of the real, rather than actively constructing ideological accounts of the social world," as Roscoe and Hight put it.[7] Yet constructing ideologically informed arguments about the social world is a central goal of the industrial film, as it is in many contemporary documentaries. Like Michael Moore's *Bowling for Columbine*, recent nonfiction films often offer arguments about the nature of social reality; in their taxonomy of documentary modes, Roscoe and Hight place such films within the expositional mode.[8] However, in contrast to films like Moore's, which takes as a main goal the foregrounding of clashing understandings about social reality in order to express the filmmaker's personal vision, industrial films use the conventions of documentaries to naturalize, and to a large extent obscure, their ideologies, which are the ideologies of their corporate sponsors and not their anonymous filmmakers. It is for the skillful simulation of documentary conventions that industrial films may be considered faux documentaries— nonfiction films that use the codes and conventions of documentaries to construct a reality that is not fictional but heavily ideologically and rhetorically interested.

My "informants" for this project are a sampling of films produced by the Detroit-based Jam Handy Organization in the 1930s, 1940s, and 1950s. Jamison Handy was an advertising promoter whose company, the Jam Handy Organization, flourished from the mid–1920s through the 1970s as a pioneer in the field of sales training films and non-theatrical motion pictures that illustrated scientific and technological innovations produced for major corporations such as General Motors, RCA, and Dupont. By 1963, the Detroit-based Jam Handy Organization was a $10 million corporate entity with production facilities in Atlanta, Chicago, Hollywood, and New York.[9] This examination is limited to films from the Handy Organization for two reasons: first, it gives the analysis a useful focus; and second, because the Handy Organization was arguably the most influential creator of industrial films, these productions may be considered the best the genre can offer.

The four short films I will examine are roughly representative of the types of industrial film the Handy Organization produced. These films emphasize a product's features (*All in One*, 1938), describe technical processes (*More Power to You*, ca. 1930s), highlight the unsung role of seemingly insignificant objects in our lives (*A Case of Spring Fever*, 1940), and finally offer a grand encomium to the role of technology in improving modern life (*American Engineer*, 1956). A review of the hundreds of industrial films available in the invaluable Prelinger Archives, a collection dedicated to the preservation of what archivist Rick Prelinger calls "ephemeral" films that would otherwise be lost, suggests the degree to which these films are representative. One could find dozens of examples of each of the four types of films discussed in this chapter, from the Handy Organization as well as the other producers in a field that, as Barnouw points out, created over 4,000 industrial films per year in the ten years following World War II.[10]

My analysis will move from the domestic front-yard play of children and animals in *All in One*, to a scripted film with adults as the main characters, *A Case of Spring Fever*, to a film that uses all of the documentary conventions note above, *More Power to You*, and finally to a film that undertakes an expansive, Whitmanesque envisioning of a powerful nation that has conquered the earth and now stands on the threshold of space, *American Engineer*.

"Men and Boys Expect Everything Good"

All in One, an eleven-minute-long text sponsored by the Chevrolet Division of General Motors, uses a range of devices to establish a straightforward documentary mode of presentation as prelude to its real rhetorical purpose.[11] The film begins as a consideration of the importance of the characteristics particular to various breeds of dog, then shifts into a meditation on the ways in which automobiles reflect — and improve upon — those canine characteristics. The opening sections of the film show different breeds of dogs engaged in work and service to humans. *All in One* establishes its documentary credentials as it unfolds with the voiceover of a narrator (an authoritative male) giving what seems at first to be factual information about sheep dogs, foxhounds, huskies, and family dogs. We see dogs herding sheep, hunting foxes, pulling a man in a sled, and finally pulling children in a cart. The settings in the beginning sections are all outdoors and naturalistic, and the scenes shift from field to barn to dogsled run with natural light, long unedited shots with a minimum of camera movement (mostly pans to follow the animals across the screen), simple cuts, and, for several minutes, no music or voiceover at all as we watch a sheep dog hard at work tending its flock. The camera appears to be a neutral observer as the narrator enumerates the admirable characteristics of the animals. Gradually these characteristics turn from the general qualities of protection, companionship, and love to more specific (and more metaphorical) features: greyhounds, we are told, represent speed and streamlining; Alaskan huskies are built for power and endurance; terriers are quick on the acceleration; collies are famous for safety; and the little Chihuahua is a model of economy.

Starting with the metaphor of the dog. *All in One* (1938) uses a range of devices to establish a straightforward documentary mode of presentation as prelude to its real rhetorical purpose.

The film then moves to a scene of a dog pulling a small boy in an unadorned wagon as the narrator intones that the child will not find style, comfort, or safety in his meager transportation. In an abrupt transition, a group of boys materialize and, beginning a sequence of actions that is more obviously scripted, set about building a car out of wood (immediately adopting the specialized roles one suspects they are destined for in the regimented adult life posited by the film: a laborer hauls materials, a skilled worker fits the steering wheel and brakes, a gawky pre-teen engineer in huge glasses solves a design problem with a snap of his fingers). Once the boys decide that harnessing six dogs to their vehicle will make it go faster than the single dog that pulled the cart previously, the narrator guides us through the recognition that "men and boys expect everything good in their dogs, and demand the same qualities of speed and protection in modern motor cars." The film presents a montage of cars similar to the montage of dogs that opened the program, though we are now given to understand, as the narrator says, "engineers did better with the automobile than nature did with the dog." As automobiles become the focus of the remainder of the film, the sophistication of the camerawork increases and the montage unfolds through wipes, dissolves of varying speed, and point-of-view shots that position the viewer behind the wheel and racing alongside the cars as they speed past the same countryside in which we earlier saw dogs working. A bouncy, lilting musical score accompanies the cars, rising to a final crescendo at the end.

All in One thus opens using several key elements of the documentary, particularly the voiceover commentary giving neutral, fact-based information about animals; a natural, outdoors setting in which unscripted events seem to take place; and minimal photographic or editing intervention. Once the viewer has processed these codes, all of which establish the appearance of a recognizable reality, the program moves away from the world of the nature documentary and begins to apply the same conventions, at least at first, to the human world that gradually replaces the one established at the film's beginning. Structurally, the dividing line between the two modes is the shot of the dog pulling the boy in the cart; after that scene, the focus on the natural world recedes and the human world assumes the foreground as, visually, the space occupied by the dogs gradually gives way first to the boys, and then to automobiles.

The narrator's observation that "engineers did better with automobiles than nature did with dogs" announces a more complex conclusion about the film's reality than the simple comparison between the safety, speed, and trustworthiness of dogs and cars. The movement from animals to boys and their playthings to automobiles (that is, men's playthings) enacts a kind of progress that puts automobiles, and the technology they represent, at a higher evolutionary step. While obscuring the role of humans in engineering certain characteristics in dogs through selective breeding by passing them off as "nature's work," the film covertly argues that nature's purpose in creating animals to serve humans is analogous to the mission of engineers to create cars of increasing sophistication to serve their owners. The comparison associates the role of the engineer with a natural process, and affirms that technological progress is as inevitable as nature, but more effective. The values of the reality that the film constructs through its documentary strategies—"everything good" that men and boys expect—are limited to a pair of features that are particular to automobiles, namely speed and protection. Within the rhetoric of the film, improving on nature means severely diminishing what society values.

"No Springs!" An Ironic Celebration of Technology

Of all the examples of industrial films discussed in this chapter, *A Case of Spring Fever* is closest to the genre of mockumentary as parody.[12] In contrast to the initial nature-documentary feel of *All in One, A Case of Spring Fever* creates a fictional reality that mirrors our own. The film follows a fictional character, Gilbert Willoughby, and his growing awareness of the importance of the humble spring in modern life, then his proselytizing for his new insight. The film opens with a shot of a woman speaking on the telephone telling the caller that Gilbert can't "play with you boys right now" because he's doing some work around the house. In the next shot the viewer learns that Gilbert is not the woman's son but her husband, caught under a sofa trying to fix the springs. After Gilbert, frustrated with his work, wishes he never saw another spring, an evil looking animated sprite who announces his name as "Coily" appears and grants Gilbert's wish. Gilbert spends the rest of the first half of the ten-minute long film discovering that without springs his watch no longer keeps time, the window shade droops, he can't call his friends because the rotary dial on the telephone doesn't move, his front door won't close, his car seat is rock hard, even the door of his glove box flops permanently open. At every discovery of what happens when springs are missing, Coily's raw and mocking cackle, "No springs!" is heard. Gilbert sees the errors of his ways, Coily relents and returns springs to the world, and Gilbert spends the last part of the film boring his golf partners with his new recognition of the importance of springs to the modern world.

A Case of Spring Fever contains fewer of the overt documentary devices we saw in *All in One*—neither voice over narration nor naturalistic settings and scenes. The first half of the film takes place in the carefully dressed, well-lit set of the Willoughbys' solidly middle class living room, and the text itself is obviously carefully scripted. Yet *A Case of Spring Fever* does incorporate documentary elements. Gilbert assumes the role of a voiceover narrator/expert explaining the role of springs in their (and by extension the viewers') lives. Though it uses a supernatural agent in the form of Coily and a dramatic approach, the film purports to offer a true version of the reality that the audience shares with the characters; the consequences of Gilbert's unfortunate

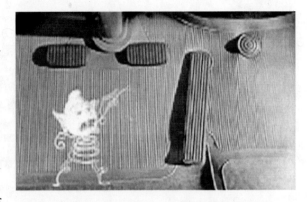

Coily in *A Case of Spring Fever* (1940) argues for the necessity of springs in an industrial film that is close to the genre of mockumentary as parody.

wish are those the audience can easily understand, as they are the homely, commonplace effects that follow from the failure of the simplest technologies that support our lives, existing below our consciousness as long as watches keep time, the window shades shut out the light when we wish, the seats comfort us in our automobiles, and so on. Clock time, personal privacy, personal comfort, and leisure form the essential elements of modern life, the film suggests, and thus whatever supports those also upholds the fundamentals of the modern age. Though the events are staged and the animated special effect of Coily insists on the production's artificiality, the film aims to portray the external world accurately—even to increase our awareness of that world, as we are meant to leave the viewing experience with a heightened understanding that the role of technology in our lives reaches to places we never notice.

A *Case of Spring Fever* also contains a considerable parodic element, as it constructs Gilbert as a comic figure and, like a mockumentary, seems to comment reflexively on its own message. Initially Gilbert is infantilized for the viewer by his wife, who says he can't "play" with the other boys until he finishes his chores. He is subsequently portrayed as a crashing bore to his golf partners by his own nonstop homage to the virtues of the spring, so single-minded in his praise of the spring that he literally puts his friends to sleep on the way home from the golf course. Yet though the representation of Gilbert is comical, the factuality of his message is never doubted; indeed, at the end of the film when one of his friends, driven to distraction by Gilbert's harping on the importance of the spring, echoes Gilbert's initial wish that he had never heard of springs, Gilbert replies, "Don't *ever* say that," with something like real fear. The irony of this production is that even as the film insists our lives are inextricably linked with modern technology, and the viewer comes to understand the role of the humble spring as a metonymic figure for that technology, the Everyman hero Gilbert becomes increasingly marginalized from the society of the film, and, insofar as we are invited to laugh at him, from the viewer as well. Thus the film's use of the codes and conventions of the documentary work to increase our understanding about our shared social world, and at the same time critique and parody Gilbert's (and, by extension, its own) attempt to communicate that understanding.

Valorizing the Fuel of the Modern Age

The final two films discussed here are closer to the "pure" form of documentary in terms of the codes and conventions they use. *More Power to You*, in particular, represents itself as a serious and detailed look at how oil is found, produced, refined, and finally used in the first third of the twentieth century.[13] The black and white images of this nine-minute film offer a full range of documentary strategies that preserve a high degree of fidelity to what Stephenson and Debrix called "a convention of reality."[14] The first striking signification of a full-fledged documentary in this film is the use (and star billing) of Lowell Thomas as the narrator. Thomas would have been well known to his audiences as a radio reporter, author, print journalist, and adventurer. He would also have been recognized as the voice of CBS news and Fox-Movietone newsreels, and a well-known guide to the life of high adventure, living and traveling in some of the most remote, exotic places of the world and bringing back from his travels images and stories in the form of documentaries and news reports. The name and voice of Lowell Thomas would thus have held for viewers of *More Power to You* the promise that the events of the film would offer a dramatic, exotic, and authoritative look at an interesting corner of reality.

Using visuals that represent the stages in the pumping and transportation of oil, the machines in operation, and animated explanations of the various processes involved, the film carefully establishes authentic-appearing settings and activities. In contrast to the initial naturalistic settings of *All in One*, and the domestic travails of *A Case of Spring Fever*, *More Power to You* represents a sophisticated viewing experience that incorporates aerial photography and long-distance shots of ocean-going tankers, oil fields, refineries, and pipelines threading through the countryside. Many of these images, such as shots of ocean liners at sea, aircraft in flight, and passenger trains barreling down the tracks, have the grainy, intertextual authenticity of documentary footage. Even the animated diagrams detailing how drills plunge through layers of soil and petroleum molecules shimmy and reform into gasoline when sufficiently heated add their own authenticity through appeals to the authoritative discourse of science. As the film roves from oil field to refinery to petroleum lab to pipelines traversing mountains and countrysides of America, the emphasis is always on a careful, clear explanation of the technical processes involved in oil exploration, production, distribution, and use. In the visuals there is never a sense that the film portrays and explains anything but an objective reality made accessible through documentary strategies.

More Power to You (circa 1930s) portrays human beings as subservient to larger mechanical processes.

Most often Thomas's voiceover supports the clear expository purpose of the visuals. On closer examination, however, the rhetoric of the language of the film reveals the production's other ideological purposes as well. The overt purpose, as we saw in *A Case of Spring Fever*, is to celebrate the role of technology in modern life. The large-scale visuals of *More Power to You*, full of impressive movement, height, and depth, certainly support that message, as the film's rhetoric consciously foregrounds and naturalizes the poetry of technology. It describes the "power of oil" to conquer heights, for example, as "the might of petroleum [pulses] in great engines that traverse the deep." It naturalizes the fields of oil derricks as "forests of derricks," and refers to the smokestacks of mid-century industry as "the pageants of industry" and the "minarets of science" (the latter a striking image, to the contemporary mind, about which I will have more to say in my conclusion). The film glorifies the ability of American industry to control the natural world. The might and brainpower that allow American capitalism to drive the technology that enhances society through both the necessities and luxuries of the modern age are on display, and the codes and conventions of the documentary energize that effort.

Yet a covert message accessible through images and language makes another kind of statement about the nature of the reality the film represents. *More Power to You* consistently privileges the mechanical over the human. In the beginning of the film, after a montage of images of modes of transportation that require oil, as *More Power to You* plunges into a close-up look at the machines, pipes, drills, rockers arms and processes involved in drilling for oil, Thomas's authoritative narration obscures the human contribution through passive verbs ("a cellar is dug," and "the rotary table ... is set in place," for example). Meanwhile, the images comply with that mystification by showing only the hands or arms of laborers performing the activities, rarely a face and never the whole person. The narration celebrates machines as the active participants through active verbs ("a steam engine drives the drilling mechanism," narrator Thomas intones, for example), while the central visual focus is on mechanical parts and processes. The machines seem to operate independent of human intervention. When the laborers are referred to at all, they are called, briefly, according to their task names ("rope chokers"), and the point makes reference only to the colorful language of the oil field, not to the workers themselves except as they are subsumed within their functions.

Later in the film, shots of scientists holding test tubes up to the light suggest that while professional workers fare better than manual laborers in the film (we see their serious and thoughtful faces, for example), *More Power to You* again portrays the human factor as subservient to the larger mechanical processes the humans serve. Even the salute to the American know-how that brought forth the power of oil obscures human agency. Waxing eloquent about how "modern magic loos'd the liquid energy from its subterranean prison," Thomas's narration metaphorically mystifies the role of the individual in the very technology the film celebrates; it is not human agency that controls the natural world, the film tells us, but a form of *magic*. In its reliance on the codes and conventions of the documentary, *More Power to You* inscribes its human participants as mere apprentices to the powerful supernatural sorcery that pries oil from the ground and turns it into the fuel of the modern age. As we saw briefly in the "natural" assumptions of tasks by the children in *All in One*, *More Power to You* also exemplifies a highly regimented hierarchy of social function.

Technology, Mass Production, and Price Reduction

If *A Case of Spring Fever* is comedy, *American Engineer* is opera.[15] The title screen of this half-hour length film sponsored by the Chevrolet Division of General Motors suggests its larger intent in conjoining the codes and conventions of both the documentary and the major Hollywood production. The words "For a Better Appreciation of American Engineers" float in script against the background of a blueprint and what looks to be a three-dimensional molecular model of a chemical element. The camera then pans down to reveal a slide rule and compass, mundane tools of the trade that, with the blueprint, establish the boundaries of the world of the film as the fact-based reality of engineers; this world, which one may measure and count, will have exact correspondences with our own. When the camera pans further down the blueprint to reveal the title, *American Engineer*, image and sound also reveal cues to the big-budget world of Hollywood: the titles "Color by Technicolor" and "Super-Scope," two relatively advanced film processes, and a celestial choir with voices soaring above strings and kettle drums. Neither the visual effects nor the orchestrations were generally available to the more limited resources of the industrial film at the time. Thus a dual expectation is set up: the viewer is prepared for a look inside the straightforward, recognizable world of an engineer, but through the lens of a sophisticated Hollywood production.

And in fact, *American Engineer* goes to great lengths to exalt the roles of engineers and the technology they create in reshaping and improving modern life. From its opening frames that show an enormous radio telescope against the snaps and crackles of space static on the sound track, the film takes the documentary stance and visual style of *More Power to You* to another level of complexity. *American Engineer* contains long, stately (and wide-screen "SuperScope") aerial photography showing the vast diversity of the American landscape, from urban centers like New York City, Pittsburgh, Chicago, and Los Angeles, cities sparkling with light and vitality and the monumental force of their skyscrapers, to the geometric precision of industrial and hydroelectric plants across the nation, to terrain dramatically resculpted by the exploding might of the machinery developed by American engineers, to

American Engineer (1956) seeks to exalt engineers and the technology they create in reshaping and improving modern life.

bustling cloverleaf highways, to cyclotrons discovering and yoking the fundamental elements, to, finally, the energetic mechanical ballet of automobile production and the shopping malls, motels, and drive-in theatres that American automobile culture made essential. With its authoritative voiceover commentary (by another brass-voiced male, though unlike Lowell Thomas this speaker remains anonymous) and panoramic, impossible-to-stage views, the film builds a persuasive vision of an America that has harnessed, multiplied, and stored the energy of the universe, then applied it to the production of the commodified modern world. The final image of the program is of Mount Rushmore, joining an icon of the American political system with its technological creations and suggesting their complex interrelationships.

As the visuals of the film impress viewers with a God's-eye perspective of the energetic nation, the rhetoric of the film explicitly connects the work of mid-century engineers with the can-do values of an America in love with its best self and all its works. Engineers, the narrator informs, "have the courage to challenge, to solve problems, to change the world." Engineers answer the call for exploration, and work to improve people's lives with honesty, curiosity, and imagination. Engineers, the narration implies, embody the national values in every respect.

When they are shown at all, which is not often, people are portrayed within the realistic context of their technical work: they are serious professionals, mostly but not entirely white males, who read gauges, gaze into microscopes, oversee labyrinths of pipes and banks of monitors and gauges, sit at their desks imagining the future, and otherwise help to create and manage the modern world. Periodically, the regular narration gives way to a second narrator, a man with a vaguely Germanic accent who talks about "enchineers" and functions as a kind of expert who legitimizes both the importance of the work engineers do and the symbolic passing of the slide rule from the Old World's dominance of engineering to an America moving forward with supreme power.

Above all, *American Engineer* celebrates the ideals of freedom and dominion over the earth. As *More Power to You* only suggested, *American Engineer* directly asserts the natural world is useless until activated by American engineering ingenuity. The narrator tells us that rivers were just randomly moving waters until engineers learned how to harness their power to move goods for the economic benefit of the many, to take just one example among a multitude of how the film constructs an identity for engineers as the benefactors of the modern world. One visual shows a close shot of roiling waters, then the camera pulls back to reveal the massive hydroelectric dam that gave such random motion purpose. Thanks to engineers, the natural world now can, as the narrator says, "delight us with mass production and make possible price reduction."

Coming early in the film, this passage reveals a shift in the nature of the reality that *American Engineer* constructs for its viewers as compared with the other films examined here. While *More Power to You* used many of the same documentary strategies as *American Engineer*, its rhetorical purposes focus on a chauvinistic, isolationist America boasting of its own industrial might. The rhetoric of *American Engineer*, in contrast, produced after the international adventures of World War II and Korea, addresses the important role of technology in improving the nation's *economy*; as the passage quoted above indicates, much is made in *American Engineer* of the causal connection between technology, mass production, and the economical delivery of goods.

Thus while the overt message of the film is the promotion of the importance of engineers and their works in the lives of Americans, *American Engineer* covertly implies that the key consequence of technology is now its facilitation of the production and consumption of goods. As the final movement of the film takes the viewer through the production of cars that we see motoring past drive-in bank windows and to shopping malls and drive-in movie theatres, the rhetoric and documentary-like visuals work together to celebrate not just the importance of technology but the nation's power to produce and consume — a constructed vision of a reality that remains recognizable and powerful to us today.

Conclusion

All of the films discussed here use the codes and conventions of the documentary to accomplish their work. To one degree or another, they use authoritative narrators as guides to the visuals and, as Roscoe and Hight suggest, shape the film's thematic structures. Even *A Case of Spring Fever*, without a formal voiceover, uses a surrogate narrator in the form of the newly enlightened Gilbert Willoughby. All four use authentic appearing, naturalistic settings and activities, represented through natural sound and lighting, even when, in *A Case of Spring Fever*, the scenes are clearly dramatized. While none used eyewitnesses, *American Engineer* offered an alternative narrator whose accent pegged him as an outsider and who functioned as an expert to legitimate the message of the film. Most of the films made use of visual intertextuality to authenticate subjects, whether with stock-appearing images or technically realistic animation.

As noted earlier, Roscoe and Hight suggest exposition as one mode of being for the documentary; films in this mode build "arguments about the social historical world."[16] The four films examined here are examples of the expositional mode in that all use the conventions of the documentary to build their arguments about the kind of world their viewers live in. As I have suggested, the films offer both overt and covert arguments. Overtly, they persuade viewers of the similarities of dogs and automobiles, establish the importance of springs, explain the steps in the process of producing oil, and valorize the importance of engineers in modern life.

Of their covert arguments, perhaps the primary one is the promotion and celebration of the role of technology in American life. All four films offer scenarios to prove that modern life is not only inextricably and positively linked with technology, but is in fact redeemed by technological advancements that make the useless useful. The films' application of the codes and conventions of documentaries gives the productions a legitimizing claim to this truth; moreover, the codes help to naturalize this particular social reality for their audiences, and serve what Lyotard called "the grand narratives" of modernity, including the emancipating power of reason and freedom and "the enrichment of all humanity through the progress of capitalist technosciences."[17] This last phrase might have come directly from *American Engineer*, so surely is it the motivating force behind that film's ideas, particularly its yoking of technology and access to cheap goods as the means for improving our lives.

A related covert argument imbricated in the films might be summarized with a line from *All in One*: "engineers did better with the automobile than nature did with the dog." The films validate the contention that modern, rational science is always an improvement over nature, whether by improving characteristics that are inherent in nature but insufficiently developed (as cars are faster and safer than dogs), by providing for the modest technological advancements that allow one comfortably to negotiate even the bumpiest country roads, or by conquering nature wholesale and turning it for human (that is, American) ends.

A third of the covert arguments of the films has to do with the nature of the social reality the films construct. This reality is predominantly male designed, controlled, and populated, and is overwhelmingly white, reflecting certainly the managerial class of the time for which the films were produced. The films also assume that technology is accessible and affordable to all who reside within its classless sphere of universal access to goods and services. There is, of course, no attempt made to problematize the role of technology in enforcing social inequities, as none are admitted into the reality the films create. *American Engineer* specifically makes the point that technology even contributes to the ideal of economic opportunity for all citizens as it briefly shows an African American male technician (the only person of color in all four films).

A final covert thematic argument that emerges from this examination of four early industrial films is the significant erasure of the human subject from the social realities portrayed. As technology improves modern life, these films covertly reduce people to ciphers within mechanical processes, fit to hold a test tube or wrap a chain around a rotating drill in an oil field, monitor a gauge, or occupy an infantilized space within their own lives, but not adequate for any starring roles in modern life, whether or not they are the ostensible focus of the film, as in *American Engineer*. The heroes of these four films are clearly the various technologies they depict. In the technosphere that they valorize, little room is left for meaningful human activity as defined in any other way than going fast and being safe, or consuming what its culture benevolently makes available.[18]

Ultimately the versions of social reality created by these four films as representative industrial films of the last century are coded, to use Gee's language from the chapter's epigraph, in highly mediated sign systems. Our postmodern understanding that all versions of reality must be seen as tentative and deeply interested no longer recognizes the arguments of these films as objective or unmediated reflections of reality. They become for us another kind of fiction.

This does not, of course, mean that we can dismiss them outright, which is a persistent danger in discussing these kinds of aging industrial films. From our contemporary perspective, it is tempting to give in to the tendency to mock their naïve, unintentionally comic representations; *A Case of Spring Fever* was once the object of postmodern ridicule on television's *Mystery Science Theatre 3000*. Yet simply to denigrate these films as flawed commercial artifacts from an earlier, less sophisticated time, occasions for congratulating ourselves on how far we have come in half a century, is pernicious. We should instead consider that our dependence on technology today is far more totalized and coercive than either the anonymous filmmakers at the Jam Handy Organization or the automotive technocrats who sponsored the films could ever have imagined seventy years ago. Along with our dependence on technology (including oil and automobiles, in particular) that those old films helped to establish and perpetuate, we are also faced with the persistence of the uncomplicated attitudes they passed down to us about how that technology was produced and consumed, and how valuable it is to our culture. Ours is an infinitely more complex world than Gilbert Willoughby faced even on the brink of World War II in *A Case of Spring Fever*, and our wisdom must be commensurate with that complexity. We must learn from artifacts like these aging films how, for example, the "minarets of science" metaphor from *More Power to You* is laden with cultural attitudes that went unquestioned in the discourse of the 1930s but that we cannot avoid when our petroleum-based society struggles with the geopolitical implications of those attitudes. Examining these four industrial films as species of faux documentaries therefore does more than simply give us the chance to poke mild fun at these obscure motion pictures. Rather, it helps to teach us about the genesis of our sense of a social reality based mainly on the virtues of technology and consumption, about how this has become so natural seeming, about its limitations—and about how we might begin to approach its reconstruction.

1. James Paul Gee, "Postmodernism and Literacies," *Critical Literacy: Politics, Praxis, and the Postmodern*, ed. Colin Lankshear and Peter L. McLaren (Albany: State University of New York Press, 1993): 280.

2. Jane Roscoe and Craig Hight, *Faking It: Mock-documentary and the Subversion of Factuality* (Manchester: Manchester University Press, 2001): 11.

3. "Rule Twelve: Special Rules for The Documentary Awards," Academy of Motion Picture Arts and Sciences, 4 April 2003, www.oscars.org/75academyawards/rules/rule12.html.

4. Erik Barnouw, *Documentary: A History of the Nonfiction Film* (New York: Oxford University Press, 1983): 213.

5. *Ibid*, p. 309.

6. Roscoe and Hight, p. 14-18.

7. *Ibid*, p. 17.

8. *Ibid*, p. 18.

9. Libby Estell, "More than 80 years ago Jamison Handy helped make sales what it is today," *Sales & Marketing Management* Oct. 1998: 112.

10. Barnouw, p. 219.

11. *All in One*, dir. unknown, Jam Handy Organization, 1938. Accessed through the Prelinger Archives section of the Internet Moving Images Archive www.archive.org/movies/prelinger. All references to this film, including quotations, come from the Prelinger Archives version.

12. *A Case of Spring Fever*, dir. unknown, Jam Handy Organization, 1940. Accessed through the Prelinger Archives section of the Internet Moving Images Archive www.archive.org/movies/prelinger. All references to this film, including quotations, come from the Prelinger Archives version.

13. *More Power to You*, dir. unknown, Jam Handy Organization, ca. 1930s. Accessed through the Prelinger Archives section of the Internet Moving Images Archive <http://www.archive.org/movies/prelinger>. All references to this film, including quotations, come from the Prelinger Archives version.

14. Ralph Stephenson and J.R. Debrix, *The Cinema as Art* (Baltimore: Penguin, 1965): 128.

15. *American Engineer*, dir. unknown, Jam Handy Organization, 1956. Accessed through the Prelinger Archives section of the Internet Moving Images Archive www.archive.org/movies/

prelinger. All references to this film, including quotations, come from the Prelinger Archives version.

16. Roscoe and Hight, p. 18.

17. Jean-Francois Lyotard, *The Postmodern Explained*, trans. Morgan Thomas (Minneapolis: University of Minnesota Press, 1992.

18. In this the facelessness of the content mirrors the facelessness of the creation of the films themselves. With the sole exception of Lowell Thomas as discussed above, these are corporate productions. No indivdual writers, directors, editors, or producers are credited, nor are any personal visions expressed. The sole credit on these films goes to the Jam Handy Organization, which reflects the corporate approach of Handy's clients (many of the company's films were created for Chevrolet and General Motors) and the worldviews promulgated by the films themselves.

6

"Documenting" Communist subversion: The Case of I Was a Communist for the F.B.I. *(1951)*

by Reynold Humphries

It came as quite a surprise to learn several years ago that *I Was a Communist for the FBI* had been nominated for the Oscar as the best documentary of 1951.[1] However, the closer one looks into the circumstances that led to the Cold War in general and the films of the Cold War in particular,[2] the more obvious it becomes that such a nomination was entirely logical. My purpose in choosing the Warner Brothers' production as the center around which this study will gravitate is to show how the politics of the 1930s and the witch-hunts that were both the cause and the effect of the prosecution of the Hollywood Ten in October 1947 converged in particular ways in the late 1940s and throughout the 1950s. One product of such a convergence can be seen in the way Warner Brothers chose to advertise *I Was a Communist for the FBI* upon its release in April 1951: by taking out a two-page advertisement in the issue of *Daily Variety* dated Wednesday, April 25, 1951.[3] Significantly, it is sandwiched between the pages reproducing the testimony of friendly witness Marc Lawrence before the House Committee on Un-American Activities (HUAC). The actual content of the ad is also significant: a compilation of reviews of the film in both the Hollywood and the national press, including editorials. Of particular relevance to us here are the following comments: "...it is not a dramatic fly-by-night, but was founded on real facts as established from the records of Congress, the F.B.I. and other official sources" (unsigned editorial in the Hearst-owned *Los Angeles Evening Herald Express*); "...there's no doubt of the facts disclosed in the story — a true story in every inch of the film" (W.R. Wilkerson, *The Hollywood Reporter*); "...a forceful and exciting true-to-life melodrama..." (*Daily Variety*).

Clearly, the aim of this ad conceived by Jack L. Warner himself is to assure readers of the factual basis of the story of the film, an aspect to which we shall have cause to return. However, other elements need to be highlighted, such as *Daily Variety*'s use of the word "melodrama" which sits uneasily with the notion of a documentary approach to a given subject but which perfectly sums up the slanted ways in which the film attempts to influence the spectator by adopting points of view that pass themselves off— with the help of newspaper articles such as these — as a purely factual recording of a pre-given reality. If we can view with grim amusement the interesting slip committed by journalist James Ratliff of *The Cincinnati Enquirier* who calls the production "An Authentic Communist Film from Hollywood," the lengthy editorial in the *Motion Picture Herald* by Martin Quigley is a far more revealing and disquieting document, in the light of the HUAC Hearings reproduced in detail by *Daily Variety* and *The Hollywood Reporter*. Quigley writes:

> The organized industry is this time avoiding the silly adventures upon which it embarked at the time of the earlier probe of Hollywood by the Un-American Activities Committee. This time it is sensibly recognizing the right and duty of the Congressional Committee to expose treason and is cooperating accordingly.

I take this as an attack on the Committee for the First Amendment launched by Philip Dunne, John Huston and William Wyler to combat HUAC in 1947 and a warning to all and sundry. Name names or suffer the penalty: the blacklist,[4] Perhaps the most revealing work in the above quote is "organized," which suggests cooperation at all levels to flush out the "termites" referred to by Jack L. Warner back in October 1947. Several of the papers quoted indulge in self-advertising by referring not only to the factual basis of the film but to the fact that it is "Timely as today's newspaper headlines" (*Daily Variety*). Thus those who produce movies and those who advertise them for the greater glory and profit of Hollywood reinforce one another and give credence to the notion that *I Was a Communist for the F.B.I.* is indeed unadorned fact. If we turn to the main character of the film, one Matthew Cvetic, we can start to grasp just what such organized cooperation entailed.

Matt Cvetic, National Hero

None of the reviews used by Warner Brothers in the ad even bothers to mention Cvetic. This, I would argue, shows that the character in the film, who existed in real life as an F.B.I. undercover agent working in Pittsburgh, functions as a signifier destined to produce a certain effect on the spectator rather than as a reminder of the real-life struggle against Communism in industrial unions that the film is supposedly representing. Numerous volumes concerning aspects of the F.B.I., McCarthy, the Cold War and witch-hunting, within and outside the film industry, devote space to Cvetic, but the most detailed single account is that of David Caute.[5] Cvetic had joined the CP in 1943 at the request of the F.B.I. and finally "emerged from his disguise in February 1950 and named about three hundred alleged Communists from western Pennsylvania...."[6] The local press immediately joined in the hue and cry by printing their names, addresses and employers, thus continuing a tradition dating from 1948 when the *Pittsburgh Press* published like information on one thousand citizens who

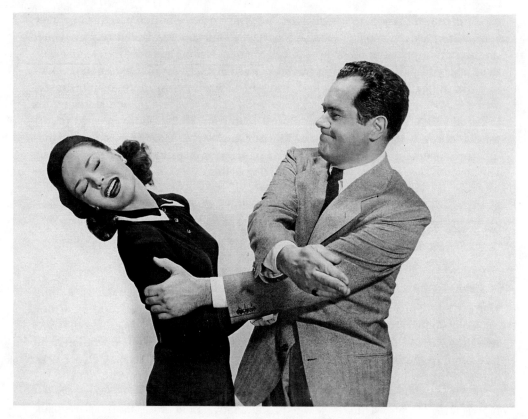

The fictional film overdetermines the portrayal of real-life figure Mathew Cvetic as played by actor Frank Lovejoy (shown here with Dorothy Hart) in *I Was a Communist for the F.B.I.* (1951).

had signed petitions in favour of Henry Wallace of the Progressive Party.[7] Workers were ostracized and their children attacked at school. "As this steel city began to boom with the Korean war orders, the fever rose: perhaps two hundred people had to leave town."[8] Given the links made in *I Was a Communist for the F.B.I.* between workers, unions and Communists, the following information is of interest: "In many cases, AFL and CIO unions demanded that persons named by Cvetic either deny the charges or resign, and some unions invited Cvetic to look over their membership lists and pick out the 'reds.'"[9]

Cvetic was part of that select group of professional informers who "made a living out of pretending to an encyclopedic knowledge of the Communist movement across the face of a vast land. On a nod from prosecutors, they sold hunches or guesses as inside knowledge, supporting their claims with bogus reports of conversations and encounters."[10] This, however, could prove an embarrassment to the informers' chief employer, the F.B.I., who risked having an informer's cover blown by another informer who had also infiltrated CP ranks. This produced moments of low comedy, such as when Cvetic denounced one Joseph Mazzei who could escape prosecution only by admitting that he, too, was working for the F.B.I. It transpired that neither man was of a high moral character or particularly reliable: certain of Cvetic's victims retaliated through the courts when it transpired that he "had been hospital-ized both for mental illness and for chronic alcoholism," although Cvetic blamed the latter on "constant harassments and smears by Communists."[11] Rather than try to decide whether this can be substantiated or is part and parcel of Cold War paranoia and Cvetic's patent megalomania, we might do better to pay heed to the informa-tion concerning Cvetic's life-long desire to be a spy since he was a boy and interpret him as a product of a fantasy that failed to distinguish between fact and fiction.[12] This suggestively evokes parallels with aspects of Hollywood's attitudes towards many of its own productions and with the very content of *I Was a Communist for the F.B.I.*, most notably its treatment of Cvetic and the various Communists on show. When one remembers the hardship Cvetic caused, aided and abetted by Hoover and HUAC, there is something distinctly distasteful about the Mayor of Pittsburgh declaring April 19, the day the film opened there, as "Matt Cvetic Day" and the film being turned into a radio show of the same name starring Dana Andrews. It is as if everyone had ended up by believing the big lie. We shall return to this in the final section.

One point must be clarified here. Whatever one's personal opinion of Hoover, Nixon, McCarthy and journalists such as Hedda Hopper and Westbrook Pegler, they were not necessarily wrong in their denunciations of Communism. Their lie con-sisted in passing off their information and analyses as objective facts, whereas they were in fact deceiving the public even when telling the truth. In other words, their concern — and this also applies to Jack L. Warner — was not with protecting Amer-ica from the Soviet Union but with protecting certain vested interests — those of big business — against the working class and with eliminating from all aspects of public life those left-wingers, particularly intellectuals, who had thrown in their lot, nation-ally and internationally, with the working-class struggle. Many such people were, of course, Communists and the relevance of that fact lies in their having been better organized than other radical groups. Just as a group working behind the scenes was evil when it was attempting to organize workers or blacks, so it was noble when made up of studio bosses and unionists like Roy Brewer who collaborated with them.[13] Just as the closed shop had to be fought in Los Angeles in order to preserve free enter-prise from Communist-inspired unions, so it had to be defended when the formula came to be synonymous with vested business interests, such as those defended by the *Los Angeles Times*.[14] Some idea of what was at stake for workers on the one hand and (studio) bosses on the other can be gleaned from the case of CP leader Steve Nel-son.

The Political and Historical Background

It is generally taken for granted that the Communist trade unionist Brandon rep-resented in *I Was a Communist for the F.B.I.* is Steve Nelson, just as the evil CP boss who organizes murder and strikes in *The Woman on Pier 13* (1949) is meant to be San Francisco unionist Harry Bridges. That the fictional characters were based on two men regularly represented as public enemies by the Right is certainly true, although I shall argue later that the situation is more complex in the later film. More to the

point surely is that it is what they stood for socially and politically that is under
attack; after all, it is much easier to attack a political notion to which one is opposed
by smearing a controversial figure who defends it than to elaborate some abstract
argument, hardly commercial Hollywood's strong point. As I shall show, *I Was a
Communist for the F.B.I.* functions systematically as a series of inversions of the real
historical situation the better to pass off the lie as a factual representation of the Communist conspiracy. Doing so was child's play, given the domestic climate and Hollywood's mastery of its own codes of narration and representation.

Steve Nelson is of interest to us here in that Cvetic testified against him; his trial
for sedition was under way in Pittsburgh at the same time as the release of *I Was a
Communist for the F.B.I.* and the transformation of Cvetic into a national hero. His
symbolic status has been summed up thus:

> ...in his desire for radical social and economic change as well as his will-
> ingness to throw himself into a movement that promised such a change,
> he was not unlike the thousands of men and women who came within the
> orbit of American Communism during the first half of the twentieth cen-
> tury....[15]

Of interest, too, are his Croatian origins, for we find here a fear of the other that
played such a crucial role in the great Red Scare in the years immediately following
World War I, a fear that finds an intriguing imaginary representation in *I Was a
Communist for the F.B.I.* in the form of the film's other real-life character, Communist Gerhard Eisler. Nelson has rendered a homage to the workers' schools set up and
run by the CP as places where workers, both American and foreign-born, were "drawn
together in a group to talk and listen, to be induced to read and study. Where else
could we get that opportunity?"[16] This, of course, was the scandal that had to be
denounced: workers organizing to oppose their exploitation. In films of the anti–Red
cycle this usually takes the form of secret meetings where the comrades have indi-
gestible texts thrust down their throats (a view of politics which functions better
when applied to Hollywood's own attempts over the decades to impose its cultural
hegemony via economic domination). Such a scene occurs in *The Iron Curtain* where
the thirst for knowledge on the part of workers is transformed into a psychological
block on the part of maladjusted intellectuals. Similarly, in *The Woman on Pier 13*,
it is the smooth egghead (obviously a cross between Dalton Trumbo and John Howard
Lawson) who attempts to get the naïve worker to think politically instead of passively
obeying his bosses at the work place.

We shall have cause to return to Nelson again, in a highly overdetermined
fictional form, when analysing *I Was a Communist for the F.B.I.* where we also
encounter Gerhard Eisler about whom a few remarks need to be made here. Eisler's
position in the States was a paradoxical one: he was as anxious to leave the country
as the authorities were to deport him, yet they refused to let him go. Why? Even if
the film had never been made, there were still plenty of reasons for him to have
become the ideal bogeyman. For a start, he had spent five years in the States as representative of the Comintern during the 1930s, although he never admitted publicly
to this, using various aliases, a fact systematically exploited when his case was mentioned

in the press: "his multiple identities made the alleged Soviet agent seem even more devious and alien."[17] Such secretive behavior lent itself perfectly to the post-war climate; the long-standing underground activities of the American CP could thus be represented as proof that they were under the control of Kremlin representative Eisler, although he no longer enjoyed that status after World War II.[18] The crowning irony lay in the fact that the man who had been in Spain at the time of the Civil War and had spent two years in a Vichy prison was detained on Ellis Island by the immigration authorities in 1941 and refused permission to continue on to Mexico because he was German and therefore an enemy alien! The post-war period, of course, still finds him a German but now it is his past Communist ties that are evoked. Schrecker points out that Eisler was in fact a refugee who risked death if sent back to Europe, a point the film ignores, preferring to use codes designating him as a Nazi.[19] Eisler himself wanted to leave the States for East Germany where he was in fact living by the time *I Was a Communist for the F.B.I.* opened in 1951. The decision to prosecute a man whom the authorities wanted to deport and who himself sought to leave the United States can therefore be seen as a piece of showmanship: use Eisler's past to expose the Communist threat, both alien and domestic. Whatever one might think of Eisler's past activities as one of Stalin's hatchet men, he was clearly yet another pawn in the Cold War power game, a useful weapon to wield against his domestic former comrades in the period 1946–9, with the press carrying out its propaganda role as it was to do for Warner Brothers in April 1951.

Where do we go from here? It would not be superfluous to attempt to sum up the situation or, at least, indicate what conclusions can be drawn from what we have seen. One theme stands apart from all others: the question of trade-union activity. It lies behind the prosecution of Nelson, the use of Cvetic as informant and the hate-filled attempt within Hollywood itself to smear, persecute and drive from their places of work anyone who refused to toe the new line, especially if they had had the tendency to toe the Party line in the past. However, I do not believe that this commitment to the creation of trade unions can be isolated from a whole set of factors to which we must turn now. I shall try to show how the struggle for workers' rights generally was intimately tied up, both for the Hollywood Left (Communist or not) and for the Right, with such related matters as the fight against racism and fascism, terms which also demand some explanation. Prior to this, however, it is necessary to turn to other films of the anti–Red cycle where both form and content are of primary importance to our argument here.

Aspects of the "Anti-Red" Cycle

Critics have drawn attention to the supposedly "documentary" nature of certain of these films. *The Iron Curtain* (1948) is based on real events, the defection to America of a Soviet spy working in his country's Embassy in Canada. *Walk East on Beacon* (1952) uses a case history of Soviet spying solved by the F.B.I. and turned into a story written for the *Reader's Digest* by J. Edgar Hoover himself. *Big Jim McLain* (1952) is about the work undertaken by HUAC investigators to weed out Communist activities in Hawaii and includes scenes with real-life members of the Committee.[20] The first two films also have recourse to an off-screen narrator and *Walk East on Beacon* was produced by "March of Time" documentary producer Louis de Rochemont, with the collaboration of the F.B.I. *The Red Menace* (1949) also has an off-screen narrator. One thinks of Welles' parody of de Rochemont in the "mockumentary" footage shot for *Citizen Kane*, a film which resembles a documentary in its content but presents itself very much as a work of fiction — and, especially, a piece of cinema — in its *mise en scène*. There can be no doubt, in the case of films in the anti–Red cycle, that the narrative device of the off-screen narrator and the presence of real-life persons or Committees, overdetermined by references to the press (whose role we have already documented in this essay), are intended to induce in the spectator the impression of watching daily reality at work. Moreover, the use of contemporary events and of real locations partakes of the tradition launched by *The House on 92nd Street* (1945), *Call Northside 777* (1947) and *The Street with No Name* (1948).[21] This last film also has the particularity of representing the work of an undercover F.B.I agent whose task is to expose and dismantle a gang and contains scenes (recounted, yet again, by an off-screen narrator) of real F.B.I. staff going patiently about their tasks, such as identifying guns and their owners via the bullets used.[22]

Certain films of the anti–Red cycle exploit therefore two tendencies within contemporary Hollywood cinema: the off-screen narrator so familiar to us from *films noirs* of the 1940s (*Double Indemnity, Laura, The Killers, Out of the Past, The Lady from Shanghai*) and the recourse to location shooting, as in the examples just cited. However, it is patent that there is a world of difference between said off-screen narrators who are also characters within the film's fictional world and invisible narrators who are seemingly just voices informing spectators step by step of how the F.B.I. goes about collecting evidence, tailing suspects, drawing conclusions, then netting the villains in one swoop. *Walk East on Beason* is such a boring experience, totally devoid of any suspense and excitement, that one is tempted to ask if this is simply the fault of director Alfred Werker or whether the film's makers were anxious to communicate to the spectators of the time the crippling boredom that comes from endless surveillance and monotonous tasks repeated *ad nauseam*. In which case spectators could react either by going to sleep or noting with pride how devoted the F.B.I. agent had to be in the war against Communism to endure such working conditions. Boredom was just one of the penalties spectators had to pay if lured from their homes to watch such dispiriting fare.

It is therefore interesting to note that *The Naked City*, the one film directed by Jules Dassin that has recourse to both an off-screen narrator (producer Mark Hellinger) and location shooting (the streets of New York) is also by far the least impressive of his works of the post-war period, and comes to life only when Dassin resorts to action and can dispense with Hellinger's laborious and often silly commentary.[23] It is also interesting to take the particular case of *The Iron Curtain*, the first film in the cycle and a relatively sober work, which does not prevent it from exploiting, less the locations and the predicament of a Soviet who finds himself at odds (according to the film) with his government and immediate superiors, than a panoply of codes of representation that give the lie to the "this is how it happened" approach adopted in the credits and the use of the off-screen narrator. The film was shot in Canada, it is "natural" that the Soviet couple should "betray" their homeland for the freedom and pleasures of the West and all the documents and messages used in the film are as presented at the trial in 1946 of the Canadians who were part of the pro–Soviet spy ring.[24] A few examples of these codes. When the Dana Andrews character visits the cipher center at the Embassy where he is to work, he passes through an iron door covered by velvet curtains, shorthand for standard devious Soviet methods.[25] At one point a seemingly cold secretary attempts to seduce Andrews in her apartment to test his devotion to duty, which both makes of her a dishonest temptress and resorts to the *film noir* character of the *femme fatale*. Towards the end of the film, after Andrews has taken the decision to defect, the Embassy staff come to his apartment to capture him and there is a shot of their feet behind the door in the lit corridor, which is presumably a reference to the killing of the Swede in *The Killers* (1946). When Andrews and his wife are visiting the city, she is deeply affected by the presence of a church (shot from a low-angle to accentuate the role of religion in their future "conversion") and the singing of hymns.[26] This is a "natural" sign of how unhappy they are with the heathen Soviet Union and takes up Leo McCarey's remark at the time of the prosecution of the Hollywood Ten the previous year that the Soviets took exception to the presence of God in his film *The Bells of Saint Mary's*. An unintentionally hilarious moment comes when another code — an extra-textual, institutional one this time — is called into play. Andrews is called out in the middle of the night and Tierney says to him: "I'll keep the bed warm for you." As they are sleeping in separate beds— the Hays Code and Joseph Breen are at work again!— one can only feel sympathy for the poor woman, having to spend the night going from one bed to the other to keep her promise to her husband.

The Iron Curtain is a typical piece of Hollywood fiction where the usual codes are re-fashioned and re-furbished to carry the necessary anti–Communist message. However, as I have stated, it is relatively sober, never quite descending to the depths of cynicism and abjection plumbed by *The Woman on Pier 13* and, especially, *The Red Menace*, *Big Jim McLain* and *I Was a Communist for the F.B.I.* John Wayne co-produced as well as starred in *Big Jim McLain* and the film is very much a work of hagiography, with totally irrelevant shots of Wayne boating in Hawaii and obviously enjoying himself on his day off from tracking down Reds.[27] This jars somewhat with his complaint early in the film, to the effect that HUAC investigators have to operate out of a tiny office. This is another example of the big lie. Sums voted for HUAC increased dramatically with the evolution of the Cold War: the Committee asked for $200,000 in 1949, twice the sum granted in 1948 and obtained satisfaction; in 1953 the record sum of $300,000 was voted. Whereas many liberals had earlier protested against the increasing power and influence of the Committee, by 1952 no liberal even asked for a roll call and the appropriations were passed anonymously.[28] Bipartisanship and consensual politics were the order of the day and we can perhaps see this at work in the film's opening where a voiceover evokes the spirit of Daniel Webster and assures him — and us— that the Union, "one and indivisible," is strong. If we turn to the career of Webster, information of another, more pertinent kind, is available:

The Iron Curtain (1948) with Dana Andrews (on bed) and Gene Tierney (reflected in mirror) is a typical piece of Hollywood fiction where the usual codes are refashioned and refurbished to carry the necessary anti–Communist message.

> The Fugitive Slave Act passed in 1850 was a concession to the southern states in return for the admission of the Mexican war territories [California, especially] into the Union as nonslave states. The Act made it easy for slaveowners to recapture ex-slaves or simply to pick up blacks they claimed had run away. Northern blacks organized resistance to the Fugitive Slave Act, denouncing President Fillmore, who signed it, and Senator Daniel Webster, who supported it.[29]

We encounter here a subject to which we shall return: the pressure exerted by Dixiecrats at the expense of blacks. First, however, we shall turn to the role played by HUAC within the film's fictional narrative and the representation and function of unions.

The opening of *Big Jim McLain* treats us to a session where HUAC members grill various witnesses about their Communist ties, past and present. Among the members are Velde, Walter and Wood, all of whom at one point chaired the Committee.[30] To the question asked each witness replies by taking the Fifth Amendment. An irate Wayne—who functions at this juncture as the voiceover narrator while appearing on the screen with the members of the Committee: the real-life status of the latter thus reinforces the status of the Wayne character and gives a "documentary" edge to a work of fiction — announces that they all walked away free. In one case, Wayne informs the spectator that the person excused will return to "a well-paid job as a full University Professor of Economics to contaminate more kids."[31] From research available, this was by no means certain. For McCarthy, anyone who invoked the Fifth could safely be considered a Communist, an attitude that he was not alone in expressing:

> ...as hysteria increased in the early 1950s faculty firings soon became frequent not only for CP membership but also for exercising the constitutional right of taking the fifth amendment before legislative committees when asked about political activities.[32]

A decision concerning the University of California that must have brought tears of joy to Wayne's eyes was that taken by the Regents in February 1950 to the effect "that those who had not signed the non–Communist loyalty oath by the last day of April would automatically sever their connection with UC as of June 1950."[33] In October 1952 the California Supreme Court declared the Regents' oath to be unconstitutional. The film's makers could not have been unaware of the number of dismissals taking place within the university system, both public and private, although private institutions "were more likely to retain Fifth Amendment witnesses on their faculties than public ones."[34] Wayne and his scriptwriters are not only indulging in a good, old-fashioned piece of intellectual baiting but using the Professor as a substitute for those Hollywood intellectuals who had already been pilloried in *The Woman on Pier 13*. Attention should therefore be drawn to the role of class in such dismissals, at least outside the film industry where the blacklist was the immediate fate of those who refused to name names and took the Fifth: "The Post Office, with its unskilled workforce and large numbers of minority-group employees, had the highest percentage of discharges. The more prestigious State Department had the lowest."[35]

Warner Brothers also produced *Big Jim McLain*, so Jack L. Warner goes down in history with the dubious distinction of having acted as public-relations officer for the F.B.I. and HUAC. In her massive study of McCarthyism, Ellen Schrecker refers to:

> ...the interconnections between superficially unrelated elements of the anticommunist crusade. When one finds references to exactly the same set of labor troubles in Supreme Court decisions, FBI reports, HUAC hearings and the memoirs and correspondence of presidential aides, important patterns become clear.[36]

Commentators have long been pointing out how information culled by Hoover's agents found its way to HUAC, not to mention the presence of former FBI investigators either as members of the Committee or as special investigators for it. In this way, films such as *I Was a Communist for the F.B.I.* and *Big Jim McLain* not only functioned to denounce Reds but also to mask the difference between fact and fiction by presenting fiction as fact. Thus, just as Cvetic was a real person and his activities as an undercover FBI agent were claimed to have taken place as shown in the movie, so McLain is played by a real-life anticommunist crusader whose presence on the Board of the Motion Picture Alliance for the Preservation of American Ideals turns McLain into someone as real as—or as phoney as—Cvetic himself. Similarly, producing a paean of praise to the FBI and dedicating another film to HUAC comes down to the same thing. A few comments on both organizations are therefore in order here.

The Anti-Communist Crusaders

If the regular and substantial increases in both the FBI's budget and the number of agents working for it is eloquent testimony to Hoover's power (of persuasion) and the general belief in the need to collect data on "subversives,"[37] more to the point is the question of bias. For Hoover, anyone advocating Marxism-Leninism "might just as well be working as an agent of a foreign power." Indeed, it was customary for FBI files to contain:

> reports about a radical's reading habits, his membership in unions and societies.... The files also contained a mire of gossip and hearsay—for example a statement by a landlady that a federal employee had kept books about Russia next to his easy chair, and a statement by his doctor that he believed in socialized medecine.[38]

Given that the prevailing attitude since the Red scare of the period immediately following World War I had been that CP members were dedicated to the violent overthrow of the American government and the country's political and economic system, the following remark takes on particular relevance:

> The concern over communism did not mean that the FBI sought to prove Soviet direction and control over the US Communist party and its affiliates. Rather, the FBI attempted to determine communist influence in a host of dissident political movements. "Communist influence" or "Communist infiltration" provided the rationale for the FBI's surveillance efforts, most notably in four areas: the federal bureaucracy, trade unions, college campuses, and the civil rights movement.[39]

Clearly, "influence" is far more vague and diffuse a term than "control." Thus a blanket condemnation of certain views, whether or not they were accompanied by acts of any kind, becomes all the easier to make and to impress on the public. It also makes it easier to understand why an intellectual belonging to the CP and interested not only in forming unions within Hollywood but also in organizing labor in general and black labor in the South in particular was hardly likely to slip through the net in the post-war years! I mention these activites as they figure prominently, but in an inverted form, in *I Was a Communist for the F.B.I.* Moreover, the question of strikes had become the main obsession of Jack Warner in the immediate post-war period.

The studio strikes of 1945–6, which particularly affected Warner Brothers, have been exhaustively researched by Gerald Horne.[40] Suffice it to say here that they pitted unions against unions, and actors against unionists in a climate of violence that drove liberal Democrat Ronald Reagan further and further to the Right and finally into the arms of the Republican Party.[41] For those on the Left, the strikes were both the logical continuation of the attempts during the 1930s to establish independent trade unions and the inevitable outcome of the close links between gangsters and those conservative elements in the labor movement favorable to the studio bosses, such as Roy Brewer. For many liberals, as well as those on the Right, the strikes showed beyond a reasonable doubt that Communists were determined to impose their point of view. The fact that the Motion Picture Alliance was launched in the summer of 1944, prior to the end of the war, indicates clearly that those who had been part of the anti–Communist crusade prior to 1939 now understood that their time had come. However, we need to look further still if we are to uncover another piece of the puzzle that will help give shape to the elements discussed up till now.

At one point in *I Was a Communist for the F.B.I.* the CP boss uses the word "niggers," to which Cvetic replies: "don't you mean 'negroes'"? Towards the end of *Big Jim McLain* one of the Hawaian Communists says "that choppin' cotton's for white trash and niggers."[42] This assimilation of Communists to racists is undoubtedly the most abject aspect of both films. Let us start by quoting Martin Dies, a Democrat from Texas and the first Chairman of HUAC, deploring in 1942 "the fact that throughout the South today subversive elements are attempting to convince the Negro that he should be placed on social equality with white people, that now is the time for him to assert his rights."[43] What is fascinating about this remark—let us not forget that the United States were now at war with Nazi Germany!—is that it hides its racism behind a question of class—"social equality"—that is in reality simply the disavowal of the fact that what Dies and his like despised and feared the most was the convergence within the person of the Negro of both class and racial equality ("assert his rights"). The "elements" that Dies is denouncing included, of course, such Hollwood Communists as future blacklist victim John Howard Lawson:

> Lawson considered racism a "dangerous cancer" that killed creativity. He dedicated himself to ending white Anglo-Saxon Protestant dominance. Twice jailed for efforts on behalf of Southern blacks during the 1930s, he found discrimination a catalyst for activism.[44]

More extreme than Dies was John Rankin, a Democrat from Mississippi and member of HUAC when it investigated the Hollywood Ten. An anti–Semite who gave in Congress the real Jewish names of such stars as Danny Kaye and Edward G. Robinson, it is Rankin who will enable us to see that the representation of the CP boss in the film is less an attack on Steve Nelson because he was a Communist than an unconscious representation of the CP's leading role over the years in fighting racism. My reasons for saying this relate to an incident involving CP leader Eugene Dennis,

> who first demanded to be heard and then, when HUAC subpoenaed him to suit itself, refused to appear on the grounds that Rankin's presence violated the Fourteenth Amendment, which stipulates that a state's representation

in Congress shall be lowered in proportion to its abridgement of the right
to vote.[45]

This, of course, was a reference on Dennis's part to Rankin's notorious white
supremacist sympathies and concomitant voting record on Negro rights. The fact that
Rankin helped condemn Lawson in 1947 reveals the blatant racist bias of HUAC and,
more tellingly, of Hollywood itself. Putting the word "niggers" in the mouth of the
CP trade unionist betrays less the racist sympathies of those who made the film than
their understanding of the racist character of the anti–Communist forces from the
1930s on.

   The Communists in *I Was a Communist for the F.B.I.* want to blame violence on
the Jews so as to set Jew and Catholic against each other, in much the same way as
they are anxious to stir up tension and unrest within the black community. For Dixiecrats blacks were happy with their lot until Communists from the North came and
stirred up trouble. Once again, the real historical role of Rankin can be perceived
here, displaced onto Communists in an inverted form: people like Lawson fought
for Negro and labor rights, whereas people like Rankin used any and every form of
repression and violence to maintain the racial status quo. The irony of this for our
study lies in the fact that the film's attempt to blame Communists for race riots
reflected faithfully the opinion of the FBI on the issue: "The FBI had trouble imagining racial change as anything but troublesome and interpreted ordinary decency
as extraordinarily radical."[46] This is nicely put and shows that, on this particular
issue, *I Was a Communist for the F.B.I.* adhered closely to the documentary tradition
in the way it reflected FBI thinking! We can safely assume that such was not the conscious intention of the film's makers, but the truth has strange ways of returning like
the repressed to plague those who do not believe in it. Thus the film suggests the CP
exploited American democracy by hiring a public hall to spread racial hatred. In 1948
the Progressive Party of Henry Wallace (supposedly controlled by the CP) found it
difficult to hire halls and the Vice-Presidential candidate Senator Glen Taylor was
prevented from speaking in Birmingham, Alabama because of a local law banning
unsegregated meetings.[47] So, quite unwittingly, *I Was a Communist for the F.B.I.* portrays the CP as being anti-segregationist, which is more than could be said for certain of the party's opponents.

   The race question is also raised with the last shot of the film: a close-up of a
bust of Abraham Lincoln, complete with the "Battle Hymn of the Republic." Even
Big Jim McLain's use of Daniel Webster pales in comparison, but it is perhaps more
germane to the question of blacklisting to insist, not on the little matter of slavery
(Rankin was also notorious for his blocking of all attempts to introduce anti-lynch
laws in Congress and for his refusal to condemn the Ku Klux Klan), but on the existence of the Abraham Lincoln Brigade, bringing together many of those Americans
who fought — and died — in Spain fighting fascism on the Loyalist side. The Left's
commitment to anti-fascism and the struggle against Franco was perhaps the single
most important element in its repression after the war: a person's presence in Spain
was considered tantamount to their being a Communist. It is worthwhile remembering that Nelson fought in Spain and that this was used against him, as if the fact

of being openly Communist was not enough, that more was needed. This in turn ties in with the theory that the anti–Communist crusade was simply put aside for the duration of the war, to be brought out of mothballs when the occasion demanded it. Films such as *I Was a Communist for the F.B.I.* are very much part of this way of thinking. Let us not forget the terms in which Roy Brewer denounced *The Best Years of Our Lives* as introducing Communist propaganda. He cites the scene where a customer in the bar where Dana Andrews works deplores the fact that Andrews' friend lost his hands in the war and claims that America "fought the wrong people." For Brewer, the scene "created the image of the American "firster" who later became the basis of the Communist attack to discredit anyone who tried to question Russia's place in the world scene."[48] This is a highly dubious mixture of lies and half-truths. For a start, those who adopted the "America first" attitude before the outbreak of World War II were isolationists opposed to the idea of America going to war over Europe and were not necessarily pro-fascist. The character in the film is plainly pro-fascist as he believes America "fought the wrong people," which surely indicates America should have joined forces with Hitler against the Soviet Union. By denouncing this character, *The Best Years of Our Lives* was defending the war effort and America's alliance with the Soviets. By denouncing the scene as a Communist ploy in terms which distort both the film and the recent historical past, Brewer reveals the basic dishonesty of the Motion Picture Alliance and his own drive to create a unique house union that would collaborate with the studio bosses.[49]

Narration and Representation in
I Was a Communist for the F.B.I.

On the most simple level the film is a lie. It presents Gerhard Eisler as being able to move around freely and as visiting Pittsburgh in 1950, which we know to be doubly false. The most fundamental parameters of the documentary are therefore flouted for propaganda reasons. The fact that the film does not even pretend to any form of objectivity is sufficient to damn it as pure manipulation. This is blatant — at least for us today, but certainly not for a public long conditioned by coding and biased press reports to take for granted the kind of representations on show — in the sequence where local CP leader Brandon holds a meeting aimed at the Negro population with the intention of creating unrest. In a documentary, the discussion would be filmed without a voiceover commentary — here thoughtfully provided by Cvetic — and various points of view would be aired. Here only one black actually speaks up, significantly to denounce Brandon for exaggerating, but he is shouted down. As he is clearly intended to represent "common sense," the film at one and the same time shows how easily Negroes can be fooled and prevents the spectator from adopting any point of view other than the hero's. It is not a question of claiming that absolute objectivity is possible, for a point of view will always be present — but not necessarily imposed — via the placing of the camera, the choice of interviewee, etc. However, surely the greatest objectivity is attained precisely where a point of view is made plain from the outset, such as in *Bowling for Columbine* where nobody would say that Michael Moore does not give full rein to his own views, while at the same time giving vigilantes the possibility of explaining their concerns.

What makes *I Was a Communist for the F.B.I.* so insidious is the way the film refers to real-life events and exploits opposition to Communists, overdetermined by unconscious racial prejudice, to invert the real situation. Thus the film evokes, in the context of the meeting for Negroes organized by Brandon, the riots that took place in Detroit and Harlem in 1943, stating they had been staged by the CP to encourage blacks to attack whites. The former were unaware, as Cvetic informs the film's audiences, that "their death warrants were signed in Moscow." If we turn to a comment on the notorious "zoot suit" riots which took place in Los Angeles that same year, a somewhat different picture emerges:

> To anyone who is young enough to think that American race riots involve gangs of black marauders attacking frightened whites, let it be recalled that in the race riots of the 1940s [Harlem and Saint Louis suffered major outbreaks too], blacks fled for their lives from pursuing gangs of whites. In Los Angeles, though, where there were still very few blacks, just beginning to immigrate to work in the arms factories and to occupy the abandoned tenements of Little Tokyo, the victims were the Mexicans, and the attackers were the United States armed forces.[50]

Referring to the documented fact that, during the period when the States were at war, Communists and Communist-controlled unions opposed strikes on the ground that to withdraw one's labor was not patriotic, George Lipsitz has written:

> Communist union leaders had favored labor-management cooperation and had been prominent advocates of more power for the labor federations and their officers. Unfortunately for them, the final consolidation of that power came only with the stimulus of anticommunism. Far from being the saboteurs, traitors, and fomentors of disruption that their enemies feared, Communists in labor unions were the unwitting and uncomprehending architects of the system that ultimately destroyed them.[51]

We can therefore draw a parallel between fictional Brandon and real-life Harry Bridges, long accused by the Right of being a Communist, a fact he always denied. The leader of the great San Francisco longshoremen's strike of 1935 was opposed to strikes during the war, so it could be argued that he was indeed a Communist![52] It is important to note, however, that *I Was a Communist for the F.B.I.* carefully avoids any mention of the war, too close for comfort and likely to trigger audience reactions diametrically opposed to those sought for by the red baiters who conceived the film: sympathy for the CP because of its patriotism and the Soviet Union because of its sacrifices.

The big lie in *I Was a Communist for the F.B.I.* consists in making the audience believe that people are free to do and say what they like in America and that Communists, both domestic and alien, take advantage of this. Numerous specialists have long pointed out that anti–Communist repression led party members to adopt the tactic of aliases and secret meetings which were self-defeating inasmuch as the F.B.I.

knew their identities.[53] This remark can also be extended to teachers with a party card. It is interesting to note that *I Was a Communist for the F.B.I.* openly states that the F.B.I. has a list of all Communist teachers, which surely indicates that the Red menace is under control. However, the film feels the urge to show how democratic the US is and assures us that such elements are allowed to keep their jobs. We see here an aspect of the propaganda of the "Red cycle" I have already referred to when discussing *Big Jim McLain*. The situation of radical school teachers or of those with a known CP past was even less enviable than that of their university colleagues:

> ...the burning issue of 1949 in New York educational circles was the Fein-berg Law, which went into effect on July 1. Henceforward a special offical in each school district would submit an annual report on the political health of each teacher. Membership in subversive organizations would count as *prima facie* evidence of disqualification, while past membership would be taken as presumptive evidence of present membership unless proved otherwise. The burden of proving his innocence would reside with the teacher.[54]

Caute adds the following revealing remark: "The Feinberg Law can be regarded as the joint achievement of the Church and the Republican Party."[55] This is of the greatest consequence, given that the author of the law was Jewish. It is common to read that red-baiters were anti–Semitic, which we have seen to be perfectly true. However, certain red-baiters were also Jewish, an argument the apologists of the anti–Communist crusade used to dismiss the charge. If we shift the argument from race to embrace class and economics, however, the situation becomes limpid. A right-wing Jew like Louis B. Mayer will side with even the most anti–Semitic red-baiter because they have one thing in common: their hatred of unions and workers' rights that threaten their vested interests.

I shall return to this crucial notion in the final section, for there are still aspects of *I Was a Communist for the F.B.I.* as phoney documentary that need to be addressed. We can take as real the observation made by various critics concerning the ways Reds in such films were represented as gangsters; however, readers may care to refer to the book by Gerald Horne referred to above to learn who the real gangsters inside Hollywood and out were and whose interests they defended by all means necessary. Our concern here is less with themes than *mise en scène* itself. Like that very different movie *The Naked City*, the film comes to life only when director Gordon Douglas has the opportunity to handle a chase sequence where all the know-how of the Hollywood professional is brought to bear to create an atmosphere of excitement and suspense that is very much part and parcel of the tradition of *film noir* to which *I Was a Communist for the F.B.I.* most definitely belongs.[56] The sequence takes place in a train tunnel and recalls the scenes in the sewers of Los Angeles in *He Walked by Night* (1948). This latter film is based on a story written by Crane Wilbur who co-authored the script, a fact that is of pertinence here: Wilbur also wrote *I Was a Communist for the F.B.I.* Like *Street with No Name*, *He Walked by Night* tends to glorify the police and the F.B.I. and to be part of a trend whose ideological implications were not immediately apparent: a justification of generalized surveillance in the name of security, which shifts from the local to the national via the introduction of the theme of Communism.[57] Indeed, the very title of the film hints at the secretive (= subversive) life of the main character who, literally, "goes underground."[58]

Thus the quasi-documentary thrust of certain Hollywood *films noirs* from 1945 on may stem from a greater interest in "realism" and "local colour" but suggests rather an increasingly repressive mode of social organization: be glad that the F.B.I. is there to protect you. Shots of the Bureau's Headquarters and sequences shot on location in *Street with No Name* suggest the need for a presence that is profoundly ideological and serves certain political interests. The opening of *I Was a Communist for the F.B.I.*, however, is closer to another tradition, the formal one of *film noir*. In the far distance a shadowy figure emerges from a lighted tunnel and advances slowly towards the camera as the film's title, word by word, flashes up on the screen. Does this juxtaposition of light and dark represent the shadowy life of agent Cvetic or the two-faced Communists he is fighting? Might we not see in this opening a reference to the credit sequence of *Double Indemnity* where the silhouette of a man on crutches advances towards the camera? Or the opening of *The Killers* where Siodmak resorts to a highly artificial — and superbly effective — use of shadow from which the killers suddenly emerge to "pose" for the spectators in order to communicate the meaning: "these are the killers"? Other instances could be cited and I offer these examples, not to claim that *I Was a Communist for the F.B.I.* is self-consciously quoting a particular movie, but to suggest that the film's entire logic of narration and, especially, representation is difficult to apprehend outside the tradition of *film noir*. Neither the documentary nor the much-vaunted "documentary style" have anything to do with this.

Finally, one scene merits particular attention because of its effectiveness and the complexity of the relationship between it, everyday life, American mythology and actual Hollywood movies. I am thinking of the moment where Cvetic gives a baseball lesson to the young son of his neighbour who, of course, interrupts this activity because he refuses to have a Commie interfering with the boy. On the simplest level this works as proof of Cvetic's sincerity and integrity: after all, only an all–American could possibly be interested in baseball; and the boy's feelings for him show just how candid the man really is! However, something much less obvious — and also more devious — is at work here and it is Stephen Vaughn who provides the clue. He refers to the two films Reagan made in 1940 that helped make him a star: his portrayal of General Custer in *Santa Fe Trail*; and the homage to football player George Gipp, *Knute Rockne — All American*.[59] The chapter that discusses Reagan's career at this point is significantly entitled "Lessons from the Past" and these lessons were certainly learned well by Warner Brothers. The fact that there is a displacement from football to baseball is perfectly in keeping with classic Freudian theory and must not hide the real significance of the information. Just as Reagan "discovered" the truth about Communists by working within Hollywood unions, so Cvetic discovered the truth about them by working within Pittsburgh unions. The fact that Reagan was already an informer for the F.B.I. before the red baiting of the post-war period is purely coincidental.

Conclusion

All of which goes to say that the "Best Documentary" nomination is a literal blind: what we see and what we are shown is there to mask the truth. Such scurrilous devices were not, however, a recent Hollywood invention; similar ones were resorted to back in 1934 at the time of Upton Sinclair's campaign to become Governor of California: the "End Poverty in California," or EPIC, campaign. This campaign took place in the aftermath of the results of the Depression, especially in Southern California: "The depression exposed the 1920s Los Angeles boom cycle, where the entire credit-based structure of easy money and financial and real estate speculation collapsed."[60] Those responsible for the crisis now joined forces to repel the common enemy, Sinclair:

> ...studio workers earning over $100 a week were assessed one day's wages to contribute to a fund earmarked for the election. The assessment financed the production of several movie "newsreels" which the studio heads sent to all the theatres in the state.
> ...The studios, which controlled the distribution outlets, could force theatre owners sympathetic to EPIC to play the newsreels under threat of losing the main feature.
> One newsreel pictured a raggedy mob scene as an announcer explained that crowds of unemployed were waiting at the border in the hope of getting into California because of the possible Sinclair victory. Though the EPIC newspaper pointed out that the crowd scenes were actually footage from other movies, almost all the major newspapers in the state failed to pick up this information.[61]

From lies about the unemployed massing to invade California to Cvetic's paranoia about the Soviets massing in Alaska to invade America and from the showing of phoney newsreels to the shooting of a phoney documentary feature is only one step. There was, however, one crucial difference due to the different dates: 1934, 1951. Whereas the baiting of Sinclair stemmed from the realization that the fundamental class structure and division of labor was threatened, the red-baiting undertaken from 1947 on, reaching a climax of sorts with *I Was a Communist for the F.B.I.*, was more complex. It was certainly dictated by Warner Brothers' wish to atone for having made *Mission to Moscow* in 1943[62] but also by the need to destroy that solidarity between liberals, radicals and Communists, between intellectuals and black and white labor, that had been so vital a force in the 1930s.

Meanwhile, *Daily Variety* and *The Hollywood Reporter* continued to document verbatim the HUAC hearings in Washington, with Hearst columnists such as Hedda Hopper and Westbrook Pegler ever ready to whip up hatred.[63] Like the press which fed it and whose hand it never tried to bite, Hollywood resorted with this film to the tactics and the values of the gutter; no lie was too big, no calumny too vile. Can the concept of cynicism help us here? It is often claimed by critics that Hollywood went on producing the films of the Red cycle despite their failure to make money. Referring to Peter Sloterdijk's "thesis that ideology's dominant mode of functioning is cynical,"

Slavoj Zizek comments: "The cynical subject is quite aware of the distance between the ideological mask and the social reality, but he none the less still insists upon the mask."[64] It was not therefore a question of Hollywood knowing the truth, yet believing the opposite, which is the psychic structure of disavowal. It was rather a question of Hollywood knowing the truth about its own lies but maintaining the mask for reasons of political and economic expediency — the survival of Hollywood in the turbulent postwar period — and continuing to make box-office flops notwithstanding because this expediency demanded it. In which case the best documentary nomination is the acme of cynicism: everyone knew the film was a big lie but expediency insisted on Warner Brothers eliminating Hollywood's past — such as pro–Soviet films — and, with that cultural past, the historical past too. The public had to be shown convincingly that the Soviet Union had always been America's real enemy, that the postwar situation was inevitable and the sole fault of Stalin and his domestic stooges. If the whole exercise stank, it did have its rationale and Hollywood kept to it up to the logical end.

1. See Stephen J. Whitfield: *The Culture of the Cold War*. Baltimore and London: The Johns Hopkins University Press, 1996, p. 134.

2. I am thinking especially, but not exclusively, of the films made in the period 1948–52. See also notes 52 and 54.

3. The ad appears on pp.8 and 9. Jack L. Warner Papers. Special Collections, USC, Los Angeles, Box 44, folder 113. My thanks to Ned Comstock for helping me research the Warner papers.

4. See Victor Navasky: *Naming Names*. London and New York, Penguin Books, 1981 (originally published in 1980).

5. *The Great Fear: The Anti-Communist Purge under Truman and Eisenhower*. New York: Simon and Schuster, 1978. The chapter on Cvetic is appropriately entitled "Hell in Pittsburgh." A radical and allegorical re-telling of the tale is, of course, *Night of the Living Dead*.

6. *Op.cit.*, pp. 216–7.

7. *Ibid.* Which only goes to show that "McCarthyism" existed prior to McCarthy.

8. *Ibid.*, p. 217.

9. Robert Justin Goldstein. *Political Repression in Modern America: From 1870 to the present*. Cambridge, Mass.: Schenkman Publishing Co., Inc., 1978, p. 345.

10. Caute, *op.cit.*, pp. 136–7.

11. Whitfield, *op.cit.*, p.135. It is interesting to note that Western Pennsylvania CP member Louis Bortz was asked by none other than McCarthy himself if he had been part of a plot to beat up Cvetic. Hearings of the Senate Permanent Subcommittee on Investigations, Wednesday, June 17, 1953, p.1384. The Hearings, via HUAC investigator (formerly of the F.B.I.) Herbert Hawkins, also informed the general public that information concerning Communist activities in Pittsburgh was obtained by an undercover agent "classified as a highly reliable source by the F.B.I." (p. 1374). This "source" was none other than Joseph Mazzei.

Bortz also refused to say whether he had ever visited Anchorage, Alaska. This question was presumably put to him because of Cvetic's delirious claim that Communists planned to invade the States via Alaska. See Nora Sayre: *Running Time: Films of the Cold War*. New York: the Dial Press, 1982, p.86. One remembers the Red scare of the late 1960s where Americans were informed that Chinese Communists were massing in Mexico prior to invading California. It is interesting to note that certain sequences of the Howard Hawks production, *The Thing from Another World* (1951), including the very opening one, take place in Anchorage, Alaska and that one of the film's subtexts concerns the Communist threat. See also below, note 51.

12. Cedric Belfrage: *The American Inquisition, 1945–1960: A profile of the "McCarthy era."* New York: Thunder's Mouth Press, 1989, pp. 198, 268 (originally published in 1973).

13. For a sobering, and depressing, history of the collaboration between conservative unionism and capital, see Paul Buhle: *Taking Care of Business*. New York: Monthly Review Press, 1999.

14. See Robert Gottlieb and Irene Wolt: *Thinking Big: The Story of the Los Angeles Times, its Publishers, and their Influence on Southern California.* New York: G.P. Putnam's Sons, 1977. We shall return to this example later.

15. Ellen Schrecker: *Many Are the Crimes. McCarthyism in America.* Princeton: Princeton University Press, 1998, p. 3.

16. Quoted in Michael Denning: *The Cultural Front. The Laboring of American Culture in the Twentieth Century.* London: Verso, 1997, p. 69.

17. Schrecker, *op.cit.*, p. 140. See also Earl Latham: *The Communist Controversy in Washington: From the New Deal to McCarthy.* Cambridge, Mass.: Harvard University Press, 1966, pp. 103–4, 229–30.

18. For full details, see Schrecker, *op.cit.*, pp. 122–30.

19. *Ibid.*, pp. 122–4.

20. *Variety*, May 12 1948, wrote "The documentary screen technique reaches the heights of timelessness in *The Iron Curtain.*" *The Hollywood Reporter*, May 7 1948, called the film "a hard-hitting documentary." *Variety*, August 25 1952, described *Big Jim McLain* as "a documentary-styled account of the Communist peril in Hawaii." PCA files on *The Iron Curtain* and *Big Jim McLain*, Motion Picture Academy of Arts and Sciences, Margaret Herrick Library, Beverly Hills, California.

21. In its review of *The Iron Curtain*, *The Motion Picture Daily*, May 7 1948, evoked "the semi-documentary format of *Call Northside 777.*" PCA file, MPAAS.

22. For a more detailed discussion of the implications of this film for the Cold War and its relation to other films of the period, see Reynold Humphries: "Investigators, undercover men and the F.B.I.: from gangsterism to Communism and back again." In *Le Crime Organisé à la ville et à l'écran.* Pierre Lagayette and Dominique Sipière (eds.). Paris: Ellipses, 2001, pp. 212–224.

23. See Reynold Humphries: "Jules Dassin: Crime and the City." In *Le Crime Organisé de la Prohibition à la Guerre Froide.* John Dean and Jacques Pothier (eds.). Nantes: Editions du Temps, 2002, pp. 145–59.

24. I find the use of the word "betray" most revelatory: could it be that it is the unconscious of the text emerging, revealing that this was precisely what Hollywood was about to ask ex–Communists to do? It certainly casts doubt on the integrity of the couple, presumably quite unintentionally.

25. It could also refer to Theodore Roosevelt's remark about the need to "walk softly and carry a big stick," but I doubt the film's makers had that in mind.

26. The wife is played by Gene Tierney, so the film can be interpreted as a Cold War version of how Laura discovered that true love lay with virile Mark McPherson and not an effete intellectual (= homosexual) like Waldo Lydecker. Think of how Bruno Anthony in *Strangers on a Train* is coded as a homosexual and behaves stealthily like a closet Red. See Robert J. Corber: *In the Name of National Security. Hitchcock, Homophobia and the Political Construction of Gender in Postwar America.* Durham and London: Duke University Press, 1993.

27. Hawaii's Chief of Police stars as himself, an attempt to remind spectators that this was the unadorned truth on show.

28. See Caute, *op.cit.*, p. 90; Richard Freeland: *The Truman Doctrine and the Origins of McCarthyism.* New York: Schocken Books, 1974 (1971), pp. 315–6; Mary Sperling McAuliffe: *Crisis on the Left: Cold War Politics and American Liberals, 1947–1954.* Amherst: University of Massachusetts Press, 1978, p. 83.

29. Howard Zinn: *A People's History of the United States.* New York: Perennial Classics, 2003, p. 181.

30. Velde has gone down in history as the person who will be remembered for calling writer/director Abraham Polonsky "a very dangerous citizen" when the latter appeared before the Committee in 1951.

31. This notion is dutifully taken up by *The Hollywood Reporter*, 25 August 1952. The heroes "go through the bitter experience of seeing proven communists go free by hiding behind the 5th. Amendment." Clippings file on *Big Jim McLain*, MPAAS. This remark suggests that only "proven communists" appeared before HUAC, whereas another argument of Red-baiters was that taking the Fifth was proof that the person was indeed a communist. So the witness was damned either way.

32. Goldstein, *op.cit.*, p. 354.

33. *Ibid.*, p. 422

34. Schrecker, *op.cit.*, p. 285.

35. *Ibid.*

36. *Many Are the Crimes, op.cit.*, xix.

37. According to Caute (*op.cit.*, p. 114), the Bureau's budget rose from $7 million in 1940 to $53 million in 1950. Another source states that there were 898 agents in 1940 and 7029 in 1952. See Athan Theoharis: *From the Secret Files of J. Edgar Hoover*. Chicago: Ivan R. Dee, Inc., 1991, p. 86.

38. Caute, *op.cit.*, p. 115.

39. Theoharis, *op.cit.*, p. 87.

40. Gerald Horne: *Class Struggle in Hollywood, 1930–1960: Moguls, Mobsters, Stars, Reds and Trade Unionists.* Austin: University of Texas Press, 2001. This splendid volume is essential for understanding the issues at stake. In particular, its sub-title says it all.

41. Reagan's Republican colleague George Murphy of the Screen Actors' Guild is the star of *Walk East on Beacon.* On the future President's career, see Stephen Vaughn: *Ronald Reagan in Hollywood: Movies and Politics.* Cambridge: Cambridge University Press, 1994.

42. PCA file, MPAAS.

43. Whitfield, *op.cit.* p. 21.

44. Vaughn, *op.cit.*, p. 151.

45. Caute, *op.cit.*, p. 96.

46. Whitfield, *op.cit.*, p. 21.

47. Goldstein, *op.cit.*, p. 313.

48. Griffin Fariello: *Red Scare. An Oral History of the American Inquisition.* New York: Avon Books, 1995, pp. 117–18.

49. Given President Truman's role in the Cold War and the fact that Brewer was a Democrat, it is of interest to note that in 1939 the future President "naively tried to enlist Roosevelt in a peace initiative with a group that viewed Hitler as a bulwark against Communism." See Arnold A. Offner: "Harry S. Truman as Parochial Nationalist." In *The Origins of the Cold War.* Thomas G. Paterson and Robert J. McMahon (eds.). Lexington, Massachusetts: D.C. Heath and Company, 1991, p. 54.

50. Otto Friedrich: *City of Nets: A Portrait of Hollywood in the 1940s.* London: Headline, 1986, p. 142.

51. *Rainbow at Midnight: Labor and Culture in the 1940s.* Urbana and Chicago: University of Illinois Press, 1994, p. 194.

52. In 1949 Bridges was indicted for perjury by the federal government who hoped to use this to break a strike led by his International Longshoremen's and Warehousemen's Union. This strike took place in Hawaii, so the "documentary" aspect of *Big Jim McLain* is as slanted as it is in *I Was a Communist for the F.B.I.* See Goldstein, *op.cit.*, p. 348. For a detailed analysis of the changing place of Alaska and Hawaii in post-war American politics, see John Whitehead: "Alaska and Hawai'i: the Cold War States." In Kevin J. Fernlund (editor): *The Cold War American West, 1945–1989.* Albuquerque: University of New Mexico Press, 1998, pp. 189–207.

53. On this question, see Schrecker, *op.cit.*, p. 140.

54. Caute, *op.cit.*, p. 434.

55. *Ibid.*, p. 437.

56. Three years later Douglas was to direct another, more justifiably famous Warner Brothers film, *Them!* The role of the F.B.I. in this film suggests that something other than the Bomb is at stake. See Reynold Humphries: *The American Horror Film: An Introduction.* Edinburgh: Edinburgh University Press, 2002, pp. 58–60.

57. *He Walked by Night* was directed by Alfred Werker who was to direct the paralytic *Walk East on Beacon.*

58. The fact that the ants in *Them!* use the underground storm drains in Los Angeles condenses the iconography of *He Walked by Night* and *I Was a Communist for the F.B.I.* and Jack Warner's description of Communists as "termites."

59. *Ronald Reagan in Hollywood, op.cit.*, p. 81.

60. *Thinking Big, op.cit.*, p. 202.

61. *Ibid.*, p. 211. Thus did big business, newspaper tycoons and studio bosses create their own brand of "closed shop."

62. See *Running Time, op.cit.*, p. 86.

63. In one of his columns, Pegler attacked John Garfield by giving his real Jewish name. It is as if World War II had never taken place and the concentration camps never existed.

64. *The Sublime Object of Ideology.* London: Verso, 1989, p. 29.

7

Teaching Fear in 1950s Science Fiction Films

by Michael Lee

Film scholars have long noted the stylistic link between the science fiction genre and what has been generally called "the documentary style."[1] While a thorough-going reworking of that argument lies outside the scope of this essay, one need only look at such seminal texts in the history of science fiction films as *Le Voyage dans la Lune* (Méliès, 1902) with its expository narration guiding the viewer through its fantastic imagery; *Things to Come* (Menzies, 1936) with its storyline subservient to a gripping exposition of futuristic society, and *Destination Moon* (Pichel, 1950) in which producer George Pal and director Irving Pichel spin out a pedantic tale of a minimally dramatic but richly detailed lunar journey. No serious scholarship on the subject of science fiction cinema neglects to mention the connections between science fiction and the documentary. With its rhetorical concern with science, science fiction's alliance to documentary (a genre where all too often the truth claims, even those supposedly based on science, lapse into fiction as well) seems built into the genre.

Similarly, claims by film historians that American science fiction films specifically of the 1950s were informed by a paranoid sensibility drawn from Cold War anxieties hardly require a detailed re-examination in this essay.[2] The allegorical relationship between alien invaders and Communists in numerous classic science fiction films of the 1950s has been thoroughly discussed even within the journalistic and fan-oriented writing about cinema. Moreover, links between science fiction texts and fear of science and in particular atomic science are explicit in the texts themselves and require no excavation.

This essay will not try and overturn these honorable critical and historical perspectives, but will try to lend some fresh light by looking not at science fiction texts from the 1950s in their entirety, but at the miniature films that often frame these films or at the tiny films imbedded within them. By examining framing devices, even those that frame the context only after the narrative portion of the film has begun, this essay will argue that the two crucial influences on science fiction during the

1950s, the documentary style and a paranoid sensibility, are not two influences but one as there is little or no boundary between cinematic pedagogy and Cold War paranoia during the 1950s. The essay hopes to show that science fiction filmmakers even rely on pedagogical cinema's unique poetics to generate fear.

For all the claims of the influence of documentaries on science fiction films, none seem interested in unpacking precisely what sort of documentary films influence Hollywood products and how. Science fiction films of the 1950s invariably offer viewers obviously narrative material meant to be understood as fictional and basically conforming to classical patterns of filmic storytelling operative in Hollywood during the period. Even the most didactic genre film of the period, *Destination Moon*, presents a linear story told through the experiences of fictional characters and shot and edited in a manner designed to draw its audience into its alternate reality. That the filmmakers wanted that alternate reality to feel as real as possible has been well documented. The film is nonetheless narrative rather than purely documentary.[3]

Yet the boundary between fictional cinema and documentary is always blurry and often more a matter of conventions of exhibition and marketing. *Destination Moon* was intended to be seen in theaters and was marketed as a "weird story." While marketing alone cannot determine a film's genre, couple this marketing with the film's narrative elements, and you have an example of narrative cinema. The connection to the documentary style seems a comparatively minor point, yet that is often where analysis of science fiction's relationship to documentary ends.

The boundary between documentary and narrative cinema was not only questioned in Hollywood. From the opposite end of the line of influence, educational films produced for American public schools use many of the same narrative strategies as *Destination Moon*, yet they appear as examples of something very different from narrative cinema. Ken Smith, in his book *Mental Hygiene: Classroom Films 1945–1970* documents that entire studios, such as Coronet Films, devoted exclusively to the production of educational films, used narrative strategies derived from classic Hollywood formulas.[4] Fictional characters are introduced to illustrate optimal solutions to generic problems. Coronet pioneered this narrative strategy in a huge number of films produced during the height of 16mm cinema in public school classrooms. The film *Shy Guy* (1947) for example, illustrates how a high school boy new to his town and reclusively interested in making a radio might successfully learn to "fit in" and make friends. Actors play the characters in conventional dramatic fashion. The titular shy guy, played by future *Bewitched* star Dick York, keeps the viewer informed about what he is thinking and feeling through first-person narration, and the entire lesson unfolds through a rather conventional cinematic narrative that illustrates one ideal and plausible solution to a more general social problem. While less dramatic than a journey to the Moon, *Shy Guy* provides a specific dramatic illustration of a didactic point: if you strive to fit in through behavior demonstrative of your interest in others, you can win new friends.

In addition to their approach to drama, an illustration of problem solving through a fictionalized performance of a solution, *Destination Moon* and *Shy Guy* share a common reliance on academic experts to maximize the pedagogical value of each film. Hermann Oberth, a leading German expert in rocketry, lent his expertise to the production of *Destination Moon*. He was one of many expert consultants hired to assist on the film. *Shy Guy* was typical of classroom films of its era in providing screen credit for an academic expert who consulted in the making of the film. The second title card of the film reads: "Education Collaborator/Alice Sowers, Ph.D./ Director of the Family Life Institute/ University of Oklahoma." Coronet, in an effort to legitimize their product in the eyes of the educators who formed their clientele, invariably credited educational collaborators for their numerous productions.

The stylistic relationship between early 1950s science fiction and classroom cinema is not easily sorted out. The genres interact rather than react to one another. Both the makers of Hollywood science fiction such as *Destination Moon*, and David Smart, founder of Coronet Films, credited the influence of the other for their approach. Coronet wanted to cozy up to Hollywood and thus make films that seemed more urgent to students[5]; science fiction mavens hoped to associate with educational cinema. While it may be needlessly reductive to claim that exhibition conventions constitute the only difference between *Destination Moon* and classroom films of the era, it is at minimum necessary to observe the indistinct path of influence linking Hollywood product and pedagogical cinema. They differ importantly in running time, production values, and the monothematic focus of the shorter educational films. Yet they share roots in the same history of filmmaking and use common stylistic elements and narrative approaches.

More important than merely claiming that *Destination Moon* strives for a documentary style is noting that the film shares with *Shy Guy*, and literally thousands of other educational films, a certain paranoid sensibility. The crisis of *Shy Guy* centers on whether the titular character will ever "fit in." Failure poses real terror for the individual who remains an outsider. *Destination Moon* deals with a journey to the Moon, but at the core of that journey is fear of domination by an unnamed foreign power. We'll return to the theme of paranoia's relationship to pedagogy before this essay is over, but suffice to say that this link between these two films is far more crucial from an ideological standpoint than their common narrative strategies, although dividing the two commonalities may prove impossible.

In order to provide some limitation to the scope of this study, we now must turn our attention not to complete science fiction texts or the vast canon of pedagogical cinema, but to the miniature films that either frame the action of science fiction or find themselves imbedded within larger films. The framing device is nearly as old as narrative. Framing devices in narrative media usually serve the purpose of lending the subsequent narrative crucial credibility for its audience. In some cases, a framing device might lay out the moral or ethical stakes present in the subsequent narrative. For example, seventeenth-century French librettist Jean-Philippe Quinault might introduce one of Jean-Baptiste Lully's *tragédies-lyriques* with an allegorical frame in which figures from mythology dispute a moral or ethical point only to have one of the interlocutor's positions illustrated in the unfolding of a tragedy played out by mortals. Readers interested in an example might read his libretto for *Armide* (1686) in which the figures Glory and Wisdom debate the hero's qualities prior to witnessing along with the audience an operatic depiction of his struggles. As King Louis XIV of France was patron to both Quinault and Lully, the necessity of allegorical frames supporting the nascent ideal of absolute monarchy figured importantly in several of their collaborations. While Quinault's approach is derived from earlier dramatists such as Pierre Corneille and Jean Racine and their approach in turn derived from Classical Greek tragedy, Quinault's work dominated French stage narrative of the late seventeenth century and informed similar narrative structures popular in Italy and elsewhere.

The moral and ethical frame gradually gave way by the nineteenth century to the framing device's potential in serving the credibility of the subsequent narrative by lending it added verisimilitude. Scottish novelist Sir Walter Scott began many of his extraordinarily popular novels with framing devices in which the narrator tells the reader how he came into possession of the story that is about to be told. Scott's plots often resemble romances, a subgenre that benefits enormously from the reader's suspension of disbelief. The novel *Rob Roy* provides a lengthy example of a framing device primarily configured along these lines and intended to lend the tale greater credibility for its having been in a certain sense discovered by the narrator rather than manufactured by the author.

Dragging Quinault and Scott into a discussion of science fiction films of the 1950s is not purely gratuitous. The framing devices they created illustrate the essential motivations for most framing devices shot for Science Fiction films: to provide a thematic or even moral context and to lend the subsequent narrative added verisimilitude. Like the romance, science fiction can easily degenerate into absurdity unless the reader suspends disbelief and enters into the escapist genre wholeheartedly. Establishing trust through a frame can be key.

We can now turn to an examination of framing material and films within films from seven classic texts of Hollywood science fiction: *The Monolith Monsters* (Sherwood, 1957), *It Came from Beneath the Sea* (Gordon, 1955), *Them!* (Douglas, 1954), *Deadly Mantis* (Juran, 1957), *Destination Moon*, *Creature from the Black Lagoon* (Arnold, 1954), and *The Mole People* (Vogel, 1956). The purpose of the following analyses boils down to advancing the claim that the documentary style and Cold War paranoia are not two influences but one as paranoia and pedagogy are necessary to complete one another. Perhaps just as importantly, we will see that in some films the poetics of classroom cinema end up serving the generation of paranoia more persuasively than the monster insects and aliens presented within the films.

The framing device for the 1957 film *The Monolith Monsters* offers a reasonable example of a framing device configured to bear the burden of lending the subsequent fantasy of a meteor striking the earth in the Mojave Desert some degree of verisimilitude. The film's narrative will tell us that this meteor is comprised of material that leeches the silicon from whatever it touches. More interestingly from a cinematic standpoint, it expands upward when it contacts water. The resulting towers of this material threaten the peaceful California town where the film's action is set. While far from the most wildly improbable of science fiction films born of the period, this story requires the acceptance of an unprecedented occurrence for the escapist fun to reach maximum impact. A frightening premise such as a world dominated by towers of pitiless minerals from deepest space toppling down on a humanity reduced to antlike stature only works if the audience identifies with the people confronting this

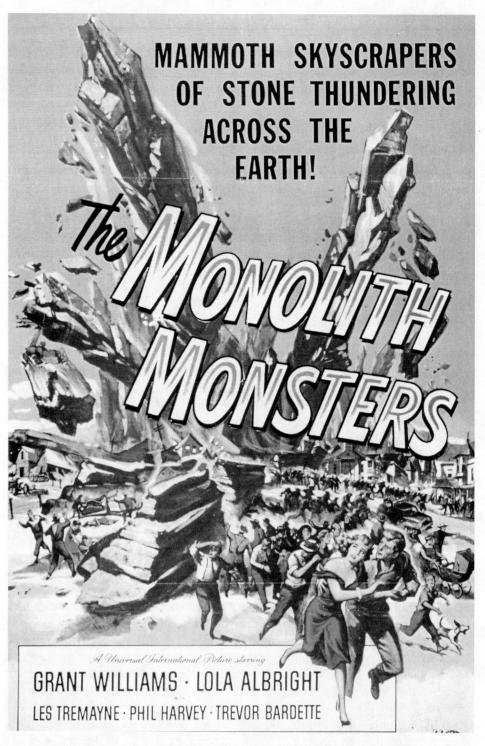

The Monolith Monsters (1957) presents one of the more plausible threats featured in a "B" science fiction film of the 1950s. This premise is aided by a framing device that draws upon the style and conventions of classroom cinema to temporarily transform the theater or drive-in into a science class.

horror in a context of believable threat. To achieve this identification, the filmmakers took pains to persuade the viewer of the plausibility of their premise so that the struggles of the human beings could take on needed urgency. While the film contains several didactic scenes during which the leeching of silicon and the effect of water interacting with the extraterrestrial minerals are explained, the framing device carries the most essential burden of establishing credibility. Stylistically the framing device is quite distinct from the narrative portions of the film. An omniscient narrator assumes the "voice-of-god" function so often used in documentary films. This narrator is heard only during the framing device thus lending the frame the status of a miniature educational film before the narrative film begins by drawing a sharp stylistic distinction between the two. As a "B" science fiction film, the target audience for *The Monolith Monsters* was likely young people who were by 1957 all too familiar with the poetics of educational cinema. The authoritative narrator, cheaply rendered graphics, and integrated stock footage used in the frame for *The Monolith Monsters* might make the local cinema or drive-in theater temporarily feel like a classroom.

The visual narration of *The Monolith Monsters'* framing device begins with a shot of the Earth from space. Initially the distance is great. Our planet appears an amorphous circle of light amid twinkling stars. The camera moves closer revealing the Western Hemisphere, although the continent of North America is rather too large and dominates too much of the planet's surface in an illustration of the American self-absorption that so galls the rest of the world, or by way of connecting the film to the often cheap and sloppy graphic design prominent in classroom films of the time. During this shot, fully eight meteors sail by the Earth. The last three strike the Earth's atmosphere and disintegrate thus illustrating a key factual point about meteors made in the shot's narration. During this shot, the narrator reads the following text:

> From time immemorial the Earth has been bombarded by objects from outer space, bits and pieces of the universe piercing our atmosphere in an invasion that never ends. Meteors, the shooting stars upon which so many earthly wishes have been born. Of the thousands that plummet toward us, the greater part is destroyed in a fiery flash as they strike the layers of air that encircle us. Only a small percentage survives. Most of these fall into the water which covers two-thirds of our world.

One could certainly object to the militaristic allusions to bombardment and invasion, however, this text is essentially accurate, although one versed in the science of the atmosphere might object to the narrator describing the gases of the outer atmosphere as "air." A common tendency in educational films of the era was to over dramatize the natural forces described in the film in order to generate interest in young viewers. Readers old enough to remember schoolrooms equipped with 16 mm projectors can likely supply their own examples. The educational film freshest in the author's mind was produced by the National Forest Service during the 1960s and remains beloved by visitors to the Cape Perpetua Visitor's Center in the Siuslaw National Forest near Yachats, Oregon. Titled *The Forces of Nature* the film describes natural processes readily visible in the area where the Siuslaw National Forest meets the Pacific Ocean. The film describes the Pacific Ocean in variously dramatic and anthropomorphic terms with such phrases as "brooding." Whether such metaphoric language is appropriate to a pedagogical film is not the concern of this essay. The important point is that pedagogical cinema indulges in language comparable to that in the framing devices for science fiction films. In a particularly exciting section of *Forces of Nature* explaining the formation of the rocky coastline, the Pacific Ocean is described as "unleashing an unrelenting onslaught against the land." Viewers of the film surely know that bodies of water cannot literally brood nor do they possess sufficient intentionality to make war on the land in anything like the sense that humans make war on one another. Applications of dramatic verbiage often found their way into classroom films. This situation might be explained by considering that classroom films so often appeared dull compared to Hollywood product. Some punchy narration could enhance the pedagogical value of the film by maintaining interest. Norman Jolley and Robert M. Fresco, the writers of *The Monolith Monsters*, similarly punch up the narration of their framing device.

During the next sequence of *The Monolith Monsters*, the narrator continues in a slightly more urgent tone as the topic turns to those meteors that strike the land. He continues:

> But from time to time from the beginning of time, a very few meteors have struck the crust of the Earth and formed craters, craters of all sizes sought after and poured over by scientists of all nations for the priceless knowledge buried within them. In every moment of every day they come from far planets belonging to stars whose dying light is too far away to be seen. From infinity they come, meteors.

Here the narration pauses for an urgent musical cue lifted from the score for *The Creature from the Black Lagoon*. The visuals change as well. A meteor is seen in a sea of stars. It grows larger in a nice rhyme of the visual material seen previously where the Earth appeared to come closer and closer to the viewer. This sequence culminates in a lovely match cut from the meteor zooming toward the camera to its impact in the California desert. Here the narrator describes the meteor, but the largely factual lesson gives way to ominous speculation: "Another strange calling card from the limitless reaches of space, its substance unknown, its secrets unexplored. The meteor lies dormant in the night, waiting."

The nature of meteors is not wholly unknown. As the narration alludes, scientists have examined many, but the fruit of this research and the speculation it can inform does not concern this framing device. Its ultimate function is not a lesson about meteors, but a framing device for a frightening fantasy about a particular meteor. The frame must appear factual, and the filmmakers draw upon the poetics and visual style of classroom cinema to accomplish this appearance. The frame's conclusion invites the audience to fear what they don't know about meteors and what in a very real sense can never be known. Jolley and Fresco take this one step further by ominously anthropomorphizing the meteor as "waiting."

What film historians have long claimed about science fiction films of the 1950s is present in this little framing film: first that they are inspired by what is rather loosely called "the documentary style" and the films are imbued with a paranoid sensibility born of Cold War anxiety. But in looking at educational films about natural occurrences that inform this framing device, we might discover that visual education as practiced during the 1950s is usually dependant on generating fear. Moreover, education and entertainment have been closely linked in the Western imagination. Plato, for example, in outlining an ideal pedagogy in *The Republic* argues for a pedagogy evenly divided between gymnastics as a means of disciplining the body and music as a means of disciplining the mind. Modern readers educated in America may find this centrality for music as difficult to understand. Plato reasoned that music's essential abstraction provided the correct discipline for understanding the forces of physics in motion, but its entertaining qualities would make it an agreeable object of study for the young.[6] Attempts to frighten through film have been a form of entertainment almost as long as cinema has existed. Fostering such entertainment within the field of pedagogy has foundations in antiquity.

While the linkage of entertainment to education helps explain the gripping hyperbole of classroom films, its effect often serves fear. To illustrate my point, let me confess that I was terrified by passages of the educational film *The Forces of Nature* as a child. The images and descriptions of the sea as violent and intentionally so certainly worried me, but worse was the film's depiction and description of sea anemones during a brief survey of tide pool life. First the film introduces a little hermit crab. The medium of film lends this particular crab some sympathy as that crab becomes specific rather than generic. Soon after its introduction, the poor thing becomes food for an anemone in a tide pool. The anemone is described in horrible terms as a viciously poisonous creature. In defense of the film's factuality, anemones are poisonous and lethally so for tiny hermit crabs, but they pose absolutely no threat to humans. Information about the degree and nature of their poison certainly would have been less dramatic and therefore less entertaining, but it would have made my childhood explorations of tide pools a less cautious enterprise and, more importantly, grounded the film in reality. The death of the particular crab coupled with narrative hyperbole about a very mildly poisonous sea creature had unintended pedagogical impact on at least one viewer. As employees of the federal government, the filmmakers had no clear motive for their hyperbole beyond a blurring of entertainment in this case achieved through inspiring fear with pedagogy. Perhaps the boundary between paranoia and pedagogy had been so thoroughly transgressed during the Cold War that teaching lessons without fear had become the exceptional approach. The structure of an American education, with its myriad potential for petty humiliations, has always depended to some degree on a general fear of failure, of being singled out as wanting. Over time fears of various forms have taken center stage. Even the motivation for learning is all too often posited in a manner configured to inspire fear. During the 1950s and 60s, high school boys in America were warned to study hard, especially in the fields of math and science, in order to contribute to Capitalism's defense during the Cold War.

This situation is illustrated in the classroom film *Why Study Science* (1955). Most of the reasons given for studying science in this film are perfectly benign, even noble.

However, behind all the film's claims is fear of the unknown. In his landmark meditation on classroom cinema, Ken Smith claims that just beneath the surface of the classroom subgenres of "fitting in" films, or driver's ed films, lies stark terror. Smith cites too many examples of fear informing cinematic pedagogy in his book to characterize them all. A striking example appears in the unlikely film *Body Care and Grooming* (1947), which preys upon young people's fear that the opposite sex won't find them attractive. Considerable emotional grief can be linked to this very urgent fear. This film rather cynically employs this fear to teach girls such routine lessons as keeping their socks pulled up. The frightening hyperbole employed seems wildly inappropriate for what really amounts to an extremely superficial lesson imposing rigid conformity and illustrates the intimacy with which paranoia was infused into pedagogy during the Cold War. Smith concludes that the application of fear to impose conformity in pedagogical cinema suggests that America was "a nation not quite in its right mind."[7]

As fear served the capitalist agenda during the Cold War, separating paranoia from pedagogy may not be wholly possible. As the science fiction film must teach its audience something in order to serve the suspension of disbelief, the technology of paranoia embedded in cinematic pedagogy inevitably comes into play. The two influences are inextricable from one another.

The framing device for *It Came from Beneath the Sea* teaches about atomic submarines rather than meteors and provides an example closely related to *The Monolith Monsters*. The important difference in these two films' framing devices lie in one explaining a natural occurrence while the other describes a man-made vehicle. The first serves as the principle threat of the film, while the latter discusses a weapon that will fail to contain the threat it confronts. Despite their differing subjects, both films utilize an off-screen narrator, teach something essentially true about the topic under discussion, and conclude with a paranoid warning about the unknown. While *The Monolith Monsters* drew from classroom cinema for its visual and narrative poetics, *It Came from Beneath the Sea* draws upon government films for its approach.

The framing device for *It Came from Beneath the Sea* appears to draw its visual material entirely from stock footage culled from material shot by the Naval Signal Corps. The narration runs this way:

> From her beginnings on a navy drawing board, through the months of secret field experiments out on the western desert, through the desperate search for new metals with properties she needed; she was designed to be man's greatest weapon on the seas: the atom submarine. Her engines were to be a miracle of speed and power, her sides strong enough to withstand any blow, her armor and firepower greater than that of any enemy she might encounter. The mind of man had thought of everything except that which was beyond his comprehension.

This framing device then elides into brash credits and a blaring score quite similar to that of *The Monolith Monsters*. We learn from this framing device that whatever the "It" is of the title, it's going to defeat "man's greatest weapon of the seas." Considering that the "it" turns out to be a giant octopus, we would understand that

introducing that concept right away might get the film off on the wrong foot by exposing its potentially silly menace, although posters had largely done that damage even
before the film began. The filmmakers invested enormous energy in creating a compelling monster octopus; showing it too early risks reducing the subsequent story to
an anti-climax. Understanding that a film about a giant octopus might find itself in
constant danger of losing the audience's suspension of disbelief, the narrator from
the framing device returns often to comment on the action and provide narrative
transitions. Yet in every instance, the narrator concludes on the theme of the
unknown. His first transitional narration comes immediately after the atomic submarine was held fast by an unknown force. Once the vessel is inexplicably released,
the narrator intones the following, illustrated by more stock footage of a submarine
docking:

> But that was only the beginning. When Commander Matthews brought the
> atomic submarine into Pearl Harbor for repairs, the Defense Department
> found itself confronted with a problem beyond the scope of navy men.

First we learned "man's greatest weapon of war" will lose; next we learn the men
of the navy will fail as well. Fortunately, they seek the help of scientists reprising a
theme started years earlier in *Destination Moon* concerning the beneficence of military and scientific cooperation.

The framing narration for *It Came from Beneath the Sea* echoes the narrative
craft of those same State Department films from which it draws so much of its footage.
A couple of famous films commissioned by the government to frighten Cold War
era Americans provide far more frightening narration than anything in the admittedly overblown narration for *It Came from Beneath the Sea*. Films on such diverse
topics as a Communist takeover of the United States to the proper use of an M-16
rifle were made by the United States Defense Department during the Cold War.
Always implied and often stated in these films is a context of fear wherein every man,
woman, and child may soon find themselves locked in a life-or-death struggle against
a horrifically inhumane and godless enemy. The immediate pedagogy of the film, be
it informing children to "duck and cover" should a nuclear blast appear or how to
cherish democratic institutions as in the daffy and paranoid film *Red Nightmare*
(1962) or something as pragmatic as the proper use of a rifle in *The M-16 Rifle: Its
Care and Use*, finds itself eclipsed by this larger imperative to paranoia.

Here we might productively turn our attention not to a framing device, but a
short film imbedded within a Science Fiction film. The most compelling predecessor to *It Came from Beneath the Sea*'s fantasy of an octopus attack was the classic of
giant monsters run amok made in the United States, *Them!*

Them! is a skillfully crafted allegory about atomic age invasion in which giant,
radioactive ants serve as surrogates for the Communist threat. The film's title, which
so ably gestures toward the central Cold War equation of "Us versus Them," unequivocally invites an allegorical reading. Film historians, journalists, and fans invariably
note this obvious reading of the film.[9] This body of writing makes an analysis of the
full film redundant. Here we look only to the short film within the film.

As the threat from giant ants reveals itself to the disbelieving agents of the Federal Government, a leading entomologist is brought in from his musty researches in the quiet of a university to aid the government as it tries to know its enemy better. To invest government officials with appropriate alarm, the professor prepares a short film about ants for which he provides a live narration. The film indulges in an interesting sort of self-reflexivity as the audience is treated to a film that self-servingly suggests that film is where one should go to learn something, or at least to learn about anything frightening.

A full recounting of the narration for the film within *Them!* might be ponderous. Suffice to say that Dr. Harold Medford provides an essentially accurate accounting of the various species, strength, and reproductive habits of ants. Just as the framing devices of the previously mentioned films begin factually then turn to fear at their peroration, *Them!* turns grimly speculative as well. Dr. Medford concludes:

> Ants are the only creatures on Earth who wage war. They campaign. They are chronic aggressors. They make slave laborers of the captives they don't kill. None of the ants previously seen by man were more than an inch in length, most considerably under that size; but even the most minute of them have an instinct, a talent, for industry, social organization, and savagery that makes man look feeble by comparison. Unless these queens can be located and destroyed by the time thriving colonies can produce Lord knows how many more queen ants.... Man as the dominant species of life on Earth will probably be extinct within, say, a year.

There are some interesting visual issues accompanying Dr. Medford's dire narration. During the early factual sections, the visuals nicely illustrate the narration. When the topic turns to waging war, the visual component can no longer support Dr. Medford's narration and is reduced to showing two ants fighting. From this point forward, vaguely suggestive is the best we can hope for from the film's visuals as they can no longer show the increasingly anthropomorphic attributes Dr. Medford claims for ants. The ant actors are simply incapable of demonstrating for the camera the "talents" they either do not possess, or possess only at a highly metaphoric level.

Language is a peculiar thing. The word "war" has a specific meaning. Ant conflicts and human conflicts might have certain very general similarities, however, considerable distinctions in the motivations of humans and ants might warrant some less anthropomorphic term describing conflicts among ants. Yet, entomologists do use war metaphors and even outright claims that ants wage war in their scientific discussions.[8] Where real life entomologists and Dr. Medford part company is where Dr. Medford blurs the distinction of instinct and talent. Humans, including Communists, demonstrate talents as an act of volition. Ants almost certainly have only instincts. Hyperbole, so typical of pedagogical cinema, serves the narration's paranoid ends. As for Dr. Medford's wild speculation of what would happen if more queen ants hatched, there we enter the ironically familiar realm of the unknown. Dr. Medford is entitled to his opinion. Given the relative ease with which the ants are dispatched during the film's final reel, his speculation appears at best alarmist even within the film's paranoid narrative. In a certain sense the film cannot deliver visual

The monster ants featured in *Them!* (1954) barely move and are badly outnumbered during the film's climax. Yet they seem frightening, in large part because the pedagogical film-within-the-film taught the audience to be afraid.

material supportive of Dr. Medford's most extravagantly paranoid claims as the largely stationary and outnumbered ants appear quite incapable of world domination. Dr. Medford's words during the film within the film end up serving the film more powerfully than the film can serve itself. These miniature educational films that reinforce the verisimilitude of the narratives that contain them really are important in teaching the audience that the threats the films present are dangerous. Pedagogical cinema reveals itself in *Them!* as the principle source, among the traditions and styles that *Them!* draws upon, that lends the film its frightening potential. Despite the criticism of the film's ending above that the giant ants on screen fail to deliver on Dr. Medford's warnings, *Them!* is a successful film. It wielded considerable influence on the genre even inspiring a thriving subgenre despite failing to provide a credible threat at the film's close. That threat seems more credible because the pedagogical film imbedded within the film and the influence of classroom cinema taught us to be afraid.

Before examining another miniature film imbedded within a science fiction film, let's look briefly at the framing device for one of *Them*'s more improbable progeny, *Deadly Mantis*. Here we find a different problem of the visuals failing to live up

The Cold War symbiosis of scientists and military men plays out in ***The Deadly Mantis*** (1957), a film whose opening draws haphazardly on classroom cinema to create a smokescreen of believability for its preposterous premise. Seated, Alix Talton; standing (***left to right***), William Hopper, Craig Stevens, and Donald Randolph.

to the promises of the pedagogical narration as the visuals and narration have next to nothing to do with one another.

The visual material found in the framing device for *Deadly Mantis* is made up of fifteen shots. The first seems drawn straight from the realm of the classroom. A map of the world is scanned for what seems an overly long time, effectively orienting the youthful target audience in the space of education. The camera pans pedantically until the words "The Atlantic Ocean" are centered within the frame, then the camera pans down the map and zooms in until a tiny, unidentified dot midway between the words "The Wendell Sea" and "The Antarctic Circle" takes center frame. The next four shots are stock footage of volcanoes. Shot six is of the map again, this time the camera pans up the map until Greenland occupies most of the screen. Since the map is a classroom favorite–the Decatur Projection map of the world–Greenland appears gigantic. The camera begins zooming in on central Greenland, until an inexplicable cut places The North Pole in the center of the screen for shot seven. Shots eight through fourteen are stock footage of icebergs in motion and great avalanches of ice into the sea. Shot fifteen shows a giant mantis under a sheet of ice with water flowing over it.

The only narration heard during this miniature film accompanies the pan up the map to Greenland and is comprised of a quotation of Newton's Third Law of Motion: "For every action there is an equal and opposite reaction." How the appearance of a giant mantis under ice is an equal or opposite reaction to a volcano is one of the daffy mysteries of the film. More important than the failure of the visuals to provide an explicit illustration of Newton's law is the interesting way that both the visual and spoken rhetoric of the classroom are marshaled in this framing device. The camera's movement over the map seems extraordinarily arbitrary. The map serves more a rhetorical function as a way of making the film seem authoritative for being connected to the accoutrements of the classroom. The quotation of Newton's Third Law of Motion has nothing to do with the appearance of a giant mantis in the arctic. It seems to have been invoked in order to attach the film's ludicrous premise to something that sounds very important and scientific, something that might be uttered in a classroom. The purpose of this framing device clearly draws upon the tradition of verisimilitude sighted earlier, but unlike *The Monolith Monsters*, there is no useful information included within the framing device. The rhetorical functions, both visual and aural of the classroom, are sufficient to lend the subsequent film its needed dose of paranoia.

Imbedded within the film *Destination Moon* is another miniature film within a film. In an effort to win support from the captains of industry, the rocket designers in the film set up a small private screening for the benefit of moneyed corporatists. The film itself features Woody Woodpecker as a skeptic about rocketry. The cartoon character's reluctance is turned to support by the carefully integrated narration and visuals. Together these elements of the film within the film demonstrate with remarkable accuracy the plausibility of a lunar voyage powered by rockets. The presence of Woody Woodpecker may remind readers who attended grammar school between 1950 and 1975 of the many pedagogical films that use animals, puppets, and other fantastical interlocutors to help fuse entertainment with learning. While classics of

Destination Moon (1950) most perfectly blurs the boundaries of pedagogical cinema and narrative science fiction film. Cold War paranoia about world domination by foreign powers informs both the pedagogy and the science fiction.

classroom cinema like *Donald Duck in Mathmagic Land* (1959) postdate *Destination Moon* considerably, the trend was started long before Disney got involved. Examples contemporaneous to the production of *Destination Moon* are legion with *Soapy the Germ Fighter* (1949) and its man-sized bar of friendly, talking soap serving as a readily available standout.

The style of introducing essentially factual information through an animated interlocutor may come from the field of pedagogical cinema, but unlike examples cited previously of that genre's interaction with science fiction, the miniature film within *Destination Moon* is faithful to the reality of rocket science. While the film is essentially accurate, the discussion following the film is not. In this case the narrative science fiction film itself and not the film within the film provides the paranoid distortion of reality. After the amused business leaders watch the film about rocketry, they are understandably confused as to the reason for its having been shown to them. Jimmy Barnes, an advocate of the project, explains that, "preparedness isn't just for the military." The filmmakers here participate in one of the central and most paranoid tropes of the Cold War era by promoting the idea that everyone is locked in this struggle. The message to the industrialists is simply that they must finance a rocket trip to the Moon because, according to General Thayer, "We're not the only ones interested in the Moon." He concludes, "Whoever controls the Moon, controls the Earth." Insofar as no entity has yet managed to control the Moon, it would be difficult to assess the absolute accuracy of the general's claim, however, no reputable geo-political theory operative today places any emphasis on lunar conquest.

With *Destination Moon*, the paranoid themes of the Cold War are located within the film itself, but their articulation within the film is largely limited to contextualizing the pedagogical miniature film within the film and to the distinctly classroom activity of discussing the pedagogical film. Pedagogical films sometimes encouraged discussion at their close. *Right or Wrong* (1951) provides an interesting illustration of this technique. More importantly, educational film companies encouraged discussion through printed teacher's guides accompanying films. In *Destination Moon*, cinematic pedagogy prompts the statement of the film's most paranoid lesson as the fictional boardroom resembles the real classroom in hosting grim predictions of a future in which America does not control the Earth, predictions prompted by an educational film.

The filmmakers of *Destination Moon* offered an alternate reality to audiences and attempted to make it feel as real as possible. Left to right: Dick Wesson , Warner Anderson, Tom Powers, and John Archer.

During the 1950s, the science classroom often found itself the locus of controversy when traditional notions about our world conflicted with emerging scientific knowledge. Some of these controversies are ongoing, for example, in the teaching of evolution. *Creature from the Black Lagoon* provides us a framing device that must contend with problems all too familiar to the public school science teacher.

The framing device for *Creature from the Black Lagoon* differs from those discussed for *The Monolith Monsters*, *It Came from Beneath the Sea*, and *Deadly Mantis*. Unlike those films, the framing device occurs after the opening credit sequence. What connects this framing device to the others under discussion here is the presence of an omniscient narrator, who, as with the narrator for *The Monolith Monsters*, is never heard from again. More importantly, it serves the framing function of providing the subsequent narrative about a surviving member of an evolutional offshoot apart from homo-sapiens but enjoying some common ancestry a certain verisimilitude. This believability is achieved through classroom cinema stylistics rather than a persuasive appeal to the intellect.

The frame opens with an extreme long shot of the cosmos. Here the narrator reads from *The King James Bible*, *Genesis* 1: 1–2. As with other framing devices discussed within this essay, the film fails to render a specific or accurate visual accompaniment to the narrative. The static shot of the cosmos indicates no action suggestive of divine creation, nor does God mentioned in the text, appear. Interestingly, this situation finds little change when the narrator turns to a more scientific account of the Earth's origins. He reads:

> This is the planet Earth, newly born and cooling rapidly from a temperature of 6000 degrees to a few hundred in less than five billion years. The heat rises, meets the atmosphere, the clouds form, and rain pours down upon the hardening surface for countless centuries. The restless seas rise, find boundaries, are contained. Now in their warm depths, the miracle of life begins. In infinite variety living things appear and change and reach the land leaving a record of their coming, their struggle to survive, and their eventual end. The record of life is written on the land where 15 million years later, in the upper reaches of the Amazon, Man is still trying to read it.

The framing device also fails to provide specific or accurate visual accompaniment to this familiar story. We do not see the miracle of life, nor do we see any living thing. The record left on the land is nothing more than footprints on a sandy beach. Indeed this narration is supported by only three shots: one of a turbulent sea, a beach, and strange footprints on the beach. These images are related to the story, but are not illustrative of it. The question, as with the visual material in the short film about ants within *Them!*, arises whether either story could be persuasively illustrated.

Glaring disagreement exists between the two narratives selected by the filmmakers to outline the Earth's origins and the rise of life on Earth. While the narrator breaks off reading *Genesis* midway through the second verse of chapter one, had he read on, some sharp contrasts would emerge. As it stands, one contrast does appear.

The biblical narration describes the Earth as having been created. The scientific narrative uses the verb "born." While one can easily imagine that the opening scriptural passage was placed in the film to placate Christians in the audience by softening the science that renders the fictional narrative its verisimilitude, there could be a deeper causality at work. As a result of their failure to illustrate their framing device persuasively, the filmmakers appear committed to neither cosmological story.

Whether the film's director Jack Arnold or his fellow architects of this sequence lack commitment to their immediate subject is not really the issue. What matters here is that pedagogical methods are invoked to set up a narrative configured to frighten its audience. More than the omniscient narrator and the introductory science lesson, the classroom is represented in this framing device by the presentation of mutually exclusive worldviews. The film, like so many high school science teachers, can take no sides in the raging debates over the origins of life and the universe. One could just as easily speculate that the inclusion of *Genesis* by the filmmakers demonstrates their commitment to evoking the classroom in their film as much as trying to placate potential viewers who might be nervous over the scientific explanation of life. Oddly, I found myself the object of lessons about evolution and the origins of life on several occasions at various stages of my public school education. In every instance, the instructor saw fit to provide at minimum a sketch of creationism as a potential alternative. The sharp contrast of the two cosmological accounts presented simultaneously and without reference to their exclusive claims in *Creature from the Black Lagoon* orients the framing device within the classroom at precisely the moment that the filmmakers are setting up their audience for a more intensely frightening film by rendering the action believable. The conflicts of the classroom inform the conflicts of the framing device.

No discussion of science fiction framing devices of the 1950s would be complete without some mention of the dizziest and most entertaining of these devices, the frame for *The Mole People.* No framing device tries harder to transport its audience to the world of the classroom than this one. The framing device takes place in a carefully appointed academic space where an actual professor of English at the University of Southern California, Dr. Frank C. Baxter, provides an extemporized lecture on Man's ongoing quest to know more of what lies beneath the Earth's surface. We find him initially consulting a small tome as the camera zooms in. Having reached some convenient stopping point, the kindly professor begins his colloquy. His presentation is extemporized lending it a certain realism for coming to us as the semi-spontaneous knowledge imparted by a distinguished member of the professoriate, rather than the hyperbolic script of a Hollywood writer. In many ways, the presentation of an onscreen educator lends this frame more authority than even the "voice-of-god" off-screen narrators of other framing devices. His casual yet impassioned delivery demonstrates that he is a seasoned lecturer. Many classroom films produced during the golden age of 16mm projectors in classrooms feature an onscreen educator. This approach was not popular at the previously mentioned Coronet Studios, but their rivals at Encyclopedia Britannica Films, who made more films on scientific subjects and fewer on social issues, made liberal use of the onscreen instructor.

Dr. Baxter opens his lecture with an extremely efficient discussion of the exploration of the Earth's surface concluding that having reached both poles, there are now "only a few square miles left that are unknown." Without granting his students–the audience–time to ponder the accuracy of this claim, he quickly moves to the topic of how much we now know about "what lies beyond, outer space." Here, the information while true leads to a dubious conclusion: insofar as we've managed in his lifetime and ours to triple the distance into space that Man has traveled, we now possess "amazing knowledge." Next comes the doubt upon which fantastical fictions depend so heavily. Throughout this section of the lecture, Dr. Baxter uses a globe as a prop. He vaguely fingers the orb and asks and answers a question crucial to the narrative that will follow "what is there beneath this globe? What is it that lies beneath our feet? No one knows, of course." This claim, plainly false, ushers in a chronological and highly selective series of speculations and historical accounts documenting Man's quest to understand what lies beneath our feet. Dr. Baxter speculates for us that primitive man retreated into caves but came out in terror to the surface with vague memories of "sighs and noises" emanating from deeper down. How this English Professor has such an intimate knowledge of the recollections of pre-literate societies gestures toward the wonderful fraudulence of the entire lecture. The good professor touches only briefly on his field of literature by mentioning Gilgamesh and Dante's *Divine Comedy* as exemplary of Man's ongoing fascination with what lies beneath the Earth's surface. Any suggestion that these allegories should be confused as anything like scientific examination seems outlandish, but the lecture's pace and the kindly yet authoritative lecturer do not allow us doubt. Dr. Baxter next illustrates some of the weirder speculations about the center of the Earth including John Cleave Simms' theory that the Earth is comprised of five globes with five surfaces. Dr. Baxter lends Simms' mad speculation credence by informing his audience that Simms died of fatigue before having a chance to test his theory by traveling to Siberia and entering the hole that connects the surfaces of the globes. Visual aids on poster board positioned on an easel illustrate the theories Dr. Baxter shares with us by way of persuading us that Man's search for answers to the question of what lies beneath our feet has been long and exhaustive. He concludes this phase of the lecture by saying "and so in this picture you are about to see, you'll see the culmination of a long series of such desires to look into the Earth." *The Mole People* probably shouldn't be described as the culmination of any mammoth human undertaking, but on that score Dr. Baxter is equally entitled to his opinion. That Dr. Baxter omits any mention of the Earth Sciences practiced with devoted professionalism at his very university indicates the filmmakers' desire to confuse rather than inform. Dr. Baxter concludes by calling the film to follow a fiction. He quickly corrects himself. "It's a fable beyond fiction." He then gives us our assignment. "I think if you'll study this picture and think about it after it's over, you'll realize that this is something more than a story told. It's a fable with a meaning for you and me in the twentieth century." Insofar as a fable can mean, "a story not rooted in fact," the good doctor is absolutely right.[10] *The Mole People*, less than most "B" science fiction films, has little symbolic potential. It's neither a legible allegory about Communism nor a moral lesson about the hubris of science. The mole people themselves provide no clear symbolic reading for while they are subjugated against their will and do rise up against their masters by the film's close, they provide the principle thrills and dangers in the film. If they are designed as central to some moral lesson about the dangers of slavery, it is an extremely unfocused and probably irresponsible lesson.

The important thing about the framing device for *The Mole People* is not its pleasurable daffiness, but its extremely clear illustration that Hollywood and specifically authors of "B" science fiction films used the field of education and most importantly the classroom film as a means of appropriating the authority of school in scaring its youthful audience. Dr. Baxter appeals to fears of the unknown when he makes the ludicrous claim that we know nothing of what lies beneath our feet. More important than the implausible conclusions drawn from the mostly irrelevant data presented within the framing device is that the filmmakers drew upon the field of education in order to increase the fear their fiction might engender.

This situation is true of all the framing devices and miniature films within films discussed in this essay. The claim that Hollywood and specifically the authors of "B" science fiction films used the ethos of the classroom to frighten, or more accurately to prime for frightening, their young audience constitutes the central claim of this essay. In these seven films, we've seen how the classroom provides the ideal context for anxiety and paranoia in an America where pedagogical cinema and Cold War paranoia provide the science fiction genre with not two crucial yet distinct influences, but one thoroughly integrated influence.

1. See for example Phil Hardy's discussion of *Destination Moon* in *The Overlook Encyclopedia: Science Fiction* (New York: Overlook, 1984): 124–125.

2. Examples are legion and this is the most introductory of lists including one standard history, one reference work, and one recent popular-press confection. Carlos Clarens *An Illustrated History of Horror and Science Fiction Films* (New York: Da Capo, 1997) 120, 130–132. Again Phil Hardy *The Overlook Encyclopedia: Science Fiction* (New York: Overlook, 1984): 124. David Skal *Screams of Reason* (New York: Norton, 1998): 180, 225.

3. The story of the filmmakers' efforts to render *Destination Moon* documentary in flavor has been well documented. To read the story see Carlos Clarens *An Illustrated History of Horror and Science Fiction Films* (New York: Da Capo, 1997) 120, or Phil Hardy *The Overlook Encyclopedia: Science Fiction* (New York: Overlook, 1984): 125.

4. Ken Smith, *Mental Hygiene: Classroom Films 1945–1970* (New York: Blast Books, 1999): 89–90.

5. Smith, p. 93.

6. For a more elaborate discussion of Plato on music and education see Armand Ambrosini and Michael Lee, *Introduction to Western Concert Music* (Dubuque: Kendall/Hunt 2003) 1–2.

7. Smith, p. 35.

8. In the August 14th, 2004 edition of the *Los Angeles Times*, for example, we find this headline "Melbourne Invaded by Giant Ant Colony." The article quotes Australian entomologist, Elissa Suhr, who uses the word "invade" in the article itself. However, the article points out that Suhr attributes a particular kind of warfare to genetics. One hopes, at least I do, that warfare is not a genetic trait in humans, but a choice.

9. Phil Hardy confirms the ubiquity of this analysis of *Them!*, then tries quite unpersuasively to claim that *Them!* lacks the paranoia found in anti-communist allegories. A contradiction of his reservation can be found in this essay's quote of Dr. Medford's decidedly paranoid narration for the film within the film. Hardy, p. 149.

10. *The Unabridged Random House Dictionary of the English Language* (New York, Random House, 1966).

8

Mondo Barnum

by Doug Bentin

Sometime after P.T. Barnum taught the world to believe none of what it heard and very little of what it saw, photography proliferated and someone came up with the notion that "the camera never lies." Fast forward to the early 1960s. World War II has been over for less than 20 years. The world has seen photographic evidence of the worst effects of the conflict. More images flooded in from Korea. The camera has proven itself once again the provider of "truth." Of course, everyone knew that movie cameras could be made to lie. Hollywood had already proved that over and over again.

Let's stop right here, before we slip into full Mondo Mode. Let's define our subject and attempt to make clear where we're headed. Notice the jocular style in the text above, the slight but clear condescension, the all-too-obvious reveling in our superiority when compared to anyone who isn't privy to our information or who doesn't share our worldview.

Mondo films of course present their own worldview, or at least their own "world," as the term mondo indicates. And it is a world that provides much insight about audience makeup and structure. After all, these are films that often edit nonfiction segments side-by-side with staged re-enactments and fictitious events. To be sure, many audiences of the 1960s probably saw the films and did not notice the variance in levels of authenticity. Others may have questioned the veracity of some sections on the simple level of narrative: do people in a different part of the world really *do* what I'm seeing them do onscreen? Should I believe it or not?

And yet there is another intriguing viewing position that the mondo films helped create, a viewing position assumed by some mockumentary viewers of today. Rather than wonder about or even take a definite stand on some anthropological point regarding a given scene—or for that matter question the narrative on its material or characterological coherence ("People don't behave that way in real life...")—the viewing position I'm describing is one where through purely cinematic means a viewer finds pleasure in proving or disproving the apparent believability of one scene versus another with the use of visual evidence. The viewer in this position becomes an arbiter of verisimilitude.

In modern terms, this position occurs when, for example, a viewer of *The Blair Witch Project* disbelieves the story that actual film students were lost in the woods as a result of certain technological problems with their "found footage." How could they keep filming day after day without recharging their limited supply of batteries? How could they film 16mm footage in low light without focusing their lens by some means and still obtain clear images? Questions of this type regarding modern mockumentaries create a viewing position in which, by gathering visual or even aural proof, the viewer engages actively with the film. Mondo films in which nonfiction footage meets fiction propose even more layers to this cinematic parlor game and do/did so in an earlier time period. And its a game which can even instill in the viewer a certain kind of superiority over the film. "More," the famous theme song of *Mondo Cane*, suggests there is "more than [we] can ever know," and yet situated in this particular viewing position it seems we can know all there is to know in the world of Mondo.

To examine how this operates let's take a look at *Mondo Cane* and the three films its primary directors, Gualtiero Jacopetti and Franco Prosperi, made as follow-ups.[1] Viewing the original Mondo canon, we find several reasons that the filmmakers would fabricate footage ranging from the practical (using faked sections to pad the running time or to be more economical than location shooting) to the "artistic" (fabricating scenes impossible to shoot for the purpose of titillation). We can readily see that there are indeed a handful of definite clues that suggest footage has been faked. These include pointless zooms, a deliberate going out of focus, impossible camera set-ups, and indoor locations to allow for shooting in a geography different than the film claims.

Mondo Cane (*A Dog's World*), is a "documentary" by Gualtiero Jacopetti[2] and Franco Prosperi,[3] with a directorial assist from Paolo Cavara, who soon left the team. It was released in 1962 and went on quickly to achieve notoriety in Europe and in the US. Marketed as a documentary chronicling odd moments in human behavior and Third World cultures, it played like Ripley's *Believe It or Not!* with the inclusion of animal cruelty and an emphasis on the anatomy of women. It was soon being described as a "shockumentary" for the inclusion of scenes of pigs being clubbed to death as prologue to a primitive feast, a piglet being suckled at a woman's breast, and other examples of barbarism, i.e., most behavior that did not adhere to the Western European cultural norm.

Front credits roll over a long tracking shot of a dog on a leash being dragged along in front of a kennel filled with barking, yipping, howling canines. A male "voice of God" narrator tells us that the material we are about to see is true. The fact he believes he needs to reassure us is itself a strong reason to in turn question him and interrogate the accuracy of what he says for the rest of the film.

After all, the first segment in Jacopetti's and Prosperi's mystery tour leaves an odd aftertaste. We are taken to the Italian city that was the birthplace of Rudolph Valentino and we see, crowded into a too-small space, dozens of the silent star's male relatives and we are told in voice over that these men exist in a state of hopefulness that they, too, may be whisked away to lasting glory in LaLaLand.

The aftertaste is secreted with the realization that this film was sold to us as a documentary and it's clear that what we have just seen was staged for the camera. We have no visible reason to doubt that these men are what the VO claims they are, but the camera has moved too freely among the crowd, giving us too many close-ups of faces that have tried to mimic the arrogant snarl of the 1920s Latin lover. It's as if someone collected all the men in the village, showed them a picture of their famous relation in full *Son of the Sheik* costume, and said, "Okay, try to look like that." Why bother? The sequence sets the stage for what is to follow by displaying quirky but harmless behavior. If some audience members think that the worst the filmmakers have in store is a collection of human eccentricities, the shocks that are coming will be that much more jolting.

The movie's second sequence is even more egregious in its fakery as the camera follows film star Rossano Brazzi, whom we are told is the contemporary (1962) equivalent of Valentino, as he goes shopping in a department store. The camera is in a place it wouldn't be for a standard documentary shot, directly over Brazzi's head, looking down. Suddenly, a group of women rush into the frame from the actor's rear and begin to force him along. Cut to a ground level shot, on his right and facing him. Dozens more women enter, reaching out to touch him. Cut back to an overhead shot of over three dozen women supposedly in the thralls of passion, clutching at Brazzi, who is then lifted and carried along, looking like Jesus on his way to the tomb. Cut to ground level, and he is swarmed by, the glamour-starved femmes clustering around him like carp around a cookie. One more cut, this one to the rear as Brazzi's shirt is ripped from his torso.

Unless the filmmakers knew exactly what was going to happen, there would be no reason for them to place their camera where they do, nor, assuming they were using only one camera, would they have been able to move it from floor to ceiling and still capture the action without staging it. In addition, study the expressions on the faces of the women. Despite the fact that they carry on in a way that makes the Bacchae look like the Dashwood sisters, their faces maintain the pleasant expressions of people who are in on a joke that you don't get. Just compare their faces to those of girls at a Beatles concert and it's obvious that the women chasing after Brazzi have been told what to do and are not caught up in the raptures of spontaneous desire.

The recent Blue Underground DVD release of *Mondo Cane* and its sequels includes a series of interviews with several of the films' makers, including the directors. These interviews were conducted many years after the Mondo craze abated so speakers have had time to perfect their stories and carefully consider their wording. Frequently the way they phrase their statements, along with their body language, provides a hint as to real meaning, but it can also disguise meaning.

Listening carefully, you become aware of contradictory statements. At one point cinematographer Benito Frattari says that shooting the films wasn't difficult. "All we had to do was face reality. Because all that we filmed was true, real."[4] Prosperi discusses the method of filming when he says, "Back then the whole world was unprepared for our shooting strategy: slip in, ask, never pay, never re-enact." No statements could be less ambiguous, but composer Riz Ortolani tells us that some of the material used in *Mondo Cane 2* was "acquired," leaving open the supposition–but only a supposition–that some of the acquired footage could have been faked.[5]

And questions of the filmmakers' verisimilitude cause responses founded on rather rudimentary documentary film theory. When accused of being subjective in his approach to the material in the film, Jacopetti replied, "Even if you're intimately, sincerely objective, the very moment that you choose the framing of a shot, automatically, your personal point of view comes out."[6] His answer is little more than a red herring, avoiding a discussion of specific scenes in the Mondo films.

While watching documentaries, one is indeed occasionally taken aback by the camera operator's luck in being set up in exactly the right spot. But this perfect camera placement occurs so often in the Mondo films, the viewer quickly realizes that these set-ups, like the ones in the Rossano Brazzi sequence, are highly unlikely when attributed purely to chance alone.

One sequence in the first film shows a speedboat full of pretty young women zooming around a U.S. Navy ship. In a shot made from above, sailors are seen rushing from one side of the vessel to the other so they can watch the women go by — but if the cameraman did not know that several buxom women were on their way to show off for the men, why was he shooting from above in the first place? There would be no reason to be in that location. That's the tip-off with many of these segments: why would the camera be where it is unless an odd or curious action was prearranged? This scene also reminds us that physical and facial types are rarely mixed in the images on the screen. When pretty girls on the beach are needed to make a point, the shot is rife with nothing but pretty girls. When elderly matrons are the point, we see nothing but. When the directors want nothing but fat, fat is all we see.

In our newfound viewing position, we have just indicted *Mondo Cane* on the grounds of being too perfect in its visual acumen. We have perceived direction beyond what we believe is possible in the visual recording of nonfiction events. Nonfiction film we believe would be hard pressed to feature such planning in the filming of unfolding events in such a repeated fashion. And yet that is what we see not only in *Mondo Cane* but also in its follow-ups.

The initial successor to *Mondo Cane* was *La Donna nel Mondo* (*Women of the World*, 1963), the least controversial and least interesting film of the series. Jacopetti and Prosperi went for pure titillation in this one, producing a documentary as it might have been imagined by Russ Meyer. Viewing this one, it is easy to get the idea that the filmmakers indulged in honest travel to pick up some B roll for future projects and, when they found something they liked, they either shot it on the spot or recreated it later.

Even the moments that appear most spontaneous quickly reveal that they have been patted into shape. Men in the Italian Army seen marching along in long or medium shot look genuine enough, but then we get a quick cut to an attractive young woman watching them on parade, her bosom captured by her bodice but struggling for release, followed immediately by a close-up of a marching soldier's face as he slides his eyes hard to the side to take in the view. The long shot is real; the close-up is staged.

Here our viewing position has enabled us to witness something more complex than a fabricated scene juxtaposed against a nonfiction one in *Mondo Cane*. In instances of this type we see that a single nonfiction scene is tainted with close-ups that reveal their fictional origin by enough variance in lighting to prove our judgment. The real and the fake have combined to create one scene, a scene that we in the end might deem in a sense to be completely fake; the addition of a single staged shot creates a slippery slope down which the entire scene and film slide.

The third film in the series is the one that seems to please Jacopetti and Prosperi the least, perhaps because it is the one that forced Prosperi to admit the kind of fakery that we (perhaps proudly) believe our visual analysis reveals without his help. One of the most startling sequences from any of the Mondo films is the self-immolation of the Buddhist monk from *Mondo Cane 2*. Watching the act unfold takes reinforced nerves and a strong stomach. Jacopetti and Prosperi build to the moment on a foundation of the apparently real. We've seen a sign forbidding the taking of photographs and the narration has underlined this point. We see conflict in the streets between soldiers and citizens. The camera shows us young Buddhist men herded together in a compound having their heads shaved with electric razors as an act of unity with the monks. It all looks like newsreel footage. But our viewing position cannot depend solely on visual analysis.

The narration informs us that "The meekest of men have been swept away by the blackest despair," as Bach's "Tocata and Fugue in D Minor" swells up on the soundtrack. "These are incredible photographs," we are reminded. Then we follow an orange-robed monk on his via dolorosa, the camera swaying to capture the soldiers and the crowd of viewers as well as the victim. Suddenly, we see the monk seated on the ground in the center of a circle of onlookers. Gasoline is poured over his head. He sits still, passively accepting the fate he has chosen as a protest to the war atrocities his country is experiencing. Flames leap up and the monk remains petrified in their midst. Once more, the camera prowls around the crowd, then we cut back to the monk's corpse, fallen over onto its back, the fire continuing to consume the remains.

The film does not identify the monk as Thich Quang Duc, who famously burned himself alive in 1963, and comparisons of the film footage with photos of Duc indicate that the two events are not the same. In fact, they can't be. The *Monde Cane 2* footage was faked. "We were making cinema," Prosperi explained. "We didn't just do documentary: if something was missing to make a scene work well, we would fix it."[7] Prosperi admitted that the monk's suicide was a total fabrication shot in Bangkok using a mannequin.

Accounts of Duc's death indicate that both before and during the conflagration the victim sat perfectly still so it would seem that many viewers of the film can't assume the burning figure's immobility is a dead giveaway—unless these accounts are drawn from watching the movie rather than from life. If descriptions of the event are based on the *Mondo Cane 2* footage, well, to quote John Ford's *The Man Who Shot Liberty Valance* (1962), "When the legend becomes fact, print the legend." But we can compare the positioning of the arms in the film and in photos of the actual event and see that they are different.

Are we to assume that the camera is hidden from the authorities, allowing the documentarians to capture forbidden images? Photos of Duc's auto de fe don't appear to be taken from concealment. And if the camera didn't have to be concealed, why

Mondo Cane 2 offers fabricated footage of the self-immolation of a Buddhist monk.

not set it up so the shots would be clear, unencumbered by spectators? The footage makes no sense, especially as the monks watching the burning body are standing still and not forcing the camera to move. Jacopetti's editing provides other clues that the footage has been staged. His cutting is used to mask what is happening rather than reveal it. We don't see the "monk" in the act of sitting down or falling over, nor can we tell who lights the fire. Finally, as we watch the prone corpse continuing to burn, we see that the arms are in the identical position they formed while the "monk" was seated upright. The hands are held chest high, palms inward, about three inches from the chest. This is not the equestrian position sometimes assumed by bodies after death, but the pose of a mannequin.

Our analysis has reached again a more complex kind of conclusion, and again we have reached it without the need of Jacopetti or Prosperi's assistance. We have used visual analysis, unveiling the reality that editing can be as deceitful in the world of Mondo as the singularity of the image. And our scrutiny has extended to an examination of materials outside of the filmic text by investigating actual photos of Duc's death.

Of course, we should pause to make clear again that ours is a privileged viewing position, one not assumed by most original viewers who were less aware of the fictional elements of what they saw. After all, the most serious charges leveled at any of the original Mondo films in the sixties were the charges of racism and murder that stuck to the fourth film, *Africa Addio* (*Goodbye Africa*, 1966). Carlo Gregoretti, who had introduced Jacopetti and Prosperi years before, accused the directors of allowing a murder to take place so they could film it.

The theme of the film is that Africa had changed beyond all recognition from the fantasyland of our most nobly savage imagination — no more H. Rider Haggard — and that the changes had resulted in bloodshed and a regression to the most ancient level of barbarism. Scenes of animal cruelty, always a staple of the Mondo films, abound, and the filmmakers delight in moments when the ignorant native peoples have overrun white settlements but don't have a clue as to how to cultivate the land or take advantage of contemporary technology. The entire continent is demeaningly referred to as a "black baby." These scenes constitute a hideous mockery of non-whites and are not unlike the more infamous moments in *Birth of a Nation* (1915).

Jacopetti and Prosperi follow a fox hunt in Kenya during which a young Kenyan is substituted for the fox as he runs cross country carrying with him a piece of a fox shipped in from England. The narration refers to him as "treacherous prey," and as he runs the camera moves along beside him, just as it does with the mounted hunters. Preparing for the hunt, black natives have been photographed with surly expressions on their faces, helping white women into their saddles. Again, camera placement is problematic as it forces us to look up at the white women as if we, and their native grooms, were beneath them.

Here again our viewing position has uncovered the hand of direction that has directed a scene beyond the normal possibilities or ethics of documentary. But what we have noticed before seems to have been faked for little reason beyond audience titillation at seeing "more" than we might have thought possible. At this juncture, we have discovered deeper purpose, and purpose that seems to justify, now as then, charges of racism.

But racism was only one of two problems many original viewers of the film raised. An accusation of murder stemmed from a moment in the film when one of the rebels is summarily executed before our eyes. One of the mercenaries turns to him suddenly, raises his pistol and shoots the man, who then drops to the ground. At some point, in describing their time spent with these white soldiers, Jacopetti had made the claim that the mercenaries did whatever the documentarians wanted them to do, and some members of the press assumed they could interpret that to mean that Jacopetti and Prosperi had instructed the whites to shoot this man just to create a stunning moment of cinema. The scandal was moving into court when the Italian judges were told that the death scenes in the film were all fabricated. "It was all a fake," Prosperi admitted, "all staged." Watch him make this confession. His body language and tone of voice are designed to give the impression that the authorities were told the scenes were staged just to get them to drop all charges but that, of course, they were authentic.[8]

But go back and watch the execution with a critical eye. Note that the victim, as soon as he is presumably struck by the bullet, drops below the bottom of the frame so we cannot see him being hit. When we cut to him on the ground, he has fallen on his stomach with his hands under his chest instead of being propelled onto his back by the force of the blow. The camera moves back to the shooter, and when it returns to the victim he has managed to raise his hips, forming a bridge with his body, but not high enough off the ground to be in danger of rolling over. Then the camera tilts up to once again to take in the triggerman, and the victim is out of the frame. After a few seconds, the camera again swings back and tilts down to discover the victim lying on his left side and facing away to the rear. Another of the mercenaries reaches down and grabs him at the waist and drags the body away. We can see the victim's chest which the bullet must have entered, and yet there is no visual evidence of a gunshot fired at point blank range. The camera has been positioned originally and then moved not to allow the viewer to witness the atrocity, but to hide the fact that no atrocity has taken place. The entire execution scene has been carefully choreographed to mislead the viewer — and it worked, at least in so far as the viewers were Italian judges.

After the accusations of racism and subsequent negative publicity that accompanied the release of *Africa Addio*, Jacopetti and Prosperi decided to respond to the criticism with another film, one that in their view couldn't possibly be interpreted as racist. They chose to explore the history and conditions of slavery in the U.S. Eschewing a Ken Burns approach, they concocted a film that would be totally fabricated but one that would resemble what a documentary might have looked like if made in the 19th century. It would be "...a movie as if staging a newsreel back in past times. It would be something bizarre because certainly in the 1800s they wouldn't conceive of documentaries," Jacopetti explained.[9]

Prosperi ingenuously added, "It was going to be a fiction, for the first time in our lives,"[10] but cinematographer Benito Frattari saw the project another way. "The film was born bad and was going to end worse."[11] *Addio Zio Tom* (*Goodbye, Uncle Tom*, 1971) is, if anything, even more brutal than the first four Mondo features, and was — presumably unintentionally — just as open as *Africa Addio*'s charges of racism. After the blistering reviews and audience indifference to their next fiction film, *Mondo Candido*, Jacopetti and Prosperi parted ways. Moving completely towards fiction upset the strange balance of reality and unreality that the mondo films created.

But even before the shattering of the original Mondo partnership, the stained and ripped screens of America's drive-ins suffered no lack of Mondo derivatives. A barrage of Mondo imitators had been gushing forth with varying degrees of competence in the filmmaking all through the 1960s. The imitations were "ghastly stuff, absurdities that people strangely would go to see," Jacopetti complained. "People confused *Mondo Cane* with all that ugly, vulgar junk."[12] And yet, whatever one thinks of their quality, the imitations closely followed the trail blazed by *Mondo Cane*.

Knock-offs like *Mondo Bizarro* (1966, d. Lee Frost), *Mondo Freudo* (1966, d. Lee Frost), *Mondo Mod* (1967, d. Peter Perry), and *Mondo Balordo* (1964, d. Roberto Bianchi Montero) borrowed the techniques developed Jacopetti and Prosperi to stage fabricated events and then disguise what they were up to. The latter film fakes "documentary" footage in a manner far more egregious than anything Jacopetti and Prosperi had been able to get away with, but seems to hope we will believe what we see because of what we hear. The voiceover comes to us thanks to Boris Karloff. *Balordo* attempts to use the familiarity of his voice to inspire trust, to instill credibility. But instead Karloff's longstanding connection to fiction seems to push us into our by-now familiar viewing position, bringing an even greater scrutiny to bear on how the film constructs its fabrications.

On the one hand, the very penetration of the term "Mondo" into so many film titles and contexts—e.g., Russ Meyer's *Mondo Topless* (1966)—rendered it diffuse and near useless. But on the other hand the term "Mondo" eventually became a signal for a cinematic brew of fact and fiction to be taken with little seriousness; it became an appropriate term to denote the viewing position we've analyzed.

Of course, a later generation of imitators mimicked Jacopetti and Prosperi in style but not title. The *Faces of Death* series began in 1978. If its own publicity is to be believed, and at this point we should be inclined not to, the original film was banned in 46 countries. But it wasn't until the video revolution of the mid–1980s that the film became widely seen in the US. The film offered Mondo-style compilations that lingered on the theme of death, whether human or animal. It's numerous successors (*Faces of Death 2* in 1981, *3* in 1985, *4* in 1990, *5* in 1995, and *6* in 1996!) offered much of the same fare. All of what we could say of the earlier Mondo films could be said of their *Faces* offspring.

Well, almost all, anyhow. One crucial element had changed, affecting forever our Mondo-inspired viewing position and perhaps all viewing positions. The proliferation of home video allowed for not only repeat viewing of entire films with ease, but also of specific scenes, specific edits, and specific shots. Our ability to stop and start a film, spreading out our viewing over hours, days, or weeks changed what it means to be a filmgoer (whose "going" leads him or her to a video rental store perhaps, instead of a theater). And it has definitely changed and increased our ability to keep images from washing over us too quickly, allowing us to perform the kinds of investigations our Mondo viewing position requires.

Of course, the legacy of *Mondo Cane* and its illegitimate brethren has become all too obvious with the proliferation of alien autopsies, Blair witches, Project Greenlights, and a slew of television "reality" programs that are, in fact, about as real as the Piltdown Man. Jeffrey Sconce, from Northwestern University, has observed that "The whole documentary wing at [the Fox Channel] uses the Mondo films as their playbook."[13]

But its legacy also means the creation of a unique way to view a film, a viewing position that can in the extreme tend towards the same jocular, condescending words that open this very essay: a position that makes us appear learned and skilled viewers, superior to that which our eyes see. It's also though a viewing position where the pleasures we gain occur due to our own initiative, through our own investigations of what is real or not, through our own game. It's a viewing position that allows us to engage with film in a manner unlike almost any other relationship of spectator to cinema. It's a Mondo-viewing position.

And as Jacopetti and Prosperi told us, it's a Mondo world. But the "more that we [could] never know," we can indeed learn and know. Because in the end, it's not *Mondo Cane* that counts, it's Mondo Barnum.

---

1. See *The Mondo Cane Collection* on DVD from Blue Underground, 2004. The eight disc set contains all five of Jacopetti's and Prosperi's Mondo films, with both the full European and edited English language versions of the films and a documentary, *The Godfathers of Mondo*, directed by David Gregory.

2. Jacopetti was a journalist before entering the world of filmmaking. He was co-founder of the magazine *L'Espresso*.

3. Prosperi's background was in cultural anthropology, in which field he studied tribal customs and taboos.

4. Interview with Franco Prosperi in *The Godfathers of Mondo*, d. David Gregory, 2003.

5. Interview with Riz Ortolani, *ibid.*

6. Interview with Gualtiero Jacopetti, *ibid.*

7. Prosperi, *ibid.*

8. *Ibid.*

9. Jacopetti, *ibid.*

10. Prosperi, *ibid.*

11. Interview with Benito Frattari, *ibid.*

12. Jacopetti, *ibid.*

13. Interview with Jeffrey Sconce, *ibid.*

9

In Search of Questions, or, A New Age Film Odyssey

by Gary D. Rhodes

The Ultimate Trip Begins

Spring, 1968. Stanley Kubrick's monumental film *2001: A Space Odyssey* quickly becomes a hit film, breaking records at numerous theaters in cities like Los Angeles, Boston, and Washington D.C. It strikes a chord with audiences spellbound by its special effects and psychedelic imagery. For many viewers at the time, *2001*'s take on evolution truly becomes the "ultimate trip."

Some four years in the making, *2001* underwent its own evolution during the production and post-production phase. For example, according to some sources Kubrick considered shooting head-and-shoulder style interviews with scientists to ground the various sections of the film with more clear narrative explanation. He also planned for Douglas Rain to read voiceover narration during the "Dawn of Man" sequence.[1] Though he did abandon such documentary techniques, his resulting film still exudes a nonfiction feel due to its extreme attention to detail and scientific accuracy. *2001*'s pacing and slow average shot lengths also feed into a documentary tradition, the camera holding deliberately on each object that it records.

The tremendous success of *2001* puzzled many in the film industry of 1968. After all, from MGM studio executives to major film critics, many viewers responded to the film negatively. Complaints were numerous, but most resulted from narrative head-scratching. What did the film mean? What was it all about? And just who or what was behind the monoliths, or "slabs" as the press generally called them at the time?

The Catholic Legion of Decency answered that second question with God, a Christian God, and endorsed the film heartily to film-going Catholics in the US. And they weren't alone.[2] *Rolling Stone* wrote about an audience member at the Los Angeles Cinerama who leapt from his seat screaming the pronouncement that "It's God! It's God!"[3] Even unimpressed critics like Dan Morgenstern at *Newsweek* suggested a traditional idea of "God" as being at play in the film.[4]

But for many viewers, the novelization of the film by Arthur C. Clarke — which hit bookstands after the film's premiere — became a kind of guidebook to unlocking *2001*'s meaning. And the answers it held hardly suggested a Christian God pulling the puppet strings of humanity. Aliens, however undefined, were at the end of the Star Gate; aliens had helped the man-apes at the very "Dawn of Man." This explanation heartened many film viewers on the film's original release, as Philip Strick wrote in his review for *Sight and Sound*. He noticed that the film was the "source of considerable pleasure as much to the UFO spotters as to the Bible readers...."[5]

When asked about this point by *Playboy* magazine in 1968, Stanley Kubrick offered a response that mediated the God-alien debate. "...these [alien] beings would be gods to billions of less advanced races in the universe, just as man would be a god to an ant that somehow comprehended man's existence.... [Aliens like those in *2001*] would be incomprehensible to us except as gods; and if the tendrils of their consciousness ever brushed men's minds, it is only the hand of God we could grasp as an explanation."[6]

Of Gods and Aliens

In 1968, as viewers screened *2001*, then-unknown Erich von Däniken copyrighted his first book *Chariots of the Gods? Unsolved Mysteries of the Past* in the United States. European editions appeared as early as 1967, though American readers had to wait until a 1969 Putnam edition.

Born in 1935 in Zofingen, Switzerland, von Däniken went to school at the Catholic College Saint-Michel in Fribourg. While there, he dedicated much of his time to reading and analyzing ancient religious works. Never finishing his degree, von Däniken began work at a five-star Swiss hotel. By the mid–1960s, he had become its managing director.[7] His interests in ancient civilizations and religions continued and increased to the point that he developed the basic theory for which he would become world-renowned. Alien visitors from outer space — "Ancient Astronauts," as von Däniken calls them — came to earth centuries ago to convey important knowledge and assistance to ancient civilizations across the globe. As he began to write and compile thoughts drawn from various texts and countries, von Däniken realized that he needed to visit the places he believed held secrets of ancient extraterrestrial influence.[8]

"Borrowing" some 400,000 Swiss francs from the hotel, von Däniken traveled to Peru, Easter Island, Mexico, Lebanon, Egypt, and elsewhere in search of proof that would support his beliefs. His pilgrimages yielded much in the way of documentary evidence, but such findings were at least temporarily bittersweet. The hotel charged him with embezzlement, and von Däniken even spent a short time in jail.[9]

But the trial came just before the initial publication of his theory and its supporting research; as a result, the publicity only buoyed von Däniken's emergent fame. *Chariots of the Gods?* hit some bookstores while the author was behind bars, and it immediately became a bestseller in Germany and then in the United States. The book would go on to sell some seven million copies and be translated into 28 languages.

Chariots of the Gods? fascinated readers with a wide array of examples supporting its thesis, but under even mild scrutiny much of what he writes fails to remain intact. Some evidence von Däniken literally invented (e.g., a falsified "ancient" clay pot), while some evidence he distorted (e.g., the Sirius-based Egyptian calendar). Biblical quotations come out of context (e.g., Ezekiel's visions), and revelatory mathematical formulas offer proof of nothing (e.g., the area of the base of the Pyramid of Cheops divided by twice its height is allegedly the figure *Pi*). Famed scientist Carl Sagan was one of many to puncture holes in the *Chariots'* wheels, a service also performed by most of the respectable book critics who published reviews.[10]

Undaunted by his detractors, von Däniken quickly produced such follow-up books as *Gods from Outer Space* (1970), *The Gold of the Gods* (1972), *In Search of Ancient Gods: My Pictorial Evidence for the Impossible* (1973), *Miracles of the Gods: A New Look at the Supernatural* (1974), and many others. At the dawn of the 21st century, over 56 million copies of his works were in print.[11] Along with print media, von Däniken has continued to pronounce his views to live audiences, having given some 3000 lectures since *Chariots of the Gods?* was first printed. Like von Däniken, thousands, perhaps millions of readers have not let critics deter their interest or belief in ancient astronauts.

The New Age Is Upon Us

Both the film *2001: A Space Odyssey* and the book *Chariots of the Gods?* offer the same suggestion, that aliens landed on earth and helped early humans. The words of Kubrick and von Däniken are strikingly similar in their descriptions of how advanced aliens would appear to be gods to early man. Considering the documentary elements of *2001* and the very questionable science brought to bear in *Chariots*, an ostensibly nonfiction work, the line between fact and fiction blurs in both texts. Both are not only similar in their basic theses, but they are also comparable in belonging to an even wider US culture in the 1960s and 1970s.

The counterculture of the sixties openly questioned traditional religion and morality while seeking and selecting new options to replace or augment the old. Often referred to as the "New Age Movement," it did not represent an organized school of beliefs with generally recognized leaders. In retrospect, it appears eclectic, fragmented, and even contradictory. Its adherents struggled for a utopian ideal, but beyond that, the polyvalent New Age was hardly bound by consistent intellectual and ideological doctrine.[12]

Clearly some of the answers the New Age sought are answers that have been asked throughout preceding centuries. The Theosophy and Spiritualist movements—at their peaks in the 1920s and 1930s—mark twentieth century predecessors to the New Age.[13] The alternative spirituality of US author and occultist Alice Bailey is an even more obvious link in the chain that leads to the 1960s New Age. In 1944, for example, she wrote that "The New Age is upon us and we are witnessing the birth pangs of the new culture and civilization."[14] Her writings became a major influence on the otherworldly pursuits of the 1960s.

Tied to past interests in occultism, psychic phenomena, magic, secret lore, Egyptology, astrology, and paganism, the New Age of the sixties embraced a variety of mystical subjects, including then-recent concerns like UFO encounters.[15] Some New Age philosophy lingered on and adopted a kind of spirituality taken from Eastern mysticism and religion. Some New Age ideas centered on the self-realizations of the individual and on the present tense, life on earth in the here-and-now.[16] Others considered the individual's ties to the greater whole of life on earth and to life after death. Anti-materialism, holistic medicine, ecology, channeling, re-incarnation: these are but a few of the various strains of New Ageism that sparked interest and controversy in an era that propelled both *2001* and *Chariots of the Gods?* to major audience acceptance.[17]

What we can take from this cursory glance at the New Age movement is that in many ways the question *becomes* the answer. In the sociopolitical milieu of the 1960s, the sheer act of questioning the status quo meant as much or more than any particular answer that might emerge from, say, studying Egyptology or UFO visitations. The unyielding ambiguity of *2001: A Space Odyssey* offers such a challenge to traditional belief systems; viewers walk away only with the ability to pose questions. And the very punctuation mark in the title of *Chariots of the Gods?* underscores the desire to question, to always question. This is the realm of the "What If?"–a realm where those two words alone are more important than any that follow.

The Chariot Race Begins

The success of the film *2001* and the book *Chariots of the Gods?* in part revealed audience interest in exploring questions related to the New Age. Their startling and challenging new questions were buttressed by traditional modes of presentation (e.g., film and print), as well as some traditional modes of communication (e.g., the documentary feel of *2001* and the scientific rhetoric of von Däniken). These texts and their audiences fueled the desire for more cinematic exploration of the question "What If?," beginning with the most likely candidate, a movie adaptation of von Däniken himself.

Appearing in 1970, the film documentary *Chariots of the Gods?* was directed by Harald Reinl and shot by Ernst Wild. Director Reinl had years earlier appeared in several Arnold Fanck mountain films and had been an assistant to Leni Riefenstahl on *Tiefland* (1954).[18] He made approximately sixty films of his own, but *Chariots of the Gods?* marked his only Academy Award nomination. Though it didn't win Best Documentary for 1970, its nomination did add an air of credibility to the film.[19]

Curiously, though von Däniken's book is credited and closely followed, he is himself not interviewed on camera or even mentioned in the film's narration. It is unknown whether or not Reinl sought to avoid at least some of von Däniken's credibility problems intentionally by changing the title, or whether or not von Däniken's lack of direct participation in terms of on-camera interviews or otherwise was connected to his jail sentence. Perhaps both factors played a role in the making of the film.

But strangely, von Däniken's absence actually helps to reinforce his book's persuasive tactics, particularly his tendency towards self-effacing third-person rhetoric. The absence of the first-person "I" gives von Däniken's prose the legitimizing tone of autonomous (and anonymous) authority. In the film, an unknown narrator (and one who changes depending on the language of the release print) helps preserve this tactic, as does the use of specific persuasive devices like passive voice. "The theory has been advanced," the voiceover offers with regard to a discussion of whether Egyptians learned embalming techniques from extra-terrestrials. Likewise, the use of an unnamed "one," because "Surely there were models—*one* is tempted to say one model—for these deities found on all continents." Retaining von Däniken's ambiguous yet authoritative tone while excluding von Däniken's physical presence encourages the impression of free floating information handed down by the classic documentarian "voice of God," rather than contestable claims concocted by a specific author.

Repeatedly, the film asks, "is this a mere coincidence?" The most obvious borrowing from von Däniken's persuasive strategies is the use of the rhetorical question, something the author once himself claimed appears in his book on 238 occasions. While the film hardly employs the tactic to such excess, we repetitively hear the narrator carefully ask questions to lead us to the hoped-for conclusion. After all, the film asks the audience, "Could their knowledge have come from extra-terrestrials?" "Is this sketch of a space module?" "Could it still be *mere coincidence*?"

Certainly some of what the film shows us is indeed more than mere coincidence, such as the infamous "primitive" electric cell that von Däniken describes in his book. Housed at a Baghdad museum, the electric cell allegedly dates to the period of Christ. The item becomes a counterpoint of discussion in the film just as it had in the book. Again Reinl both adapts and adopts the foibles of von Däniken, because the item is a fake, made by an Iraqi paid by von Däniken himself.

To strengthen von Däniken's arguments of visual similarities between ancient artwork and modern spacecraft, Reinl uses editing in tandem with narration to persuade the audience. "Doesn't that look familiar?" the narrator asks when Reinl shows a Biblical sketch showing angels which have metallic-like legs and then offering a photograph of a NASA lunar lander. In Reinl's hands, even a Russian building jutting into the sky edited against a similar angle on a NASA rocket (both being examples of "man reaching for the sky") visually connects such disparate material in a manner beyond what von Däniken achieved in his book.

These editing choices accelerate in complexity as the film progresses. Whereas Reinl initially takes us from one country to the next, he later repeats imagery from several countries in an attempt to suggest that, beyond mere alien visitation, artwork and descriptions around the globe stem from the inspiration of the same basic visitors. The editing shifts from image to image, which are no longer attributed to their geography or culture, and blurs them into a visual menagerie suited to the film's argument.

"We thought it impossible that more compelling evidence for the visitations by extra-terrestrial beings existed, but they do." So the narrator tells us at our last major geographical destination: the Nazca lines of Peru, large ancient drawings on the landscape, visible in their entirety only from the air. That they are landing strips guiding alien visitors is the additional evidence to which the narrator refers. But what is fascinating is that when the narrator speaks about "compelling evidence," it is the first time the film overtly adopts the thesis of "God was an astronaut." The script has carefully kept a precise thesis at bay just as it has attributions for the use of passive voice. The caution of rhetorical questions is replaced finally with the film accepting responsibility for its own argument, finally placed boldly before the audience.

All of these tactics—adopted from von Däniken and re-imagined through Reinl's strong visual sensibilities and editing skill — are couched within a documentary film that couples cinematography shot over much of the globe with a traditional male voice as narrator. Almost no head-and-shoulders interviews carry the story. *Chariots of the Gods?* roots its startling thesis in the traditional and longstanding documentary approach of Grierson, of Lorentz, and of the *March of Time* newsreels. Imagery and utterance combine to lead the audience to a monolithic conclusion to their esoteric questions: the exalted truth, rendered impersonally and without apparent bias. The cinematic apparatus of the past supports the New Age questions of the "now."

The Bright Rays of the Sunn

The box-office and subsequent televised broadcast success of *Chariots of the Gods?* vividly illustrate the widespread and continuing audience interest in seeing the "What If?" unfold on the screen. Sunn Classic, a small Mormon-owned company based in Salt Lake City, understood the success of *Chariots of the Gods?* and the potential in making "documentaries" based on subjects of the unknown and mysterious.

Sunn also understood movie audiences of the day, and throughout the 1970s surveyed filmgoers in shopping malls with the question "Which of the following movies would you see based on the title alone?" Their demographical field research served them well, as Sunn Classic found strong box office success throughout the 1970s, in part due to the inexpensive nature of their films and in part due to their ability to provide audiences with what they seemingly wanted to see.[20] *The Life and Times Grizzly Adams* (1974) and *Hanger 18* (1980) brought audiences to the theaters in respectable numbers, but it was the form of documentary that allowed Sunn to tap into New Age questions most clearly. And the enormous success of their first, a Bigfoot film called *Mysterious Monsters* (1975), paved the way for an entire series of Sunn Classic "What If?" productions.

Mysterious Monsters begins with a pre-credits discussion by narrator Peter Graves, who essentially repeats one of the major lines from some *Chariots* publicity, that the "film you are about to see was filmed by many teams of cameramen in more than 100 locations around the globe." He adds that: "Scientists representing the world's foremost research centers took part in the examination of the evidence. The facts that will be presented are true. This may be the most startling film you will ever see." It is only after these words are spoken that the Sunn logo appears and the title sequence begins. The film actually attempts to step outside of itself and add commentary on its proceedings in order to convey verisimilitude and a serious tone.

Of equal importance is the fact that the pre-credits sequence is spoken by Graves, a recognizable actor who is the audience's source of information and much onscreen action. Not only is Graves posed as existing outside the film in its opening moments, but he also exists outside the film to the degree that he plays himself as host. Graves-as-host depends on our familiarity with him as he exists apart from and prior to *Mysterious Monsters*. We know him, so therefore we should believe him. If we are uncertain of the latter claim, Graves tries to buttress it at various stages of the narration. "Some of you *like me* may have been skeptical about these reports...." Graves is thus positioned as the formerly skeptical observer partaking in audience reservations and objections. By implication, if Graves shared viewers' concerns and was converted, then they should feel confident in removing their skepticism as well.

The film attempts to further Graves' credibility by placing him into the geography where Bigfoot sightings have happened, and–even more commonly–into environments sporting signs of science and education. He appears in various labs where Bigfoot sound recordings or hair samples are tested, for example. But most notably, he appears in the Sunn Classic office of knowledge. Bookcases line the wall behind a large important looking desk along with charts and maps. Such trappings would become crucial in future Sunn documentaries. Signifiers of intelligence and academic authenticity envelope the onscreen host in order to reflect their ethos back on him.

As with *Chariots of the Gods?*, *Mysterious Monsters* uses a carefully chosen array of words in the narration script to support its claims. Sometimes it is the lack of attribution ("Some claim..."), sometimes it is using legalese to seem more believable ("Exhibit A"). We hear unnecessary details that attempt to sound important or credible, such as irrelevant details about the "135mm telephoto" lens and "spring wind" camera used to film one bit of footage. And we get bizarre logical formulations like the following: "If this [Bigfoot home movie] is legitimate, then there can no longer be any question about Bigfoot's existence."

Mysterious Monsters leaves the subject of Bigfoot during its middle third to discuss the Loch Ness Monster and the Abominable Snowman, providing found footage, photos, and artifacts onscreen to convince us that these creatures do exist. The film's argument in large part actually becomes one through which we should believe in Bigfoot because the film has proved Nessie and the Yeti exist. And if two monsters exist, a third surely must. Like *Chariots of the Gods?*, the film most clearly states its thesis during its closing minutes. The final words of *Mysterious Monsters* do not ask if Bigfoot exists, but — having "proven he does" — ask whether he is "Man ... or Beast?"

But the Sunn Classic style departs notably from the world of von Däniken when it repeatedly uses recreations of Bigfoot encounters. Handheld camera becomes Bigfoot POV, as the monster stalks the Pacific Northwest, stumbling across some of the same people we see in quick "eyewitness" head-and-shoulder sound bites. Many of these people go unnamed, so their status as anything more than bad actors is definitely in question. And the recreations of Bigfoot events—which dominate much screen time and much of the evidence pool — are never even acknowledged as re-enactments.

This collection of questionable data, logical fallacies, and cinematic tricks won over audiences in a way that exceeded the promise of *Chariots of the Gods?*, raking in millions of dollars at the box office.[21] Whether or not they actually believed the film's evidence, audiences certainly seemed to enjoy sharing the questions the film posed. Future Sunn "documentaries" of the same ilk posed questions about everything from ESP and near death experiences to the precise location where Noah's Ark docked land. And in doing so, they relied on much the same logical structure and cinematic style of *Mysterious Monsters*.

For *The Amazing World of Psychic Phenomena* (1977), Sunn hired actor Raymond Burr to fill Graves' shoes as host. The bulk of the time, however, they relied on Brad Crandall, more familiar by his baritone voice than by name. For films like *Beyond and Back* (1978), *In Search of Noah's Ark* (1976), *The Lincoln Conspiracy* (1977), *Encounters with Disaster* (1979), *The Bermuda Triangle* (1979), and *In Search of the Historic Jesus* (1980), Crandall helmed the desk and bookshelves, pointing to charts of everything from the coast off of Florida to the Shroud of Turin.

The persuasive tactics of these films follow largely the pattern set forth in *Mysterious Monsters* and *Chariots of the Gods?* Slippery slopes abound, as in sentences like "Since we've already determined *The Bible* is archeologically accurate...." And these films pose cautious language in their narration ("Some [unnamed] scientists...") until the final minutes, shifting to a clarity of thesis and belief in it. Submitted evidence of Noah's Ark by the final reel is, after all, "overwhelming." Crandall speaks in rhetorical questions with some regularity. And as Graves told us earlier, we hear Crandall say again and again at the beginning of Sunn films: "The motion picture you are about to see may be the most startling...."

Stock footage marks these films, from nonfiction footage of NASA rockets and World War II aircraft (e.g., *The Bermuda Triangle*) to clips from earlier fictional films of Roman battles (e.g., *In Search of the Historic Jesus*), replete with scratches and pops. On the one hand, this material — as well as historic photographs — allowed Sunn to take up screen time inexpensively. On the other hand, worn film footage and black-and-white photographs or newspaper headlines attempt to bestow a kind of authenticity to the films.

We can easily point to faked material in these documentaries too. Crandall stands in front of an obvious fake of Jesus' tomb for *In Search of the Historic Jesus*. Faked aerial photos of Noah's Ark appear for *In Search of Noah's Ark*. And even faked sound bites, with actors portraying actual people, appear in films like *The Bermuda Triangle*. A reel-to-reel recorder plays an actor's voice in *The Bermuda Triangle*, with no indication that the material heard is anything other than "real."

But by far the most common faked material in these films appears in the form of recreations of actual events. Though featuring limited special effects and generally poor acting, these re-enactments are never indicated as being just that: re-enactments. Granted, few would be fooled by these scenes, particularly when they are historical events of more than a century old: Lincoln's assassination, for example. But it is the historic setting in tandem with cheap production values that reveals these fakes, never the Sunn films themselves.

What the Sunn "documentaries" managed to do with admirable box-office success is to give the "What If?" audience of *Chariots of the Gods?* similar storylines that questioned the status quo of accepted science. And these films posed their striking questions by coupling the rather traditional documentary forms of *Chariots* with on-

The reliance on low budget "recreations" in Sunn Classic films can be seen in this image from *In Search of Noah's Ark* (1976), with Vern Adix as Noah (woman uncredited).

camera narrators and the budget-conscious recreations of historical events seen in many classroom/educational films.

Seeing Tommorrow Today

By 1980, the Sunn Classic documentaries were essentially at an end. Perhaps it was the sheer proliferation of Sunn product and their various imitators during the 1970s that saturated the market.[22] By 1980, Robert Guenette — director of *Mysterious Monsters* and a cofounder of the International Documentary Association — directed *The Man Who Saw Tomorrow* based on the predictions of Nostradamus. He made the film for Warner Brothers rather than Sunn, although the formula was identical. Orson Welles acted as the onscreen host in the mold of Brad Crandall and Peter Graves, with recreations and historic footage carrying much of the running time. But unlike Graves in *Mysterious Monsters*, Welles distances himself from the viewer and the film as much as possible, forcing into the narration a line of dialogue that conveys his disbelief and even disdain in Nostradamus' predictions. Welles' skepticism shows that even a salaried actor could not be convinced to give credence to the questions.

Perhaps the traditional rhetorical and cinematic paradigms of persuasion were by then too ingrained in the mind of increasingly sophisticated audiences. Perhaps US viewers had become so accustomed to questioning the status quo in the wake of the counterculture movement and Vietnam and Watergate that "What If?" was more commonplace than startling. And perhaps some yearned for what Reagan and the 1980s promised: a return to Truth and Trust and Values that could return to a Status Quo that needn't be questioned at all.

Of course these "perhaps" are themselves locked in questions, such as the extent to which audiences believed anything Sunn and von Däniken told them. Watching "What If?" hardly means subscribing to specific answers like alien landing strips or Bigfoot hair samples. Trustworthiness isn't nearly as necessary to pose a question as to give detailed talks on near-death experiences or the Shroud of Turin. *2001: A Space Odyssey*, after all, seems more "real" to many of us than any segment *Chariot of the Gods?* or *The Bermuda Triangle*.

At the least, though, these alleged documentaries, with all their cinematic slight of hand tricks, echoed onscreen the questions offered by *2001* and von Däniken and the New Age. And like the hyper real sensibilities of 2001, they situated themselves somewhere between the Fiction of Méliès and the Nonfiction of Lumière, a cinematic nether region in which the question was the most important answer.

1. LoBrutto, Vincent. *Stanley Kubrick: A Biography*. New York: Da Capo, 1999: 278–279.
2. "Catholics Doubt *2001* For Kids." *Variety* 17 Apr. 1968: 7.
3. Quoted in LoBrutto, 312.
4. *Newsweek*, 15 April 1968: 97.
5. *Sight and Sound*, summer 1968: 153–54.
6. Phillips, Gene D. *Stanley Kubrick Interviews*. Jackson: University Press of Mississippi, 2001, p. 50.
7. "Erich von Däniken." Available at www.mnsu.edu/emuseum/information/biography/uvwxyz/vondaniken_erich.html. Accessed on 2 Feb. 2004.
8. *Ibid*.
9. Souter, Gavin. "The Disappointing But Profitable Mysteries of Erich von Daniken." *The Advertiser*. 31 Mar. 1973.
10. *Ibid*.
11. "VP Highlights Mystery-Park's Advantages in Wall Street Transcript Interview." Available at www.twst.com/notes/articles/lav014.html. Accessed 2 Feb. 2004.
12. Sutcliffe, Steven J. *Children of the New Age: A History of Spiritual Practices*. New York: Routledge, 2003: 9–17.
13. Heelas, Paul. *The New Age Movement*. Cambridge: Blackwell, 1996: 44–45.
14. Sutcliffe, p. 49–54.
15. *Ibid*, p. 66.
16. *Ibid*, p. 114–15.
17. Heelas, p. 15–38.
18. "Harald Reinl." Internet Movie Data Base (http://imdb.com/name/nm0718243/). Accessed 2 Feb. 2004.
19. Kaplan, Mike, ed. *Variety Presents the Complete Book of Major Show Business Awards*. New York: Garland, 1985: 69.
20. Nelmes, Jill. *An Introduction to Film Studies*. 2nd Edition. New York: Routledge, 1999: 47.
21. Unfortunately little has been written on the history Sunn Classic films.
22. Their imitators include, for example, *Mysteries From Beyond Earth* (R.C. Riddell and Associates, 1975) and *UFOS: It Has Begun* (Gold Key, 1979, with Rod Serling, Jose Ferrer, and Burgess Meredith as narrators).

10

Artifice and Artificiality in Mockumentaries

by Gerd Bayer

Even though mockumentary films represent a rather recent sub-genre of the history of cinema, they already come in a number of different shapes and flavors. Some simply try to amuse, others aim for more parodistic effects. Some allude in a reverential manner to earlier films, others introduce a more skeptical note into the discourse on the role of cinematic texts. This essay will concentrate on the latter variety, on mockumentary films that provide a commentary, through their parody, on the state and role of visual media. Since mockery and parody rely heavily on the delivery of precise verbal gestures, the question of style is of prime concern to an understanding of the subtle workings of mockumentaries. Whereas documentary films claim to present to their viewers real events, mockumentaries refer less directly to the everyday reality of their audience. The precise relationship between the filmic text and its purportedly genuine object is determined by its level and degree of artificiality, that is, by its artfulness.

This chapter, then, will outline some of the aesthetic strategies used in such different mockumentaries as Woody Allen's *Zelig* (1983), Rob Reiner's *This Is Spinal Tap!* (1984), Rémy Belvaux, André Bonzel, and Benoît Poelvoorde's *Man Bites Dog* (1992), as well as Peter Jackson and Costa Botes's *Forgotten Silver* (1997), commenting also on the films by Christopher Guest. The machinery for creating both the humor and the criticism inherent in mockumentary films rests on a stylistic program that emphasizes the constructedness of film, its artifice, with the intention of glossing over its artificiality. In an ironic twist on viewers' expectations, mockumentaries make use of the mediatory qualities of film for heightening the alleged veracity of their content, or rather, for emphasizing the unavoidable status of film as a mediation and therefore interpretation of reality. I argue, first of all, that the ostentatious use of artifice in mockumentary films functions as a means to lessen the sense of artificiality usually attached to cinematic texts and, in a second step, that this emphasis on the mediality of film derives from the metanarrative criticism of mockumentaries.

Most mockumentary films undermine their viewers' critical disbelief through the use of standard attributes of documentary film making, such as interviews with "genuine" experts on the themes portrayed in the films or the interweaving of "authentic" documents. In addition to including generic clues derived from documentaries' project of "representing reality," to follow the title of Bill Nichols's important book, mockumentaries make the production side of filming visible, thereby creating in their viewers a conscious awareness that they are indeed watching a film, that is, a constructed reality. This flaunting of a film's artifice ironically heightens the sense that what is witnessed must indeed be a genuine document, since it is not so much *represented*, but rather *presented*. The presentational characteristics of mockumentaries include a range of stylistic features: frontal camera shots in which the objects acknowledge the presence of the camera, mirrors that disclose the actual film equipment, and, most frequently, unstable camera moves that aim to emphasize the unstaged and spontaneous filming process. As a result, the viewers are drawn into the cinematic narrative. This leads to an overlap of realities between the lived experience of the viewer and the presented reality within the film. Mockumentary films thus recreate the aesthetics of cinéma vérité films from the 1960s. However, as critics at the time were already quick to point out, the intended veracity of this style should not obscure the fact that even cinéma vérité films are representations: "The issues of mediation were not removed by the new style. Shots were still framed. Films were still edited. Stories were still created."[1] The realization of this mediated role of cinema returns again with the emphasis that mockumentaries place on a film's artifice. This time around, though, the mediation itself becomes a central concern for the makers of mockumentary films.

It is within the context of artifice that mockumentary films approach the relationship between film and reality. There seems to exist an unexpected contradiction between the effects that artifice and artificiality have on viewers: mockumentaries take pride in their artifice; they present their constructedness. By doing so, they manipulate their viewers' perception, causing them not simply to suspend disbelief, but rather to discard all skepticism. Within the framework of mockumentary film making, the presence of staged artifice disavows a film's actual artificiality. Whereas the cinematic aesthetics of fiction films—through its perfected hyperrealism of imagery—clearly if subconsciously indicates that the visual representations really must be artificial, the absence of this perfection within the (mocku-) documentary genre aims to indicate that reality is presented in its actual form. It is partly through the inclusion of intentional imperfection that mockumentaries create their false sense of reality, a process which relies heavily on genre traditions that viewers decode into specific expectations. As a number of critics, such as Jane Roscoe and Craig Hight in *Faking It*, have already pointed out, the question of a film's generic affiliation is answered to a significant extent by the knowledge and behavior of its viewers. It is they who determine — during the act of watching the film, and based on their specific expectations— what the film will be. In order to come to an appreciation of the parodistic and hence critical characteristics of mockumentaries, viewers need to be aware of the cinematic traditions that are being mocked.[2]

The Camera Lie

Despite some shared strategies, the films considered here present a range of different approaches to subverting the genre of documentary film making. For example, Rob Reiner's film *This Is Spinal Tap!*, a "rockumentary" about a British band, opens with ostentatious indicators of its "documentary" character. However, the viewers grow increasingly suspicious, mostly because of the ubiquitous use of satire, that what they are watching must be fiction after all. In the process of satirizing its topic, the film exaggerates the portrayal of rock music clichés to the point where the humoristic side of the presentation outbalances the initial willingness to see the film as a documentary. It ends up being, predominantly, a mockery of its topic. As one of the earliest and most successful examples of the mockumentary film genre, *Spinal Tap* already incorporates many aspects that will resurface in later mockumentaries, most importantly the projecting of the process of film making onto the screen. The first minutes of the film emphasize the artifice of *Spinal Tap* through the commentary by the film's (alleged) director, Martin DiBergi, played by the actual director, Rob Reiner. The film also makes visible the film-making equipment and acknowledges on the screen the presence of the film crew, thereby accentuating the mediated nature of the presented images.

The presence of the camera on the movie screen as a device that reminds the audience of the constructedness and mediality of the cinematic image follows in a

This Is Spinal Tap! (1984) exaggerates the clichés of rock music within a documentary style. Back row, *left to right*: David Kaff, R.J. Parnell. Front row, *left to right*: Tony Hendra, Harry Shearer, Michael McKean, and Christopher Guest.

tradition that dates back to the beginnings of cinema. Dziga Vertov, in *Man with a Movie Camera* (1929), repeatedly returns to the image of the cameraman with his apparatus. During one sequence, Vertov shows the actual filming of scenes that were seen earlier, and will be seen again later in the film. In another part of the film, he famously includes the process of film cutting and editing, thereby emphasizing that filmmakers have significant control over the outcome of their work. In a similar fashion Zacharias Kunuk's *Atanarjuat* (2001), a postcolonial response to Robert Flaherty's *Nanook of the North* (1922) that implicitly questions the imperialistic aspects of the earlier film, finishes, while the credits are already scrolling across the screen, with footage shot during the making of the film. Not only does the presence of high-tech equipment on the arctic film set provide a contrast with the traditional life-style of the film's characters, the modern clothes of the actors, along with the disclosure of the camera, also emphasize the filmic medium. The superimposition of cinema as medium onto the film, as in *Man with a Movie Camera*, and the insistence on the mediality of the camera, as in *Atanarjuat*, stand for a metanarrative tradition in the history of cinema that also characterizes the parodistic intertextuality of mockumentaries.

With the (lying) camera established as a medializing apparatus, viewers can now actively participate in the films. In Woody Allen's *Zelig*, the cinematographic trajectory follows other fake documentaries, such as Mitchell Block's *No Lies* (1975),[3] but both the filmic environment and the impressive trick photography raise not so much the question of reality and satire,[4] but more, in the tradition of Orson Welles's *F for Fake* (1975), the question of the reliability of film sources in general. While the opening scene presents Susan Sontag, who along with other public intellectuals lends the film "credibility," the first appearance of the film's eponymous object — the human chameleon Leonard Zelig, played by Woody Allen — signifies that the movie is at best a re-enactment. (Most viewers will indeed watch *Zelig* knowing from the outset that it is a fiction film by Woody Allen.)

In *Zelig*, then, the viewer is taking pleasure in being fooled, and rejoices in the idea of a false sense of reality, more so, maybe, than in a regular feature film. Allen's film thus sheds further light on Bill Nichols's concept of "epistephilia" as found in the reception of actual documentaries.[5] Nichols argues that part of the attraction of documentary films lies with the enjoyment of learning. This epistephilic joy undergoes a specific metamorphosis in the context of mockumentaries that corresponds with the meta-critical attitude of the genre. Since the content of mockumentaries is by definition fabricated, the pleasure of viewing such films stems from learning about the making — and artifice — of mockumentaries, and by extension, of cinema and the media industry at large. With this almost epistemological tendency of mockumentaries in mind, *Zelig* might even be said to recreate the original sense of wonder that the first audiences of moving pictures must have felt, knowing that they are watching an aesthetic and technological representation of reality and, simultaneously, that it has its own powers of reality.[6] Extending Trin Minh-ha's statement that "[t]here is no such thing as a documentary,"[7] one could therefore argue that cinema truly exists in the form of the mockumentary, that is to say, as a medium whose exact relationship to reality remains suspended.

Indeed, mockumentaries should be viewed as semiological commentaries on the textual practice of cinema. John Fiske points to the fundamental stylistic differences between documentary and dramatic conventions of film making: "The documentary conventions are designed to give the impression that the camera has happened upon a piece of unpremeditated reality which it shows to us objectively and truthfully: the dramatic conventions, on the other hand, are designed to give the impression that we are watching a piece of unmediated reality directly, that the camera does not exist."[8] Both traditions comment on the project of representing reality; both are engaged in a mimetic task. However, the choice of genre in and of itself does not guarantee a specific epistemological position, as Erik Barnouw argues: "Some artists turn from documentary to fiction because they feel it lets them get closer to truth. Some, it would appear, turn to documentary because it can make deception more plausible."[9] Yet others, one might add, turn to mockumentaries to address the original problem of cinema: its mediated, or symbolic, referentiality.

As David Banash noted in his essay on *The Blair Witch Project* — a fake documentary film about the search for a supernatural presence in a remote forest area that ends with the death of the film team — part of the fascination with mockumentaries stems from the viewers' (epistephilic) realization that they witness the failure of the omnipresent media spectacle to represent and capture reality.[10] This breakdown of the mimetic task lies at the center of the satirical relationship between mockumentaries and documentaries; and it has a long pre-history. In this context, it might be more appropriate to state that Flaherty laid to rest the genre of documentary film making which he is often credited as having invented. The mockumentary tradition follows in his footsteps, and presents staged imitations of reality that nevertheless contain an element of authenticity, often using only roughly-sketched scene outlines and relying heavily on impromptu dialogue.[11] Given Flaherty's habit of treating his films' objects with a generous dose of creativity, it is no great surprise to find that people in his immediate circles already used the term "mockumentary" when they saw his *Man of Aran* (1934).[12] They emphasized with this neologism Flaherty's departure from previous conventions of film making since the early developments of photography — and the first attempts at film — were inspired by the wish to document, truthfully and objectively, aspects of the real world such as astronomical events, animals in motion, or, in the case of Louis Lumière, people leaving or arriving at various locations.[13] However, footage of staged and fake events was already infiltrating the documentary tradition of cinematography in the first decade of the twentieth century.[14]

Later in the century, the title of Woody Allen's *Zelig* harks back to one of the earliest fake films, which presented staged footage of Theodore Roosevelt on an African hunting trip produced in 1907 by William Selig, using a *doppelgänger* of the president. Allen's film thus continues in a long tradition of appropriating the alleged truthfulness of visual testimony for creating a situation of artificiality. Therefore, a list of the direct antecedents of *Zelig* has to include *Citizen Kane* (1941),[15] in particular the fake newsreels early in the film, as well as Welles's subsequent, somewhat apologetic master piece, *F for Fake* (1976), to which Allen refers in *Zelig*, for instance through the inclusion of aviation stunts and historical footage from public parades through New York Cities.

Citizen Kane (1941) and its use of a faked newsreel should be seen as a direct antecedent to the modern mockumentary film movement. (Pictured center: Orson Welles as Charles Foster Kane.)

As these examples show, the problem of the veracity of filmic documents has accompanied cinema from its earliest days. In what Bill Nichols calls reflexive documentaries this tendency once again gains momentum[16]; the same trend is noticeably at work in mockumentary films. In the former the mediality is acknowledged, whereas in the latter it becomes the central concern of the texts' message. With their emphasis on cinema's problematic relationship with reality, mockumentaries thus continue a long-standing discussion. Christian Metz has famously pointed out that cinematic art has always already been characterized by its specific branch of artificiality. The filmic text he describes as an imaginary signifier and therefore states: "Every film is a fiction film."[17] With this assertion, Metz predates Trinh Minh-ha's view that documentary films are an impossibility. The arguments by both critics might lead to the assumption that there is nothing unique about the genre of fake documentary movies, and yet their recent popularity begs the question of their specificity.

At least on some level mockumentaries can be understood as cinema's equivalent to literature's narcissistic narratives, as the postmodern filmic version of self-reflexive fiction.[18] The sub-genre of the mockumentary indeed forms a response to cultural and philosophical phenomena of the late twentieth century. In particular, mockumentaries relate to the discourse on the non-referential nature of signs, what

Banash, writing about *The Blair Witch Project*, describes as the "the horror of confronting a world that cannot be represented."[19] The unavoidable deferral of meaning that characterizes all logocentric systems leads (postmodern) artists almost by necessity to an engagement with the medium of communication. In mockumentaries, precisely such a fascination with the mediality of cinema occurs.

This interest in the discursive and medializing nature of cinema explains why mockumentaries return to a style of cinematic representation that emphasizes the presentational character of the visual image. This textual strategy intends to increase the willingness of the viewer to decode the presented text as a medialized image of reality. In addition to using "real" people, as Woody Allen pretends to do in *Zelig* by interviewing well-known intellectuals, the style of many mockumentaries creates a link to an earlier form of cinematic veracity. By engaging in this kind of stylistic anachronism, mockumentarians do not try to escape or to avoid the problematic situation of contemporary documentary film making, but they address through their narrative framework and chosen stylistic form the postmodern epistemological crisis of textuality.

One consequence of this crisis is an active engagement with the history of cinema that leads to the typically postmodern stylistic eclecticism of form. The genre of the mockumentary to some extent is in accordance with the principles of early documentaries as laid out by Grierson: "With Flaherty it became an absolute principle that the story must be taken from the location, and that it should be (what he considers) the essential story of the location."[20] Films like *Zelig* or *This Is Spinal Tap!* surely fulfill this demand and present the essential reality of the environment they portray. While the individual music bands in *This Is Spinal Tap!* or *A Mighty Wind* (2003) are fake, their environment, the music industry and the fan circuit, is recreated with great accuracy.

Commenting on a similar moment of cinematic mimicry, Kurt Scheel emphasizes that Woody Allen's *Zelig* is particularly successful in re-creating the style of documentary filming through the inclusion of ostentatiously flawed material. Mentioning the shaky camera work, the very poor sound quality, and the jump cuts, he concludes: "all this is of the *perfect* faultiness of documentaries that actual documentary material cannot have."[21] Scheel sees in Allen's film a comment on the process of adaptation and assimilation that characterizes human history in general and the Jewish diaspora in particular.[22] Indeed, *Zelig* is, in the opinion of Ruth Perlmutter, the "most radical deconstruction of cinema"[23] by Allen.

Writing about the dialogical principle in *Zelig*, Robert Stam sees in the "reciprocal hybridization" occurring between Zelig and his environment an important aspect of the film,[24] which points to the syncretic structure of issues such as ethnicity or race. The film's presentation of the inherent multi-valency of any individual provides guidance for the attempt to decode the structure of the mockumentary film as such. In the same way as Woody Allen's Zelig seems to float between various personalities, the generic location of *Zelig* falls between the feature film and the documentary, taking its inspiration from both, and leaving both changed in the process. The film's stylistic and generic identity replicates the content of the movie, and both combine to provide criticism of the project of mediated representation. Sam Girgus contends in *The Films of Woody Allen* that this tendency is by no means limited to this film by Allen, who repeatedly questions "the processes by which films mediate and validate experience."[25] By adding to *Zelig* the question of generic affiliation, Allen turns the film into a quest for cinematic form. While retaining a ludic tone, his mockumentary also contains a critical perspective.

Mockumentaries as Critical Fiction

The critical leanings of many mockumentary films, evident in their tendency to provide a meta-documentarian commentary on the limitations of medialized representations, also emerge in the Belgian film *Man Bites Dog* (1992). This low-budget movie made by film students pretends to portray the daily life of a serial killer. It uses the generic and stylistic framework of documentary films and thereby speaks out against the fascination with violence that increasingly dominates the television screen. The film's ideological proximity to Oliver Stone's *Natural Born Killers* (1994) emphasizes the meta-critical intention of *Man Bites Dog*. It furthermore lends credibility to the claim that mockumentaries should be thought of as meta-documentaries that criticize the generic conventions and discursive expectations viewers bring to the question of truthfulness in visual media.

The opening scene of *Man Bites Dog*, with its candid portrayal of a murder on a train, sets the tone for the film to follow: on the one hand, its content violates the professional code of journalistic or documentary work by making the film crew implicit (and, eventually, actual) accomplices of the murderer. The generic and stylistic cues of the film, on the other hand, indicate that the film follows the framework of documentaries. The black and white film stock, the shaky camera moves, the single point of view, the occasional in-frame presence of the crew, and, finally, the (metanarrative) discussion of the film within the film: all these emphasize the alleged status of *Man Bites Dog* as a documentary film. The parodistic side of the movie provides a subtle challenge to its generic affiliation. The omnipresent sense of humor often borders on the outrageous but rarely crosses into the unbelievable. Ben, the serial killer and object of the film, proves himself to be a seriously disturbed and unbalanced character, suffering from a myriad of phobias and prejudices, thereby making it all the more likely that he could, maybe, behave in the way presented in the movie. As an interview included in the DVD version of the film makes clear, the sense of reality accompanying the film derives to some extent from the real world struggles of making a low-budget film, featuring the actual filmmakers playing themselves. The contrast between the stylistic proximity to documentary film making and the ethical conflict surrounding the chosen object of the film points to the problematic relationship between ethics and visual representation, in particular to the question of whether documentary films exacerbate and even profit from the social ills they chose to present. Above all, the film presents, in its form and style, a serious engagement with the contentious nature of documentary film making.

Yet, *Man Bites Dog* is after all a documentary film of sorts, presenting evidence about film making and thereby adding to the metanarrative tendencies of mockumentary films. It is not by coincidence that documentary truthfulness exists only on the level of the narrative framing of the film and not in the story presented therein. This shift in emphasis reinforces the earlier claim that mockumentary films are predominantly interested in questions of narrative, that is, in film's power of framing a story. As Welles has so cleverly shown in *F for Fake*, the success or failure of art depends on the verdict of the critics. Accordingly, one of the characters in his film asks: "But if there weren't any experts, would there be any fakers?" The importance of framing for any aesthetic work is one of the central concerns of Welles's film. It repeats the structural claims present in mockumentaries' insistence on addressing the fragile nature of represented reality. Art itself is presented by Welles and the makers of mockumentaries as both always and never a fake. The ultimate decision on this issue has to be made by the audience. Authors, however, can also directly address the question of an artwork's veracity. Welles "quotes" Picasso in his film as saying: "I can paint false Picassos as well as anybody." For *Man Bites Dog* this means that its affiliation to the documentary tradition depends on various aspects, including both the critical verdict by viewers and the artists' intentions. Its indebtedness to different genres shapes the film's aesthetics. As with other mockumentaries, however, its emphasis on artifice raises suspicions that an inherent artificiality is being either covered up, or ironically brought to the fore.

During a deadly shoot-out in an empty industrial building, the film's sound man is shot and killed. With remarkable attention to detail the film turns silent for a few seconds because the body of the injured technician covers the microphone, blocking all sound. In a similarly ostentatious gesture, the film ends with pictures from a camera dropped to the floor as a result of yet another shooting involving both the object of the film and the film crew. Both the visual and the aural physicality of the film thus stress its medial nature: the artifice of filming and its lack of immediacy. The recurrent reminder of the mediacy of the image, supported by the presentational character of the narrative, denies the audience the possibility of immersing themselves in the picture's simulated reality. Akin to Woody Allen's technique in *The Purple Rose of Cairo* (1985), where actual viewers of the movie are watching a film character go to a cinema watching a character in another film watching somebody else, we are reminded of the layering and framing of the presented image as well as of the passivity that characterizes the audience of a spectacle. Yet, *Man Bites Dog* rarely steps outside its ironic and parodistic tone. But lest the viewers forget that they are watching a fictional film crew following a fictional serial killer, halfway through the film they witness an encounter with another film crew, following its own criminal. This on-screen replication of the film's narrative framing brings back to memory the very presence of framing. It also visualizes the role of the spectator.

A very dramatic version of this anti-spectacular tendency is at the center of the short film *No Lies*, in which a film maker interviews a young woman in her apartment. The camera is visible from the first moment, revealed in various mirrors and following her object through various rooms. The filmmaker speaking from behind the camera lens places the audience in a position of complicity. When the film's dialogue surprisingly reveals that the young woman had recently been raped, and when the subsequent insensitive questioning by the interviewer brings her to tears, the ethics of such "reporting" is implicitly challenged. Viewers learn only at the very end of *No Lies* that the two people are actors, and the film fictional. By linking the potentially exploitative nature of documentaries to the mediality and artifice of cinema, as done through the content and style of *No Lies*, the movie subscribes to the critical and metanarrative tradition of mockumentaries.

The emphasis on a film's mediality implies a heightened awareness of the role of the author and director of a film, which might explain the motivation behind the presence of a film maker in *No Lies* or *This Is Spinal Tap!* Other mockumentaries involve the creator of artifice in a different manner. Both *Blair Witch Project* and *Man Bites Dog* end with the death of the on-screen film makers. The text terminates the author. The criticism implied in this development is directed against the position of the author within the context of documentary film making. Similarly, in *Forgotten Silver*, a film within the film shows the last moments of the alleged cinema pioneer Colin McKenzie, filmed by the camera he had placed on the ground during a skirmish in the Spanish War. These gestures imply that the camera is almost independent of the film maker and that the camera eye represents reality in a subjective and direct manner. The director appears to possess only limited powers over the final product. On a superficial level, it is the ultimate statement of the film's veracity, emphasizing in a grand finale the artifice of the presented text, thereby reassuring viewers of the authenticity of the mockumentary content. The amount of irony involved in this process, of course, is enormous: in order for the film material to be developed, edited and cut, and finally put into presentable form, another director had to take over. What the on-screen death of the "film-maker" therefore demonstrates is the insidious presence of yet another level of framing and, therefore, of control. From this critical relationship to the discourse of power derives the fascination many viewers develop for mockumentary films.

The End of Artifice

Contrary to Bill Nichols's observation that more recent tendencies in documentary film making emphasize the representational character of the filmic medium, for instance through voiceover or interview passages, the mockumentary style often engages in the earlier, presentational mode, where the object of the film is allegedly presented directly to the audience. However, the self-reflexive mode that Nichols observes also features prominently in the mockumentary artistic palette, most prominently through its visual and aural style. The inclusion, for instance, of a director's board early in *The Blair Witch Project*, the in-frame presence of both the film crew and their equipment in *Man Bites Dog*, as well as the blending of different filmic and print media such as news reports, amateur video footage, and interviews in *Zelig* and *This Is Spinal Tap!*—all, of course, staged — add to the cinéma vérité quality of authenticity. The connection between a film's style and its appeal as a genuine document is very predictable, as Stella Bruzzi explains: "The less polished the film the more credible it will be found."[26] The first mockumentary films appropriated the audience's generic viewing habits, shaped by documentary films, for their own purposes.

This chapter has repeatedly described as one of the central aesthetic devices for the creation of the mockumentaries' false sense of authenticity the making-visible of the artifice of the filmic text. The emphasis on the constructedness of the cinematic representation harks back to the postmodern awareness of the discursivity of all texts, but reaches its own ironic reversal in the mockumentary mode. The antagonism between presentation and representation, allegedly sublated in the deconstructionists' understanding of the deferential meaning of all signs, is reinstated in the conscious appropriation of the medium of film for the process of creating believable fiction. It remains debatable whether the aesthetic and critical interest behind mockumentary films stems from their alleged topics, such as the dog show in Christopher Guest's *Best in Show* (2000), or from the fact that a select audience of cognoscenti enjoys the satirical portrayals of the films' clichéd characters, bringing treats of everyday average life to the screen. Read in such a way, mockumentaries present a return to the original motivation behind early film making, that is, they once again take the mundane as their central topic. Mockumentary films indeed follow the theoretical program outlined by Kracauer as the true domain of cinema: "Film renders visible what we did not, or perhaps even could not, see before its advent."[27] The medium of film is at its best, so argues Kracauer, when it portrays the more ephemeral characteristics of life. Cinema should thus focus on the unintentional and unscripted: "Street crowds, involuntary gestures, and other fleeting impressions are its very meat."[28] To this documentary quality of (early) cinema the mockumentary genre returns in the sense that it also focuses on peripheral discourses and often relies on unscripted dialogue.

Whereas many postmodern documentarians are in disagreement about the historical and ideological truthfulness of their films and may well wonder about the possibility of reaching an adequate level of objectivity,[29] the makers of mockumentaries move this discussion to a different plane. Rather than joining to the political or historical project of documenting actual events, they choose to fabricate events. In doing so they contribute, inadvertently or not, to the discussion about the status of documentary film making. By preemptively removing, through their parodistic tone any claims of authenticity, films like *Best in Show* or *Forgotten Silver* deflate the documentary project and bring to the fore the high potential for manipulation inherent in the medium of film. Recent technological developments that enable film makers to present as "truthful" pictures computer-generated fabrications further exacerbate the manipulative risks inherent to cinema. Ten years before *Forrest Gump* (1994), the technical bravado of the recreated historical film material in *Zelig* and *This Is Spinal Tap!* is put in the service of mocking the alleged truthfulness and veracity developed during the reign of cinéma vérité aesthetics. Since they address the process of film making as such, mockumentaries can be called meta-documentaries or, to follow Linda Hutcheon,[30] un-"reel" documentaries. After all, they see as their aim not the documentation of a real-life event, but rather the questioning of documentary film making per se. Implicit in this project is the active participation of a film's audience.

A comparison between mockumentaries and a certain type of recent special effects films such as the Wachowski brothers' *The Matrix* (1999) makes obvious that two different strategies of viewer immersion are at work in the two genres. While the high-tech spectacle of freeze shots and bullet time in films such as *The Matrix* casts the audience into a strictly passive role, following the lead of the camera's unrealistic yet smooth movements, the repeated emphasis of the camera's physical presence in the mockumentary film reminds the viewers that they are indeed watching a created reality. In Christopher Guest's *Waiting for Guffman* (1996) and *Best in Show*, for instance, the tongue-in-cheek parody and mockery of not only filmic genres but also professional and social peculiarities encourage a decoding of the films that is more active and participatory. The predictability of the individual characters as well as the returning cast of actors in Guest's mockumentaries both resist a fully immersive response to the films. Rather, the on-screen narrative unfolds parallel with the audience's enjoyment of the parody and, in the process, with the metanarrative of the mockumentary.

When watching a mockumentary as a mockumentary, this simultaneous duality of response creates a sense of stereoscopic enjoyment, what Barthes might call the pleasure of a writerly cinematic text. In Woody Allen's *Zelig*, viewers familiar with Allen's work and with the generic form of the documentary watch the film simultaneously on different levels. Indeed, it is questionable whether mockumentaries can be watched in any other way since viewers either are aware of the false claim of the truthfulness of the "document," in which case they are watching a mockumentary on the multiple levels just described, or they do not realize that the film presents fictional information, in which case they would have to believe they are indeed watching a documentary.[31] In other words, viewers would no longer watch the film as a mockumentary. The generic pointers to specific generic and formal traditions, what Genette calls a work's architextual references,[32] remain important throughout, since the framing of any film will determine how a naive audience reacts to it.[33] When *Forgotten Silver* was first shown on New Zealand television, many viewers initially reacted to the film as they would to a genuine documentary, even though a number of them must have realized that the claims presented in the film were simply too outlandish to be true. Those who decoded correctly the ironic content probably also detected the parodistic genre; they ended up watching a mockumentary.

Another example for the writerly qualities of mockumentaries exists in the form of a short cartoon documentary about "The Powerpuff Girls," shown on the Cartoon Network in January 2004. While the average child watching the film might believe to find in the narrative a "truthful" document, the occasional grown-up viewer watching alongside surely realizes not only that the nature of animated film contradicts any claims to veracity, but also that the film's mockumentary tendencies, such as the cinéma vérité quality of its images and the on-screen presence of a (fake) film maker, poke fun at the documentary genre. This cartoon mockumentary exemplifies the importance of the audience in the process of allocating to a film its genre and hence the appropriate way of reading.

Due to the instability of a film's generic affiliation, it is not surprising that the original emphasis on artifice within the first mockumentaries has since given way to a more assertive and less artificial presentation of mockumentary films. Since the early days of *Zelig* and *This Is Spinal Tap!*, mockumentaries can claim their own heritage and therefore no longer feel required to signal to the audience their hybrid qualities.

Though the band in *The Mighty Wind* (2003) is fake, its environment, the music industry, and the fan circuit are recreated with great accuracy. (*Left to right*: Harry Shearer, Michael McKean, Christopher Guest.)

Rather, these second-generation mockumentaries proudly locate themselves within the parodistic tradition that was started by the first films of that new sub-genre, but they no longer follow the aesthetic framework initially developed. Gone is the artifice and gone is the ironic proximity to the cinematic language and style of documentary film making.

A good example for this subsequent strategy is Guest's third film, *A Mighty Wind*, which refuses throughout the film to make any claims to being a documentary. It can afford to do so because of the formation of a new genre, the mockumentary, and the concomitant formation of an audience both trained in the generic tradition and its appropriate reception. One of the last remnants of the documentary legacy of those later mockumentaries is the inclusion of on-screen names and professions for the films' characters. Having dropped all pretenses of being a genuine, historical document, *A Mighty Wind* proceeds without overt stylistic references to the genre of documentary film making and its claims of veracity. Guest's first two follow-up films to *This Is Spinal Tap!* were already released as mockumentaries: other than the original rockumentary, they did not attempt to create a narrative framework that includes the documentarian, and they did not follow the cinematic style of vérité camera work and sound. Rather, they came with the glossy shine of "normal" feature films. Even in the advertisement campaigns to *Waiting for Guffman*, *Best in Show*, and *A Mighty Wind*, all deception was dropped. None of the three films is presented as a documentary. Without the need to employ artifice to fool their audiences about their own artificiality, the most recent mockumentaries present themselves as proud members of a new genre.

For their help and advise during the writing of this essay, I would like to thank Luis José Bustamante, Omri Yavin, Jane McGonigal, Tim Damon, and Florin Berindeanu.

1. Brian Winston, "Documentary: How the Myth was Deconstructed," *Wide Angle* 21.1 (March 1999): 70–86; 75.

2. The necessity to "know" cinema lies at the bottom of an understanding of mockumentary and parodistic films: "La perception de l'effet parodique tient beaucoup aux connaissances du cinéphile qui doit savoir comment un documentaire est fait; donc, d'un cinéphile qui peut mieux mesurer la distance entre le modèle et sa variante parodique." Gilles Thérien, "Constitution du sujet parodique dans l'imaginaire du cinéma," *Dire la Parodie: Colloque de Cerisy*, eds. Clive Thomson and Alain Pagès (New York: Lang, 1989): 341–359, 351.

3. *No Lies* opens with a scene in front of a mirror, thus introducing the camera from the very first moment.

4. The role of satire is emphasized in Francesco Spagnolo Acht, "'Doin' the Chameleon': Strategie testuali e strategie di sopravvivenza in *Zelig* di Woody Allen," *La Rassegna mensile di Israel* 62.3 (Sept.–Dec. 1996): 70–120.

5. See Bill Nichols, *Representing Reality: Issues and Concepts in Documentary* (Bloomington: Indiana University Press, 1991): 178–180.

6. Tom Gunning describes this two-part response when he writes about the early film audiences: "Far from credulity, it is the incredible nature of the illusion itself that renders the viewer speechless." Tom Gunning, "An Aesthetic of Astonishment: Early Film and the (In)Credulous Spectator," *Film Theory and Criticism: Introductory Readings*, eds. Leo Braudy and Marshall Cohen (New York: Oxford University Press, 1999), 818–32; 822.

7. Trinh T. Minh-ha, "The Totalizing Quest of Meaning," *Theorizing Documentary*, ed. Michael Renov (New York: Routledge, 1993) 90–107, notes 214–215; 90.

8. John Fiske, *Television Culture* (London: Routledge, 1994) 30.

9. Erik Barnouw, *Documentary: A History of Non-Fiction Film* (New York: Oxford University Press, 1974): 288.

10. David Banash, "*The Blair Witch Project*: Technology, Repression, and the Evisceration of Mimesis," *Postmodern Culture* 10.1 (1999).

11. See the interviews with Lynn Geller, "Christopher Guest," *Bomb* 29 (Fall 1989): 38–41, and Richard Grant, "Nowt so Queer as Folk," Weekend Magazine of *The Guardian* 10 January 2004: 26–33.

12. See Winston, "Documentary," 73.

13. Barnouw, *Documentary* 3–11.

14. Barnouw, *Documentary* 25; see also Brian Winston, "'Honest, Straightforward Re-enactment': The Staging of Reality," *Joris Ivens and the Documentary Context*, ed. Kees Bakker (Amsterdam: Amsterdam UP, 1999): 160–170.

15. The relationship between these two films is investigated by Douglas L. Rathgelb, "Faces in the Newsreel: Illuminating *Citizen Kane* through Woody Allen's *Zelig*," *Post Script* 6.3 (Spring–Summer 1987): 31–44.

16. See the historical classification of documentary modes in Bill Nichols, *Blurred Boundaries: Questions of Meaning in Contemporary Culture* (Bloomington: Indiana University Press, 1994) 92–106, as well as the critical reply by Stella Bruzzi, *New Documentary: A Critical Introduction* (London: Routledge, 2000).

17. Christian Metz, *Psychoanalysis and Cinema: The Imaginary Signifier* (London: Macmillan, 1983): 44.

18. See, for instance, the works of Linda Hutcheon, *Narcissistic Narrative: The Metafictional Paradox* (New York: Methuen, 1984), and Robert Stam, *Reflexivity in Film and Literature: From Don Quixote to Jean-Luc Godard* (Ann Arbor: UMI Research Press, 1985).

19. Banash, "*The Blair Witch Project*," paragraph 7.

20. Forsyth Hardy, ed., *Grierson on Documentary* (New York: Praeger, 1966): 148.

21. Kurt Scheel, "Filme: Eine Kolumne," *Merkur: Deutsche Zeitschrift für europäisches Denken* 38.4 (June 1984): 437–442; 441, my translation; emphasis added.

22. The impact of the Jewish diaspora on the film also interests Robert Stam and Ella Shohat, "Zelig and Contemporary Theory: Meditation on the Chameleon Text," *Enclitic* 9 pp. 1–2 (Fall 1987): 176–193.

23. Ruth Perlmutter, "Woody Allen's *Zelig*: An American Jewish Parody," *Comedy/Cinema/Theory*, ed. Andrew Horton (Berkeley: University of California Press, 1991): 206–221; 215.

24. Robert Stam, "A Tale of Two Cities: Cultural Polyphony and Ethnic Transformation," *East-West Film Journal* 3.1 (December 1988): 105–116; 115.

25. Sam B. Girgus, *The Films of Woody Allen* (Cambridge: Cambridge University Press, 1993): 71.

26. Bruzzi, *New Documentary* 6.

27. Siegfried Kracauer, *Theory of Film: The Redemption of Physical Reality* (New York: Oxford University Press, 1960): 300.

28. Kracauer, *Theory of Film* ix.

29. See, for instance, the essay by Linda Williams, "Mirrors without Memories: Truth, History, and the New Documentary," *Film Quarterly: Forty Years — A Selection*, eds. Brian Henderson, Ann Martin, and Lee Amazonas (Berkeley: University of California Press, 1999): 308–328.

30. See Linda Hutcheon, *The Politics of Postmodernism* (London: Routledge, 1993): 108–110, where she discusses *Zelig*; see also Loes Nas, "The 'unreel' in Woody Allen's *Zelig*," *Literator* 13.3 (November 1992): 93–100. Concern over the Germanic nihilism allegedly at play in Woody Allen's film expresses Allan Bloom, *The Closing of the American Mind* (New York: Simon and Schuster, 1987): 144–146.

31. In a short essay included in the official *Spinal Tap Companion*, Justin Meadows is quoted as remarking that viewers of the film *This Is Spinal Tap!* wondered why the director had chosen "a terrible band" for his film (119).

32. Gérard Genette, *Palimpsests: Literature in the Second Degree*, trans. Channa Newman and Claude Doubinsky (Lincoln: University of Nebraska Press, 1997): 4.

33. See Dirk Eitzen, "When Is a Documentary?: Documentary as a Mode of Reception," *Cinema Journal* 35.1 (Fall 1995): 81–102.

11

"It Ain't the Movies! It's Real Life!"
Cinematic Alchemy in
Woody Allen's "Woody Allen"
D(M)oc(k)umentary Oeuvre

by Robert Sickels

"Woody Allen." Those two simple words are unique in American filmmaking for a variety of reasons, not the least of which is the mental image they invariably conjure, that of a small man with a largish nose and thick black rimmed glasses struggling mightily to lucidly say a sentence without stumbling over his words. This mental response makes him anomalous among directors in that rather than thinking of his movies, when people hear his name, they think of *him.* Other directors have widespread name recognition — Spielberg, Tarantino, and Scorsese for example — and many folks likely even know what they look like, but when they hear their names, they don't react in the same way; people don't react as though they know them and that's because they don't, at least not in the same way they think they know Woody Allen. Scorsese and Tarantino occasionally appear in the films they direct, but their movies just aren't about them, while Allen's seemingly always are, even in a few of the rare instances in which he's not in them. With Allen the temptation to see his "real life" writ large in his movies is immense, even though, as Maurice Yacowar sensibly suggests, "the conventions of fiction should preclude this judgment."[1] But what if the "Woody Allen" the films are about isn't the Woody Allen who lives an intensely private off-screen life, but the fictional Woody Allen persona who inhabits the real Allen's films? If that's the case, then in watching Allen's films we *do* get the entire biography of the Allen persona. If we are to consider the Allen character in this way, as a kind of recurring narrative touchstone that reappears in film after film after film, then the way we view his oeuvre is very different than the ways in which we consider the bodies of work of other filmmakers, especially as concerns the relationship of Allen's work to documentary and it's various incarnations, including, perhaps most prominently, the mockumentary form. While most of Allen's individual films aren't obviously documentaries, or even mockumentaries, they can nevertheless collectively be seen as a blending of the two styles, as well as straight fictional filmmaking, that forms a biographical d(m)oc(k)umentary chronicle of the Woody Allen character.

As Julian Fox notes, "Woody Allen stands today as the most extensively documented film comedian-auteur after Chaplin. It is even possible that, taken simply as a public personality, he has attracted more print and media analysis within a relatively shorter time than any other comic performer of the twentieth century."[2] While this may be true, it's also important to understand that while Allen is sometimes compared to Chaplin, there is a major fact that separates the cinematic personas of the two. As Sam Girgus writes, "in contrast to Chaplin, who usually performed as The Tramp, Allen invariably plays himself, thinly disguising himself as various characters who are themselves fictionalized versions of Allen's own manufactured identity as Woody Allen."[3] Accordingly, perhaps a better comparison to Allen is not Chaplin but Cary Grant.

An old story about Grant (which may well be apocryphal), goes something like this: Once Grant was asked by an interviewer what it was like to be Cary Grant, to which he supposedly replied, "I have no idea," the point being that no one could live as fabulously suave and debonair a life as Grant typically played onscreen. Allen too, though playing a character on the polar opposite end of the social spectrum from Grant, has long been accused of continually playing what is essentially the same version of himself. And just as in Grant's case, despite what may be some similarities, the cinematic Woody Allen isn't the real one, plain and simple. But that doesn't mean people don't believe that he's real, which is tantamount to the same thing. Accordingly, as Girgus posits,

> ...over the years, the invented identity of Woody Allen, auteur director, actor, and urban neurotic worked as a self-fulfilling system to help make Allen successful. The name and picture of Allen conjured up images and ideas, notion and values that provided a basis for developing his fictional screen characters. The composite Allen public image functioned as a ghostly alter ego to identify and situate the fictional Allen character portrayed in the film's story.[4]

Not surprisingly, while some critics subscribe to Yacowar's prudent cautioning about drawing straight lines between Allen's filmic characterizations with his real life, many critics do so anyway, and not without good reason. As Peter J. Bailey observes, "responsible criticism of Allen's work must also recognize how insistently a few of his films ... intrude the issues of autobiography into their narratives as inescapable components of the films' constructions. In essence, none can be adequately interpreted without critical attention being paid to the ambiguous role that Allen's self-extrapolation of a protagonist in the movies plays in relation to him."[5] The continuing debate over what extent biography plays in Allen's work and how much weight one should give it is endlessly played out in an ocean of extant criticism of Allen's work. But there is another way to look at it. It is my contention that the biography that matters most in Allen's work is not the off-screen life of Allen himself, but the ongoing biography of the onscreen lives of the closely connected characters he's played over the years. In approaching Allen's films this way, there is no reason to try and extrapolate from journalistic and/or tabloid accounts of Allen's life how his real life plays out in his fictional films. Instead, if we consider the various characters he plays in his films as being of a piece, then we get all the information we need to assemble a complete biography of the onscreen Woody Allen. Furthermore, when one considers his work as a whole, a complete and detailed picture emerges; we can view his various individual films as symbiotic parts in what collectively functions as a multipart biographical d(m)oc(k)umentary that relates the continually evolving tale of the onscreen Woody Allen persona.

Allen's connection to documentary style filmmaking, specifically the mockumentary form, is long and varied and

Beginning with *Take the Money and Run* (1969), Woody Allen established himself as not only the most prolific mockumentarian, but the most diverse as well.

spans the length of his career. Beginning with *Take the Money and Run* (1969) and continuing to the release of *Sweet and Lowdown* (1999), Woody Allen has established himself as not only the most prolific mockumentarian in movies, but as the most diverse as well. Allen has made mockumentaries on subjects ranging from a career criminal (*Take the Money and Run*) and a so-called "human chameleon" (*Zelig*, 1983) to an unsuccessful talent manager (*Broadway Danny Rose*, 1984) and a pathological jazz musician who fears only Django Reinhardt (*Sweet and Lowdown*). And, as Girgus notes,

> Allen's development of the documentary style over so many years in such a variety of forms to dramatize a diversity of stories, subjects, characters, and themes indicates not only a natural proclivity toward this form in his work but also an instinctive appreciation for the centrality of documentary to film in general. His repeated use of documentary form to structure works of fiction suggests his interest in the documentary nature of all film as well as his insight into the intrinsic relationship in film between documentary and fiction.[6]

His "natural proclivity" towards the documentary form is such that he can't seem to get away from it; that documentary shades his every film stems from the fact that, as Joseph Mills writes, "[a]lmost all of Allen's work deals self-consciously with form

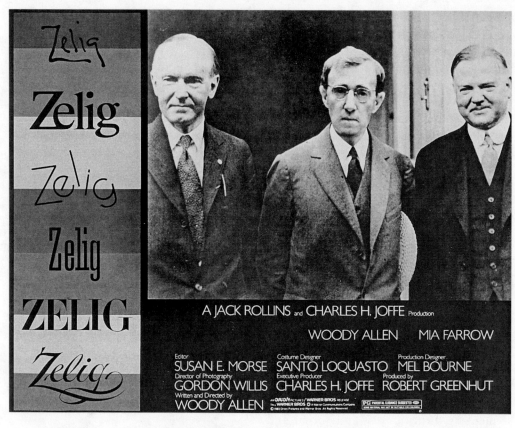

Woody Allen satirizes the "archival documentary" in his 1983 film *Zelig*. (*Left to right*: Calvin Coolidge, Woody Allen, Herbert Hoover.)

and genre.... Allen utilizes genre conventions to invoke certain audience expectations which he then refuses to satisfy."[7] Allen's constantly playing with genre conventions in and of itself does not make his films feel like documentaries; after all, many of the directors who came of age in the freewheeling American cinema of the 1970s acknowledged genre conventions while at the same time flaunting them. However, when coupled with the visual and narrative style of his films, Allen's willingness to subvert audience expectations becomes something else again.

As a documentarian, Allen is best known for his mockumentaries, which, as the *Oxford English Dictionary* states, is a film "which adopts the form of a serious documentary in order to satirize its subject."[8] Although the curtness of the *OED*'s definition doesn't do the richness of the genre justice, it does cut to its essence. While in his discussion of the genre Thomas Doherty concedes that the first mockumentaries may have occurred as early as the films produced at Edison's studio in the late 1800s, he argues that "the locus classicus — the first truly authentic exemplar of the fake documentary in American Cinema — was conjured by that media con artist par excellence, Orson Welles ... whose fake screen obituary in *Citizen Kane* (1941) unraveled the stiff formal wear of the bombastic Hollywood Newsreel."[9] As concerns mockumentaries that follow the form of the archival documentary as perhaps first practiced by Welles, "CGI [computer generated imagery] launched a true revolution in motion-picture perception, giving forgers the means to replicate, with a fidelity undetectable to the naked eye, the look of the archival blueprint."[10] This kind of archival documentary mockumentary undoubtedly reached its apotheosis in 1983 with the release of Allen's *Zelig*, a film about the fictional Leonard Zelig, a "human chameleon" (played by Allen) who assumed the physical and social attributes of whomever's company in which he found himself, whether it be an Asian man, an African-American jazzman, or a jackbooted follower of Adolph Hitler.

While *Zelig* is easily among the best of its kind, it stands alone in Allen's cannon. He hasn't really made any other archival mockumentaries nor has he made any of the fly on the wall style verité mockumentaries that seem to dominate the genre and have become so ubiquitous as a result of the rise of reality television. Instead, he has focused primarily on what one might call, for lack of an accepted term, "anecdotal reenactment mockumentaries," perhaps best evidenced by *Sweet and Lowdown*, in which interviews with real and faux "experts" recalling tales of 1930s jazz guitarist Emmet Ray (Sean Penn) are intercut with reenactments of events that may or may not have happened. Indeed, in one instance we get not one, but two versions of how Ray may have inadvertently ended up at the scene of a gas station hold-up.

In his numerous films that are easily recognizable as intentionally informed by documentary filmmaking, Allen adheres to the parameters of the genre. According to Eric Simon, documentaries typically tell "the story of whoever, or whatever" and frequently incorporate

> ...interviews with living persons who have germane input towards the subject. These sessions usually show the interviewee well lit, in a medium shot, seated on a chair or a couch. And ... often include brief segments of old photographs, or maybe stock footage if it's a subject that has been the focus of a previous documentary. These days, the photographic stills/stock footage aspect can come to include the increasingly popular "recreations."[11]

With the notable exception of *Zelig*, Allen doesn't do much with stock footage (or faux stock footage as the case may be), but he repeatedly uses the devices of interviews and reenactments in many of his films. Furthermore, his camera doesn't usually move much, especially when compared to his contemporaries, whose cameras frequently move more frenetically and less purposefully. Instead, while not unwilling to experiment, Allen is something of a cinematic classicist, preferring to leave his camera on his actors and let them convey the action and emotion of a scene. As a result, "action and speech flow beyond the frame. That is to say, life continues beyond what a particular scene may convey."[12] This feeling that life is happening all around the frame, and not just within it, greatly enhances the documentary feel of his films, especially in the countless New York location exteriors in which he's had his characters converse over the years.

Stylistically, Allen's films closely parallel "real" documentaries, not only visually, but in tone as well. In his mockumentaries, even though we know we're being put on, there's a fierce narrative and emotional realism that makes them seem much closer to "real" documentaries than do other mockumentaries. Furthermore, many of the stylistic hallmarks Allen has appropriated from documentary filmmaking — including first person into-the-camera narratives, voiceovers, interviews, and title-cards — remain consistent no matter what his subject, which, I would argue, greatly expands the number of his films that can be considered mockumentaries, or at least mocking in tone and "feeling" as though they are documentaries. As Yacowar notes,

> ...Woody Allen developed his film artistry through forms of genre parody ... [and] Allen's nebbish persona provided a continuity across the wide range of film types that he parodied.... As a result his series of formal frolics seemed like a running autobiography, the candid, self-exposing confessions of a loser whose garb of heroic and romantic aspirations just did not fit. Each new chapter widened and deepened his audience's identification with his image.[13]

As Allen matured as a filmmaker his films became more sophisticated, but they never really varied much stylistically or strayed from his love of parody and they've almost always featured a similar version of a character played by Woody Allen, which is why, perhaps more than the work of any other filmmaker, his films collectively feel as though they're part of a continuing story. Therefore, any number of his films — including such works as *Husbands and Wives* (1992), *Bullets over Broadway* (1994), *Mighty Aphrodite* (1995), and especially *Deconstructing Harry* (1997) — can be reconsidered as examples of Allen's works that blur the lines between mockumentary, documentary, and more traditional comedy in their pursuit of his primary interest, which, as reflected in nearly all of his films, is faithfully documenting the Woody Allen character's perceptions of life and love in late 20th century America.

In discussing Christopher Guest's trilogy of mockumentaries, *Waiting for Guffman* (1997), *Best in Show* (2000), and *A Mighty Wind* (2003), Doherty observes that the films display "the always double-edged relationship of parody to the original; both parasite on the host and slave to the master."[14] The same can be said of virtually all of Woody Allen's films, the difference being that the "master" is neither people enmeshed in dog show culture nor over the hill folkies trying to recapture their brief moment in time; instead, the "master" to which the films are "slave" is the Woody Allen character, who often seems to be onscreen even in films in which Allen doesn't appear. Kenneth Branagh's character in *Celebrity* (1997) is clearly modeled on the Allen character, but there are many other examples, including John Cusack's playwright in *Bullets over Broadway* (1994) and Sean Penn's neurotic guitar player in *Sweet and Lowdown*, both of whom Allen likely would have played were he a younger man when the respective films were made. As Barbara Schapiro writes, "Allen's personality dominates every character and every one of his films as a whole, and the fragmented voices of all of the characters reflect the tenuous structure of that determining personality."[15] Schapiro's point of view is absolutely right, so long as the "personality" to which she is referring is the personality of the recurring Allen character and not the real life Woody Allen. There is no leap of faith to make if you look at the films in this way; the evidence is right there on screen, from film to film, most of which are dominated by the fictional Allen persona.

Julian Fox argues that "[i]n Woody's case, any discussion of his work, as comedian or filmmaker, is bound to take cognizance of a life and its concerns which, more than for any other contemporary film artist, seem to have been so overtly reflected in his movies that we feel we know him better than we actually do," which is true as concerns the real Woody Allen, but belies the fact that we *do* intimately know the Woody Allen character and his desires, obsessions, and tics perhaps better than any other screen character in history.[16] While the Allen character has been around since the beginning of his career, what we can call the mature or fully developed Allen character didn't come to fruition until 1977 and the release of *Annie Hall*. It was in the writing of this film that, as Ryan Gilbey observes, "Woody Allen created Woody Allen. The character proved so resonant that its creator would never be required to trade it in for a jazzier model. Although he augmented or modified it over the decades, the essence of that persona could not be negotiated," nor can it be said that that real Allen has shown much interest in working over or subverting the fictional Woody Allen.[17] And why would he? For those who love him, the character works (although, it should be noted, that there are people — my wife immediately comes to my mind — who vehemently despise Woody Allen's films simply because they can't stand the Allen character, which becomes an insurmountable problem as there just isn't any escaping him because he's always onscreen and he rarely shuts up).

The Allen character as born in *Annie Hall* and depicted ever since is eternally neurotic, compulsive, and obsessive. In discussing Allen's major films of the late 70s and early 80s, Barbara Schapiro claims that they typically feature "both the lack of self and the obsession with self ... all reveal an obsessive fear of death, of fragmentation and self-disintegration, an alternation of idealized, grandiose self fantasies with expressions of contemptuous self-deprecation, and a similar alternating idealization and contempt for women."[18] Her assessment holds equally true of the films made since the publication of her article in 1986. In fact, the number of recurring tropes and themes, not to mention actors (especially Diane Keaton and Mia Farrow) and music (most notably the classic jazz of the 30s and 40s), in Allen's films is immense and would require a book length study in order to do their importance in his work justice. To illustrate, a cursory look at *Deconstructing Harry*, which arguably contains the most self-reflexivity and intertextual elements of all the films featuring the Woody Allen character (in part due to its coming so late in the sequence and in part seemingly intentionally so), provides a sense of how recurrences in his work can be seen to unify his films into a comprehensive d(m)oc(k)umentary study of the filmic Allen persona.

The film opens with repeated viewings of Judy Davis' character leaving a taxi and heading towards Harry's (played by Allen) apartment building. We see the scene over and over again, and each time it feels a little different. This opening recalls the Allen character's voiceover of his attempts to begin a novel at the outset of *Manhattan* (1979), an allusion that is made even more clearly at the end of *Deconstructing Harry*, at which time Harry is sitting in front of his typewriter and we hear his voiceover as he types out the premise of his new novel. The use of voiceover is recurrent in Allen's work and it's used in a variety of ways. Sometimes it's in a straightforward documentary fashion such as in *Take the Money and Run* and *Zelig*, but it's also frequently used to give his audience insight into his characters, thus making audible their interior monologue as in the case of *Hannah and Her Sisters* (1986) and several other films.

Of course we see both the young version of Harry, played by Tobey Maguire, and Allen's Harry in the office of a psychiatrist. Psychiatrists and characters talking about psychiatry and their experiences with it are everywhere in Allen's films; as Schapiro argues, "[c]onsidering the fact that Woody Allen has himself been in analysis for some twenty years, it is not surprising that his on-screen personas use clinical terms that note their own neuroses."[19] In *Deconstructing Harry*, Harry actually goes so far as to marry his analyst (played by Kirstie Alley). At one point they get in an argument, during which she raises her hand up towards Allen's mouth and says "don't speak." While the context is very different, one can't help but recall Dianne Wiest's Oscar winning turn from *Bullets Over Broadway* in which her character's notable tagline was "don't speak."

As many of Allen's films do, *Deconstructing Harry* goes back and forth in time, and not just to the recent past, but to a past so much earlier that it requires a different actor to play a particular character. And Allen and a former wife, in a magical, *A Christmas Carol* kind of way, drop in on his brother and sister to see how they talk about him when he's not around, an instance that recalls *Annie Hall* in which Annie Hall (Diane Keaton) and Alvy Singer (Allen) drop in on younger versions of themselves to see how they acted.

In *Deconstructing Harry* there is a heavy metafictional aspect. Harry's stories (he's a writer, an occupation often held by the Allen character) are thinly veiled fictional accounts of things that have happened in his "real life" (remembering of course that Harry himself is fictional), so we sometimes get reenactments of "actual events" featuring Harry's fictional characters living out fictionalized versions of "real" events. And then we see the "real" characters and hear their versions of the same events. And eventually Harry's fictional characters start appearing in his "real" life, culminating in a surreal climax in which Harry imagines himself in conversation with all the characters he's ever created. This metafictional (or is it metafilmic?) blurring of the "real" and "imagined" happens all the time in Allen's films. For example, in *Radio Days* (1987) Allen's voiceover, in recounting an earlier event, apologizes for the rain but says "that's the way I remember it." In *The Purple Rose of Cairo* (1985), a character from a movie walks off the screen and into real life to woo an audience member who eventually makes her way up into the world on-screen. And *Bullets over Broadway* is a film about the putting on of a play narrated by the playwright himself — rarely does his voiceover match what the audience sees on-screen. And in *Stardust Memories* the blending of film director Sandy Bates' (played by Allen) real and fictional lives with his films is also very much in keeping with Allen's frequent use of a metafictional motif.

Towards the end of *Deconstructing Harry*, Harry comments that the universe is expanding, which directly recalls *Annie Hall*'s young Alvy Singer (the child version of the adult played by Allen) refusal to do his homework for what is essentially the same reason. After all, if the universe is ultimately going to break apart, why bother? While sitting in jail after being charged with solicitation of a prostitute, possession of marijuana, and kidnapping, Harry has an imagined discussion with Richard (Bob Balaban), a character who had died earlier in the day. As Harry laments that he's "a failure at life," Bob tells him that as a writer he's created his own moral universe, a comment that not only recalls several characters making the same claim in *Bullets Over Broadway*, but has larger implications concerning Allen's work as a whole.

Love triangles abound in Allen's films; in fact they form the narrative crux of most of them. And rarely are the members of the triangles strangers. Instances of friends "stealing" the lovers of their friends happen all the time. Even more disturbing is the recurring motif of men having sexual relations with the sisters of their wives. Both instances of a love triangle are socially anathema and would likely result in one's being permanently cast out from his or her social circle. But as an artist, the real Woody Allen has indeed created his own moral universe at work in his films and its rules seem far less stringent than those on the real planet earth, especially as concerns punishment. When Harry ends his relationship with his wife's sister Lucy (Judy Davis) by dumping them both and taking up with a twentysomething aspiring writer, Lucy threatens to kill him, going so far as to fire a few rounds at him. But it never seems very threatening and it is all played for laughs. Furthermore, in a fantasy sequence in which Harry visits the ninth plane of hell (a gag that was originally to have appeared in *Annie Hall*) Satan is played by Billy Crystal, who in "real life" is set to marry the young woman for whom Harry had left his wife and her sister. Hell, whether real or not, is a place of banishment for those who have egregiously sinned in life, but in *Deconstructing Harry*, it too is played for laughs. Allen's moral universe is much more amoral than not, but as it's fictional, most folks don't get hurt too badly, regardless of the seriousness of their varied legal and/or social offenses.

Over the course of the narrative we also learn that Harry likes sports, which is also a recurring obsession for the Allen character, so much so that Allen's character's profession in *Mighty Aphrodite* is that of sportswriter. But perhaps the most famous example of the Allen character's love of sports occurs in *Annie Hall*, in which Alvy retreats from a stuffy cocktail party into a bedroom with a TV so he can watch his beloved Knicks (a team at whose games Allen himself is often present). When his wife comes into the room and protests, saying that staff members of the *New Yorker* are in the other room, Alvy is unmoved, although he does try to have sex with her. And the idea that the kinds of intellectuals who might work at or subscribe to the *New Yorker* (a magazine in which Allen has published repeatedly over the years) are beneath his interest also fits squarely into the trajectory of Allen's cannon, in which intellectuals have often received rocky treatment.

The onscreen Allen has always had a contentious relationship with erudite types. In the fantasy sequence that concludes *Deconstructing Harry* a literature professor and, especially, a grad student offer readings of Harry's novels that draw attention to what is the ridiculousness of some literary criticism; similarly, in *Annie Hall*, a college lecturer going on about what he knows while standing in line to see a movie is famously called out by Alvy, who contends the guy has misread the theories of Marshall McLuhan. In a sublime moment, Alvy calls in McLuhan himself to discount the claims of the snobby teacher. In *Stardust Memories*, the only people who come off worse than the audience of filmmaker Sandy Bates' films are the critics. In *Zelig* the narrator backhandedly mocks the French critics who were so much in vogue in the early eighties, commenting that in Leonard Zelig the French intellectuals "see in him a symbol of everything." As Karen Blansfield writes, "[o]ne of Allen's favorite targets has always been the world of academia and pseudo-intellectualism, a world which divides the so-called educated and sophisticated from the ignorant uncultured. He ridicules abstruse scholarship and critical overreaction...."[20] However, one has to take the Allen characters' mocking of intellectuals with a grain of salt, because his humor, while having a generous share of high hat one-liners, also depends heavily on the erudition of the audience to be familiar with the highbrow things he likes to knock down. Furthermore, a number of noted academics and thinkers appear as experts in his films and come off quite well, such as Susan Sontag and Saul Bellow in *Zelig*. Ultimately, Allen remains

> ...an intellectual's comic, even though, like Shakespeare, he is also accessible to lesser educated audiences by virtue of his linguistic versatility and comic strokes. He ridicules the obscurities, pretensions, and profundities of high culture, yet he nevertheless admires and respects the realm of learning on which such culture is founded, from art to literature to philosophy. He has always shunned the charge of anti-intellectualism and continually denies that he is attempting to do anything more than simply be funny.[21]

Nevertheless, despite Allen's films' frequent intellectual posturing and the scholarly attention it garners, what is often missed by scholars is that most of his films are at heart just plain funny. As Daniel Green asks "[w]hy is it ... that in order to appreciate Woody Allen it is necessary to pretend that he isn't a comedian? Or that a comic film can't be 'clearly focused intellectually?' Is comedy only a 'safety net' in Allen's best films?"[22] The people in *Stardust Memories* who say they prefer Sandy Bates's "earlier, funnier films" have identified the best part of the onscreen Allen persona; he's funny and his presence makes the films funnier than they would be without him. Allen's straight dramas have been met with decidedly mixed reviews by academics and they've been despised by audiences, and to some extent rightfully so; it's not that films such as *Interiors* (1978) *September* (1987), and *Another Woman* (1988) are entirely without merit, it's that they're without humor, and perhaps more importantly, Allen himself, or at least an Allen like persona. This gets back to Doherty's comment about the slave and master. The screenwriter, director, and actor Woody Allen has done such an amazing job in creating and playing the onscreen Woody Allen persona that his films rarely succeed without him. In his best films, Allen is able to still address issues every bit as serious as those found in films like *Interiors* and *Another Woman*, but as Dianne Vipond observes, he explores "the big questions ... with a seriousness made palatable by an aesthetically distancing overlay of humor."[23] Indeed, of all the myriad recurring things in Allen's work none aside from the Allen character himself recurs more frequently, or more effectively, than humor, and Allen's comedy at its best, "like that of most great humorists, is essentially tragic, lamenting the gap between the ideal and the real, between exquisite hope and sordid fact which exists in our world, our culture, and our everyday lives, and acknowledging the impossibility of ever closing that gap."[24] But the key to that humor working is unequivocally the presence of the onscreen Woody Allen persona.

In the end, as Mary Nichols argues, "[a]ny interpretation of Woody Allen's movies, especially one that takes as its concern such serious topics as truth and virtue, runs the risk of over interpretation. Allen himself often mocks those who look for more meaning in films than is there."[25] Accordingly, it would be foolish to argue that a film such as *Deconstructing Harry* is a d(m)oc(k)umentary because in and of itself it's clearly not, at least not in the way that more overt examples of the form such as *Take the Money and Run, Zelig,* and *Sweet and Lowdown* clearly are. However, if one looks at the many Woody Allen films that also feature the Woody Allen persona, then it's not so crazy to see *Deconstructing Harry* as an important piece in a larger cycle of films — an Allen d(m)oc(k)umentary chronicle — which cumulatively documents the life of the onscreen Woody Allen persona that has become so well defined and easily recognizable over the years. I would argue that if we view these films as parts of a larger piece that in its entirety forms a kind of documentary, then it's clear that a mockumentary element comprises a large chunk of our metaphorical pie. And while many things are treated mockingly in Allen's films, what gets mocked most of all is Woody Allen himself, or at least the character he plays in his movies. It is that ceaselessly funny (but bittersweet) mocking of the Allen persona that in turn leads us to think about some of the more challenging issues in the movies of the writer/director Woody Allen. At its root, "the mockumentary is ... a soothing genre. It repays a lifetime of arid channel surfing with an oasis of cool attitude and flatters spectators.... Americans may be hazy about the dates and details of real history but a nation of televisual scholars boasts an encyclopedic knowledge of the tropes and turns of history-by-the screen."[26] And as concerns our "encyclopedic knowledge" of Woody Allen, there is nothing we know better than Woody Allen himself. Or at least the character he plays in the movies.

1. Maurice Yacowar, "Beyond Parody: Woody Allen in the 80s," *Post Script: Essays in Film and the Humanities* 6.2 (Winter 1987): 32.

2. Julian Fox, *Woody: Movies from Manhattan* (Woodstock, New York: The Overlook Press, 1996): 7.

3. Sam B. Girgus, *The Films of Woody Allen* 2nd ed. (Cambridge: Cambridge University Press, 2002): 1.

4. Girgus, p. 4–5.

5. Peter J. Bailey, *The Reluctant Film Art of Woody Allen* (Lexington, Kentucky: The University Press of Kentucky, 2001) 185.

6. Girgus, p. 9.

7. Joseph Mills, "Roller Coasters, Aristotle, and the Films of Woody Allen," *Literature/Film Quarterly* 29.1 (2001): 40.

8. "Mockumentary," *Oxford English Dictionary (Online)* New Edition, draft entry Sept. 2002 Oxford University Press, 21 December 2003 http:// dictionary.oed.com /cgi/entry/00313007?single=1&query_type=word&queryword=mockumentary &edition=3 e&first=1&max_to_show=10.

9. Thomas Doherty, "The Sincerest Form of Flattery: A Brief History of the Mockumentary," Originally printed in *Cineaste* 28.4 (Fall 2003): 22–24. Accessed online via InfoTrac Web. 8 pp. but N.P. 17 December 2003 http:// web2.infotrac.galenet.com/itw/infomark/676/343/ 44779893w2/purl=rc1_ EAIM_0_A110266867&dyn=3!xrn_2_0_A110266867?sw_aep=whitman.

10. Doherty.

11. Eric Robert Simon, "Tracing the Evolution of the Satirical Mockumentary from 1969 to

1992 through Three Auteurs and their First Films: How *Take the Money and Run*, *Real Life*, and *Bob Roberts*, come Together as a Trilogy that Moves Progressively towards a Plausible Reality," M.S. Thesis, Boston University, 1999, p. 12–13.

    12. Yacowar, p. 33.

    13. Yacowar, p. 29.

    14. Doherty.

    15. Barbara Schapiro, "Woody Allen's Search for Self," *Journal of Popular Culture* 19.4 (Spring 1986): 49.

    16. Fox, p. 8.

    17. Ryan Gilbey, It Don't Worry Me: The Revolutionary American Films of the Seventies (New York: Faber and Faber, Inc., 2003) 159.

    18. Schapiro, p. 47.

    19. Schapiro, p. 48.

    20. Karen C. Blansfield, "Woody Allen and the Comic Tradition in America," *Studies in American Humor* 6 (1988): 147.

    21. Blansfield, p. 150.

    22. Daniel Green, "The Comedian's Dilemma: Woody Allen's Serious Comedy," *Literature/Film Quarterly* 19.2 (1991): 71.

    23. Dianne Vipond, "Crimes and Misdemeanors: A Re-Take on the Eyes of Dr. Eckleburg," *Literature/Film Quarterly* 19. 2 (1991): 99.

    24. Blansfield, p. 145–146.

    25. Mary P. Nichols, *Reconstructing Woody; Art, Love, and Life in the Films of Woody Allen* (Lanhan, Maryland: Rowan & Littlefield Publishers, Inc., 1998): 1.

    26. Doherty.

12

"That's Really the Title?" Deconstructing Deconstruction in The Positively True Adventures of the Alleged Texas Cheerleader-Murdering Mom *(1993) and* Real Life *(1978)*

by Harvey O'Brien

This essay examines two films that expand the boundaries of the mockumentary. Both not only satirise their subject through an intentionally inauthentic representational framework, they consciously engage with and deconstruct documentary and docudrama discourse on terms of referentiality, indexicality, and facticity. In the manner of Bill Nichols' self-reflexive mode of representation in documentary these films "prompt the viewer to a heightened consciousness of his or her relation to the text and to the text's problematic relationship to that which it represents."[1] Transposing schisms in documentary methodology and epistemology onto stories in which the discourses of truth and reality are central precepts, these films draw attention to the core relationships between subject and audience.

Eschewing even the parodic proposition of "objectivity" typical in the mockumentary genre, both films explore subjective contact between the texts and those who created them by throwing the actual filmmakers into the mix. In Roscoe and Hight's terms, these films represent the third of three degrees of relationship with factual discourse constructed by individual mockumentary texts,[2] representing "the 'hostile' appropriation of documentary codes and conventions, and can be said to bring to fruition the "latent reflexivity" which we argue is inherent to mock-documentary's parody of the documentary project." It is my contention that through such an actively polemical (or 'hostile') attitude to the conventions of representing reality in documentary and docudrama, *The Positively True Adventures of the Alleged Texas Cheerleader-Murdering Mom* and *Real Life* bring a quality of discursive engagement commensurate with self-reflexive documentary to fictional or "fictionalized" texts. They find in mockumentary a mode of address which facilitates their exploration of the limits of communication between film maker and subject, and in deploying and simultaneously exposing specific techniques of 'documentary' construction, they implicate the viewer in the process of their deconstruction.

Claiming the Real

In 1995 Brian Winston published his critique of the Griersonian documentary *Claiming the Real.* In it he argues that in the age of digital imagery, "Digitalisation destroys the photographic image as evidence of anything except the process of digitalization."[3] (In the light of such a crisis in indexicality, though the documentary film may be used as a tool for exploring aspects of human experience, Winston argues that its value is rooted in the abandonment of the claim on "the real" inherent in the Griersonian conception of the form.

For Winston, the cultural and ideological factors which influence the subjectivity of the filmmaker negate any possibility of the objectivity required to gain access to "reality." He argues that in maintaining the illusion of objectivity, the Griersonian tradition deludes the naive spectator into accepting subjectivity as objectivity. It is often, he argues, a matter of aesthetics. Especially with regard to direct cinema techniques (most frequently employed by mockumentary films to signify documentary practice), he points out:

> The pretension to a superior representation of the real is deeply encoded in the dominant documentary style. Handheld, available light, available sound, long take, jump cut, direct gaze, minimal graphics—all these signify "evidence." This signi-fication is the reason why direct cinema film makers *say* they are being subjective, but their aesthetic practice *says not.*[4]

The only hope for documentary as a form of discourse, he argues, is in embracing the reflexive mode exemplified by Errol Morris' *The Thin Blue Line* (1988). In Winston's terms, the practice of a self-reflexive mode of representation would ideally contribute to a liberated form of fact-based film making which "should be constrained only by the needs of the relationship of film maker and participant."[5] Winston is speaking of documentary proper, of course, and his concern for "the participant" revolves around questions of ethics and victimisation which though not entirely irrelevant to the present debate are at least complicated by the participation of actors rather than interviewees. The point is still a useful one though, given that it suggests that a post–Griersonian reflexive documentary practice has a duty to engage its material with due reference to the needs of more than one party. Ideally, as Nichols points out, reflexivity also engages the viewer, creating a participant hermeneutic in which deconstruction serves as part of the process by which discourse takes place.

In *The Positively True Adventures of the Alleged Texas Cheerleader-Murdering Mom* and *Real Life* we see just such a process at work within a mockumentary context. As Roscoe and Hight indicate, this level of reflexivity is actually comparatively uncommon in the form. Though all mockumentary may be seen to be reflexive on some level, the target is rarely the epistemology of reality itself: "The mock-documentary form seems to be more typically used by filmmakers to parody aspects of popular culture, particularly media culture, than to encourage viewers to question their adherence to the assumptions and expectations associated with documentary."[6] The rarity of what they term "degree 3" mockumentaries suggests "both the potential of the mock-documentary form to serve as a site for the active subversion of factual discourse and the degree to which this potential has remained relatively underdeveloped."[7] In this chapter, I would like to explore how these two films realise these potentials and challenge our expectation of the limits of discourse in mockumentary film.

Positively True Adventures

"Next on HBO," the announcer begins in her soothing, beautifully modulated performance voice, "*The Positively True Adventures of the Alleged Texas Cheerleader-Murdering Mom.*" There is a pause, followed by the voice of a studio engineer in the background saying, "Terrific. That's great." We hear a rustle of paper. The announcer, a touch of disbelief in her now everyday speaking voice, says "That's really the title?" The music begins and the credits roll on director Michael Ritchie and writer Jane Anderson's 1993 made-for-cable "true story" based on the notorious Texas Cheerleader case of 1991.

Wanda Holloway, divorcée and mother of two from Channelview, Texas, allegedly attempted to hire a hit man to eliminate her daughter's Junior High cheerleading squad rival. Though Holloway was initially convicted of solicitation of murder, based largely on the evidence provided by her former brother-in-law, Terry Harper (who had co-operated with the police and recorded their private conversations), the judgment was invalidated on a technicality. Holloway went free, and began a series of legal proceedings against various media organisations and others who had sought to capitalise on the story.

The case had been the subject of numerous local and national news documentaries, and the first made-for-TV "dramatization" followed quickly. On 8 November 1992 ABC broadcast *Willing to Kill: The Texas Cheerleader Story* directed by David Greene and written by Alan Hines. It featured Leslie Ann Warren as Wanda, Tess Harper as Verna Heath, mother to the offending cheerleader and one of Wanda's alleged intended victims, and William Forsythe as Terry Harper. This straightforward rendering of the story was based on rights to Terry Harper's version of events. Meanwhile HBO had already begun production of their version, the rights for which had come from Terry's brother, Wanda's ex-husband Tony Harper. Wanda confined herself to appearing on talk shows, including *Donahue* where she continued to protest against the exploitation of her life by the media.

HOLLY HUNTER   BEAU BRIDGES

THE POSITIVELY TRUE ADVENTURES ★ ★ OF THE ALLEGED TEXAS ★ ★ CHEERLEADER-MURDERING MOM

The Positively True Adventures of the Alleged Texas Cheerleader-Murdering Mom (1993) exemplifies the synthesis of self-reflexive documentary and fictional text.

    The Positively True Adventures of the Alleged Texas Cheerleader-Murdering Mom first aired on 10 April 1993, taking a skewed perspective on not just the story itself, but the story of the story. In addition to giving based-on-testimony-and-transcript details about the alleged crime itself, the latter part of this film was concerned with the media circus surrounding the case and the subsequent squabbling between family members over the rights to sell their story. It starred Holly Hunter as Wanda, Elizabeth Ruscio as Verna, and Beau Bridges as Terry Harper. The writer of the film, Jane Anderson, appears in it as herself, interviewing, respectively, Verna, Terry, and Tony (the latter portrayed by Gregg Henry).

In discussions of the film, Anderson, a former stand-up comic, describes her encounter with the subjects during the research phase as having been central to the attitude taken towards them: "they were just a heinous bunch of human beings," she comments.[8] Her personal skepticism about these individuals, particularly Tony Harper, feeds into the ease with which the film slips from one register to another. The question of whom exactly is exploiting whom is raised quickly, particularly in scenes where Tony negotiates with agents and journalists for photographs of his children, "valuable family heirlooms" as he calls them. At one point Tony confronts Anderson about the upcoming network television version, saying he had heard from Terry's writers that "Theirs is going to be REAL." Anderson nervously responds "Never believe what a writer tells you."

The sense of confusion of boundaries characteristic of the mockumentary is central to the film's polemical stance. It is not strictly a parody of documentary, nor is it a pastiche of stylistic elements of either documentary or docudrama. Yet the film addresses, critiques, and deconstructs the process of its own making, drawing the audience's attention to the codes, conventions, and techniques by which it has been put together. In doing so it forces the viewer to engage with the subjectivity with which its version of this "true story" has been constructed, and, by turns, to respond to the ambiguities inherent in the discourse of facticity in docudrama in general.

The film is framed by a clever structuring device, which Anderson credits to Michael Ritchie, whereby the "story" is punctuated by an "interview" with Wanda (Hunter) seated in a studio flanked by her attorney (Matt Frewer) and her daughter Shanna (Frankie Ingrassia). As the reconstruction unfolds, "Wanda" provides perspective on events in her responses to questions posed by the off-screen director of the "documentary" she is making. Hers the the 'real life' commentary on the "fake" reconstruction.

The script draws further attention to the problematic nature of documentary indexicality by beginning with quasi-informal technical set-up in the studio. The opening shot is a blurry close up of a camera operator's white shirt, followed by awkward zooms, make-up checks, sound tests, and Frewer's complaint to the floor manager about a gel used on the lights behind Wanda which casts shadows resembling prison bars. "This is meant to be a documentary, not Geraldo," he protests.

A point of comparison is made here between the perceived "objectivity" of a documentary and the kind of sensational tabloid journalism commonly associated with Geraldo Rivera. Yet from its opening title montage, *The Positively True Adventures of the Alleged Texas Cheerleader-Murdering Mom* demonstrates an awareness of the exploitative triviality of its own subject matter. The white-on-black titles are intersped with newspaper headlines charting the progress of the Holloway case, substituting images of the actors for the individuals they portray. What is interesting is what else is in those papers, and partly through the actual layout of the newspapers themselves and partly through camera movement and angles, the audience's attention is also drawn to this.

The events took place during the build up to and outbreak of the First Gulf War. This and other stories of world significance were part of the everyday fabric of the lives of the people in this film, and television and radio reports remind the audience of this throughout. The opening title montage juxtaposes headlines such as "Battles rage along front" in *The Houston Post* of 2 Feb 1991 to "I want her gone!" (an alleged quote of Wanda) in *People Weekly*, and, in terms of an internal juxtaposition within one newspaper, *The Houston Post* of 27 August 1991 carries the lead story "British hostage in Beruit freed" on the top right with a sub story "Cheerleader Trial: States witness says Holloway requested hit" to the left. By the time the credits end, the headline from *The Houston Chronicle* of 1 November 1991 reads "Cheerleader Mom's murder plot to become TV movie" over an image of a Bush/Quayle rally in Texas to the left and the headline "Arabs, Israelis trade insults and accusations" to the right.

President George Herbert Walker Bush makes more than one appearance in the film, most notably following a key conversation between Wanda and Terry where Terry jokingly suggests she ship Verna and her daughter off to Iraq to "let Hussein deal with them." A radio announcement tells us that Bush's deadline for war is 24 hours away, followed by the sound bite to the effect that the situation in the Persian gulf is plainly one of "good and evil, right and wrong." In a world of such real world moral absolutism, this dramatization shows a rather more ambiguous type of morality being negotiated on the micro level in Bush's own home state.

Nichols makes the point that an impression of moral ambiguity is usually not characteristic of a documentary mode. It is more in keeping with a European art house cinema, where "realism combines an imaginary world rendered through a blend of objective and subjective voices with patterns of authorial overtness."[9] *The Positively True Adventures of the Alleged Texas Cheerleader-Murdering Mom*, which is "fictive," operates in just such a middle ground between reconstructive interpretation and audience positioning, a blending of perspective in which the self-conscious and deconstructive authorial presence guides the viewer towards inconclusive reading of its referentiality and the indexicality of the image in general terms.

The film's most powerful weapon in this regard is Hunter's Emmy Award-winning performance, the force of which comes from the actor's ability to refuse conventional dramatic characterisation. For Nichols, the presence of the actor is the final nail in the coffin of docudrama relative to the documentary endeavour. The actor, he notes, is "a body too many."[10] between the text and the referent, "it reduces representation to simulation."[11] Hunter's portrayal of Wanda Holloway is far from simulation though. This is explained in another self-referential scene where Jane Anderson speaks with Elizabeth Ruscio (in the role of Verna Heath) as they walk in a park.

Asking who is to play Wanda in the movie, "Verna" is surprised to hear that Anderson has written the part with Holly Hunter in mind. "She's not right" she muses. Her preference is for Susan Lucci, long-time star of daytime TV's *All My Children*: "She is Wanda" says "Verna." The levels of encoding here are fairly transparent. Not only is one actor commenting on the casting of her co-star in the presence of the writer, a Texas housewife is expressing a preference for a soap-opera star to play the woman who allegedly tried to have her killed, also in the presence of the writer. That writer, meanwhile, is playing herself at a moment earlier in time than that in which the scene has actually been shot. The movie is "documenting" an intimate moment in its own creation, drawing the attention of the viewer to all of the various aspects of that moment which have implications for how they respond to what they see.

Ritchie films the scene in long and medium shot, refusing the close-up view which might provide the reflexive thespian wink to the audience. As Anderson notes, Ritchie, director of deadpan satires *The Candidate* (1972) and *Smile* (1975) explained that the secret of great comedy writing is that "the characters have to take themselves absolutely seriously."[12] Likewise Hunter's characterisation of Wanda is crucial in maintaining the balance between outright parody and deconstructive reconstruction. She creates a distinctively "neutral" reading of Wanda. Through a series of intense, virtually unreadable stares and long pauses, and a combination of precise movements, gestures, and vocal modulations, she brings a quality of ambiguity to her portrayal, an ambiguity which restores epistemological uncertainty to the viewer's response to the "truth" of this true story.

Both in the "interview" and "reconstruction" segments, Wanda's motivation is easy to see but difficult to draw conclusions from. She is fiercely self-possessed, certainly, clearly driven by an inferiority complex and intense jealousy, but scene after scene reinforces the sense that there may be a great distance between what is visible on the surface and what is going on underneath.

In one key scene Wanda is lying on the couch watching television with her son Shane (Frederick Koehler), daughter Shanna, and Shane's friend Pete (Giovanni Rabisi). Pete and Shane are talking about a girl at school they don't like and jokingly speculate about killing her. Pete maintains that loosening the bolt on the drive shaft of her car would be a good way to do it. They laugh. Wanda seems to take a sudden interest in this conversation. She says "You know who I'd like to see dead? [Pause] Verna Heath." Pete laughs nervously, then Wanda asks him how he would go about doing it. Shane says he would put explosives in her baton, a remark Wanda dismisses icily with "That's not practical, Shane. How would you do it, Pete," turning her attention back to the other boy with a quick movement of her mascara-darkened eyes. Increasingly uncomfortable, Pete murmurs vaguely that he'd have to think about it. There is a long pause before Wanda bursts into laughter, dissipating the tension.

In the "interview" segment which follows, Wanda points out that everyone has, at one point or another, said "I'd like to kill that person," or "I'd like to see that person dead," arguing that only when she says it do people "come out of the woodwork" and attest to her murderous intentions. Again Hunter's controlled projection of self-conscious neutrality is vital here, communicating a reasonable point with facial expressions which say everything and nothing. Holly Hunter the actress gives Wanda Holloway the character the benefit of the doubt, and thereby forces the audience to examine its own response to her actions in terms of how they come to a conclusion regarding Wanda's guilt.

This quality of ambiguity is, of course, as Nichols says of the indexicality of documentary imagery "a self-substantiating claim akin to the remonstration by the Cretan that he is telling the truth as he tells us that Cretans always lie."[13] It is a

performance, and as such an interpretation in itself, yet because that thespian, directorial, and written interpretation directs the audience towards an ambiguous reading of the character, it subverts expectation and throws light back upon the other
deconstructive elements of the script. This strategy holds throughout, and the result
is indicative of the core of epistemological doubt sustained by the film, with which
it challenges the subject positions of film maker and audience.

In framing this story amid moral, ethical, and political crises on both the micro
and the macro levels, and organising these through a superstructure which folds in
on itself by exploring its own construction, the film blends form and content without significantly distorting the superficial entertainments of a made-for-cable "true
story." Its deconstructive nature becomes pronounced by degrees, by which time the
audience, immersed in one level of self-conscious parody through the presence of
the "interview" segments, finds itself addressing questions of broader context of
'truth' and 'reality' at its core.

A final factor worth pointing out is one of shooting style. Apart from the opening moments of the "interview" scenes which show shifting focus and awkward
zooms, the "interview" is largely shot entirely stationary and on video. The quality
of the video images is distinct from the 35mm used in the "reconstruction." More
significantly though, the docudrama sequences are shot entirely with hand-held cameras. As Winston indicates, hand held photography is often taken as a signifier of
authenticity in direct cinema documentary, and, as noted earlier, is a common stylistic reference point in mockumentary. The degree of hand-heldedness can vary
depending on the desired effect, from the "observation" style used throughout *This
Is Spinal Tap!* (1984) to the frantic POV shots used in *Man Bites Dog* (1992) and *The
Blair Witch Project* (1999).

The Positively True Adventures of the Alleged Texas Cheerleader-Murdering Mom
never draws attention to its hand-held camera, but the aesthetic has the significant,
subtle effect of orienting the viewer in an "observational" frame (in traditional documentary terms). Without making this a pronounced feature as most mockumentaries do, the presence of the filmmaker (coded as absence) signified by the hand-held
camera is here appropriated to draw attention to their nominal absence (enhancing
the impression of "reality" in a staged environment). Meanwhile in the "interview"
sequences, the stationary camera and off-screen questions attest to an organising
presence. The juxtaposition of the two styles functions almost subconsciously, but
with the repeated return to the questions of media exploitation and representation
raised by the "story" itself, the film rarely allows the audience to ignore its constructed nature.

This returns us to Nichols, who notes that "observational" film making gives
rise to particular questions. "Since the mode hinges on the ability of the filmmaker
to be unobtrusive, the issue of intrusion surfaces over and over within the institutional discourse."[14] This question of "intrusion," which also raises the matter of
"presence" reminds us that the use of an observational documentary aesthetic is
inherently bound up with a critique of the fictive nature of the practice. This brings
us to *Real Life*, where the topic is addressed directly.

"Their House Is Really Burning!"

In one of his frequent appearances on *The Tonight Show* comedian Albert Brooks portrayed a mime artist who narrated his routine. Not at all sure that actions spoke louder than words, the character would point out exactly what each gesture was meant to represent, just in case the audience didn't get it. In the process of doing so, he deconstructed the art he supposedly practised. Brooks, a screen actor since Martin Scorsese's *Taxi Driver* (1976), brought this same attitude to his feature-directorial debut *Real Life*, a mockumentary inspired by the television documentary serial *An American Family*(1973).

The premise of the film (co-written by Monica Mcgowan Johnson and *This Is Spinal Tap!* co-star/writer Harry Shearer) is that Albert Brooks, noted comedian and now filmmaker, has come to Phoenix, Arizona to observe and record the life of an ordinary American family, the Yeagers (played by former *Candid Camera* actor Charles Grodin, Frances Lee McCain, and non-professional child performers Lisa Urette and Robert Stirrat). Under supervision by the National Institute for Human Behaviour, the principle of the project is that everything is transparently real, right down to the acknowledged presence of the crew. The title scroll boasts that this is "the next step" after *An American Family*: "It documents not only the life of a real family, but of the real people who came to film that family and the effect they had on each other."

It is clear from the opening that the film is using the methodology of fly-on-the-wall as the basis of a deconstructive parody. As even Craig Gilbert, director of *An American Family*, acknowledges, the "absence" and "non participation" of the crew was one of the most problematic elements of the production of the original series:

> But in the end I held to my commitment to make *An American Family*, as far as possible, a series of films about the Louds, not about how the Louds interrelated with a film crew from NET. I knew damn well that no matter how we conducted ourselves we could not avoid having some effect on the family. But I was adamant about trying to keep that effect to an absolute minimum.[15]

Real Life explicitly reverses this procedural and ethical principle. Instead of pretending they do not exist or minimising contact, the crew are very much in the frame during this "observational experiment," particularly Brooks. Like the mime on *The Tonight Show*, Brooks the character explains while Brooks the director deconstructs.

He spends the film's opening section cheerfully and slightly condescendingly explaining exactly how the film is going to be made. He emphasises the costs, the cutting edge technology, and the weight of intellectual and academic weight being brought to bear behind the scenes under his direction. Seated on the steps of the National Institute for Human Behaviour, he points out that this means that not only does he have a chance of an Oscar for this, but a Nobel Prize too.

Science is used throughout the film as a guarantor of worthiness and as signifier of authenticity. The latter is a point Winston draws particular attention to as part of the documentary's claims to evidentiality (which, needless to say, he dismisses). He observes that the implicit assumption that the film camera operates like a scientific instrument is often used to justify the "findings" of documentary film on the same terms as those of scientific research. The typical attitude, he notes, is that: "Watching 'actuality' on the screen is like watching the needles dance on the physiograph: the apparatus becomes transparent; the documentary becomes scientific inscription — evidence."[16]

The "science" of film making and the science of evidence-gathering are consciously juxtaposed in *Real Life* in terms Winston would probably sympathise with. Brooks the character demonstrates the operation of the experimental cameras used to film the family's life, firstly a set of Japanese heat-sensing panel-mounted devices placed unobtrusively around the house and secondly, the monstrous "Ettinauer 226-XL" cameras worn over the heads of cameramen and making them look like astronauts or Martian invaders. The contrast between the conceptually "realistic" wall cameras and the intentionally ridiculous Ettinauer draws attention to the technological limitations of the process of unobtrusive observation. In one scene Mrs. Yeager is seen riding a tandem bike with a cameraman wearing his Ettinauer cycling from the second seat. Particular note is made of the life-like qualities of the Ettinauer, which "sees" "like a human eye" through a lens in the helmet which takes the place of the cameraman's face, and "hears" like human ears through microphones mounted where the cameraman's own ears would be. Brooks the character's excited, patient introduction to this exclusive and expensive hardware makes a point of the fetishisation of such objects within documentary practice. The hereby affirmed biomechanical qualities of the camera also call to mind Vertov's theories of the Kino-eye, where the perfection of the machine improves on the weakness of the flesh: "We cannot improve the making of our eyes, but we can endlessly perfect the camera."[17]

Also during the opening section of the film, significant attention is given to the "scientific" process by which the "ideal" family was chosen for the project. Brooks the character provides lists of largely meaningless statistics and the viewer is shown 'filmed excerpts' from some of the tests. These range from a parent/child role-reversal scenario where a father eventually responds violently to his son's provocative simulation of his controlling character to the machine designed to measure the on-screen presence of a potential subject, which gives a bespectacled, balding man a 'charisma rating' of 4.2.

During filming, as the cameras gather their "evidence," Brooks' scientific advisors are shown to be observing his own behaviour. Skeptical from the outset, especially when Brooks performs a song for the assembled townspeople of the Fifth District of Phoenix, where the "documentary" is to be filmed, consultant psychologist Dr. Ted Cleary (portrayed by J.A. Preston) constantly questions Brooks' methods and makes notes for an article in *The Journal of American Psychology*. When Cleary finally leaves the project in disgust and Brooks asks "What about the journal?" Cleary's response is "Their field is science, not buffoonery."

But who is making the film though, the "scientist" or the "buffoon?" The mocking sincerity of Brooks' characterisation is stylistically reminiscent of Rob Reiner's later portrayal of "Marty DiBergi" in *This Is Spinal Tap!*, but, importantly, in calling the character "Albert Brooks" and referring to actual aspects of Brooks' own life (he is introduced at the town meeting with Brooks' actual professional background, including reference to *The Tonight Show*), the film invokes (and parodies) the self-inscriptive dimensions of autobiographical or performative documentary, and uses this as a means to address questions of intervention and the role played by the film maker in the film making process.

Jim Lane tells us that autobiographical documentary does not use reflexivity "to eradicate the real,"[18] but rather to strengthen the film's claims to referentiality by acknowledging the place and function of the film maker in interpreting the world. He observes:

> By shifting away from the promise of the immediate truth of direct cinema, autobiographical documentaries acknowledge the problem of the grand model of historical reference. Consequently, these films and videos move between life and representation, scene and narrational acts, where authorization reflexively declares its own position in the work. This declaration involves an awareness of a representation of the self and the viewer's stake in such a discourse.[19]

The acknowledgment of the presence and the person of Albert Brooks in *Real Life* ("declaring his position" to use Lane's terminology) is a doubly referential device. The film uses Brooks "honesty" about himself and his role to make a claim for authenticity and ethical transparency, and yet, as the film shows, his presence as a character significantly disrupts the "reality" of the other characters' lives.

During filming Brooks the character seems to devote as much time to himself as to the Yeagers. He is shown explaining the project to his participants, reviewing the progress with the crew, arguing with his consultants, pondering his own appearance on screen (probing a research consultant on whether he looks "heavy" on camera), and, purely because of the character's pride in his achievement, he treats us to details of how he furnished his brand new house (his first, we are told). Apart from these "incidental" presences, the character is also shown attempting to actively engage with the Yeagers life in ways which directly affect their participation in the film. In one scene he dresses as a clown to cheer them up and in another he attempts to talk Mrs. Yeager (McCain) into having an affair with him in order to create on-screen drama during a particularly slow and depressing time in the family's life.

By the end of the film, Brooks the character realises that his experiment is an utter failure: his "reality" has been tainted by what is revealed to have been his personal desire to create an ideal family. Abandoned by his scientific advisors (who explain he is filming "a false reality"), vilified by his confused studio backer (Jennings Lang) who asks (via speakerphone) "where the hell is Paul Newman?," and rejected by the family, who are now being hounded by the news media, he is plunged into despair. In an outburst of hysterical realisation, he decides to save the film by giving the audience what they want: a big, fake ending. Inspired by the burning of Atlanta in *Gone with the Wind* (1939) ("Was David O. Selznick crazy?" he asks), he sets fire to the family home screaming triumphantly "It's real. Their house is really burning." As the movie ends he sits on the lawn and watches his subject's home go up in flames.

The double irony of all of this is that though the audience is aware that Brooks the character and Brooks the film maker are not one in the same, the film never explicitly acknowledges a schism between the "real" Albert Brooks, director of the mockumentary they are watching and the on-screen 'Albert Brooks' the character who is directing a documentary. Brooks the character nominally aims to film "real life" while unconsciously deluding himself about his motivations. Brooks the director aims to deconstruct the notion of documentary objectivity and referentiality though employing and parodying documentary conventions. Brooks the character "eradicates the real" from within, initially unconsciously, then, (cathartically) consciously, while Brooks the director exposes the methodologies of representation through which "the real" is usually constructed.

The "performative" dimensions of the film are thus doubly encoded. Because Brooks the director allows the character to share aspects of his own life experience, the audience is asked to acknowledge the crossover between fact and fiction and to engage with the argument being made with regard to the "truth claims" of documentary on the whole through the auspices of a mockumentary film. As Roscoe and Hight note, it is not merely the conventions of popular culture which are being mocked here (though these conventions are in question, specifically those of the "reality show" itself), the film encourages viewers "to question their adherence to the assumptions and expectations associated with documentary."[20]

The film is revealed to be, in Nichols' terms, literally a documentary of wish-fulfillment instead of one of social reality. The ego-centric "Albert Brooks" is so blinded to his own subjectivity that when confronted about a difference in attitude between them by Dr. Cleary, who says "We are not the same person," Brooks replies "I have to disagree." The performance of self designed to acknowledge the presence of the film crew in the production of documentary becomes a revelation of the inherent subjectivity of a film maker's world-view. In a final, viscously polemical turn, the film then concludes with its cataclysm of fire in which deconstruction becomes literal destruction and Brooks the character celebrates the reality of the film maker's encounter with the subject — he sends it up in flames.

As Roscoe and Hight observe of *Man Bites Dog* (1992), the film:

> ...seems to suggest that there is a kind of obscenity, or at least a question-able moral attitude, underlying the ideological pretensions associated with factual discourse. The distanced, objective view which the documentary genre claims to hold is revealed as a thin veneer covering a far more mundane and easily corrupted moral agenda.[21]

The moral agenda in question is one of an idealised view of the American family, but also of the means by which such an ideal can be represented and the purpose which that representation serves. Following his departure from the project, Dr. Cleary writes a book criticising the project using terms like "mind control" and "psychological rape" to describe what he calls the "Nightmare in the Desert" (the title of his book). It is interesting to note that Brooks began work on this film not as a parody of documentary, but a more conventional mockumentary on the charismatic but manipulative leader of a fictional self-help organisation modelled on Werner Erhard's est.

Questions of how American society moulds its conscious and unconscious mind run throughout the film, and there is an implicit argument that the ability to look closely and honestly at the self is beyond the means of American filmmakers.

The most explicit statement of this is the sequence in which Brooks the character, liberated by Dr. Cleary's departure, follows the family on a series of cheerful escapades including trips to a fun park and other wholesome indoor and outdoor activities connoting family togetherness. All of these are depicted in a slow-motion montage which Brooks explains in the voice over will "show the French what a montage is really about." The acknowledgement of the limitations of both form and content relative to the stated aim of the sequence (it is clearly cheesy Americana and a false reading of the reality of the life of the family the audience have been observing) is dual layered. It draws attention to the artificiality of this "vision" of the American family and the methods of film making used to render it. The sequence is also in intentionally gross contrast with the filming style used elsewhere throughout the film, as if the strain of maintaining the aesthetic rigour of documentary has finally proved too much for the meagre abilities of Brooks the "documentarist."

The film also questions the ethics of its fictive maker in a key scene where Dr. Yeager (Grodin), a veterinarian, over anaesthetises a horse during surgery, killing it. Clearly overly-conscious of the hovering Ettinauers as he mistakenly orders the anaesthetic twice over, Yeager commits an act of professional negligence captured (and caused) by the cameras. Seated in his office afterward, Yeager makes an impassioned plea to Brooks to exclude the scene from the final film. Brooks, who throughout has rigidly stuck to the axiomatic presumption that nothing that happens can hurt the film because everything is real, is reluctant, but tells Yeager "As far as you are concerned, it's out." The viewer realises that this is not true because they have just seen the scene in question, and when Yeager asks if Brooks could put that assurance in writing, Brooks firmly but politely refuses on the grounds that if he did, it would trouble him as a film maker.

The complicity between film maker and viewer (and thus the awareness of the viewer of their place in this tangle of axiographic space) is cemented by the shooting style throughout these scenes. The roving, hand-held style used in shooting the operation increases our awareness of the presence of the crew, and thus we can empathise with Yeager when he is distracted by them. The stationary, observational mid shot used to film the conversation between director and subject thereafter reinforces the sense of a voyeuristic intrusion into a private exchange on matters of ethics and legality "behind the scenes." Like *The Positively True Adventures of the Alleged Texas Cheerleader-Murdering Mom*, the film constantly reminds the viewer that there is an "on" and "off screen" space, both of which they have privileged access to, alongside the film maker, whose perspective they are ultimately invited to share.

Conclusion

By providing a deconstructive fictive space in which to engage the viewer, the mockumentary potentially offers a powerful discursive form through which to analyse and criticise the mechanisms of construction employed in the representation of reality. With the jaundiced eye of the self-aware satirist, it is possible for the mockumentarist to invite even an unattuned viewer to participate in the process of epistemological deconstruction. A heightened awareness of the codes via which evidentary claims to reality made by filmic representation is an important step towards the liberation of reality formats from the perceived rigour of the Griersonian concept of 'documentary.' As such we can see in mockumentary a potentially progressive, subversive, and yet discursive form of film making which, though not consistently explored to its fullest potential, is at least increasingly aware of the additional dimensions of the practice which do exist.

    1. Nichols, Bill. *Representing Reality: Issues and Concepts in Documentary*. Bloomington and Indianapolis: Indiana University Press, 1991: 60.
    2. The "degrees" in question are: 1) Parody, representing the bulk of mock-documentary, including *The Rutles* (1978), *Zelig* (1983), *This Is Spinal Tap!* (1984), and *Waiting for Guffman* (1996); 2) Critique and Hoax, a more involved degree of specific attack on media exploitation such as in *Bob Roberts* (1992) and *Alien Abduction — Incident in Lake County* (1998); finally 3) Deconstruction, which is our case here and which Roscoe and Hight discuss relative to *David Holzman's Diary* (1967), *The Falls* (1980), and *Man Bites Dog* (1992). See Jane Roscoe, and Craig Hight. *Faking It: Mock-documentary and the Subversion of Factuality*. Manchester and New York: Manchester University Press, 2001: 100–180.
    3. Winston, Brian. *Claiming the Real: The Griersonian Documentary and Its Legitimations*. London: BFI, 1995: 259.
    4. Winston, p. 254
    5. *Ibid*, p. 258
    6. Roscoe and Hight, p. 160–161.
    7. *Ibid*, p. 161.
    8. Quoted from a public interview given at the WGA awards 2002. Transcript available online from www.wga.org.
    9. Nichols, p. 166.
    10. *Ibid*, p. 249.
    11. *Ibid*, p. 249–250
    12. *Ibid*.
    13. *Ibid*, p. 151.
    14. *Ibid*, p. 39.
    15. Gilbert, Craig. "Reflections on An American Family." *New Challenges for Documentary*. Ed. Alan Rosenthal. Berkeley, Los Angeles and London: University of California Press: 1988: 200.
    16. Winston, p. 137.
    17. Vertov, Dziga. "The Resolution of the Council of Three, April 10, 1923." *Kino-Eye: The Writings of Dziga Vertov*. Ed. Annette Michelson. Trans. Kevin O'Brien. Berkeley and Los Angeles: University of California Press, 1984: 15.
    18. Lane, Jim. *The Autobiographical Documentary in America*. Madison and London: University of Wisconsin Press, 2002: 18.
    19. Lane, p. 23
    20. Roscoe and Hight, p. 161.
    21. *Ibid*, p. 178.

13

Man Bites Dog:
Deconstructing the
Documentary Look

by Jane Roscoe

Man Bites Dog is a multi-layered mock documentary made in 1993 by three Belgian film students; Remy Belvaux, Andre Bonzel and Benoit Poelvoodre. It is a feature length film about a serial killer and the documentary crew who are engaged in filming his everyday life and killings. The crew starts off by simply filming him, but end up becoming fully implicated in his horrendous deeds. *Man Bites Dog*, in its use of the mock documentary form and documentary style, is very consciously engaging in a debate about documentary and in particular, the authority of the documentary look. The polemic also highlights the obsession of "actuality" programs with the extraordinary or bizarre. The title itself, *Man Bites Dog* underlines this focus by referring to the journalistic desire for entertaining and newsworthy stories[1] (Winston, 1995: 214).

Man Bites Dog plays ruthlessly with the codes and conventions of the documentary screen, in particular that of the observational form which favors non-intervention on the part of the film maker with less emphasis on exposition (Nichols, 1991: 38–39). It is perhaps the observational documentary which best illustrates the documentary ideology in terms of what it claims to promise and what we as viewers, expect from it. Documentary seems to have such an obvious purpose as to warrant closer scrutiny unnecessary. In its objective to document the socio-historical world the importance of any documentary text lays in its referentiality. That is, what is indicated about the social world through its sounds and images; in the way in which documentaries leave behind traces of the (real) physical world.

> The core mode of documentation from the 1930's through to today is the employment of the *recorded images and sounds of actuality* to provide the viewer with a distinctive kind of "seeing" and "hearing" experience, a distinctive means of knowledge [Corner, 1995: 78 original italics].

Corner suggests that this way of "seeing" or "looking" is distinctively different from the "fictional gaze" and relies on the notion that what is seen is evidential (real) rather than constructed (not real or fake). This is particularly important in the case of observational documentaries which expect viewers to take part in the pretence that the camera is not there and to accept the film maker's presence as absence. Further, we are asked to participate in the belief that the events presented to us, would unfold in exactly the same way if the camera had not been present (Nichols, 1994: 95). "The cameras apparently neutral gaze gives the impression that we are simply being shown what is there..." (Britton, 1992: 26).

It is documentary's (referential) relationship with the "real" that has secured its key position within society as the screen form that can gain direct access to, and present, the most accurate and truthful accounts of the social world. The "documentary approach" claims to show reality as it is, unmediated, unconstructed and objectively and as Van Lier suggests through this "a documentary can *reach the core of things*" (Van Lier, 1993: 3, my italics). It is a look that claims to penetrate to the very factual heart of the matter. Of course this idea that documentary is unmediated has a certain ideological power. Documentary works to present issues and events as naturally occurring rather than as constructed. Its moral or ideological standpoint is subtly cloaked in the rhetoric of "naturalism" and "realism" and tends to go unquestioned.

Establishing a Documentary Mode of Engagement

"Documentary suggests fullness and completion, knowledge and fact, explanations of the social world and its motivating mechanisms." (Nichols, 1993: 74) It is this "documentary look," the look that bears knowledge, fact and truth, that is deconstructed and destabilised within *Man Bites Dog*. To allow this deconstruction it first has to co-opt viewers into a documentary mode of engagement. While audiences[2] are encouraged to (although it is not assumed that they will) enter into a documentary mode of engagement when viewing *Man Bites Dog* , this is not to say that viewers are duped into thinking that this is a real documentary. Rather, the film attempts to position viewers *as though they were watching a documentary*. It is not only that documentaries make certain claims concerning their ability to gain direct access to the real, but that viewers also have expectations of documentary which are brought to any particular viewing context. We expect documentaries to present the "real"; to give direct access to "facts" and specialized knowledge and we expect some attempt towards objectivity and balance. These promises and expectations frame the way we as viewers evaluate certain types of visual material.

Documentary has developed a repertoire of specialized codes and conventions to promote and reinforce its claims of objectivity, access to the real and its truthfulness. These have now become so familiar as to seem "natural" and unconstructed themselves. Through the utilization of conventions such as the objective "third person point of view," a documentary gaze or look is set up. As the film opens we watch Ben, the killer and subject of the film, strangle a woman on a train. Framed within such a gaze, it has the appearance of reality, a far cry from the choreographed violence (complete with special effects) of Hollywood blockbusters. With no evidence of the presence of the film crew we are allowed direct access to that which is usually hidden. We become voyeurs, but at a safe distance. Documentary relies on there being a distance for its claims to objectivity. This distance, no matter how small, reinforces the notion that what is being seen is evidential and that we are 'onlookers' rather than participants in the sphere of action.

The "realism" of the film is heightened in several ways which works to certify this objective documentary look. As well as being filmed in black and white, which serves to give an air of authenticity to the film, it also has a "camcorder" feel to it. Camcorder footage[3] is very popular within current documentary and 'actuality' programming working to promote the idea of immediacy and the experience of being a "fly on the wall." The camcorder is a central component of Reality TV, which Dovey describes as factual programs which use camcorder footage together with reconstructions to construct "a raw high energy and sensationalist 'tabloid TV'" (Dovey, 1995: 104) *Man Bites Dog* both embraces this and comments on it. The film takes as its subject matter a serial killer and joins reality television's fascination with the perverse, yet at the same time refuses to sensationalize its subject. *Man Bites Dog* invites viewers to take up this opportunity to engage with these screen forms at a different ideological level, rather than be passive consumers of them.

Continuity editing, long and mid-range shots are used most effectively in the scenes where Ben is shown at home, with his family at their shop and during the disposal of the dead bodies. The use of long seamless shots allows the "look" to be suitably distanced. The repetition of these scenes and situations works to reinforce their "reality" by locating them in the historical facticity of time and place (Nichols, 1991: 41). A capturing of "naturalistic" sound and lighting, and the use of real people, rather than (paid) actors further works to promote a sense of realism and factuality. This final point is underlined by the knowledge that the three students who made the film also star in it and use their real names, Benoit Poelvoode plays Ben the serial killer and so on.

Throughout *Man Bites Dog*, the "direct address" is used effectively as means by which Ben can impart his philosophical wisdom (especially within the context of his local pub). This direct address has the effect of calling into existence an audience for Ben and his life. In an early scene Ben addresses the camera and crew directly when discussing his methods for the removal of dead bodies. Looking them straight in the eye he explains the importance of assessing the weight, size and bone density of victims to ensure the correct ratio between the bodies and materials used to weigh them down. His information conveys the idea that this procedure ensures that bodies will remain safely at the bottom of lakes and rivers. Documentary participants usually address viewers directly in the knowledge that they are being invited to act upon information being shared with them. While giving the impression of a documentary mode of direct address, Ben is not really addressing us, the audience of the film. Rather, Ben seems to be ignoring the audience, not giving much consideration as to how we may react to what he says or what he does. The film's deconstruction of the documentary look is successful in part because of this refusal to acknowledge the

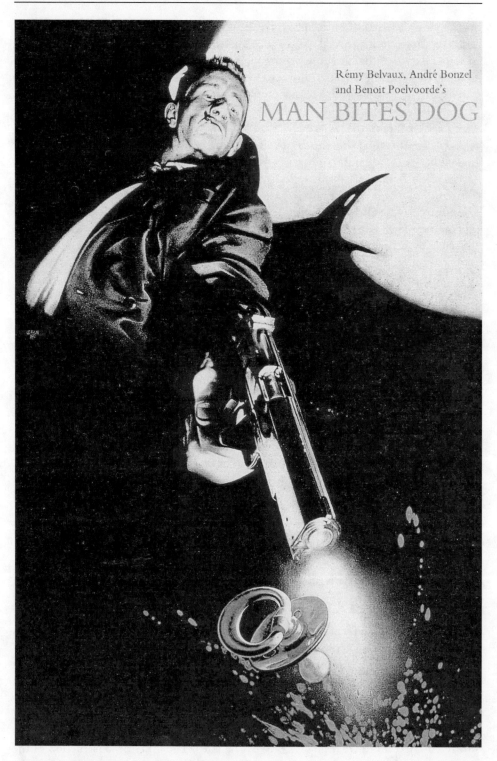

Rémy Belvaux, André Bonzel
and Benoit Poelvoorde's
MAN BITES DOG

The mock-documentary *Man Bites Dog* (1993) examines the ethics of documentary observation.

implications of a direct mode of address. This has three possible implications. First, it positions the crew as part of the action and narrative, rather than being detached and outside of it. Second, it allows the viewer to recognize both Ben *and the crew* as the object of the documentary gaze/look and, third there is ambiguity as to exactly what knowledge viewers are being invited to act upon.

Deconstructing the Documentary Look

While the film attempts the establishment of a documentary mode of presentation, early on that very form is de-stabilized. This is attempted through parody and burlesque as well as through a subversion of the traditional conventions. Often these moments are funny, but they also have a more serious implication in terms of the way in which they can draw attention to the constructed nature of documentary's truth claims and myths. In this next section the ways in which *Man Bites Dog* attempts to deconstruct the documentary look will be explored.

The early observational style scenes which allow lingering, but static, shots of Ben and his family soon give way to moments in which this "documentariness" is disrupted. For example, while filming Ben dumping a body over a bridge, the camera (and our look) wobbles thus alerting us of the actual presence of the camera. In a following scene, Ben attacks a postman in a darkened shop doorway. In the outer edges of the shot, the crews reporter Remy can be seen and heard shouting "Lights!." Thus we are made aware, not only of the camera, and of the crew, but also of the artificial nature of such observational documentary moments.

Documentaries' claims of objectivity is perhaps one of its most treasured and protected myths and one that *Man Bites Dog* moves to dismantle. The film charts the movement from the crew as "objective recorders" to active participants and allows consideration of the implications of this, thus, deconstructing one of documentaries central myths. As the film progresses the crew's presence becomes more central to the events. At first it is just a fleeting acknowledgment that they exist. For example, Ben makes a visit to Jenny who is a prostitute. As Ben rings the bell he turns to the crew and asks if they "got home ok" after their evening in the pub. He comments that they "must be bushed." In Jenny's flat the crew's presence is once again acknowledged when she turns to them and asks what they would like to drink. These early signs of existence soon give way to scenes in which the crew begin to participate more fully. After Ben has killed a black man on a building site, he recruits Remy to help him to move the body. Remy starts to appear more consistently within shots and the crew seem to be moving from "outsiders" looking in on the events, to "insiders" who are part of the action. The distance between the camera (viewer) and object begins to diminish both metaphorically and literally and the documentary look starts to be de-objectified.

The crew's participation in the events allows for some humorous moments. Ben has chosen as his next victim, an old lady living in a block of flats. Ben recruits the crew in his bid to gain entry to the old woman's flat. As the woman opens the door he introduces himself as part of a television crew who are making a documentary on "loneliness in high rise apartments." As he sits down next to the old woman he requests the crew to start filming the "interview." This is funny not only because they themselves are in fact a documentary crew, but also because of the way it draws attention to the reputation that some documentarists have for using deception to gain access which would otherwise be denied.

The crew is not merely recording Ben in the act of killing the woman but are themselves part of those acts. After Ben has killed the woman, he and Remy are shown searching the flat for cash. Ben remarks, to Remy's obvious delight, that there will "be plenty for everyone!" It is as if these events seal the new relationship between Ben and the crew. Outside, in the street, the status of this new relationship is explored. Ben declares that killing the old woman has "whet his appetite" and offers to take the crew for a celebratory meal. Remy seems keen yet the crew hesitate, pondering the implications of this new relationship. Just as it looks as though they are about to reclaim their status as (objective) outsiders, the next shot reveals the crew and Ben in the restaurant.

Documentaries are often criticized for exploiting "real" people for their own ends. The participants don't get paid, they have little editorial control and are often in a powerless position. In *Man Bites Dog,* this is consciously subverted. During the restaurant scene Remy tells Ben that they are running out of money and may not be able to carry on with the film. To this Ben replies that he will fund the film, thus ensuring himself a screen presence. Ben's position changes from that of a powerless "object" of study through to position of power and control. This has the effect of once again, subtly shifting the object of study from himself to himself and the crew.

During a shoot-out in a disused factory, the soundman, Patrick is shot. Patrick's body is disposed of without ceremony and as usual, the days events are subject to a post-mortem in the local pub. Once again, it is both Ben and the crew who are the object of scrutiny. Ben and Remy share the screen space whilst the presence of the cameraman, Andre is indicated through his glass of beer which lies on the counter.

The death of Patrick allows for a moment of parody. On returning from the pub, Remy sets up the camera and delivers a memorial monologue. With a bottle at his side and tears in his eyes Remy proceeds to explain that the job was always tinged with danger; death is an occupational hazard that could strike any of them. However, they would continue the film for Patrick, his girl friend Marie-Paul and for their unborn child (this is particularly funny because Remy gives the almost word-for-word same speech when a further crew member is killed). This moment specifically parodies the authors of war documentaries and reportages who seem so willing to put themselves in obvious danger in order to bring the stories and the truth back home to the public. Here, there is little talk of courage or sacrifice, the death is almost trivialized, Patrick did not die for the "truth." This parody not only makes fun of such documentary claims but, also points to their insincerity.

Until now the crew have only been indirectly involved in the killings. As yet they have not actually killed anyone themselves. As they become more actively involved with Ben so they become more and more detached from their original roles as observers. As they cruise a suburban street Ben challenges them to choose a house and the next victim. It is a choice that has consequences and the crew is expected to play a part. This is an interesting moment as their victims, the members of a white, middle class nuclear family are the typical (ideal) viewers of television documentary. As the crew participate, their complicity forces a collapse of the audiences' distance from the subject. Once inside the house, Vincent, the new sound man, heightens Ben's enjoyment of killing by capturing the sound of Ben breaking the husbands neck and, Andre uses his camera and lights to help track down the young boy who has run off into the dark night. However, it is Remy who has a direct taste of murder. Once Ben has caught the young boy, it is Remy who effectively suffocates the child by holding down the pillow over his face. These events could be read as the symbolic death of the ideal television documentary viewer and of the safe distance which they are usually guaranteed through the participation in the discourses of objectivity. Here, this objective distance implodes back on to the audience. As we get closer to the subject, we become more aware of the constructed nature of the documentary look and we can no longer take for granted its promise to allow access to the real without the consequences of having been there.

The final loss of Ben and the crew's original roles and positions is symbolically played out in a scene in Ben's hideout, an old derelict warehouse. As they arrive in the building they hear movements in the floor above and Ben tells Remy that "The Nightingale" (presumably an enemy of his) is present. Gunshots ring out and a second crew member is shot down (Franco). A chase across rooftops presents a spectacle that would not look out of place in any "Reality TV" program. On return to the house, Ben and the crew encounter another documentary crew, there to film "The Nightingale." They are clearly "rivals" working on video rather than film and possibly from a network "Reality TV" program. Ben is quick to point out the evidence of a bigger budget and asks Remy whether he would like their equipment. They take what they want, leaving the video crew, their tools of the trade taken, impotent. Without their cameras they have no protective lens from behind which they can vicariously take part in the action. Further, they no longer have any legitimate role to play and so they are killed literally, but also symbolically rendering them, and all they stand for, dead.

There has been an almost total inversion of the situation at the beginning of the film, the dead film crew representing what was, in contrast to what is. This is taken to its logical ending when Ben *et al* go on what can only be described as a rampage. Remy and the new soundman, Vincent are fully implicated now and are shown in the pub playing a game called "dead baby boy." This game involves an olive and a sugar cube tied together with a piece of string which is then dropped in a gin and tonic. The aim of the game is to have your "baby" rise to the surface last. It symbolizes the "ballasting of corpses" and during the game Ben refers to his earlier lecture on this subject, testing Remy and Vincent. Once again Andre's presence is indicated only through his glass. After several rounds they leave the pub in search of action. They stop at an apartment block and as Ben dances in a drunken stupor we see for the first time the silhouette of Andre and his camera. They climb the stairs and burst into the kitchen of a young couple, caught naked. What follows is a brutal gang rape of the woman with the man forced to watch. Everyone takes a turn, including Andre whose face we never see.[4]

After Remy has raped the woman the camera frames him for a brief moment. There is a look of total disgust on his face. Its as if he has suddenly realized what he has done and what he has become. But it is also a look that realizes there is no turning back. The whole scene seems gratuitous and unnecessary and as they wake up in the morning surrounded by death, there is little room for humor. As Remy comes to realize what he has done, so too, we as viewers begin to realize what we have been watching.

"The camera gaze that actively sides with agency of death legitimates itself through the same codes as the taking of life in the first place" (Nichols, 1991:85) The documentary gaze and our voyeurism are implicated in the deaths.[5] Documentary asks us not only to engage with its representations, but to also act upon that knowledge. Perhaps *Man Bites Dog* is unsettling because it is presenting to us, truths or knowledge we would rather not engage with or act upon.

The Documentary Look — A Moral Look?

There are other ways in which the authority of the documentary gaze is destabilized. Documentaries do not merely present the social world, but comment upon it. Since the early days of the Grierson movement, documentarists have not only "recorded" but have interpreted, analyzed and commented upon the social world (Winston, 1995: 11). Even the purest observational documentary has at its core an argument which may give indications of the ideological or ethical perspective of the documentarist but also produces certain ideological or moral subject positions. That this moral positioning may be overlooked is in itself an indication of how successful documentary has been in passing its versions of reality as naturally occurring from that reality rather than a construction of it.

One of the unsettling aspects of *Man Bites Dog* is its refusal to fully take up a position in which Ben and the killings are explicitly condemned. Its not that the film takes an *amoral* stance on the murders, but rather it is ambiguous about its position. In effect it refuses to speak with the authoritative moral voice. Instead it leaves us with a series of ambiguous moments from which we as viewers have to construct our own moral response to it. The representation of the "serial killer" within the film is perhaps one way in which a moral stance is refused. There has, over the last few years developed, what one might describe as the "cult of the serial killer." Hollywood has presented us with a continuous supply of films in which these figures are paraded.[6] What is central to many of these portrayals are killers who are represented as pathologised individuals, often from broken homes or as victims of child sexual abuse. In these representations these films reinforce the stereotype of the serial killer as an abnormality outside of mainstream society. In doing so, they take a particular type of moral position which has certain political and social implications. In *Man Bites Dog* a very different representation is made available. Ben is represented as a cultured and educated middle class male. Far from being a product of a deviant upbringing, his family embody "normality." Further, Ben himself is in a long-term stable relationship and seems to have no other anti-social traits. This "normalization" of the serial killer is reinforced by the repeated shots of Ben with his family, with his partner and in the pub, all 'normal' everyday ways of being. This normalization of Ben attempts a subversion of the usual moral positioning that is produced by the documentary gaze. It works against what we expect a documentary to do, that is comment upon (and condemn) what society has deemed evil.

Conclusion

Man Bites Dog invites us to participate in a documentary mode of engagement, *as though it were a documentary*. In doing so, it creates a space within which viewers can negotiate a reading which deconstructs the documentary look. This is not a one-sided critique of the documentary form, but rather a deconstruction which questions, not only the authority of documentary, but also the position of documentary makers and viewers. Old dichotomies such as the objective/subjective and insider/outsider that have shaped both the production and reception of the documentary are challenged within *Man Bites Dog* specifically through the complicity of the film crew in the killings. As the distance between the subject (Ben) and the observers (the crew) disappear the documentary look finds a new subject. The whole process of documentary production comes under scrutiny and open to question. In joining Ben in his "work," the crew lose the safety of their outsider status and so too, we as viewers are left without the protection of the documentary look. A look that is supposed to be objective and distanced, allowing voyeurism without the risks of being located within the action.

We, as viewers, are forced to reconsider some of the assumptions and expectations that frame our documentary watching. *Man Bites Dog* is not only uncomfortable to watch because of its explicit violence, but because of the ways in which it implicates us in its construction of "reality." As a tool through which documentary can be explored, questioned and problematized, *Man Bites Dog* is a powerful film and one which raises other issues concerning the future of documentary. Mock-documentaries such as *Man Bites Dog* may indicate a transformation stage in the development of documentary. "The present significance of generic transformation as a creative mode reflects the feeling that not only the traditional genres but the cultural myths they once embodied are no longer fully adequate to the imaginative needs of our time" (Cawelti, 1986: 200).

Documentary may not conform to the traditional notions of genre that Cawelti refers to, but there is a considerable body of work that we now regard as "Documentary." There is certainly an institutional framework with its own specific language and practices (including the notion of "documentarists"), particular commonalities across a body of texts and importantly, a collection of audience expectations concerning documentary that frame the viewing. It is also the case that the documentary project has been with us since the birth of cinema and is, as such, the oldest of genres.

It is then, perhaps not surprising that documentaries (like many other genre) have been subject of such transformative elements such as parody and the burlesque as can be seen in *Man Bites Dog*.[7] What is surprising is that for so long documentary has been a sacred space with very little questioning of its authority.

Documentary has already spawned a variety of hybrid forms such as drama-documentary and "reality TV." Film makers have been, for some time, pushing the boundaries, looking for new ways to move beyond the limitations of traditional documentary. Institutionally, the safe haven for documentary within the public network has been disrupted and funds are increasingly hard to come by. Audiences, media literate and sophisticated, require the novelty of new forms. New technology is starting to undermine the sacredness of the document and photograph, and this is having serious repercussions for the documentary form. Documentary is in a state of flux and is in the process of transformation (Hughes, 1995: 45). As we celebrate one hundred years of film, mock documentary is one site where the documentary can be contested and questions debated about how the social world can be represented. As move into the next century, documentary has to find new ways of answering those questions.

1. Dog bites man is not news, but man bites dog is. Journalists are required to hunt out man bites dog stories.

2. There are serious problems associated with talking about idealized viewer positions. In recent years those undertaking textual analyses have been criticized for their reliance on the idealized spectator, assuming universal readings and neglecting to explore the full complexities of the "making sense process." Stacey (1993) has pointed out that much film theory talks of the audience without ever having felt the need to undertake empirical research on actual audiences. Here, it is argued that this analysis of *Man Bites Dog* would benefit greatly from some empirical audience research. Any film text can be seen as polysemic offering a range of subject positionings and readings (Roscoe et al., 1995). Clearly not all viewers will take the particular reading offered here.

3. The "camcorder look" can be characterised as one which is grainy, has a cluttered screen, disconnected edits, narrative discontinuities or incompletion and so on.

4. It is perhaps through the character of the cameraman, Andre that the audience is implicitly implicated in the action throughout the film.

5. However, it also the case that this same gaze could be seen as commenting on such discourses. See for example, David Monaghan's discussion of his documentary *Executions* which has caused much controversy for breaking a screen taboo by showing real deaths. "My bloody documentary is the antidote to the Hollywood hype dumbing and dripping blood from the shelves of our video stores" (Monaghan, 1995: 31).

6. *Silence of the Lambs*, *Seven*, *Copycat* and *Natural Born Killers* to name just a handful of the most high profile of these films.

7. *Man Bites Dog* is not alone in its parody of the documentary. New Zealand's Television One recently screened an exceptional mock documentary, *Forgotten Silver* (made by Peter Jackson and Costa Botes). For a fuller discussion of this programme, see J. Roscoe and C. Hight (1996) "Silver Magic" In Illusions No. 25 pp. 14–20.

Works Cited

Britton, A. (1992) "Invisible Eye" *Sight and Sound* Vol 10: 2.

Cawelti, J.G. (1986) "*Chinatown* and Generic Transformation in Recent American Films" In B.K. Grant (ed.) *Film Genre Reader* University of Texas Press, Austin.

Corner, J. (1995) *Television Form and Public Address* Edward Arnold, London.

Dovey, J. (1995) "Camcorder Cults" *Metro* No: 104: 26–30.

Hughes, P. (1995) "The Documentary Caught in a Web?" *Metro* No: 104: 45–52.

Monaghan, D. (1995) "Executions" *Metro* No: 104: 30–36.

Nichols, B. (1991) *Representing Reality* Indiana University Press, Bloomington and Indianapolis.

Nichols, B. (1994) *Blurred Boundaries* Indiana University Press, Bloomington and Indianapolis.

Nichols, B.(1993) "'Getting to Know You...' Knowledge, Power and the Body" In M. Renov (ed.) *Theorizing Documentary* Routledge, New York and London.

Roscoe, J., Marshall, H. and Gleeson, K. (1995) "The Television Audience: A Reconsideration of the 'Taken-for-granted' Terms 'active,' 'social' and 'critical.'" *European Journal of Communication* Vol 10: 1 87–108.

Stacey, J.(1993) "Textual Obsession: Methodology, History and Researching Female Spectatorship" *Screen* Vol 34: 3 260–74.

Van Lier, M. (1993) Editorial *Dox* No: 0 Winter.

Winston, B. (1995) *Claiming the Real* British Film Institute, London.

14

Stanley Kwan's Centre Stage *(1992): Postmodern Reflections of the Mirror Within the Mirror*

by Wayne Stein

> Stanley Kwan was doing research two years before the film
> started. So he has this pile of information and tapes, and we
> were in Shanghai for four months and the first two were just
> getting into the part, so it was vary rare for Hong Kong — I felt
> that to do that part properly and well, I must know it well. I
> would even fall asleep thinking about her. She really haunted
> me for those four months. — Maggie Cheung, interview[1]

When young and famous film stars die at the height of their careers, they often become legends. Rudolph Valentino, James Dean, Marilyn Monroe and Bruce Lee all belong to this category of stars that died young at the height of their fame. The death of such icons seduces us. These figures become ghosts, reborn into our imaginative tales, transformed within a multitude of articles, short stories, books, plays, and films which continue to haunt the public's imagination. Chinese audiences would add the name of the great silent film star, Ruan Ling Yu (1910–1935) to this list.[2] At the age of twenty-five and at the height of her fame, her suicide guaranteed her place as a legend in Chinese cinema. Furthermore, her death seemed to mirror the suicide of the character that she portrayed in her last picture: *The New Woman* (1935). Life imitated cinematic fiction as she committed suicide right after the release of this film.

Some fifty years later interest in her life and death continues to grow in Asia. Hong Kong director Stanley Kwan (1957–) explored the death and short life of the legendary Ruan Ling Yu in his film *Centre Stage* (1992). The director gathered an outstanding team of well known Hong Kong actors to make what looked to be an interesting docudrama, examining the historical links of Hong Kong filmmaking to the past. *Centre Stage*, however, is not your typical docudrama, for there is a key distinction to make about docudrama when compared to other film genres. In a docudrama,

Maggie Cheung as the Chinese actress Ruan Ling Yu in death in Stanley Kwan's *Centre Stage* (1992).

the "representation of history does not pretend to be documentary in nature."[3] Thus, a docudrama is not a documentary which tries to record the factuality of history. However, are such distinctions always clear in film practice? Stanley Kwan's treatment of the legend of Ruan Ling Yu seems to be both a docudrama and a documentary. The film mixes actual photos and footage of the original silent film actress along with interviews conducted by the director with contemporaries who knew Ruan Ling Yu including Chinese actors Li Lili and Chen Yan Yan. Both acted in Ruan's films and later had success in their own films. Furthermore, the film contains interviews with the stars of the film. Even an interview with a biographer of Ruan Ling Yu is interjected into the narrative. Though this integration of documentary techniques, especially the use of interviews, recalls other dramatic films such as Warren Beatty's *Reds* (1981), it differs due to the constant integration of "factual" documentary techniques with "fictional" narrative devices associated with docudramas.

In the opening sequence of *Centre Stage*, Stanley Kwan comments on the impact that the 1935 death of Ruan Ling Yu has had on Chinese popular culture today, some fifty years later. Thus, the film opens with the documentary technique of using voiceover narration over a series of old movie stills of the actual silent film star, since most of her original films are now lost. The audience hears that her death came at the age of 25. Kwan explains that it wasn't until she starred in a film made by Hong Kong's Lienhua Studio in 1929 that she made the transition from being a bit actor to becoming a true star. Lienhua Studios and its left-wing film makers changed Chinese cinema in the 1930s by creating more realistic films that focused on the working class and on re-defining Chinese women. Such Western-like films that focused on the average person appealed to Chinese audiences. These films contrasted sharply with the popular Wuxia Pian or martial arts films, with their fantasy sword fights that were born from the Peking Opera tradition. *Crouching Tiger, Hidden Dragon* (2000) is a contemporary example of this genre.

After the opening narration, Kwan introduces another documentary technique — that of the interview. He asks Maggie Cheung (1964–), who stars as Ruan Ling Yu, if she wishes to be remembered some fifty years later. Cheung looks into the camera and replies that she does, but in a different manner because Ruan remains a legend while Cheung is just starting to play more serious roles.[4]

For Stanley Kwan, the film could have been just another docudrama narrating the tragic fall of yet another film star. Like so many other docudramas, its purpose could have been "to re-tell events from national or international histories, either reviewing or celebrating these events" or "to re-present the careers of significant national or international figures."[5] However, the death of Ruan Ling Yu stands as the crowning event in an incredible career which was engulfed by nationalistic fervor, for her last films were created in an attempt to define a much needed national cinema in order to combat the colonial and invading forces within China. According to Asian film historian Shuquin Cui, "the 1930's saw the transformation of early Chinese cinema into a socionational practice."[6]

The integration of documentary-like techniques changes *Centre Stage* from being just another docudrama. This integration is not as seamless as the computerized techniques used to allow a central character to "meet" historical figures, as in Robert Zemeckis's *Forrest Gump* (1994), but the film displays many of the documentary techniques found in mock documentaries. Mock documentaries use "transparency within the work itself in order to reveal its constructed nature" as a way to criticize and "subvert" social or political norms.[7] Though *Centre Stage* does not employ humor as mock documentaries can, the docu-techniques do allow audiences to be more critical of the exposed social norms, as mock documentaries do. The docu-techniques help to explore the cause of Ruan Ling Yu's death by exposing the irony of her rise to fame as an actress who played liberated, modern women on-screen while off-screen societal norms expected her to be the traditional subservient Chinese woman, dedicated to both man and family.

Jane Roscoe, one of the authors of *Faking It: Mock-documentary,* stated in an interview about the meaning of the genre: "What mock documentary does is it plays with something that's very sacred to the documentary form, it says, 'Don't believe everything you see because we can make something real but it's actually fake, it's fictional.'"[8] Questioning reality stands as an important aspect of *Centre Stage.* Kwan's film offers his audience a new way of examining an old legend. But the film does maintain the familiar characteristics of the standard Hollywood narrative by creating a "linearity and unobtrusive" illusion which "creates the effect of a closed diegesis, a seemingly autonomous fictional world which the viewer can access fantasmatically, as a privileged and invisible guest."[9] Furthermore, the format of *Centre Stage* is meta-cinematic in nature.[10] According to Stephen Teo, Stanley Kwan's format created a "dialectical, self-critical text in an attempt to 'write' film criticism within the context of his own work, while at the same time providing a historical pre–1949 or precommunist view of Chinese cinema."[11]

The many mirrors and windows found in the film represent the perfect voyeuristic metaphor for a film star concerned with her appearance. At the same time, the use of docu-techniques works to maintain a meta-cinematic appeal which is also reinforced with the mirror imagery. The meta-cinematic apparatus becomes all too apparent as we observe the process of filmmaking. While such techniques reveal the invisible camera, they also expose the "invisible guest." We, as the complacent audience, become more than mere viewers, for we are made aware of our own vicarious involvement by observing the production process.

The camera itself gains significance during an interview in which Maggie Cheung talks to Stanley Kwan within the frame of a mirror. At the beginning, we view a close up of Cheung's face as she asks about the relationship between Ruan Ling Yu and her husband, Chang Ta-min. We learn in the film that Chang Ta-min came from a wealthy family. Ruan Ling Yu's mother had been a maid for his family when Chang and Ruan fell in love. That would have been fine if he had married someone else and Ruan Ling Yu had become his mistress, but to marry the maid's daughter as he did meant disgrace for his family. Consequently, his act of marriage became an act of rebellion and he was cut off from his family's wealth. For Ruan, this should have been an act of love that any young woman would dream about, but Chang was not much of a provider and he was addicted to gambling. She became an actress to support them and his gambling. Chang used Ruan's sense of guilt over his sacrifice for her throughout her remaining years. For example, there is the strange scene where she has bought a ring and tries to put it on his wedding finger but it doesn't fit. This scene captures how traditional Chinese gender roles were reversed in their relationship.

Returning to the key scene with the camera reflected in the mirror, about half of Stanley Kwan's face is shown within it while he is partially out of focus, listening. As the camera pulls back slightly and pans to the right, Kwan begins to answer Maggie

Maggie Cheung, Stanley Kwan, the cameraman's assistant, and the camera as reflected within a mirror.

as he comes into focus. Maggie's face goes out of focus, and her image moves partially out of the frame to the left. Then we see first the cameraman's assistant, and then the camera itself along with the cameraman. All four individuals and the camera are now bound within the frame of the mirror. This scene captures the collaborative nature of filmmaking as well as the interplay between the time and space of the film's production and the biographical narrative of Ruan Ling Yu's life.

The presence of mirrors and windows establishes itself in the first scene where Maggie Cheung acts as Ruan Ling Yu in *Centre Stage*. The camera pans through the glass house that is Lienhua Studios as Cheung sits in front of three mirrors placed on a dresser looking ghost-like because of the white face make-up necessary for a silent film. It is 1929, and Ruan is 19 years old. In this scene a star is reborn. The cycle of death and rebirth begins to turn in this moment of cinematic samsara, a Buddhist concept describing the eternal cycle of human existence. The reflecting surfaces reinforce the cyclic nature of death and rebirth. The triple mirrors reflect Cheung as the replicated image of Ruan Ling Yu in an instant of cinematic samsara in which the former silent screen star is brought back to life through the contemporary film star's performance.

For Buddhists, the reflective elements found throughout the film represent the mind. Often water is the popular metaphor for reflection. For example, the reflective image of the moon on the pond (mind) symbolizes reality being reflected in the mind. In an impure mind, clouds (confusion in the form of desires and attachments) often fog over the image of the moon. Only when the reflection is free from the distortion of waves, does the clear mind have the potential for enlightenment. A clean mirror reflecting reality without distortions symbolizes purity and wisdom. Though Ruan Ling Yu's cinematic roles often embodied the ideal of the emancipated modern woman, Ruan Ling Yu's life remained rather traditional while she desired to be liberated and wise. In *Centre Stage*, whenever the images in the mirrors are unclear, the mind of Ruan Ling Yu or others seems unclear.

In the film, mirrors often reflect the emotional and psychological states of the characters. In a key scene, Ruan Ling Yu breaks up with her husband, Chang Ta-min, and moves in with her new lover, Tang Chi Shan, who also happens to be married. Mr. Tang was a rich businessman who enjoyed investing in films and meeting young film stars who became his mistresses. Ruan became just another of his conquered prizes. After she moves in, her husband, Chang Ta-min, visits the new house when everyone has left for the day. He asks for a tour of the house, ending up in the room she shares with her new lover. Once they enter the room, Chang Ta-min looks at Ruan Ling Yu, who is out of frame, while to his back stands the dresser with a mirror. Though Ruan is out of the frame, the image of her face is reflected in the mirror; however, it is a featureless, though radiant, blur of light, which represents her emotionless feelings toward him. We hear her monotone replies from this oval radiance of light. He claims to care for her, but his real motivation is to get an advance on the final settlement of monthly installments that she has promised to pay him. This rather out-of-focus image of Ruan captures the reality of their out-of-focus relationship.

In another important sequence involving a mirror, Ruan Ling Yu goes to Chang

Ta-min's dilapidated place to confront him. She knocks, and he lets her in. She stands with a dresser mirror directly behind her. In the next shot, the mirror becomes the center of the shot while she stands to its right with the darkness to the left. This scene parallels the use of the mirror as part of the *mise-en-scène* when Chang Ta-min visited her bedroom earlier. The centered mirror becomes the focal point of the shot reflecting no one as it lies partially in the *noir*-like emptiness with only a small water container reflected in the mirror. She confronts him verbally while he responds violently, breaking the glass table — a reflective surface — before him. He then states that he still loves her. Without looking at him, she replies that she does not love him. He walks to the window and looks down, noticing a crowd gathering. As she walks toward the window and as the camera views them together from the outside, the empty mirror again comes into complete view, centered between them momentarily. Though the couple sees each other, they have become invisible to each other's heart in this arranged *mise-en-scène* with the dirty window in the forefront and the image-less mirror in the background. The dirty window parallels the opaqueness of their relationship while the broken glass reinforces the fragmented nature of their relationship. The scene shifts and becomes an interior shot with the dirty window in the background. Seeing the crowd below, Ruan Ling Yu screams and cries, asking why he brought the public crowds into their private lives. She came wanting sympathy and wanting him to stop selling lies to the tabloids; she left distraught though she tried to maintain her composure when passing through the gauntlet of eyes on the street below.

The original source of the mirrors comes from Ruan Ling Yu's last film, *The New Woman* (1935). Ruan played a music teacher, Wei Ming, who became a successful writer. Kristine Harris points out how in one scene from *The New Woman*, the car window becomes like a mirror reflecting scenes from Wei Ming's memory by transforming into "a screen for a film within a film.... She becomes, in effect, a spectator within the movie, watching herself critically."[12] Stanley Kwan constructed *Centre Stage* to be a continuation of *The New Woman*. Mirrors become visual metaphors of the mind. Contrast the scene containing the facelessness of Ruan Ling Yu featured in the mirror when Chang Ta-min visits her new house to the scene of the human-less image in the mirror when Ruan visits Chang's house to the scenes of the clarity of the images in the mirrors found throughout the film, especially those of her final death scene.[13] The mental composures of the characters are captured in such sequences.

On March 8, 1935, on International Women's Day, just one month after the film *The New Woman* was released, Ruan Ling Yu committed suicide with sleeping pills because the press had revealed that she was living with a married man while still married to another man, a common practice for men at the time, but unacceptable for women, even film stars. The left-wing critics made her into a martyr for their cause by claiming that she was killed by the feudalism that imprisoned a country. Thus, "from a victim, Ruan Ling Yu was transformed to a heroine who was courageous enough to wage war against the corrupt social structure by sacrificing her life."[14] She became but another woman used by men, for:

women bore signs and codes signifying larger socionational issues.... As a displayed object, she not only provided physical evidence of and persuasive witness to social oppression, but also legitimacy of male intellectuals' cultural mission. In fact, the voice that spoke from women's issues came from male intellectuals rather than from women themselves.[15]

In reality, Ruan Ling Yu died because she wanted to avoid the trial and public humiliation that would turn her private life into a circus before the world.

The gossip in the tabloids painted differing images than the strong matriarchal images found in her films. Chinese film historian Laikwan Pang points out that while the left-wing films she starred in emphasized the independence of the new modern woman, they also emphasized a woman who represented a strong motherhood.[16] She died because the stories about her being unfaithful to her husband contradicted the characters she enacted in her films, where she would die for her family. During the suicide scene in *Centre Stage*, Ruan Ling Yu writes that she is not afraid of death but that she only fears malicious gossip. It was the press that had originally attacked *The New Woman* because within the film, the press is blamed for the death of Wei Ming. Indeed, in retaliation for this depiction, the press had demanded that the film be edited and then started to attack its star. With the death of its star in real life, the press possessed the perfect story with which to seduce its readers. Wei Ming dies cinematically on the hospital bed proclaiming, "I want to live. I want revenge." Ruan died in reality only wanting her privacy. Kristine Harris contends that the death of Ruan Ling Yu symbolized:

> an irrecoverable loss of public innocence. On a local level, this was an instant of recognition that the press, film studio, star, and audience were mutually implicated in the production and circulation of images— process of commodification and consumption that could strip away or reconfigure whatever fragile boundaries exist between artifice and nature, romantic and real, public image and private life.[17]

In real life, when Ruan Ling Yu died, the public felt a great sense of lost and partial responsibility for her death, for their mourning conceded a duplicity in their consumption of gossip and a complicity in her last act of self-destruction.

In a further irony, *The New Woman* mirrored and re-enacted the recent death of another star, Ai Xia, who had committed suicide after the release of a film she had written and starred in called *A Modern Woman* (1934). In *The New Woman*, Wei Ming's life becomes tragic as she becomes poor and enters into prostitution to help pay for her ailing daughter's medical needs. The press finds out about her becoming a prostitute and reports on the details of her life. Though she stops herself from being a prostitute, she knows the fatal consequences that such an act will have on her daughter. She can withstand the poverty but not the humiliation caused by the press, so she commits suicide. The film's director, Cai Chu Sheng (1906–1968) wanted to direct *The New Woman* as a film of remembrance for Ai Xia and as revenge against the press that did not support her. In the film, *A Modern Woman*, Ai Xia played the typical Chinese woman trying to please the men in her life but in the end she rejected submission to patriarchy in order to become an emancipated woman. The film was supposed to showcase left-wing ideology which fought against the backwardness of Chinese traditions and the oppressiveness of European and Japanese colonialism. Furthermore, the film was supposed to represent a model of the new independent Chinese woman. However, when Ai Xia committed suicide, not only did the tabloid press have a feast about her failed romance, but even the left-wing critics attacked her suicide and her last film as signs of feminine weakness.[18] Since "the left-wing cinema needed a new revolutionary-woman image to represent a new China,"[19] Ruan Ling Yu was chosen for *The New Woman* to re-present that image, something that Ai Xia had tried to do.

Quietly and voyeuristically throughout *Centre Stage*, Ruan Ling Yu looks into mirrors and through windows at others, some of whom are asleep. She has distanced herself from reality. Indeed at one point, she walks in a dream-like state into the bedroom of her mother and daughter to momentarily watch them sleep. Even during her last act alive, she watches her latest love, Tang Chi Shan, sleeping. Thus, like a sleepless ghost, Ruan Ling Yu experiences the joys and pains of those she views, but they do not experience the joys and pains of her life. The film captures her ironic solitude even though she is often surrounded by people. This time she watches Chi Shan as she commits the final act to join permanently the purity of all those who are "asleep" by taking sleeping pills. Finally, she tries to wake him up to ask him if he loves her. As he quickly regains his full consciousness, it is too late, for she is now unconscious, nearing death or already dead. The recurring shots through mirrors and windows instill and reinforce a haunting voyeurism throughout the film. I agree with Ackbar Abbas, a critic who lives in Hong Kong, that the film's methodology "is a way to representing the ghost [of Ruan Ling Yu] as an actress."[20]

Throughout the film, the ill fate of the Shanghai film industry is examined, for the death of Ruan Ling Yu became a symbol of its demise. She is not just the ghost of a starlet who haunts us, but the possible specter of a film industry. Furthermore, her death brought about crucial questions concerning the future of Hong Kong cinema. Hong Kong was in search of its own identity in the early 1990's as it experienced the end of colonialization and a return to Chinese authority on July 1, 1997. Asian film scholar Kristine Harris has commented on Hong Kong's return to China's control and notes the parallels between 1930's and 1990's:

> On a psychic level, the splendor and fear of the 1930's semicolonial Shanghai on the eve of war matched the sense of fin-de-siecle uncertainty accompanying the British colony's imminent reunification with Mainland China. Will Hong Kong's energetic local film industry, which has thrived on commodified stars and all manner of action, romance, and fantasy films since 1949, perish under unfamiliar new censorship regulations?[21]

At one point in the film, Ruan and others from Lienhua Studios, sensing the end of an era, escape momentarily to Hong Kong while the Japanese attack Shanghai.

Throughout the film, the docu-techniques combine with the motif of reflection to enhance the meta-cinematic experience. Shuqin Ciu points out how the "(meta)-narrative-cinematic structures" embody the "slippery concept" of Hong Kong's postmodern, fragmentary essence.[22] The blending of documentary and narrative formats that Kwan utilizes in *Centre Stage* connects the postmodernity of contemporary Hong Kong with the modernity of 1930s Shanghai. The problem with "post"-modernity for China is that modernity, with its elevation of the individual, never quite ripened. Though Shanghai welcomed the arrival of modernity, the historical travesties — such as the Japanese invasion and the rise of Marxism — prevented modernity from maturing. As Sheldon Lu explains:

> Contemporary China consists of multiple temporalities superimposed on one another; the pre-modern, the modern and the postmodern coexist in the same space at the same moment.... Spatial co-extension, rather than temporal succession, defines non–Western post-modernity. Hybridity, uneveness, nonsynchronicity, and patishe are the main features of Chinese postmodern culture.[23]

Being a filmmaker in colonial Hong Kong, while possessing more artistic freedom than your Chinese communist counterparts, was a little too ironic in a post-modern/post–1989 city where Hong Kong artists remained colonial figures, never enjoying political freedom.

The 1989 massacre in Tiananmen Square created a crisis for the Chinese psyche, becoming an ominous sign-post of things to come. This event awakened the Hong Kong masses and influenced the need to make films like *Centre Stage*.[24] In Tiananmen Square, students began to make pro-democracy proclamations during the early part of May to replicate the May 4th movement of 1919 in which students had gathered to protest against the Versailles Treaty that had given Chinese land to Japan. On June 4, 1989, Tiananmen Square was the site of a bloody slaughter of protestors at the hand of the Chinese government. This event occurred just like previous demonstrations, such as the March 18, 1926 protests against the Chinese government for the concessions it had made to Japan. The date of March 18 is heard early in *Centre Stage* and the voices of the intellectuals involved in the original May 4th Movement were also heard in such Lienhua films as *The New Woman* (1935).

The meta-cinematic samsara — the death and rebirth cycle — experience of *Centre Stage* along with the use of documentary techniques transforms the historical transition from modernity to post modernity into a meditation on the process of interdependence. During the funeral wake, in a contrapuntal fashion that cuts back to the farewell party, many of Ruan Ling Yu's directors recall her final moments. The farewell party is for Mr. Skinner, an American sound technician responsible for allowing Lienhua Studio to begin producing talkies. Mr. Skinner's farewell party becomes Ruan's farewell party. The farewell party becomes an overview of her career at Lienhua Studios as she thanks and gives the directors of her films two kisses, one on each cheek. The meaning of the two kisses for director Cai Chu Sheng differs from the kisses she gives to the others. The shot of her kissing him situates the pair of figures side by side next to the windowed door to their left, which acts as a doubling reflective signifier by enhancing the visuality of the longest and the most endearing kisses that Ruan gives anyone. It also records Cai Chu Sheng's awkwardness and embarrassment at the moment of Ruan's endearment. At the funeral wake, many directors regret not being able to show her how they appreciated her contributions to the richness of their own lives and careers. Director Cai Chu Seng alone nearly collapses but is held up by his friends.

The end of an era marks the beginning of another era. The grand funeral of Ruan Ling Yu in 1935 symbolized more than the death of a star, for it became the funeral of an industry as the 1937 invasion of Japanese forces caused many directors and stars to flee to Hong Kong. The 1930's helped to transform, invigorate, and create Hong Kong cinema because of the infusion of Shanghai talent. Directors like Cai Chu Sheng and actors like Li Lili and Chen Yan Yan would make Hong Kong their home. This transformation parallels the exodus of Hong Kong talent to Hollywood that began in the 1990's. Thus, the re-birth of Hong Kong cinema as a global cinema occurred out of the fears of the post–1989 tragedy and speculations about post–1997 realities brought about by Hong Kong's return to mainland China.

Though *Centre Stage* acts as a meditation on the death of a star who is reborn as a legend, the film also documents the irony of normalcy that entraps Ruan's life. During the film, in her moments of privacy, the shots are often engulfed in darkness, with window frames creating shadows on the walls and her face, appearing to be behind prison bars. These *noir* effects foreshadow the unhappy ending often associated with *film noir*. As she gains more power and more control over her career, she loses more power and more control over her own life.

Ruan Ling Yu's last act of suicide signifies her desire to regain control through an act of liberation from her suffering. The image of herself in the large mirror before her is lucid, paralleling her resolve. However, as we experience this visual clarity we know things are not clear in her mind, for her perception of the moment is cloudy. Though we are emotionally drawn to the moment, we are also detached due to the docu-techniques that often distance us from the events of her life. We recall other mirror scenes, especially when Stanly Kwan and Maggie Cheung discuss Ruan Ling Yu's relationship with her husband. Things are not what they appear to be. Kwan's style in *Centre Stage* leads us to question reality and the choices that Ruan makes.

When she starts to live with another man, Tang Chi Shan as played by Chin Han, the pervasiveness of the *noir* style evaporates as an abundance of light enters her new house. However, Ruan Ling Yu seems lost in her private labyrinth of light and space. She seems happy. With each improvement in her life, she experiences a rebirth of sort, a temporary forgetting of past sufferings that might also be thought of as analogous to a little-death. But before long, the suffering returns, even stronger than before. She realizes that the great film star is just a typical mistress to a rich businessman, who has had famous actresses as mistresses before. Even though he treats her mother and daughter like his own family, something is wrong. Even though he tries to carry her over the threshold of the new house, he still remains married to another woman. Ruan is not the liberated and powerful matriarchal figure she symbolized to so many fans in her cinematic incarnations. Something is wrong. In reality, she is quite vulnerable, quite lonely, and quite desperate for love. Indeed, later she even confesses her feelings for director Cai Chu Sheng and tries to escape with him, but he refuses. Something is amiss.

Towards the end of the film, Ruan Ling Yu stands before the smoke rising up

Maggie Cheung re-enacts a scene from the 1934 film *A Sea of Fragrant Snow.*

from a row of red incense sticks burning before the altar of Buddha in a temple in a reenactment of a scene from *A Sea of Fragrant Snow*. The film's director, Fei Mu (1906–1951), played by Stanley Kwan, tells her that her character has prayed hard and has promised to become a nun if the lives of her husband and child are saved from the turmoil of war. Later, when her prayers are answered and her family is safe, they want her to come back to them, but she is content with the blissfulness of the temple and has made a sacred vow to become a nun. At the same time, she wants to return to her family. In trying to maintain a solemn presence for the scene, Ruan Ling Yu pretends to hold back the tears. When the director yells cut, real tears pour out from the current pains of her life. The pull of the fictional family's life evokes the pain of Ruan's own unfulfilled family life: living with a married man and an adopted daughter — a postmodern familial construct in a simulated modernity. This sequence marks the continuing birthing pains of a new awareness in Ruan Ling Yu's mind that her own life is not complete. She realized that she did not love Tang Chi Shan and, even more important, she realized that if he loved her, he would have divorced his wife. In her own life, there is no true love or true family.

In Chinese temples, the flames of the candles and the smoke of red joss sticks represent the impermanence of life where all sentient beings struggle only to die and be reborn within the wheel of samsara. While at any moment, the light of the flame or the smoke from the incense stick may seem to have died down, such a symbolic death is merely momentary and illusionary since the light continues to flicker or be re-lit. Light becomes a metaphor for life, extinguished one moment and reborn in some other fashion in the next. Lamps, holders of light, are another variant of the metaphor. In a cinematic fashion, the light in the projector (lamp) flickers the images of life onto the screen of theaters and the mind of a culture. We enjoy viewing cinema because it is a mirror of ourselves.

The final death scene of Ruan Ling Yu in the film *The New Woman*, concludes in sadness and tears, as the character Wei Ming proclaims, "I want to live. I want revenge." Director Cai Chu Sheng yells cut on a Shanghai stage. We see the crew, the camera, and its apparatus. Still continuing to cry because of the pains in her own life, Wei Ming transforms into Ruan Ling Yu. Then Cai Chu Sheng approaches the bed to soothe Ruan Ling Yu, but she just continues to cry even louder. Then the real director, Stanley Kwan, yells cut on a Hong Kong stage. Director Cai Chu Sheng and the great silent film star, Ruan Ling Yu, transform into Tony Leung Ka Fai and Maggie Cheung, respectively. We see the crew, the camera, and its apparatus. A new shot appears as Stanley Kwan and camera crew begin to relax and go about their business. The shot changes to monochrome, looking grainy and old. Next, images of Ruan Ling Yu as Wei Ming appear as she dies in the hospital saying, "I want to live. I want revenge." Thus, we leave the postmodern mirror of *Centre Stage* and return to the reflection within the modern mirror of the *The New Woman*, reflecting the interdependence of the 1990's filmmakers and actors with those of the 1930's film crew and actors, standing before the mirror within the mirror and recording the rhythmic turning of cinematic samsara.

During the final death sequence, the voice of Ruan Ling Yu is heard over the silence of the solemn moment explaining the reasons for her suicide while she watches her lover, Tang Chi Shan, sleeping. As he is awakened and after she enters the pure land of unconsciousness, we return to the final moments of the funeral wake. The film then shifts to the next scene as the camera pans right across the glass windows of Lienhua Studios and then zooms and enters into its empty space. In the next black and white scene, the camera again pans right across the actual ruins of the Lienhua Studios as they appeared in 1991. An eerie feeling pervades these sequences as if the wandering ghost of Ruan Ling Yu is traversing the empty cinematic landscape. Finally, the film ends with an actual black and white photograph of Ruan Ling Yu from her funeral wake.[25]

Somewhere center stage between a docudrama and a narrative fiction lies this meta-cinematic film by Stanley Kwan, incorporating the duel elements that act both as a celebration of the life and death of a film star and as a subversive commentary on the state of Chinese society and cinema. Though film stars may come and go, though film studios may come and go, and though entire film industries may come and go, the wheel of samsara turns as impermanence abounds. Liberation from the wheel of samsara is possible. A film about meta-cinema becomes a film about meta-awareness, hinting about liberation. Finally, when the projected light of the film ends, the real light of life commences, and we are reborn to our reality.

The mirror of our mind reflects our interdependency with the community that views our lives. As actors, we are trapped within our own life dramas. As actors, we are sensitive to criticism. Who writes the malicious lies about us? At times, we forget we are actors. We are haunted by the ghosts we once were in our previous films (lives). Suddenly, a momentary taste of nirvana emerges when we cut through the thought clouds of our memory. As we clean the mirrors of our mind, we remember the fragments of our forgotten lines we once memorized or the lives we once lived. Death, the illusion, never stands as the final act, but promises a rebirth that returns us to a life of suffering, the pathos of dramatic tension. Returning to the cinematic world of the reel samsara, we face the mirror within the mirror, again and again, reflecting genre within genre. It's showtime. Action!

I want to thank Ching Hua Luong and Callie Lee for their assistance in the translation of key scenes from Centre Stage *along with the intertitles from* The New Woman.

1. Maggie Cheung, interview with Miles Wood, *Cine East: Hong Kong Cinema Through the Looking Glass.* ed. Miles Wood (Guildford, England: Fab Press Publications, 1998) 35.

2. Chinese names are written with the family name as the first name with no comma as in Ruan Ling Yu. However, when Chinese adopt a Western name, it comes first and then the family name, as in Maggie Cheung. This is how the names are written in this paper.

3. Steve N. Lipkin, *Real Emotional Logic: Film and Television Docudrama as Persuasive Practice* (Carbondale: Southern Illinois University Press, 2002): 45.

4. The film, *Centre Stage,* earned Maggie Cheung two awards for best actress: the Hong Kong Film Awards and the Silver Berlin Bear from the Berlin International Film Festival. She was best known in the West for being a damsel in distress in Jackie Chan films including the successful *Police Story* series. In 2003, she refused to reprise her role in the latest sequel of the *Police Story* series, stating that she had previous commitments.

5. Derek Paget, *No Other Way to Tell It: Dramadoc/Docudrama on Television* (Manchester: Manchester University Press, 1998): 61.

6. Shuquin Cui, *Women Through the Lens: Gender and Nation in a Century of Chinese Cinema* (Honolulu: University of Hawaii Press, 2003): 9.

7. Paget, p. 87.

8. Jane Roscoe, interview with Michael Cathcart, "Faking It: The Mockumentary." National Radio. Australian Broadcasting Corporation. 12 March 2001 www.abc.net.au/arts/film/stories/s452476.htm.

9. Miriam Bratu Hansen, "Fallen Women, Rising Stars, New Horizons: Shanghai Silent Film as Vernacular Modernism," *Film Quarterly.* 54.3 (2000): 11.

10. Julian Stringer, "*Center Stage*: Reconstructing the Bio-Pic," *Cine Action* 42 (1997): 28.

11. Stephen Teo, *Hong Kong Cinema: The Extra Dimensions* (London: British Film Institute, 1997): 192.

12. Kristine Harris, "The New Woman Incident: Cinema, Scandal, and Spectacle in 1935 Shanghai," *Transnational Chinese Cinema: Identity, Nationalhood, Gender,* ed. Sheldon Hsiao-peng Lu, (Honolulu: University of Hawaii Press, 1997): 282.

13. In another sequence with a mirror, the mouthless image of Chang Ta-min appears in the mirror during a scene which represents the lies his mouth transmits and will transmit in the future. In this scene, Chang breathes into a mirror where the condensation leaves a blur, an interesting signifier of a mouthless man in the mirror.

14. Laiwan Pang, *Building a New China in Cinema: The Chinese Left-wing Cinema Movement 1932–1937* (New York: Rowman and Littlefield Publishers, 2002): 125.

15. Cui, p. 13.

16. Pang, p. 118.

17. Harris, p. 297–8.

18. Pang, p. 122.

19. Pang, p. 123.

20. Ackbar Abbas, *Hong Kong: Culture and the Politics of Disappearance* (Minneapolis: University of Minnesota Press, 1997) 47.

21. Harris, p. 298.

22. Cui, p. 30–32.

23. Sheldon Lu, introduction. *China, Transnational Visuality, Global Postmodernity* (Stanford: Stanford University Press, 2001): 13.

24. Another film that examines the future of Hong Kong by reflecting into the past is by Tsui Hark. He wrote and directed the revival of the Wong Fei Hong series (*Once Upon a Time in China* 1991–7) that re-invigorated Jet Li's career. In *Wong Fei Hong II,* the clock symbolizes the end of one era and the start of another. This film featured the Boxers who opposed Modernity and who believed

they could withstand bullets and maintain traditions. Some critics did not like Jet Li playing the legend because of his Mainland China origins; however, this series foreshadows the return of Mainland China's influence on Hong Kong.

25. In many ways, *Centre Stage* is a remake of Stanley Kwan's *Rouge* (1987) as Abbas points out. In that film, an opera star during the 1930's commits suicide with her lover and returns some 50 years later as a ghost to Hong Kong to find her lover who survived. The recent, though unrelated, deaths of the two stars of the film, Leslie Cheung (April 1, 2003) and Anita Mui (December 30, 2003), has become fuel for gossip for the tabloids. Leslie committed suicide while Anita died of cancer.

15

Fool's Gold:
New Zealand's Forgotten Silver,
Myth and National Identity

by Ian Conrich and Roy Smith

1995 was the year that cinema celebrated its centenary. Histories of national achievements in filmmaking were produced with particular interest in the birth of cinema. It seemed then, for a period, that film's pioneers were of popular interest with their cultural value growing from the work of enthusiasts, historians and archivists. The pioneers were being rediscovered and reassessed and cinema's centenary appeared to offer the greatest exposure. Within this context, the New Zealand Film Archive, like other national film archives, was conducting a nationwide search for old celluloid. Peter Jackson and Costa Botes's 1995 fake documentary, or "mockumentary," *Forgotten Silver*, led the viewer to believe that New Zealand had unearthed its own lost filmmaker of world significance, Colin McKenzie. It was claimed that old silver nitrate film had been recovered from a chest at the bottom of a garden, belonging to the neighbor of Jackson's parents, in Pukerua Bay.

McKenzie may be regarded as a cross between Forrest Gump and Woody Allen's Zelig, but *Forgotten Silver*'s filmmakers exhibited a technical expertise and an understanding of documentary conventions of narrative and exposition.[1] They created a seemingly legitimate mode of presentation, which aided the film's basic premise of authentic rediscovery. Produced by WingNut Films, in association with the New Zealand Film Commission and New Zealand On Air, this one hour long documentary was first shown on Television New Zealand, in the respected *Montana Sunday Theatre* slot, on 29 October 1995, and was watched by an estimated audience of 400,000.[2] Despite the film's far-fetched claims regarding McKenzie's achievements, many New Zealanders were prepared to accept it as historically veracious. As co-director and co-scriptwriter Costa Botes said, "[a]ll the clues were ignored. The 'hoax' was swallowed hook, line, and sinker by a sizeable majority of that first night audience."[3]

.We have screened *Forgotten Silver* as part of a workshop in a variety of places. One workshop was for a group of Danish teachers attending a New Zealand weekend session in Skanderborg, Denmark, and, here, more than half the audience were duped by the program and believed the fictitious account of McKenzie to be fact. On being informed that they had been deceived all appeared to warmly accept the film as playful and humorous and to congratulate it as exceptional entertainment. In contrast, many viewers of the 29 October broadcast, upon later learning of the hoax — what Geoff Chapple describes as "New Zealand's biggest-ever hoax"[4]— expressed outrage, and if the letters received by New Zealand's *Listener* are an indication, then a majority disapproved of the film.[5]

It is the willingness, even desire, of the New Zealand public to accept *Forgotten Silver* as documentary truth, that is of interest. Public gullibility and naivety can be set within the context of a broader seeking of identity among New Zealanders. The negative response that the filmmakers experienced, once the hoax was revealed, highlights the extent to which many New Zealanders wanted the story to be true. This raises questions relating to issues of myth and aspects of New Zealanders' self-consciousness and psychological security.

Invention

Accounts of early film are centered on skilled inventors, technological advances, developments in film's mode of representation and the vision of film directors and performers. Histories have established a "cinema of firsts," which has promoted a "landmarking" of achievements. In Britain, the work of camera-maker Augustin Le Prince was again spotlighted during cinema's centenary. It has been argued that Le Prince, who lived in Leeds, invented cinema and that he was the first to screen project film, but he mysteriously disappeared in 1890 and his body has never been found. One hypothesis is that Le Prince was disposed of by his competitors and the thought that his family never financially benefited from an invention that pre-dated the achievements of Thomas Edison and the Lumière brothers, is mournful yet, at the same time, captivating.[6]

If *Forgotten Silver* is accepted as presenting historical truth, then New Zealand's Colin McKenzie was responsible for an astonishing series of "film firsts." We are informed that he invented the first tracking shot, he was the first to employ the close-up and, in 1911, an early color process. He also produced the first feature and was the first filmmaker to use synchronized sound film. *Forgotten Silver* has the viewer believe that cinema and the history of film technology is not anchored in the workshops of Britain and France and the heavily financed American laboratories of Edison, but in the ingenuity of a young man from New Zealand's South Island community of Geraldine. McKenzie's innovations were surrounded by comic ill fortune — his first synchronized sound film had one "fatal flaw," and audiences "walked out in droves" as the dialogue of his Chinese actors had not been translated into English — and are shown to have had little effect on the international film community of the time. Days after his second marriage, which signaled a recovery from a period of disillusionment, he died during the Battle of Málaga, in the Spanish Civil War.

Peter Jackson

Perhaps some viewers should have stood back from *Forgotten Silver* and thought about the source of invention. A part of this documentary's identity is the work of one of its directors, Peter Jackson, whose films include *Bad Taste* (1988), *Braindead* (1992) and *Heavenly Creatures* (1994). Jackson's films have been marked by a strong juvenile tendency, excessive comic-book violence and a striking mixture of comedy and gory horror, that some have termed "Splatstick." *Heavenly Creatures*, which gained tremendous critical and popular praise, may have indicated a new maturity for Jackson, but there clearly still remains within his work an element of the trickster, prankster or magician. The fantasy "Fourth World," Borovnia, imagined by the two female protagonists of *Heavenly Creatures*, is an exquisite private garden that the viewer is also able to enter.

With *Forgotten Silver*, Jackson and Botes presented a romanticized history of early New Zealand film that both enchants and seduces the viewer. The illusion is sustained by the use of supposed photographic evidence, old newspapers, references to historical events, such as Gallipoli, the first flight by air and the Wall Street Crash of 1929. Furthermore, figures of authority are employed: respected commentators and experts, such as the film critic Leonard Maltin, the actor Sam Neill, John O'Shea, New Zealand's most important post-war filmmaker, and the head of Miramax Pictures, Harvey Weinstein, as well as so called eyewitnesses, such as McKenzie's widow.

The Pukerua Bay neighbor is Hannah McKenzie, Colin's widow, and the chest of celluloid film in her garden shed enthralls the childlike Jackson. There is a sense of boyhood fantasy about "young Peter" and his journey to an area of his elderly neighbor's garden; an adventure that is later mirrored, but also magnified, when we see him, accompanied by Botes and colleagues, hacking through the bush of the South Island West Coast — we are informed, a three day trek from Hokitika — and uncovering a biblical lost city built by McKenzie. Jackson retraces McKenzie's historical path but there is a striking similarity between the actual and fictional filmmakers. As Barry Keith Grant suggests "McKenzie may be seen as something of a fictional alter ego."[7] Jackson, himself, said that "[t]here are a lot of things in Colin's life I recognize in my own."[8] The twelve-year-old McKenzie stole eggs—"2000 Dozen"— to produce photo-sensitive celluloid emulsion (an early clue to the film's absurdity and fake credentials); Jackson, aged ten, made his first 8mm short film, *The Dwarf Patrol* (1971), and pricked pin-holes in the film to suggest a gun-shot effect. McKenzie constructed a concrete city and engaged a cast of thousands for his biblical epic *Salome*; Jackson has produced a spectacular three-part film adaptation of the monumental *The Lord of the Rings*, employing 15,000 extras and recreating Middle Earth with the aid of digital technology. *The Lord of the Rings* is, for Jackson, "the holy grail of cinema."[9]

Myth

There is a deep irony in many New Zealanders believing that within such a short Pakeha history there could actually exist a lost city. As Jackson's team of pseudo-archaeologists progress on their expedition into the bush they uncover a series of (concrete) steps which direct them to a city of magnificent proportions and the discovery of a vault containing incredible treasures—reproduction biblical artifacts employed for McKenzie's production of *Salome*, and another chest containing cans of silver nitrate film. A film archivist's fantasy.

Appraising the (fake) McKenzie films, voices of authority declare him to be a genius. In the documentary, he is compared to Orson Welles and D.W. Griffith, and the American critic Leonard Maltin declares that McKenzie "now belongs ... in the pantheon of great cinema artists and innovators." What this "mockumentary" attempts is a re-drawing of film's map. Early New Zealand film was, largely, localized and often drew on the various communities for both content and economic survival.[10] Yet, in *Forgotten Silver*, this film community is re-positioned to a central world location and is depicted as being at the heart of film innovation and development, and able to attract finance from Hollywood and, more incredulously, the Soviet government, who instruct McKenzie to produce a Social Realist rewriting of the Salome story, with all the religious references removed.

Much of the hoax is facilitated by the utilization of documentary conventions, but the process of deception is dependent upon the employment and construction of national myths and issues of identity. Costa Botes said that this documentary was "a full-blown celebration of Kiwi ingenuity."[11] It could also be read as destabilizing a society by the creation of a questioning of the believability of New Zealand's national myths, through a figure that initially appeared real, but is revealed to be fictional. There is also a demonstration that social and cultural beliefs can be invented and manufactured; part of a post-colonial pattern of myth-exposure. This can lead to an uncertainty of the "real" New Zealand which, as Ruth Brown, following Fredrich von Schiller, argues "all national identity formation is to some extent a scam."[12] An important factor for assessing viewers' outrage is how they were manipulated into observing such a disclosure.

Inherent within New Zealand culture are the myths of the white-settler pioneer and the mastering of nature, of a rural or pastoral paradise, the DIY Kiwi bloke, and an enterprise culture that favors a "have-a-go" spirit. New Zealanders were able to recognize McKenzie as they were able to recognize the myths. McKenzie is also a character that the viewer, New Zealand or otherwise, would find extremely sympathetic. Jackson has said that people "cried when Maybelle [*Salome*'s lead and McKenzie's first wife] died."[13] William J. Schafer writing on New Zealand argues that there is "at its centre a sense of mateyness, of sharing, of communal work, fortune, and misfortune."[14] Many New Zealanders would have found the story of Colin McKenzie very seductive, and would have shared in his moments of success, for he is distinctly Kiwi. The viewer would have felt proud of McKenzie's achievements for they belong to the nation. And at the moments of failure, New Zealanders would still be there sharing "their mate's" misfortune. Crucially, the McKenzie tale operates upon colonial myths and a search for nationhood that is, arguably, most relevant to Pakeha identity.

McKenzie is the archetypal resourceful Kiwi Bloke; the New Zealand male who supposedly can repair anything with a number 8 fencing wire. In 1900, aged 12, McKenzie built a movie camera and produced his own film stock. An enterprising man, he exhibits all the traits of the "have-a-go" Kiwi, who despite numerous set-backs and difficulties—charges of exhibiting "smut" and being sentenced to hard labor, filmmaking on the West Coast and being hampered by the worst rain and the hottest summer for thirty years—he trudges on. The New Zealander, apparently always on the look out for a good opportunity is, here, adroitly characterized as the ingenious filmmaker battling to succeed, to complete the four-hour epic *Salome*.

For *Salome*, this son of a South Island farmer constructed New Zealand's largest man-made structure. McKenzie repeatedly shows the resilience and spirit of the pioneer settler, mastering the landscape and penetrating deep into the harsh vegetation, whilst enduring discomfort and physical burdens. He is a national hero, and as Jackson mischievously suggests "this guy should be appearing on our banknotes. They should create a $3 banknote just to put his face on it. He is postage-stamp material."[15]

Reaction

An interesting effect of the first broadcast of *Forgotten Silver* was the extent to which people had been taken in by the hoax. Also of significance was the negative reaction from a large number of viewers who seemed to take the duping as a personal affront. Jane Roscoe and Craig Hight have considered the public response to the screening as reflected in letters written to the Editor of the *Listener*.[16] Although this was a relatively small sample of the overall audience, the number of letters demonstrated that the broadcast was a potent issue and a clear majority, of roughly three to one, disapproved.

Some highlighted how impressed they were by the character of McKenzie. He was described as "truly inspirational—worthy to stand alongside Rutherford and others in New Zealand's legend."[17] The film made reference to another national figure, Richard Pearse, whom many New Zealanders argue was the first aviator. This possible event was exploited for *Forgotten Silver*, with the alleged discovery of film footage of Pearse's flight. With the aid of a digital enhancer, the date of a newspaper, being carried in the film in the back-pocket of a spectator, was declared to be conclusive proof that Pearse had flown nine months prior to the Wright brothers. This aspect of the documentary's hoax was subject to particular criticism, and reflects the regard in which such people are held. One disgusted writer from Christchurch said that "after a lifetime of interest in film, [I] have resigned my membership of the Film Society." The Pearse connection

> was tasteless and left many in South Canterbury disappointed and angry.
> It also may have the effect of discounting any claim that he might have of

being the first to fly, for many may now dismiss his life as part of the hoax that the film has perpetrated.[18]

Other letters point to a broader disquiet and aroused distrust and questioning of previously accepted voices of authority —

> I do not wish to reveal my score on a gullibility rating of 0 to 100 percent. Suffice to say, I was not entirely surprised to discover it was a hoax, but was also profoundly disturbed by the discovery that I had been duped. If on this, then on what else? God, the Pope, the integrity of *Fair Go*, Richard Long, Judy Bailey, the last shreds of Paul Holmes; all disappearing down a gurgling plug-hole of lost credibility.[19]

Here, it seems, some viewers took the deception of *Forgotten Silver* as a portent of a possibly grander conspiracy of fraud and manipulation — "One Network News admitted that last night's *Montana Sunday Theatre* was a hoax. Well, all credibility has gone down the tubes—I won't be believing in TVNZ's news anymore."[20] Suggestions of this "mockumentary" being indicative of a deliberate attempt to fool the New Zealand population beyond its transmission time may appear fanciful. However, when one considers the level of involvement in this deception by the broadcaster and the *Listener*, in setting the scene for the program, a certain level of culpability is apparent. The media is an essential element of myth projection and sustainment and observing it to be part of a process of national deception could create considerable offence and fury.

It seems that the undoubted achievement of producing a film with the technical sophistication to successfully challenge a nation's preconceived view of its own history, is insufficient to find acceptance as a source of national pride. The very fact that people were led to believe the basic premise of the "documentary" is evidence that this was work of the highest quality.

The Filmmakers' Response

With the exception of the particular disappointment expressed by a grand-niece of Richard Pearse, who "watched *Forgotten Silver* in great excitement," believing the legendary flight to have been substantiated, there were no other regrets from the filmmakers.[21] Interviewed by Geoff Chapple, Botes said that people should "wake up and see what's in their backyard."[22] Jackson adds "[t]here's a lot of Colin McKenzies out there, and a lot of such backyard people are nobbled in New Zealand. They're nobbled by the 'go out and get a proper job' brigade. The negative reaction to our program seems a very good example of that."[23]

Criticism of Jackson and Botes is neatly countered by the highlighting of what they consider to be a negative trait within elements of New Zealand society. They identify with the subject of their film not only by way of their shared professions but also in the way in which they experience an under-valuation of their originality, innovations and skills. Both filmmakers say that "the people who have dumped on them are the same who would have dumped on McKenzie."[24] *Forgotten Silver* claimed to have discovered a filmmaking genius and this documentary is as much a record of the lost McKenzie as the arrival of its directors Peter Jackson and Costa Botes.

1. See Barry Keith Grant, *A Cultural Assault: The New Zealand Films of Peter Jackson* (Nottingham: Kakapo Books, 1999), p. 22; Jane Roscoe and Craig Hight, "Mocking Silver: Re-inventing the documentary project (or, Grierson lies bleeding)." *Continuum* 11:1 (1997), pp. 67–82. (Roscoe and Hight wrote the similar article "Silver Magic," *Illusions* 25 [Winter 1996], p. 14–19). See also Jane Roscoe and Craig Hight, *Faking it: Mock-documentary and the subversion of Factuality* (Manchester: Manchester University Press, 2001), p. 115–119, 144–150.

2. Roscoe and Hight erroneously write that the documentary was broadcast on 8 November 1995. "Mocking Silver," p. 68; "Silver Magic," p. 14.

3. Costa Botes, "Made in New Zealand: The Cinema of Peter Jackson" www.nzedge.com/hot-/ar-jackson.html.

4. Geoff Chapple, "Gone, not forgotten," *Listener* 25 November 1995, p. 26.

5. "Letters," *Listener* 25 November 1995, p. 12.

6. See, Richard Howells, "A movie murder mystery," *The Times Higher Education Supplement* 23 July 1999, p. 18–19.

7. Grant, p. 22.

8. Denis Welch, "Heavenly features," *Listener* 28 October 1995, p. 32.

9. Mike Houlahan, "Jackson Scores 'The Holy Grail of Cinema,'" *The Dominion* 26 August 1998, p. 11.

10. A striking example are the short community comedies that filmmakers such as Edwin Coubray and Rudall Hayward produced in the 1920s and 1930s—films such as *Daughter of Christchurch* and *Suzy of Stratford*. These are parodied by Jackson and Botes, who create another fictitious character, Stan Wilson, for *Forgotten Silver*. We are informed that during periods of financial hardship, McKenzie produced a number of successful, yet spiteful, Stan the Man candid-camera-style comedy shorts—*Stan the Man in Taihape, Stan the Man in Levin*, and *Stan the Man in Rotorua*.

11. Chapple, p. 26.

12. Ruth Brown, *Cultural Questions: New Zealand Identity in a Transnational Age* (London: Kakapo Books, 1997), p. 3.

13. Chapple, p. 26.

14. William J. Schafer, *Mapping the Godzone: A Primer on New Zealand Literature and Culture* (Honolulu: University of Hawaii Press, 1998), p. 11.

15. Welch, p. 32. For the centenary of cinema, New Zealand film was commemorated on a set of four New Zealand postage stamps, with individual images from *Hinemoa* (1914), *Broken Barrier* (1952), *Goodbye Pork Pie* (1981), and *Once Were Warriors* (1994).

16. Roscoe and Hight, "Mocking Silver," pp. 73–76; "Silver Magic," pp. 17–18. See also Ian Pryor, *Peter Jackson: From prince of splatter to lord of the rings* (Auckland: Random House, 2003), pp. 169–173; and the short documentary *Behind the Bull: Forgotten Silver*.

17. Letter from G.A. De Forest, *Listener* 25 November 1995, p. 12.

18. *Ibid.*, letter from W.J. Gaudin.

19. *Ibid.*, letter from I. McKissack.

20. Letter cited in Chapple, p. 26.

21. Chapple, p. 26.

22. *Ibid.*

23. *Ibid.*

24. *Ibid.*

16

Before Big Brother, *There was* Blair Witch: *The Selling of "Reality"*

by Fincina Hopgood

The Blair Witch Project is a model example of the emerging style of "post-cinema" movie-making.[1] More of a "total package" than a film, *The Blair Witch Project* represents a fusion of independent filmmaking with blockbuster marketing strategies, which creates a dispersal of narrative across several media (film, television, the Internet, comics, books, music), while exposing a mainstream multiplex audience to documentary and avant-garde aesthetics. This essay investigates *The Blair Witch Project* both as a film (the 87 minute feature screened in theatres) and as a popular culture event (the "mythology" and the marketing), which may be regarded as symptomatic of the changes in cinema leading up to the twenty-first century. In particular, the film's blending of genres (documentary, horror and avant-garde) together with its wilful blurring of the boundaries between fact and fiction cast it as an exemplary postmodern cultural product. Throughout this essay, reference is made to the context of the film's reception in the United States and Australia, as gleaned from reviews, interviews and articles in mainstream newspapers and magazines. This sociohistorical analysis is buttressed by reference to theories about documentary and avant-garde aesthetics, as well as more general discussion about postmodern cultural production and the challenges for film in the digital era. This assembly of various discourses demonstrates the necessity for a pluralist approach towards a film like *The Blair Witch Project*, with its dispersed, multimedia narrative and its persistent cross-over of boundaries between genres, between independent production and mass-market distribution, between reality and its representation.

The Blair Witch Project: *The Hype*

> *It's the little movie that could and people like that —*
> *that's an underdog story — we are nothing but underdogs.*[2]

The Blair Witch Project is already regarded as a landmark film by virtue of being the most profitable cost-to-gross film in the history of cinema.[3] The question of economics is central to the film's aesthetic and how it was marketed.[4] From the outset, before the film's first theatrical screening at the Sundance Film Festival in 1999 and its sale for distribution, the directors Daniel Myrick and Eduardo Sánchez had conceived of using the Internet as an adjunct to the film.[5] This was not simply to generate interest in the film, but to further the narrative — the "back story" — behind the footage they had shot. They also screened "trailers" on a cable TV show featuring independent filmmakers, hosted by John Pierson.[6] On both the original site and the trailers, *The Blair Witch Project* was presented as "found footage" of three student filmmakers who went missing in the woods in October 1994 while filming a documentary, and were never found. Neither the site nor Pierson's show mentioned that this was a (fictional) film directed by Sánchez and Myrick. Thus the "myth" of *The Blair Witch Project* began.

With an already-established cult following (all four screenings at Sundance were sold out)[7] and Internet chat sites debating whether the story was "true" or not,[8] Artisan Entertainment recognised the commercial potential of the film and bought the rights for worldwide distribution for $1 million (US) at Sundance.[9] Artisan invested heavily in improving the sound mix and, more crucially to their marketing strategy, expanding the web site. With a target market of teenagers and university students, Artisan supplemented the film's on-line presence with advertisements in university papers and the posting of "Missing" notices featuring photographs of the three filmmakers; this latter strategy was another idea that began with Myrick and Sánchez, who had posted similar notices throughout Park City during Sundance.[10] Apart from select screenings to college audiences and a screening at Cannes (where it won the Prix de la Jeunesse), the film was not shown for six months until July 14, 1999.[11] It was only in the final weeks before the film's commercial release that Artisan utilised more "traditional" marketing techniques of cinema trailers (June 11), newspaper advertisements (July 4) and radio and television promotions (July 5 & 16).[12]

The key to any successful marketing strategy is word-of-mouth, which in this case was greatly assisted by rapid and extensive dissemination across the Internet. After opening in 27 theatres on the weekend of July 16, *The Blair Witch Project* opened in more than 2,000 theatres two weeks later.[13] One month after the film's opening and after fourteen months on line, the official website had received more than 75 million hits.[14] By the time the film opened in Australia in December 1999, US box office takings had reached $150 million (US).[15]

The Mythology and the Marketing

> The Blair Witch Project *blends the timeless terror about the*
> *evil that lurks in the woods at night with current fantasies*

In October of 1994
three student filmmakers disappeared
in the woods near Burkittsville, Maryland,
while shooting a documentary...

A year later their footage was found.

THE BLAIR WITCH PROJECT

The Blair Witch Project (1999) represents a fusion of independent filmmaking and blockbuster marketing strategies dispersed across a variety of media.

*about instant indie successes and current
confusions about cinematic fact and fiction.*[16]

The film *The Blair Witch Project* relates only a portion of the entire narrative of the Blair Witch legend created by Sánchez and Myrick. Early in the film, Heather Donahue, the director of the project, interviews people in the township of

Burkittsville (formerly Blair) who relate some of the key events in the 200-year-old legend. On the website, these events are related in greater detail, as part of "a time-line of major events in the history of the Blair Witch."[17] This timeline includes hyper-text links to excerpts of footage from the film, but also—and more signi-ficantly—these links include drawings and photos of historical documents, newspa-per clippings, maps, newsreel footage and interviews with "experts" such as the "Exec-utive Director of the Burkittsville Historical Society" and a "Professor of Folklore." None of this material appears in the film itself.[18] Sánchez and Myrick have created an elaborate back story that draws upon conventions of historical documentation and expert testimony, thereby further distorting the distinction between fact and fiction, history and myth.

The official website maintains the film's central conceit—that this is the footage of three missing filmmakers—by including biographies and photos of the three stu-dents.[19] In addition to the back story of the legend, the website picks up the narra-tive where the film left off: with the ensuing police search for the students.[20] The site includes further interviews with the town sheriff, a "Professor of Anthropology" and a private investigator hired by Heather's mother to investigate the students' disap-pearance. The chronology of the search is related with photographs of police evi-dence (the students' reels of film and sound recordings found buried in the woods) and with excerpts from local news broadcasts. Thus, this fictional narrative "mas-querades" as fact through the combined authority of police, academic and television news discourses.

The website includes a key character development absent from the film. Excerpts from Heather's journal reveal her obsession with the project, her insecurity about her role as a female director in charge of her two men crew, her frustrations and ambi-tions. The journal articulates her increasing fear and paranoia, which in the film were expressed mainly through tears and hysterical screaming. The journal thus pro-vides motivations for the behaviour we see on screen, and was perhaps designed to engender sympathy in order to counter audience perceptions that Heather was "bitchy" or "bossy."[21] Perhaps even more importantly, the journal counters the argu-ments of those viewers who, like Mike and Josh, are increasingly frustrated by the "un-real" behaviour of Heather refusing to turn the camera off when their lives are in danger:

> As long as I keep shooting, I feel like all of this has a purpose. Maybe not
> at the moment, but eventually. Shooting is the only way to make this sit-
> uation good for something as soon as we get out of here.[22]

Heather's self-analysis as to why she continues to film, and the reactions of Mike and Josh, will be discussed further in an analysis of the film's use of documentary aes-thetics.

The significance of *The Blair Witch Project*'s website is that it used the Internet for movie-marketing in a manner that was completely different from the "traditional" Hollywood movie website. Most mainstream films have a website that features clips, or at least images, from the film, together with biographies of the principal cast and crew, and the opportunity to win prizes or purchase related merchandise. The website is thus part of the studio's larger strategy of conglomeration, whereby the website supports the promotion of the film and its related merchandise tie-ins, such as books, t-shirts and CDs.[23] Where *The Blair Witch Project*'s website differs from other movie websites is in its maintenance and supplementation of the film's fictional narrative, through interview clips, historical background and further "plot" developments.[24] In the case of an "R" rated movie in the US — which means teenagers can only see it if accompanied by an adult — the website also serves to expand the film's audience through offering teenagers unsupervised access to a "watered down" version of the film.[25] In order to maintain the illusion that "this is real," merchandise is not available through the Blair Witch site itself. Only by clicking on a link to Artisan's site can browsers "break" the fiction and enter the *Blair Witch* "shop."[26] Even here, something of the film's fictional premise remains; the traditional merchandise of posters, t-shirts, stickers and videos (featuring *Blair Witch* iconography and images from the film) is supplemented here by merchandise based upon the three characters. The "companion album" for the film is a CD of a compilation tape found in Josh's abandoned car, known as *Josh's Blair Witch Mix*. Shoppers can also click on images from the film and connect to an on-line store that stocks beanies just like the one Heather wore, flannel shirts just like Mike's, or the camping mattress we see on the back of Josh's pack.

Several books and comics have been published that continue the film's narrative, either through closer examination of the events surrounding the disappearing filmmakers or by providing more information about the legend of the Blair Witch and related mysterious events in and around Burkittsville, Maryland.[27] As the blurb for one book notes, the film "was only *part* of the story,"[28] while another declares "the story isn't over...."[29] The film's fictional premise is maintained by publications such as *The Blair Witch Project: A Dossier*, compiled by "noted journalist D.A. Stern and private investigator Buck Buchanan," who accessed "the official police reports to compile the first fully detailed and illustrative investigative report on one of the most disturbing cases in Maryland history."[30] The legend of the Blair Witch is elaborated in further detail by a graphic novel that narrates the stories of Elly Kedward, the woman accused of witchcraft and banished into the woods of Blair (later renamed Burkittsville), and Rustin Parr, the man who killed seven children because the voice of the witch told him to.[31] These are figures uncovered by Heather in her research, but in the film they are mentioned only briefly during her interviews with the townspeople, prior to entering the woods.

As the website demonstrates, a significant portion of the Blair Witch legend is narrated not on the cinema screen, but on computer screens and in books. Many of the excerpts of interviews on the website also appear in a television "documentary," *Curse of the Blair Witch*, which screened on the Sci-Fi Channel in the week prior to the film's release.[32] Perhaps this is the documentary that Heather was trying to make all along. The "documentary" includes footage of the woods with an ominous female voiceover, interviews with "the man on the street" as well as local experts, and moody background music. When Sánchez and Myrick first conceived of the idea for the Blair Witch, they wanted to recapture the style of the *In Search of ...* documentary series, which focused on myths and legends such as Big Foot and the Loch Ness Monster.[33] Their television "documentary" even includes a clip from "Mystic Occurrences," a (fictitious) documentary-style program on the occult, complete with faded colour footage and the copyright logo of 1971, in obvious homage to the *In Search of...* style. The postmodern aesthetic of pastiche is clearly at work here,[34] in the directors' imitation and emulation of the 1970s pseudo-documentaries they grew up with. Their familiarity with the televisual aesthetic also demonstrates the collapsing boundaries between film and television styles.[35]

The marketing strategy outlined above has, in turn, become part of the film's "mythology." After its successful opening weeks in the United States, the popular press was touting *The Blair Witch Project* as the film that "brought [an industry] to its knees"[36]: "Through cunning use of the Internet, [Artisan has] been credited with revolutionising the way films are sold."[37] Tom Bernard, co-president of Sony Pictures Classics, said *The Blair Witch Project* was "the first time someone used the Internet to draw an audience into theatres—as opposed to just providing information. It's woken up the studio system and the independent world to the Internet as a marketing tool that's much more powerful than a billboard."[38] While members of the press seemed keen to stir up the debate—"If Artisan can create an avid audience on cable and in cyberspace, why is Fox or Warner Bros. spending tens of millions on advertising in the papers and on prime time?"[39]—members of the filmmaking industry, both studio and independent, were more pragmatic in their response: "The studios are owned by conglomerates; no part of that mechanism is to run the risk of failing."[40] According to Ray Price, president of American Zoetrope, there is nothing new about using the Internet to market films, mounting grassroots campaigns on college campuses or creating such market-specific tie-ins as comic books and television specials.[41] The consensus seems to be that the Internet worked so well for *Blair Witch*'s marketing strategy because that was where the distributors would find their target audience of 12-to-17 year olds and "Generation Xers who grew up with the Internet": "the Net may not work the same way for a movie like *Runaway Bride*."[42]

"Guerrilla" Filmmaking and Beating Hollywood at Its Own Game

A veritable David and Goliath story in which a very small, almost amateur work, half shot on video, managed to muscle into a commercial industry dominated by blockbusters.[43]

Changes in filmmaking technology have increased the accessibility of cameras and other recording equipment for the no-budget filmmaker. Leading this filmmaking revolution is the Hi8 camcorder and the advent of digital technology.[44] The majority of the footage in *The Blair Witch Project* is shot not by Josh's 16mm camera (this is reserved for the students' planned documentary) but by Heather's Hi8 camcorder, or "shaky cam," in reference to the shakiness of the image as she walks or runs with the camera. The sound is recorded either by Michael's DAT (digital audio tape) machine, or by the microphone built into Heather's camcorder. The breakthrough for independent, low-budget filmmaking — also known as guerrilla, DIY, or credit card filmmaking — is that the affordability and user-friendliness of this new technology allows "wannabe" filmmakers to bypass the traditional path of film school and official funding sources.[45]

Increasingly, video is proving the preferred medium for both independent and documentary filmmakers.[46] Although it has become less expensive to actually make a film, the costs of distribution and promotion remain prohibitive.[47] Those few low-budget films that manage to secure sales for distribution rarely do "big business" at the box office, hence the significance of *The Blair Witch Project*'s takings. Steve Montal, from the American Film Institute, believes *The Blair Witch Project*'s commercial success is largely due to the combination of 16mm and Hi8 footage providing the suitable aesthetic for its subject matter. The film's concept — "emulating an experience of being lost and scared in the woods" — perfectly matched its rough shooting style: "That gimmick is essentially what made the film. Without a suitable aesthetic style, it's difficult for a DIY feature to be successful."[48]

The legacy of *The Blair Witch Project* may be the opening of doors for independent filmmakers looking to team up with studios for distribution. In the opinion of Amorette Jones at Artisan, "suddenly, retailers and licensees realise there's an opportunity with independent cinema. So instead of just instantly dismissing (a small film) because you don't have an 'A' star with a $100 billion dollar budget, people are taking notice that there is some power here."[49] In contrast, John Pierson, whose cable show screened the first trailer for the film, believes "it's not an independent-film phenomenon. What you really have is a convergence of old and new media."[50] As Lynden Barber notes, the DIY movement "started long before *Blair Witch*."[51] He cites *El Mariachi* (Robert Rodriguez, 1992) and *Clerks* (Kevin Smith, 1994) as examples of US low-budget films that "showed ... you could make a feature without spending millions of dollars and demonstrated to the powers-that-be that there was money to be made from them."[52] The key difference with *The Blair Witch Project*, as Michael Hutak notes, is "that no indie hit ever made so much cash from so little investment."[53] Questions of profit aside, the technological impact of video and the commercial success of a handful of independent films mean that, in Rick McCallum's view, "at least now there's going to be a group of people who can work within the system for very, very little money."[54]

Documentary Aesthetics and the Representation of "Reality"

> *What seems like amateurish, occasionally out-of-*
> *focus footage taken by inexperienced and very scared*
> *filmmakers lost in the woods is actually amateurish, occasionally*
> *out-of-focus footage taken by actors playing inexperienced*
> *and very scared filmmakers lost in the woods.*[55]

To achieve the "reality effect" they were seeking, Sánchez and Myrick trained their three actors to use the two cameras, then sent them into the woods for eight days' shooting. The actors kept their own names and improvised their dialogue, according to plot lines which Myrick and Sánchez left at various drop-points during the shooting. The crew would shadow the cast's movements and scare them at night with strange noises, while reducing their daily food rations and making them hike all over the woods. These techniques were based upon the training program for the US Army's Special Forces:

> Normally your conscious mind insulates you from extreme fear. But if we could wear down the actors mentally and physically, by the end of the film when really intense things are happening, they'd tap into a part of their psyche they normally don't touch. The "insulation" would be stripped off and they'd react in a primal way.[56]

For many reviewers, these techniques succeeded in achieving the film's "realism": "The raw, amateurish-seeming scenes that result, with their repetitiveness and lack of focus, only pull us deeper into the film's illusion that what we're seeing really happened."[57] In its depiction of three actors pretending to be filmmakers, who are nevertheless hungry, tired and scared "in real life," *The Blair Witch Project* "examines the boundary between the real and the imaginary, the amateur and the professional, the sincere and the manufactured."[58]

By eschewing a detailed shooting script and letting the cameras capture the actors' "spontaneous" reactions, Sánchez and Myrick drew upon the conventions of the *cinéma-vérité* style, pioneered by documentary filmmakers in the 1960s. The *cinéma-vérité* movement in France, the Observational Documentary in Britain, and the Direct Cinema movement in the United States, all emerged from the technical revolution heralded by lighter, more portable cameras and sound-recording equipment. While each movement operated according to different principles,[59] they shared a number of common features: they valued "immediacy, intimacy and 'the real,'" while rejecting "the glossy, 'professional' aesthetic of traditional cinema." In fact, if their images "were grainy and wobbly and occasionally went out of focus," as they frequently do in *The Blair Witch Project*, "these 'flaws' in themselves seemed to guarantee authenticity and thus became desirable."[60]

These days, *cinéma-vérité* is more of a style than a movement, its techniques having been co-opted by the feature film industry. As Kevin Macdonald and Mark Cousins note, *cinéma-vérité* has become "a vague blanket term which is used to describe the *look* of feature or documentary films—grainy, hand-held camera, real locations—rather than any genuine aspirations the filmmakers may have. As so often, what started as a revolution, has ended up as a style choice."[61] Nevertheless, this style is still used as a mark of "realism" in both documentary and fiction films.[62] E. Ann Kaplan suggests that "the same signifying practices can indeed be used for different ends.... Taken simply as a cinematic style, which can be used in different genres (ie. documentary or fictional), realism does not insist on any special relation to the social formation."[63] Her argument is borne out by Andrew Eaton's observation: "With the rise of 'reality' TV shows, we've begun to accept the documentary as an entertainment format, no longer caring if it's actually 'real' or not."[64]

As a fiction presented as documentary, *The Blair Witch Project* has been labelled a "mockumentary," in the tradition of films such as *This Is Spinal Tap!* (Rob Reiner,

1983), which chronicles the come-
back tour of a (fake) heavy metal
rock band. Mockumentaries are
usually characterised by a tone of
irony or sarcasm towards their
subject, thus making them the
ideal vehicle for political satire.[65]
Despite the apparent absence of
this comic tone, *The Blair Witch
Project* succeeds in mocking the
documentary form itself and its
claims to the "truth." The convention of the investigative reporter
directly addressing the camera,
assuming a position of authority
and expert knowledge, is parodied by Heather's solemn, self-
important narration as she stands

Presented as "found footage," the *Blair Witch Project*
(1999) illustrates a dramatic use of handheld camera
shots, as shown in this image of star Heather Donahue.

in the Burkittsville cemetery, talking of stories "etched in stone." The documentary
filmmaker as "obsessed" is implicitly critiqued in Heather's persistent filming, despite
requests from Josh and Mike to stop. As Amy Taubin notes, in privileging filming
over trying to find a way home, Heather "fails in her primary responsibility—to
bring her boys home safely."[66] Both Josh and Mike persistently confront Heather
about her attachment to the Hi-8 camcorder:

JOSH	Put the camera down! This is not funny.
HEATHER	Do I look like I'm laughing at all?
JOSH	No, but you're going around doing your documentary thing, man. [At which point, Mike walks towards the camera and tries to take it off Heather. The field of vision is blurred as they wrestle each ot her.]
MIKE	Turn the goddamn thing off! [sounds of wrestling] If you bite me one more time, I'll throw you in the fuckin' woods!
HEATHER	You touch my camera again and I'll bite you again!

In another scene, as Josh films Heather through the Hi-8, he says he under-
stands why she likes the video camera so much: "It's totally like filtered reality, man.
It's like you can pretend everything's not quite the way it is." Finally, as tensions
increase, Josh "attacks" Heather with the camera, zooming in and out towards her
tearful face, yelling at her "there's no one here to help you. *That's* your motivation!
... *That's* your motivation!" When Mike tells him to back off, Josh replies "no, she's
still making movies man. That's my point." A tearful Heather yells back: "It's all I
fuckin' have left OK?"[67]

As Michael Hutak notes, throughout *The Blair Witch Project*, Mike and Josh dis-
avow the value of Heather's Hi-8 camera: "will you quit shoving that fucking camera in my face?"[68] In Mike's wrestling with Heather and Josh's tormenting of her, the

camera is both assaulted and assaulting. Despite their attempts to turn the camera against her, it remains a source of comfort and protection for Heather, as she increasingly talks to herself "through" the camera, leading to her famous "confession" scene in the tent, delivered straight to camera, with tears streaming down her face: "I'm so sorry."

In this way, *The Blair Witch Project* problematizes the relationship of subject to camera at the heart of documentary filmmaking. In Direct and Observational Cinema, the camera is intended as an invisible, unacknowledged witness to events that would have happened the same way regardless of the camera's presence.[69] Many documentary filmmakers, since the demise of the Direct Cinema movement in the late 1970s, have become aware of the impossibility of the camera remaining unacknowledged; hence the emergence of new, more "reflexive" modes of documentary narration.[70] *The Blair Witch Project* emphasises the intrusiveness of the camera, while at the same time demonstrating its incapacity to capture the very subject it seeks to record: the witch herself.

Avant-Garde Aesthetics and the Horror Genre

Like watching a snuff film.[71]

While Heather fails in her attempt to "document" the Blair Witch, the film itself succeeds in conveying the essence of horror. Documentary evidence, or "proof," lies in the image, what is seen ("I'll believe it when I see it"). While the camera records the students' fear, the source of their terror remains elusive. However it is precisely this 'unseen menace' that is at the heart of *Blair Witch*'s ability to terrify. In a style more typical of avant-garde aesthetics than mainstream 1990s horror, terror is conveyed in *The Blair Witch Project* through long minutes of darkness and an expressive soundtrack, ranging from piercing screams to heavy breathing. The 'image' of horror is deflected onto totemic symbols of rocks and twigs, as portents of things to come, and conveyed by the wild-eyed terror on the faces of students. For Michael Hutak, *The Blair Witch Project* recalls the early years of horror, "especially German avant-garde classics of the 1920s such as *Nosferatu*."[72] *The Blair Witch Project* shares Expressionism's interest in the psychological aspects of horror and the externalised expression of fear and paranoia.[73] Through its use of grainy, often pitch-black, footage, it evokes "the uncanniness and unease generated by such supposedly 'raw' images and sounds."[74]

1990s horror films, such as Wes Craven's *Scream* trilogy (1996–2000), are characterised by explicit representations of violence, sex and gore, often with elaborate special effects and make up, and a prevailing tone of irony in their various homages to the slasher films of the 1970s.[75] In these films, the audience always sees the monster, sometimes before the victims, and often the camera privileges the monster's point of view.[76] *The Blair Witch Project* challenges these generic conventions through its use of avant-garde aesthetics; specifically, its site of generic revision is the image, rather than the narrative. In using the term "avant-garde" to describe certain aspects of *The Blair Witch Project*, I am drawing upon Noël Carroll's observation that "to say a film is avant-garde is to say something about the form of a film"; in particular, interpreting a certain film as avant-garde "demands that one establish how it deviates from existing practice."[77] In my view, *The Blair Witch Project* deviates from existing practice—where we take existing practice to be the conventions of the 1990s horror genre—by refusing to show the source of the horror, the face of the monster. More specifically, the film chooses to represent its horror obliquely, through the soundtrack rather than through the image.[78] The cinematic image is reduced, at times, to total darkness; at others, to blurred, unsteady images as the bearer of the camera runs through the woods. There is the persistent sense that the image of horror is just off-screen, about to jump out in front of the camera or be glimpsed in the corner of the frame. This constant state of anticipation is the source of the film's horror. In these unconventional images, I place *The Blair Witch Project* in the genre that Carroll reserves for young structuralist filmmakers, whose films are "not really repudiations of prevailing practices but rather merely repetitions or amplifications of the existing, well-entrenched stylistic frameworks set forth by [avant-garde filmmakers] like Frampton, Gehr and Snow."[79] What *The Blair Witch Project* shares in common with these films is its "stylistic deviation" from "a larger, more dominant form of cinema."[80]

The essence of *The Blair Witch Project*'s avant-garde aesthetic lies in its challenge to the viewer to make meaning from the image:

> the audience has to piece things together from sequences that stop in the middle, or gaze for a long boring minute or so at a shot of weeds while, the camera momentarily forgotten, the characters argue. We never get quite enough information to figure out what's happening, but ... we always get enough to dread what's coming next.[81]

Several reviewers commented on the "minimalist" aesthetic of the film: "The 'real' footage comprising the film—both the stark black-and-white 16 millimetre and the low-tech video—comes to carry a spooky, unsettling effect in its very texture."[82] Others suggested that the aesthetic style of *The Blair Witch Project* recalls the principles of the Dogma manifesto, used in films such as Lars von Trier's *The Idiots* (1999) and Thomas Vinterberg's *Festen* (1999).[83] All of these films were made "with a hand-held, high-definition video camera in 'real' time with no separately recorded sound track and actors deeply involved and improvising much of what they say and do."[84] As these examples demonstrate, despite its commercial success, *The Blair Witch Project* has also been discursively positioned as an avant-garde film. This blurring of the boundaries between the mainstream and the avant-garde is a hallmark of post-cinema visual culture.[85]

The Blair Witch Project *as Postmodern,*
Post-Cinema Cultural Product

The literary and aesthetic theorists of a previous era would
surely have gone mad trying to figure out exactly what kind and

degree of "willing suspension of disbelief" is involved in
the consumption of such expanded, multimedia fiction.
Hence the uneasiness of some of the reactions to the Blair
Witch *juggernaut: is it the fruit of a youthful, boundless*
"postmodern" imagination, or just an elaborate trick to
win a few, fleeting moments of celebrity attention?[86]

As Adrian Martin observes, *The Blair Witch Project* is "very much a case of narrative in the age of the CD-ROM ... a central storyline is only a starting point for branching off into other 'extensions.' A self-contained plot is replaced by an ersatz mythology."[87] *The Blair Witch Project* has created a legend with both a history and a future, ensuring plenty of material for prequels and sequels, as well as spin-off web sites.[88] Contemporary visual culture is characterised by the generation of new forms of audiovisual intertextuality.[89] *The Blair Witch Project* may be regarded as an example of this new audiovisual intertextuality; in the interrelations between the film, the books, the website, and the DVD, we see the convergence of "old and new media."[90] This intertextuality demands greater interaction on the part of the spectator, who is required to synthesise the narrative of the Blair Witch legend from a range of diverse audiovisual material.[91]

The Blair Witch Project's mixing of documentary and fictive modes, and its juxtaposition of heterogenous genres, are just two of the reflexive strategies identified by Robert Stam as definitive of postmodern aesthetic practice.[92] In its use of a genre associated with "reality"—the documentary—to narrate a fiction, *The Blair Witch Project* is an exemplary postmodern cultural product: reality is simulated and the resulting image is no longer a guarantee of "truth."[93] Lloyd Rose compares the film's "hoax" with Orson Welles' 1938 radio broadcast of "The War of the Worlds": "Like that youthfully-impetuous, near-hoax, Myrick and Sanchez's movie is a work that *plays*—with form, technical possibilities, audience expectations and the idea of a show as a *magic trick*."[94] Rose's choice of the words "magic trick" seems apt in an era where scholars are drawing comparisons between the current post-cinema visual culture and the pre-cinema sideshow culture, or "cinema of attractions."[95]

In this analysis of *The Blair Witch Project*, I have drawn upon a range of theoretical approaches concerning diverse subject matters: the documentary film; the avant-garde film; film in the age of digital media; film in the age of postmodernism. While the discussions of theory in each area have, of necessity, been brief, I hope this has demonstrated the utility of a pluralisation of film theory in understanding the production and reception of a particular film text. As Robert Stam argues, "the question is not one of relativism or mere pluralism, but rather of multiple grids and knowledges, each of which sheds a specific light on the object studied."[96] To simply "read" *The Blair Witch Project* as "a documentary film," "an avant-garde film" or "a horror film," is to misread the complex intersections between these genres that account for the film's meaning. And to approach *The Blair Witch Project* simply as "a film," and not as a multimedia product of postmodern visual culture, is—in merchandising parlance—"only half the story."

1. *The Blair Witch Project*, dir. Daniel Myrick and Eduardo Sánchez, perf. Heather Donahue, Joshua Leonard and Michael C. Williams, 1999, prod. Haxan Films, distrib. Artisan Entertainment (US).

2. Actor Heather Donahue (who plays "Heather") quoted in Michael Hutak, "*The Blair Witch Project*," *Juice* [Australia] Nov. 1999: 50.

3. Michael Hutak, "The Horror and the Hype," *Juice* [Australia] Dec. 1999: 105.

4. The relationship between economics and film aesthetics will be discussed later in the section on "Guerrilla Filmmaking."

5. The website <http://www.blairwitch.com> first appeared on the Internet in June 1998, seven months before the film premiered at the Sundance Film Festival (Andrew Eaton, "Cheap Thrills," *The Big Issue* [Australia] 15 Nov. 1999: 26).

6. Michael O'Sullivan, "All the Fright Moves: *Blair Witch*'s Crew Romps through the Chilling Fields," *Washington Post* 11 Jul. 1999: G2.

7. O'Sullivan, p. G1.

8. Anthony Kaufman, "The *Blair Witch* Directors on the Method to their Madness," *Village Voice* 20 Jul. 1999: 50.

9. Bernard Weinraub, "A Witch's Caldron of Success Boils Over," *New York Times* 26 Jul. 1999: B1.

10. Richard Corliss, "Blair Witch Craft," *Time* 16 Aug. 1999: 58.

11. Corliss, p. 58–9.

12. *Ibid*, p. 59.

13. *Ibid*.

14. Edward Guthmann, "Under *Witch*'s Spell: Hollywood rethinking its strategies after small film's huge success," *San Francisco Examiner-Chronicle* 29 Aug. 1999: 63.

15. Hutak, "The Horror," p. 105.

16. Amy Taubin, "Spelling It Out," *Village Voice* 10 Aug. 1999: 68

17. "Mythology," *The Blair Witch Project* official website, Haxan Films, 1999, 18 Nov. 2003 <http://www.blairwitch.com/mythology.html>.

18. Originally, Myrick and Sánchez intended the film to include the search for the students and further information on the legend of the Blair Witch, in keeping with the feel of a "mock documentary." After editing the material together, they decided to remove this additional historical background footage and retain solely the footage shot by the students (the actors). These "outtakes" thus became the source material for the website and the television "documentary" *Curse of the Blair Witch*, dir. Daniel Myrick and Eduardo Sánchez, Artisan Entertainment, 1999 (Corliss 62).

19. "The Filmmakers," *The Blair Witch Project* official website, Haxan Films, 1999, 18 Nov. 2003 www.blairwitch.com/filmmakers.html>.

20. "The Aftermath," *The Blair Witch Project* official website, Haxan Films, 1999, 18 Nov. 2003 www.blairwitch.com/aftermath.html.

21. In their commentary for the DVD release, Myrick and Sánchez note that they made changes to the film's final edit for commercial release following the premiere at Sundance, after audience response suggested Heather was an unsympathetic character and too "bitchy": Directors' Commentary, *The Blair Witch Project*, digital video disc, Artisan Entertainment, 2001.

22. "The Legacy," *The Blair Witch Project* official website, Haxan Films, 1999, 18 Nov. 2003 www.blairwitch.com/legacy.html.

23. Shu Shin Luh, "On the Web, Rags to Witch's: Unsophisticated *Blair* Site Built the Mystery for Teens," *Washington Post* 19 Aug. 1999: E8.

24. A more recent example of innovative website design that maintains and expands upon a film's fictional universe is the official website for *Donnie Darko* (Richard Kelly, 2001) 18 Nov. 2003 <http://www.donniedarko.com>. Like the *Blair Witch* website, this site uses fragments of "documentary evidence"—police reports and pages from philosophical books—to provide a back story to the film's main narrative and to strengthen its "mythology" (in this particular case, the mythology of time travel and parallel universes).

25. Luh, p. E8.

26. This link would take browsers to the following URL http://store.artisanent.com/cgi-bin/storeArtisan/bwstore/index.html>. However, since this essay was first published in 2001, this page has been removed from Artisan Entertainment's website (as at 18 Nov. 2003). Indeed the Arti-

san site no longer includes an online shopping forum. In 2001, *Blair Witch* merchandise was also available at blairwitchdirect.com, but the registration for this domain name has expired (as at 18 Nov. 2003).

27. Despite the demise of the *Blair Witch* online shops noted above, *Blair Witch* fans can still purchase a range of DVDs, videos, books, comics and soundtracks through the online department store Amazon www.amazon.com. (as at 18 Nov. 2003).

28. D. A. Stern, *The Blair Witch Project: A Dossier* (Onyx Books: 1999) back cover, my emphasis.

29. Jen Van Meter et al., *The Blair Witch Chronicles*, graphic novel ed. (Oni Press: 2000) back cover.

30. Stern, back cover. Although now listed as out of print, used copies are still available through Amazon (as of 18 Nov. 2003).

31. Van Meter et al. This book is also still available through Amazon (as at 18 Nov. 2003).

32. *Curse of the Blair Witch* is available for purchase on video (released 2000) through Amazon (as at 18 Nov. 2003), and comes as a bonus feature on the DVD release of *The Blair Witch Project*.

33. Weinraub, p. B5.

34. Susan Hayward, *Key Concepts in Cinema Studies* (London: Routledge, 1996) 262–63.

35. Hayward 266; Robert Stam, *Film Theory: An Introduction* (Malden, Mass: Blackwell, 1999) 315.

36. Guthmann, p. 63.

37. Corliss, p. 56.

38. Guthmann, p. 63.

39. Corliss, p. 58.

40. Randolph Pitts of independent film distributor Lumière Films Inc., Los Angeles, quoted in Luh E8.

41. Guthmann, p. 63–64.

42. Luh, p. E8.

43. Adrian Martin, "Pity it's phooey," *The Age* [Melbourne] 2 Dec. 1999: B3.

44. Kevin Macdonald and Mark Cousins, *Imagining Reality: The Faber Book of Documentary* (London: Faber and Faber, 1996) 352–53; Stam 322.

45. Lynden Barber, "Guerilla Cinema: How a few thousand dollars and a digital video camera can change the (film) world," *The Weekend Australian* 11 Dec. 1999, "Review": 8.

46. Wim Wenders' 1999 documentary *Buena Vista Social Club* was shot on video (Barber 8). According to Barber, other filmmakers planning digital features include Spike Lee, Gus Van Sant, Mike Figgis and Eric Rohmer.

47. Barber, p. 9.

48. *Ibid*, p. 9.

49. Guthmann, p. 64.

50. Corliss, p. 62.

51. Barber, p. 9.

52. *Ibid*, p. 9.

53. Hutak, "The Horror" 105.

54. Barber, p. 9. Rick McCallum, producer of the *Star Wars* series, is described by Barber as a "high-profile fan of DIY."

55. O'Sullivan, p. G2.

56. Producer Greg Hale, quoted in the on-screen production notes included as a bonus feature with the DVD release of *The Blair Witch Project*.

57. Lloyd Rose, "*Blair Witch*: A Spell of Pure Terror," *Washington Post* 16 Jul. 1999: C5.

58. Sandra Hall, "*Blair Witch* a lesson in hard spell," *Sydney Morning Herald* 9 Dec. 1999: 17.

59. There is insufficient scope to go into details here of the differences between the American movement of Direct Cinema and the *cinéma-vérité* of Jean Rouch, suffice to say that the former eschewed all intervention on the part of the filmmaker, while Rouch was more interactive towards the subjects he was filming. For more detail, see Macdonald and Cousins 250–51 and Bill Nichols' discussion of what he terms "the observational mode" (Direct Cinema) versus "the interactive mode" (*cinéma-vérité*) in *Representing Reality: Issues and Concepts in Documentary* (Bloomington: Indiana University Press, 1991): 35–56.

60. This paragraph is a summary of the overview of *cinéma-vérité* presented by Macdonald and Cousins 249–51.

61. Macdonald and Cousins, p. 251.

62. As examples of the *cinéma-vérité*/realist aesthetic in feature films, Lizzie Francke cites the work of Wayne Wang (*Blue in the Face*, 1995), Warren Beatty and Trevor Griffiths (*Reds*, 1981), Oliver Stone (*JFK*, 1993 & *Nixon*, 1995) and the social realist films of Ken Loach (Francke quoted in Macdonald and Cousins 341).

63. Kaplan quoted in Nichols 68.

64. Eaton 26. For further discussion of "Reality TV," see Nichols, "At the Limits of Reality (TV)," *Blurred Boundaries: Questions of Meaning in Contemporary Culture* (Bloomington: Indiana UP, 1994) 43–62.

65. Francke in Macdonald and Cousins pp. 342–43.

66. Taubin, p. 68.

67. In a parody of the ethics of investigative journalism that propel the reporter in the search of "truth" (the public's right to "know"), Heather's journal, posted on the film's website, provides further insight and self-analysis about why she continues filming. These comments point to the role of documentary film as proof that something "really" happened: "Whatever is chasing us has to be documented.... If something is going to harm me that I can't stab or kill and if I am defenceless in the face of it, the least I can do is capture it so that people will know that it is real." And later, "Documents. Documenting. Documentation. Verifying existence. That makes sense right. I am verifying that I am still here." See the link to Heather's Journal in "The Legacy," *The Blair Witch Project* official website, Haxan Films, 1999, 18 Nov. 2003 <http://www.blairwitch.com/legacy.html>.

68. Hutak, p. 105.

69. Macdonald and Cousins 250; Nichols 39.

70. See Nichols, "The Reflexive Mode of Representation," *Representing Reality* 56–68.

71. Director Daniel Myrick quoted in O'Sullivan G2.

72. Hutak, p. 105.

73. Hence the influence of German Expressionism on both horror films and *films noir* (David Bordwell and Kristin Thompson, *Film Art: An Introduction*, 3rd ed. (New York: McGraw-Hill, 1990) 380–81).

74. Martin, p. B3.

75. Martin B3; Corliss, p. 60.

76. Corliss, p. 60–61.

77. Noël Carroll, "Avant-Garde Film and Film Theory," *Millennium Film Journal* 4–5 Summer-Fall (1979): 136.

78. This use of sound rather than image as the source of horror recalls Jacques Tourneur's masterful work in *Cat People* (1942).

79. Carroll, p. 137.

80. Carroll 136 & 137. Richard Zoglin puts forward a similar view about *Blair Witch's* avant-garde status: "the scariest cinematic moments for the most part have come courtesy of low-budget independent films that, like *The Blair Witch Project*, arrive unheralded from outside the Hollywood mainstream to chill us with their grungy lack of artistry" (quoted in Corliss 62). Zoglin's other examples include George Romero's *Night of the Living Dead* (1968), Roger Corman's films, David Cronenberg's early films, Tobe Hooper's *The Texas Chainsaw Massacre* (1974) and John Carpenter's *Halloween* (1978).

81. Rose, p. C5.

82. Martin, p. B3. Both Edward Guthmann (63) and Richard Corliss (56) describe the film as "minimalist." In his discussion of "Digital Theory and the New Media," Robert Stam notes "an uncanny affinity between the new media and what used to be regarded as *avant-garde* practices": "low-budget video-makers can deploy a kind of cybernetic *minimalism*, achieving maximum beauty and effect at minimum expense" (322–23; my emphases).

83. Stan James, "Bewitching the mind," *Adelaide Advertiser* 11 Dec. 1999: 20; Barber 8.

84. James, p. 20.

85. Stam, p. 317 & 322.

86. Martin, p. B3.

87. *Ibid.*

88. Following the popularity of the official *Blair Witch* site, a spin-off website emerged <http://www.rustinparr.com> which cast doubt upon the validity of the confession and trial that saw Rustin hanged for the murder of seven children in 1940. Since this essay was first published in 2001, the counter-narrative provided by this website has ceased to exist (as at 18 Nov. 2003) while the official *Blair Witch* site is still on line. Sánchez and Myrick's production company, Haxan Films, was commissioned in 1999 to begin planning a prequel or sequel as part of their "ongoing development" relationship with Artisan Entertainment (Guthmann 64 & Kaufmann 52). Myrick and Sánchez served as Executive Producers on the sequel *Book of Shadows: Blair Witch 2* (2000), directed by Joe Berlinger. Berlinger co-wrote the screenplay with Dick Beebe, based on characters created by Sanchez and Myrick. As an award-winning documentary filmmaker, Berlinger was touted by Artisan as a bringing to the project "a unique understanding of the blurry line between truth and fiction that is a key element of the Blair Witch series" (<http://www.artisanent.com/ComingAttractions/bwp2.html> 18 Nov. 2003). However, when *Book of Shadows* failed to recapture the critical and commercial success of its predecessor, production plans for *Blair Witch 3* — a prequel to be scripted and directed by Myrick and Sánchez — were shelved. *Blair Witch 3* was listed on the Internet Movie Database <http://www.imdb.com> for some time as being "in production" (last updated 18 February 2001) but its listing has since been removed (as at 18 Nov. 2003).

89. Stam, p. 324. This new audiovisual intertextuality — the use of multiple mediums to narrate a popular fiction — is evident in *The Matrix* trilogy (Andy & Larry Wachowski, 1999 & 2003), where the mythology extends over three feature films, several animés (including one, *The Final Flight of the Osiris* (Andy Jones, 2003), that provides a narrative link between the first and second films), and a video game *Enter the Matrix* (Andy & Larry Wachowski, 2003) that includes extensive live action footage using the same actors and locations as the feature films.

90. Recall John Pierson's comment, quoted earlier in the section on "Guerrilla Filmmaking."

91. Stam, p. 323.

92. *Ibid*, p. 303.

93. *Ibid*, p. 319.

94. Rose C5, my emphases.

95. Stam, p. 318–19. Regrettably, it is beyond the scope of this essay to discuss the parallels between pre- and post-cinema in greater detail. Nevertheless this discussion was influenced by the insights of Tom Gunning and Miriam Hansen in their consideration of contemporary visual culture and its similarities to early silent cinema, especially the privileging of spectacle over narrative and the reception of the cinematic text in the context of a variety of other forms of entertainment, such as vaudeville and magic shows. See Tom Gunning, "'Now You See It, Now You Don't': The Temporality of the Cinema of Attractions," *The Velvet Light Trap* 32 Fall (1993): 3–12; Miriam Hansen, "Early Cinema, Late Cinema: Transformations of the Public Sphere," *Viewing Positions: Ways of Seeing Film*, ed. Linda Williams (New Brunswick: Rutgers University Press, 1995) 17; Hansen, interviewed by Laleen Jayamanne & Anne Ruthford, "'The Future of Cinema Studies in the Age of Global Media': Aesthetics, Spectatorship & Public Spheres," *The UTS Review* 5 (1999): 94–110.

96. Stam, p. 330.

17

Chasing the Real: Reality Television and Documentary Forms

by Leigh H. Edwards

Reality television is well known for its cannibalistic impulses towards the genre of documentary. But what is most interesting about its appropriation of the form is that it tries to reendow documentary with the status of "truth." While theorists and filmmakers have long remarked on the inevitable merger of fact and fiction, witnessing and interpretation in the non-fiction film form, reality television wants to change course and make documentary synonymous with "authenticity." Viewers are aware that the actual content of these programs consists of, at best, what Erik Barnouw would term "provoked action" and, at worst, scripted situations performed poorly by nonprofessional actors.[1] But instead of asking viewers to believe in the content, reality programming asks audiences to believe in the form.

By staging their own fantasy version of "documentary," where blockbuster shows mime formal techniques such as single-camera interviews, black and white surveillance sequences, and voiceover narration, these programs pretend to deliver on the marketing promise of their "reality" moniker. Documentarians know that a filmmaker changes a system as they observe it, merging subjectivity and objectivity into two sides of the same coin, revealing observational expression as always already motivated, coming from a particular perspective rather than a universalized view. But reality television wants to downplay that knowledge, at least for the sake of marketing. And perhaps their success in merchandizing reveals more about audience nostalgia for the "truth" claims of film and video as visual forms than anything else. Emerging audience studies give us empirical evidence that viewers know many reality shows are loosely scripted but they still see reality programming as at least "moderately" real.[2]

In this essay, I explore how particular shows and subgenres merge non-fiction with narrative fiction techniques, how they refit documentary features to traditional televisual formats like the family situation comedy, and how they sometimes change documentary. Reality programming is obviously not the only television genre to adapt documentary elements, but it does make its own unique, elaborate truth claims. John Caldwell argues that when "reality soap" programs like *The Real World* use documentary techniques, they only ever reveal the fictional construction of the genre, i.e. the shows do not document the verity of "seven people picked to live together and have their lives taped," they document, rather, the fabrication of the series, replete with story-boarding, editing into narrative arcs, and some loose scripting.[3] I agree with Caldwell, but I also see a different dynamic at play here too, one that deserves more inquiry. I will show how reality TV develops an elaborate fantasy version of documentary that itself becomes a visual, formal analogy or metonym for "the real," one that records audience nostalgia for the outmoded idea that visual technologies can picture ontology. I will explicate how the genre makes formal truth claims through its imagined model of "documentary," which is full of standardized techniques adapted to serial television. My argument focuses on the recent reality programming trend ushered in by MTV's *The Real World* in 1992, though actuality format shows have, of course, a long history on television from the medium's inception (to understand reality TV's present, you have to understand its past, like observational cinema classics such as PBS's *An American Family* [1973] and the on-going *Candid Camera*).[4]

In the process of imagining "documentary," reality television is playing a high stakes game in the sense that it stages resistance to our critical deconstruction of the ontological claims of visual representation. It also raises important questions about genre and hybrid forms. We might ask, for example, how do we make meaningful distinctions between non-fiction and narrative film? Can any film or video profess to be a documentary simply because it presents itself as non-fiction? And to beg more questions of genre, to what degree is it possible to see reality television and documentary as discrete entities? Bill Nichols explains how documentary film as a discourse can assert verisimilitude but only in a limited way, calling it a "discourse of sobriety" that makes truth claims, much like science, economics, politics, and history.[5] As in these other fields, though, we know the mimetic impulse is inevitably mediated. Even more than that, we know that the merger of "factual" and "fictional" forms permeates our everyday lives; part of the draw of reality television is its meditation on how we understand our experiences through stories, that narrative fiction form that structures our very sense of what is happening around us.

As a case in point of the problems with "authenticity" in representation, documentary filmmaker and theorist Jill Godmilow discusses how "reality" becomes a generic formal convention of documentary. Godmilow explains why she dislikes the term "documentary" and only uses it for the sake of convenience:

> Because everybody *thinks* they know what the term means, because everybody has seen some television programs labeled documentary — either televisual "white papers," that is so-called objective journalistic presentations of social problems, or history programs that chronicle certain social movements, or portraits of famous artists or historical figures and the like. Unconsciously embedded in these forms called documentary is the conceit

of "the real," which substantiates the truth claims made by these films. These general notions about documentary film produce a fairly limited understanding of what non-fiction cinema can be and do.[6]

Godmilow goes on to question the effectiveness of the alternative term "non-fiction" and to debate the current status of non-mainstream practices in the genre. Nichols himself resorts to defining documentary based on context, linking style and the uses to which the film is put, emphasizing function over "reality," or accurate mimesis.[7] Leaving aside debates within documentary film studies about the current state and future of the medium, my concern here is to question how reality television programs use these "embedded truth claims" in documentary to position themselves as "authentic" representations of reality.

If, then, reality television uses documentary to signal "the real," to what effect? Many programs use documentary forms to reinforce their product. That product ranges from being the program itself, or an image — such as a celebrity's "private" life offered up for "public" consumption, or the viewer-as-product to be sold to corporate advertisers.

I will focus my argument by examining one particular documentary technique, direct address, and how it has been used by two different types of reality programs: first the celebrity subgenre, with series such as *The Osbournes*, *The Simple Life*, and *The Surreal Life*, and second MTV's youth culture shows such as *The Real World*, *Road Rules*, and *Tough Enough*. Reality television uses the direct address technique of speaking to the camera in two main ways: voiceover narration (in the mode of direct address documentary style offscreen narration) and castmembers talking directly to the camera, either in the midst of action sequences or in set-up single camera interviews (where the speaker sometimes mentions the audience explicitly and sometimes does not). Celebrity reality shows use direct address to reinforce the status of "celebrity" in their televisual world, using documentary techniques to mimic the performance and form of camera-mediated stardom. MTV's youth shows, meanwhile, use the technique in documentary-style interviews aimed at the camera, often presented as "confessionals," to establish a particular ideology in their castmembers— an ideology of personal growth towards liberal pluralist consensus, creating a subjectivity for cast and viewers that allows MTV to deliver a specific kind of audience-as-product to their corporate advertisers. In the first case, where direct address signals "celebrity," the form establishes the cultural value of an image as the show's product. In the second case, where direct address enacts pluralist consensus on youth shows, the form establishes an ideology as a way to fashion the viewer as product. After a word on the interplay of form and content in the genre, I will turn to analyze both cases and their ramifications for representations of documentary and visual evidence.

Form and Content

Any account of reality television's version of "documentary" must first attempt to grapple with the multifarious, juxtaposed interaction of form and content in the genre. These television serials combine elements of different formal techniques, from the "talking head" set-up interviews of expository documentaries to observational cinema's surveillance of people's behavior (using both direct cinema and cinéma vérité), though they tend to eschew the reflexive or diaristic approaches now common to many documentary films. In direct cinema mode, programs avidly trail a castmember through the events they are experiencing and imply an invisible "fly on the wall" vantage; most shows mix in cinéma vérité sequences, where producers provoke the action and set up situations, drawing on the paradox Barnouw identifies in this approach, the idea "artificial circumstances could bring hidden truth to the surface."[8] As the shows purport to deliver "reality" through their visual vocabulary, they imply they will even sometimes be absolved from doing so through their content. For example, the forms "single-camera interviews" or "direct address interviews" frequently signal "reality" rather than the actual content of those interviews. Sometimes a castmember might deliver a particularly moving speech full of content that induces viewer sympathy for what seems an accurate representation of that person's life. But more often than not, if that interview is unconvincing or even boring, the visual frame of the subject in a chair delivering a direct address message to the audience will signal to viewers that what they are watching is "real life," not completely fake, even given the mediation and editing viewers know is part of the image they see.

There are abundant examples of reality programs using documentary set-ups to make ontological claims even when the episode's plot or dialogue is obviously fabricated. On the one hand, televangelist Tammy Faye Messner (formerly Bakker), starring in *The Surreal Life*, gives a moving direct address interview about how her religion saved her from suicide; her emotional words and delivery frame her as a candid truth-teller and the WB Network's message boards light up with praise for what a down to earth, believable person she is.[9] Yet, on the other hand, Paris Hilton, in *The Simple Life*, sits at the kitchen table of the Arkansas family hosting her (the premise for this reverse Beverly Hillbillies, fish out of water story of a celebrity party girl living with rural Southerners), and says "What is Wal-Mart? Do they sell wall stuff?"[10] We know she is delivering a put-on. In a later print interview, she admitted she knew what Wal-Mart was, saying "I was just playing a part. If I knew what everything was, it wouldn't be funny."[11] Hilton discloses that she was enacting an interesting persona for the camera rather than expressing her "actual" reactions to "real-life" situations. But her televisual world is presented in cinéma vérité style; the cameras follow her around the table, picturing the family from her perspective and vice versa with several shot/reverse shot images, all intercut with footage from Hilton's later direct address single-camera interview commenting on the action and explaining her difficulty in understanding her hosts. Thus, we get to experience pleasure in the visual "forms" of reality, even when the content cannot approximate the "real" half as well itself.

Documenting "Celebrity"

In celebrity reality programs, U.S. culture's obsession with fame has found a new way to satiate itself. What would it be like to be a superstar? We have our vicarious answer. A camera locks its gaze on luminaries, and we get to follow them beyond the velvet ropes, into the VIP area, to scrutinize their daily lives behind the idol façade. But as we are invited to look under the media construction, to see the man behind the Oz-like curtain, we do not so much abandon our belief in celebrity as find new ways to reinforce it; when a program offers to display to audiences the "private" person beneath the constructed "public" persona, it reinforces the very existence and cultural capital of that "public" persona (particularly when the private persona is equally constructed).

Direct address functions as part of the central framework of such series, encoding "celebrity" as a visual performance involving an intricate ballet of cameras, microphones, booms, wires, and a semi-reluctant, semi-willing, semi-famous star. The subgenre emphasizes observational cinema approaches to suggest immediate access to the stars. Not surprisingly, the celebrities usually get to speak for themselves too, meditating on the minutiae of their lives. Single camera interviews let them comment on the events pictured, sometimes accompanied by black and white flashbacks of earlier sequences—which are accorded the status of confirmed visual evidence. NBC's *The Apprentice* offers a good example of voiceover narration in the subgenre. Slamming hapless contestants, hawking products, or intoning business philosophies, Donald Trump narrates the show as castmembers compete to run one of his companies, and his voiceover identifies the show with his "celebrity" point of view.

Notably, celebrities break reality genre taboos. Witness spontaneous direct address moments during the action sequences (versus clearly delineated interview sequences), where stars interrupt the action to talk to the camera, insistently drawing attention to the crew or the videotaping, sometimes breaking the fourth wall by referencing the audience explicitly. Other reality subgenres render that behavior strictly forbidden. Castmembers on shows like *The Real World* or *Survivor* are instructed not to interact with the camera crew or speak directly to the lens except during set-up interviews. I would argue that celebrity shows encourage their casts to violate the invisibility conceit because those moments confirm celebrity by having the castmembers perform it. The stars are at pains to reestablish the contours of their "natural" mediated habitat, which consists of dodging film crews, reporters, and paparazzi, embodying the object of the camera's gaze, being the center of media attention. When castmembers tell the television cameras to "get out of their faces" or insist that the producers "turn the camera off," they reassuringly enact celebrity identity.

For example, in *The Osbournes*, producers use direct address interviews to establish the pop idol status of their objects of study and to signal that viewers are gaining access to their "private" reality, but also to establish the cultural cachet of the series itself, bringing *The Osbournes* into the realm of celebrity object while also making the claim of "documenting" the show on a meta level. The series has been a smash hit for MTV, a home run precisely because it ironically juxtaposes Ozzy's bat-biting Prince of Darkness rocker persona with a private persona, one MTV narrativizes as the addled domestic sitcom patriarch of "America's favorite dysfunctional family." From the insider story the docu-style coverage tells, we learn our character lessons: "the Dad" is loveable but poignantly disoriented and barely functional, partly

Documenting the "private" reality of celebrity life: *The Osbournes*.

from years of drug abuse and the heavy metal lifestyle; "the Mom" is in charge and manages their business interests with a mafioso's iron fist; the teenage kids run amok, trying to find themselves amidst a series of family tragedies and escapades. A typical American family, except famous? MTV offers that conceit. If Ozzy breaks the direct cinema mode when he should not, we are to believe he does so because of his characteristic confusion; he must ask the camera crew where he lives or he would never find his way home. But more than that, the direct address technique bestows the fetish of fame on both the family and the show. In a scene that performs this double function, Sharon Osbourne launches the program's second season with a direct address speech to the camera in which she gleefully exhibits all the magazine covers and press attention their show garnered during its first season.[12] The episode shifts from documenting this media sensation through direct address to following Sharon and her children around music industry events using direct cinema style. The truth claims of the direct address scene attempt to blanket the rest of that episode's footage, and the series itself, in "authenticity" as well as confirmed celebrity.

By contrasting *The Osbournes* to other televisual representations of this family, we can see precisely how the program uses its own version of "documentary" to sell its product. One notorious episode in season three, for instance, features startling footage of Ozzy immediately after a motorized All Terrain Vehicle (ATV) accident that almost killed him.[13] Through its documentary gestures, what this episode dramatizes, more than Ozzy's near-death experience, is MTV's ability to capture real-life events on camera because of its reality format. MTV jams documentary-style footage into its domestic sitcom narrative, combining black and white footage of the event with direct address clips of Ozzy joking about the accident later — the episode's narrative frame situates him as affable father in the family tragicomedy. In contrast, ABC's *Primetime Thursday* newsmagazine contemporaneously aired a Diane Sawyer interview with Sharon and Ozzy.[14] This interview is obviously in a different format, a journalistic two-camera live video with a host conducting the discussion, but it also differs markedly from *The Osbournes*' representation in that it uses a much more serious, traumatized tone to focus on how severe the accident was. The ABC news division tries to achieve journalistic credibility by adding on-camera interviews with Ozzy's doctors and shots of his X-rays. Both shows are constructed narratives. But *The Osbournes* lays claim to a higher level of actuality. The newsmagazine attempts to verify the facts of what happened with expert testimony and reportage, but significantly, it uses MTV's clips as visual "evidence" of the accident itself. The reality show, meanwhile, tries to capture the actual experience, since their marketing promise involves their potential to document the entire lives of their subjects on video.

The MTV sequence in question illuminates how *The Osbournes* uses documentary forms to signal actuality. As advertisements for this episode imply that MTV will show audiences Ozzy almost dying on camera, the program's documentary-style footage is a clear marketing technique. However, the episode does not show the moment of his crash but rather implies that it could have. The sequence moves from a comical shot of Ozzy haphazardly steering his ATV around a field to an intercut, sped-up aerial shot of his bike racing across the terrain, to a jerky black and white shot of Ozzy's prone body on the ground, his body guard desperately trying to revive him as other ATVs race to the scene. The crash occurs in the offscreen space. The image of Ozzy on the ground is a hand-held camera moving frame shot from the point of view of someone following on an ATV. In the next shot, the program self-servingly draws attention to itself, breaking the direct cinema conceit by having the camera man speak, recorded by the in-camera microphone, and put his camera down on the ground to run for help. Here, MTV wants viewers to know they abandoned filming to help Ozzy, contrasting themselves with other reality programs criticized for their ethics, as when a camera crew films the action rather than helping the hurt castmember (as *Survivor* creator Mark Burnett infamously instructed his crew to do).[15] This shot of Ozzy is from the camera man's subjective point of view whereas the program elsewhere uses a limited omniscient point of view. The camera keeps rolling, silently watching, giving us a canted frame image of Ozzy lying unconscious on the ground. Hearing the camera man's agitation is another marker of authentic proof that this event really happened — the camera saw it, as did its operator. The absence of a crash picture as well as the sudden shift to a subjective point of view highlights the program's more omniscient gaze elsewhere. This sequence suggests the panoptic power of MTV's cameras — they can give you access to the ocular proof and then take it away; they can retain the power to picture a near-death accident as well as the moral position of not doing so. Here, reality television's documentary techniques signal "truth claim" ability.

The Surreal Life *as Paradigm*

The Surreal Life is another popular reality program that verifies the "celebrity" of its product through visual and narrative forms taken from documentary. The series warrants extensive analysis because it explicitly meditates on fame as well as the rituals of camera-mediated stardom, illuminating how its celebrity product is coextensive with its documentary form. The program provides an extensive catalogue of this form I am calling reality television's "imagined version" of documentary, or, let us say, "reality documentary," and it also reveals some of the larger ramifications of this cultural practice. A self-conscious program like *The Surreal Life* interrogates what visual evidence has come to mean in this context, often questioning then partially reasserting the idea that the visual image is equivalent to actuality. Such programs register a deep awareness of how media construction of images works, and they uncover some profound ambivalences about this procedure, particularly concerning audience identification with the celebrities and the process of turning an image into a commodity.

The dance of identification and disidentification in these programs is an elaborate one. Viewers must identify with the celebrities but not too closely, otherwise the cast's star status is lost. Shows offer the stars as screen surrogates at times but at others, they disrupt that process of identification. For instance, *The Surreal Life*'s premise establishes its documentary setting and its method for enacting celebrity: cameras track a flock of B-list stars brought together to live in a house in a fine example of Barnouw's "provoked action." In each episode, the stars are asked to perform tasks, such as putting on talent shows or flipping burgers at a fast food restaurant, while we follow their every move. In an episode during season one, erstwhile child star Corey Feldman instigates a fight with his costars on a tour bus and suddenly demands that the crew stop filming, brushing the microphones and cameras aside with his arms, covering the lens with his hands. The text, which in that scene had been operating in direct cinema mode, pictures Feldman breaking into that format, making you aware of the camera in order to establish the forms of stardom on which the franchise depends.[16] In case some viewers were worried, perhaps understandably, that Feldman could no longer claim movie idol status, they can be reassured by these iconographic visual moments that perform "celebrity" for him, distinguishing him from the viewers.

As it pictures stardom, this subgenre stages both the lure and the frustration of entering what Sut Jhally terms the "commodity-image system," where the mass media fetishizes visual commodities, flattening out a person into an icon.[17] The reality genre accelerates the process of image commodification, even as it creates new "celebrities." After all, one *Surreal Life* castmember's only claim to fame is that she appeared on a previous reality series (Trishelle Cannatella, from MTV's *Real World: Las Vegas*). The series critiques how the media in general and reality programming in particular create those commodity images precisely by reducing a person to a single trait, one that is amplified, over-circulated, and over-exposed. As *Joe Millionaire* contestant Sarah Kozer complains of reality TV editing conventions, "I've been to law school, traveled the world, but now I'm the girl in the bushes" with Joe Millionaire.[18] Yet *The Surreal Life* cheerfully enacts that convention to sell itself. Its opening credit montage encourages you to interpret people as types, introducing each castmember first with a graphic of a stereotyped moniker, then with their name. Erik Estrada becomes "The 70s Heart Throb," Cannatella "The Reality Vixen," and Ron Jeremy "The Porn King."

The *Surreal Life* thus ironizes how media images work, yet it banks off the titillation of reality TV conventions. The series' conceit is that celebrity itself is surreal in the age of mass-mediated hyperreality. It ridicules how television produces stars. In the second season, the group house includes Warhol-style portraits of each media personality in their heyday, designed to capitalize on the visual irony of a 1970s television actor like Estrada trying to recapture his youthful glory years. The series sympathizes with castmember Rob "Vanilla Ice" Van Winkle who continually expresses deep pain and frustration with his media image; his fleeting fame as a white rapper in the early 1990s was followed quickly by his wholesale denigration for being a trite media construction rather than a musical talent. The camera follows him as he spray paints over his Vanilla Ice portrait, saying "I'm sick of being perceived as that image that wasn't even me."[19] But *The Surreal Life* continues to sell that image, since it is the basis for his fame. As the show's narrative arc for Van Winkle incorporates his ambivalence about that earlier reductive media image of himself, it simply makes a new narrative for him here — he is no longer just the talentless white rapper, he is the washed-up singer angry about his media image. The series turns the celebrities' discomfort with controlled media images into a marketing narrative, as when it pictures the self-reflexivity of fame in each episode by having the cast read about what they will be doing that day in a fake tabloid newspaper.

We know "Porn King" Jeremy is there to titillate, the pairing of him and "Televangelist" Tammy Faye a walking punch line, though the series fails to provoke conflict in its headliner odd couple, who establish a lingua franca of tolerance, becoming fast friends. But in its portrayal of Jeremy, *The Surreal Life* makes a larger point about voyeurism and genre. It analogizes the voyeurism of viewing pornography with that of watching reality television, again deconstructing reality TV conventions while also using them for marketing. The extremely rapid title sequence montage mixes the show's footage of each star with old television or film footage of them, still photos, and animated graphics. Jeremy's segment begins as an animated red curtain wipes across the frame, revealing a movie theater graphic with an old image of Jeremy emblazoned up on the cinema screen in the background, a frame within the frame.

A red graphic of the letters "XXX" superimposes itself on Jeremy's nude torso, making sure to identify the image as a porn film. At the same time, a still video shot of an almost-nude woman's torso with cropped head is superimposed to the right of the frame, over theater seats. Her image then dissolves, through an iris-in shot of her almost-bare breast, to reveal the lens of a movie camera, implying that we have been watching her from the point of view of the filmmaker. We then transition to a shot of that same film camera, seen in full, now gazing at a still video image of Jeremy, bathrobed and drinking in a hyperreal graphic of a *Surreal Life* bedroom, replete with champagne bubbles peppering the air. If these celebrities are living in a fishbowl for our entertainment, it is one filled with champagne, not water. The movie screen curtain again wipes across the screen and we transition into a still video shot of a clothed, grinning Jeremy, from *The Surreal Life* footage, with a graphic of a ruler superimposed near his crotch, and we hear an audio clip of him discussing his adult film career. Using juxtaposition and counterpointing, this quick montage links several viewer subject positions: the audience at a porn film is like the audience watching *The Surreal Life*, just as the porn and reality TV filmmakers are one in the same. As the program registers the pornographic nature of the pleasure of looking in the reality TV genre, its critical awareness is in line with Mulvey's application of Freud's scopophilia concept to Hollywood film.[20] Yet even as it ironizes that structure of seeing (and making), the series also banks off of these kinds of images, advertising such plot twists as a trip to a nudist colony and a pool party with Jeremy's adult film cohort, then gazing on their pixilated naked bodies.

In spite of elements that self-ironize televisual images and media stardom, *The Surreal Life* also asserts actuality. Through its own version of "documentary," it invites you beneath the celebrity persona to see the "real" person with whom you are asked to sympathize, often precisely through the structure of direct address interviews. For instance, throughout an episode in which a psychic visits and conducts a séance, action sequences are intercut with direct address cast interviews, allowing the stars to comment on and spin the events, eliciting viewer sympathy. These monologues, done one-on-one in their bedrooms, are offered as sober, confessional "reality" as opposed to the kitschy séance.[21] Similarly, the season finale pictures a staged Sally Jessy Raphael talk show in the house, replete with a studio audience. Grandstanding, Sally Jessy shows us *Surreal Life* clip reels and trashes the stars' morals and tears her hair out over their behavior, making the idols furious. We then see "behind the scenes" footage of angry castmembers and a matter-of-fact Sally Jessy, whose attitude is 'this is what you signed up for, kids, get used to it!' As it deconstructs the fake talk show, the program implies that these direct address interview moments after the staged talk show are "real" reactions.[22] Now for further insight let us turn to Tammy Faye's crying eyes, the true stars of the talk show. There as elsewhere in the series, Tammy Faye moves her peers to tears, her emotional testimonials ringing like a Pavlovian bell, here one that makes her castmates hungry to confess.

The Eyes of Tammy Faye

From her leopard-print dresses and impossibly thick make-up to her emotional break-downs, Tammy Faye is a spectacle. And *The Surreal Life* positively devours her.

It at once ridicules her persona, a charming version of the "church lady," and also tries to elicit viewer sympathy for her moral views and what it presents as the "real" Tammy Faye. The serial's clearest depiction of celebrity through a documentary-reality hybrid form comes in its fixation on her. The show mimes earlier documentary and journalistic footage of her when it focuses on images of her in tears. It is Tammy Faye's crying eyes that have become a media fetish, and both she and *The Surreal Life* producers know it. TV viewers will likely be able to recall video journalistic coverage of her then-husband Jim Bakker's Praise the Lord (PTL) ministry embezzlement scandal in 1989 — endless reels of Tammy Faye sobbing, her mascara running down her face, transforming into a garish mask of pain. Accused of embezzling 158 million dollars from PTL, Jim Bakker went to jail — Tammy Faye went to the Betty Ford Clinic. Tammy Faye herself has made a living by creating her own media self-representations, helping build the three largest Christian television networks and hosting several television programs.[23]

Its direct address interviews with her while she is weeping work to establish both documentary-style truth claims for the show and her status as a "celebrity" hounded by cameras in her moments of "authentic" suffering. The program is self-conscious about how it achieves its mixture of fact and fiction by juxtaposing old and new media images— old television show and movie images enjoy the status of "fact" because they are part of our collective pop culture consciousness. A 1970s image of Estrada from *CHiPs* takes on the same status as a journalistic shot from Tammy Faye's scandal days. But the show depends on those hybrid images even as it ironizes them.

By mixing earlier journalistic footage of Tammy Faye with its own reality docudrama footage, *The Surreal Life* wants to achieve the status of accurate reportage too, translated into the terms of reality show mimesis. In her title sequence, an old scandal-era image of Tammy Faye appears, Kleenex in hand, bedecked in blonde hair, a huge diamond ring, and tears tinged with mascara. This still video image is superimposed in front of a graphic of a church with an animated red sky, while a graphic reading "The televangelist" appears in the bottom left of the frame. We pan right to an animated cross and graphics of three angels with the face of Tammy Faye (circa 1989) fly into the sky, one after the other. Next, recent video footage from the current show appears, picturing her with red hair and large black sunglasses. She raises her hand to her sunglasses, then tilts them down to peer over them with a knowing glance and a smile, a movement the sequence comically repeats at high speed. As the current Tammy Faye tilts her sunglasses, the last of the three angel figures rises on the screen as if emerging from her hand. The montage suggests that *The Surreal Life* Tammy Faye can summon the angels of her past at will.

The sonic and visual landscape of the show thus draws direct parallels between the old and new Tammy Faye, the journalism coverage and *The Surreal Life* coverage, the footage of her "authentic" responses to historical events and the program's own documentary forms. *The Surreal Life* invokes those earlier journalism images as "objective" visual truth. Both sets of images, the sequence implies, have the status of accurate reportage. In fact, the audio track encourages viewers to collapse those images with its use of two sound clips. The first plays while the old image of

Tammy Faye is on the screen, and we hear her say in voiceover: "God has gotten ahold of my heart," the second accompanies the new Tammy Faye: "I said I'd never cry on TV again, well so you made me cry." Although the sequence implies that the first audio clip is from her PTL days, both are actually drawn from *The Surreal Life*, from direct address speeches she makes in the midst of action sequences. The first clip comes when she refuses to consult the visiting psychic. The "never cry on TV again" audio clip is from the episode that sends the celebrities to a nudist camp, at which point Tammy Faye balks and weeps, an historically significant act, as she notes—one implying that *The Surreal Life* is documenting a moment in television and pop culture history similar to the journalism coverage of Bakker's embezzlement scandal. In a direct address set-up interview, Tammy Faye herself claims to be "the original reality TV star" because of her talk shows and scandal coverage.[24]

Those crying eyes have warranted their own documentary, *The Eyes of Tammy Faye* (2000).[25] Comparing that film with *The Surreal Life*, we can see how the television series does not problematize the truth claims of the documentary techniques it scavenges and retools, even though many documentary films do so themselves. In the documentary, filmmakers Fenton Bailey and Randy Barbato explore Tammy Faye's status as a gay icon and her camp appeal, replete with voiceover narration by celebrity cross-dresser RuPaul. The film is a situated cultural argument that admits it wants to make a sympathetic intervention on her behalf; it argues that televangelist Jerry Falwell betrayed the couple, stealing their ministry, and that the embezzlement accusations were false. Pondering her visual iconography, the film pictures Tammy Faye delivering the self-aware revelation: "Without my eyelashes, I wouldn't be Tammy Faye. I don't know who I'd be, but it wouldn't be me." A critical analysis of this documentary would treat it as a mixture of fact and fiction that can only make qualified, contextualized truth claims, ones that inevitably question ontology. But *The Surreal Life* does not admit that it is itself a cultural argument and instead deploys stock documentary techniques to make its own unproblematized truth claims.

During the psychic episode, direct address interviews with Tammy Faye establish the shows ridicule as well as its embrace of her, a knotty mixture of identification and disidentification. The documentary techniques here organize her celebrity persona, the folksy religious diva who is outlandish but is nevertheless trustworthy and has a high moral character. Calling to mind Dana Carvey's earlier madcap satire of a "church lady" stereotype on *Saturday Night Live*, *The Surreal Life* deliberately eroticizes their televangelist, trying for a jolt of scandalous energy. The series objectifies her body and offers it up for visual consumption, with close-up body shots of her, clips of other cast-members telling her she "has a great body," and viewer posts on the WB website proclaiming "she's stacked!"[26] The psychic sequence begins with a shot intercut from Tammy Faye's later direct address interview in which she disparages psychics and séances. Her interview continues in voiceover narration as we watch the action sequence begin, and the form consequently encourages audiences to share her viewpoints. The focus on Tammy Faye continues throughout this sequence and the subsequent group séance sequence, since she gets the most interview face time of anyone.

But the most striking moment of direct address used to establish viewer sympathy with Tammy Faye is an unusual long shot of her during the action sequence involving the psychic. When asked to go meet with the psychic, Tammy Faye has an emotional break-down in the house living room. She delivers a teary confessional to her castmates explaining that she can not breach her religious views, though she would not judge others who believe in psychics. An extended long shot of her tumultuous speech sharply contrasts with the quick jump cuts and brief shots standard to the series. Tammy Faye speaks both to castmembers and directly to the camera, sobbing imploringly:

> ...God has gotten ahold of my heart. And he has kept me from committing suicide. Has kept me from ... from things that could have killed me. And has given me peace in spite of the horrible circumstances I've faced. And I like that lady, she's a nice lady, but I'm not going to her for advice. I'm going to get on my knees for advice and ask God to tell me, because he can tell me anything she's going to tell me if he wants me to know it.

The scene begins with a medium shot of Tammy Faye; as she begins to cry during her speech about turning to Christianity rather than to psychics for revelations, we cut to a close-up of her face, intercut with reaction shots of her castmates, all looking serious and supportive, like an adoring audience gathered around her. After the séance, the episode transitions to a scene where the cast is partying and drinking into the night, but it intercuts a grainy high-angle surveillance camera shot of Tammy Faye going to bed, and the editing privileges her genial moral avoidance of the party. Like her later emotional confessions on the staged Sally Jessy talk show, the breakdown scene situates Tammy Faye in terms of the therapeutic discourse Mimi White isolates as a dominant rhetoric shaping subjectivity on television talk shows and television more generally.[27] Her testimonials have the effect of bringing her castmates and audience into cathartic sympathy with her and her viewpoints. Indeed, a protective Jeremy is so moved by Tammy Faye's testimonials that he angrily tells Sally Jessy he would "kill anyone who tried to take [Tammy Faye's] Bible from her."[28]

Throughout this series, Tammy Faye explains her appeal, in direct address interviews, by saying "she's a real person" and she "tells it like it is." Such direct address moments provoke viewer sympathy even as they consistently reference her fetishized cultural image. One fan posting on the WB's discussion boards notes she "used to view Tammy Faye as a caricature," but after watching the show has "so much respect and admiration" for this "sweet, tolerant lady" who is "the first one you'd think would be a diva and she's actually the most agreeable person in that house."[29] In a clear paradigm of how "celebrity" documentary works in this subgenre, the show thus encourages viewers to accept their direct address interviews and footage as accurate depictions of "reality," a reality that merges Tammy Faye's public image with her purportedly "true self"—a straight-talking "authentic" woman.

Youth Shows and Ideology

MTV's *The Real World* puts a cast of attractive 18-to-24-year olds in a house-as-sound-stage setting and asks them to reveal themselves, and consequently human nature, for the camera. Here, direct address helps deliver a different kind of product: the 18-to-29-year old viewer demographic (sometimes defined more broadly as a 13-to-35-year old demographic) drawn to MTV's visions of consumerism.[30] *The Real World* features two kinds of direct address interviews: a diary confessional room where castmembers enter and activate a static camera themselves, and interviews conducted by a producer or director (who in some seasons has also been a clinical psychologist), taped as direct address to the camera with the staff and their questions edited out. Savvy about how to hail both their young cast and their viewers, creators Mary-Ellis Bunim and Jonathan Murray note how they wanted it to appear as though the castmembers "were talking directly to ... the viewer at home."[31] In the video diary segments, explicitly termed "confessionals," castmembers embark on a Foucauldian journey in which they internalize their own discipline by adapting to the program's dominant ideologies. And their confessors sit listening in the living rooms of America. The staff-conducted interviews, meanwhile, shape Bildungsroman narratives that trace the castmembers' psychological development and how their identity is being formed by the show and its staged experiences. Fashioning the audience as their product by drawing on the appeal of this complex narrative process, *The Real World* pulls viewers in by playing on a desire to fetishize narrative, to reify the process of imagining one's life as a story. A show like *The Real World* delivers an image of the "model viewer" on the screen, i.e. castmembers who participate in a saturated MTV consumer "reality" situation and mirror home viewer desires. Audiences can identify with the cast members they see on the screen. Founder Robert Pittman created the channel in 1981 as an on-screen "pure environment" for his commercial messages with a "zero-based" programming strategy — he profiled his market and then tried to recreate their lifestyle desires in his channel's content.[32]

The text constructs this screen surrogate by creating MTV's ideology of liberal pluralist consensus, one that sells the viewer group to corporate advertisers. The franchise focuses on interpersonal conflicts and social tensions, the fights and fits that fuel its ratings, yet its overriding narrative encourages castmembers to arrive at a pluralist resolution. The show's plotline frequently follows a teenager who learns to abandon views such as racism and homophobia, but their "change" is often superficial. They learn to feel their roommate's individual pain at racist comments without critiquing the institutional structures that support and promulgate racism. This superficiality serves what critics have termed "corporate multiculturalism" or liberal pluralism that purports to deliver "diversity" but fails to do so in any substantive way, thus maintaining existing social hierarchies of race and class; corporations make "diversity" or "difference" into a product to sell to consumers. In the show's version of pluralism, it upholds a vision of American culture in which minority groups are included and represented, but only at the margins. *The Real World* casts a balance of men and women but includes a clear majority of white characters and tokenizes the people of color on the cast. The franchise's model reflects the kind of pluralism Lisa Lowe has critiqued for masking "the existence of exclusions by recuperating dissent, conflict, and otherness through the promise of inclusion."[33] Indeed, the series is an instance of what Robert Stam would term a "liberal-pluralist" form of multiculturalism, which "develops a patronizing etiquette of tolerance and inclusiveness, a paternalistic exhortation to 'be nice to minorities,' what Peter Sellers once satirized as the spirit of 'Take an Indian to lunch this week.'"[34]

Reality Television Meets bell hooks

What would bell hooks say if she were appearing in a reality television show? MTV pretends to find out. In an episode that advertises itself as pedagogy by flashing a title card at the beginning warning viewers of a "frank" discussion of race, *The Real World* uses a visual image of a bell hooks book as a stand-in for a structural critique of racism, all on their way to establishing their liberal pluralist ideology based on possessive individualism rather than the kind of wide-ranging critique of institutional racism hooks actually gives us.[35]

On *The Real World: San Diego*, the lone black male castmember, Jacquese, finds himself having to confront Robin, a white female castmember who uses the "N word" during a bar fight. The episode establishes Jacquese's personal pain in a sympathetic framing of him in direct address interviews. In both "diary" direct address footage and later interview footage, Jacquese expresses how troubling it is for his roommate not to understand that the racial epithet is offensive and painful. In jump cuts of the action, Jacquese confronts a drunk Robin at the bar as she argues she should be able to use the epithet, then the show intercuts a later direct address interview with fellow castmate Brad (from a staff-conducted set-up interview), a white man, saying he does not think it is ever right to use that word. The sequence then cuts back to shots of the housemates returning home, the other housemembers comforting an upset Robin, leaving Jacquese to call his mother for support. She tells him he cannot turn into a stereotype of an "angry black man" and should instead have patience with them because they simply do not know or understand how racism works.

Jacquese consults the internet for information about racism and the camera pans over quick shots of the stacked spines of his books on his shelves, including bell hooks's *Talking Back* and Angela Davis's *Women, Race, & Class.* Jacquese has a house meeting with everyone, explaining he has had his feelings hurt, but the meeting dissolves when Robin becomes distraught, insisting she has emotional issues about racial identity because a black man raped her, but she never meant to hurt anyone's feelings. Ja comforts her and they both bond about their mutual understanding of shared pain.

As the editors intercut the action sequences with direct address interviews, the program encourages the viewers to empathize with a reading of the situation that rejects racial epithets because they hurt the individual's feelings. The episode does not include any verbal account of structural racism, only gesturing towards such analysis by picturing books or internet pages, very brief images of them. Thus a shot of a bell hooks book is a substitute for the structural critique the show does not make. Similarly, in *The Real World: New Orleans* season, an episode devoted to the "N word" pictures a white man, Jamie, learning to question his own racism when a castmate who is a woman of color, Melissa, explains why the word hurts her feelings, and his character development is staged in direct address interviews.[36] The program insisted on this story arc even when Jamie claimed he was misrepresented.[37]

Direct address encourages viewers to identify with the person speaking to the camera as they model behaviors, hailing audiences to join their imagined pluralist community. *The Real World* and its peers turn this documentary form into a truth claim meant to fashion ideologies with which viewers can identify. These programs also make meta truth claims via tie-ins, behind the scenes documentary-style videos of "the real world you never saw," "the really, real world." Buy them to chase the ever-evaporating real. Similar to their original reality shows, produced by the same companies, these meta-reality TV texts promise even realer documentary, like VH1's *Reality T.V. Secrets Revealed*, billed as an exposé of how "producers, editors, and contestants use clever methods to get big ratings."[38] Documentary keeps getting positioned as the "real," able to provide a self-exposé meant to change viewer's minds about what reality TV is. Reality TV markets nostalgia for photographic truth even while it registers visual representation's constructedness.

Reality TV's use of documentary reveals multifaceted, competing agendas. It uses the "authenticity" of documentary to work through specific cultural problems, like the relationship between celebrity and subjectivity, popular culture and personhood. Simultaneously, shows fashion a consumer identity, a viewer-as-product to be sold to corporate advertisers. Their cultural work often is to formulate social constructs like subjectivity or multiculturalism in ways most amenable to capitalism. These multiple agendas are fashioned through reality TV's reshaping of narrative and documentary techniques.

1. From his discussion of cinéma vérité, in Barnouw, *Documentary: A History of the Non-Fiction Film*, 2nd Rev. ed. (New York: Oxford University Press, 1993): 254.

2. Robin L. Naby, Erica N. Biely, Sara J. Morgan, and Carmen R. Stitt, "Reality Based Television Programming and the Psychology of Its Appeal," *Media Psychology* 5 (2003): 303–330.

3. John Caldwell, "Prime-Time Fiction Theorizes the Docu-Real," *Reality Squared: Televisual Discourse on the Real*, ed. James Friedman (New Brunswick: Rutgers University Press, 2002) 259–292. I join critics like Susan Murray who aim to assess what functions reality TV's use of documentary serves, not whether it debases or expands documentary in what John Corner terms "post-documentary" culture. Murray, "'I Think We Need a New Name for It': The Meeting of Documentary and Reality TV," *Reality TV: Remaking Television Culture*, ed. Susan Murray and Laurie Ouellette (New York: New York UP, 2004) 43–44. Corner, "Afterword: Framing the New," *Understanding Reality Television*, ed. Su Holmes and Deborah Jermyn (London: Routledge, 2004) 297.

4. Jeffrey Ruoff details how *An American Family* combines documentary sound conventions with those from broadcast television at the time, asserting that this kind of combination, rather than calling the actuality series' bluff, reveals the constructedness of all film. Ruoff, "Conventions of Sound in Documentary," *Sound Theory/Sound Practice*, ed. Rick Altman (New York: Routledge, 1992): 220, 217–234.

5. Bill Nichols, *Representing Reality: Issues and Concepts in Documentary* (Bloomington and Indianapolis: Indiana University Press, 1991), see also Nichols, *Introduction to Documentary* (Bloomington and Indianapolis: Indiana University Press, 2001).

6. Jill Godmilow, in conversation with Ann-Louise Shapiro, "How Real Is the Reality in Documentary Film?," *History and Theory* 36.4 (December 1997): 80–81.

7. Nichols, *Representing Reality, Introduction to Documentary*.

8. Barnouw 255.

9. "Return of the One-Eyed Monster," *The Surreal Life*, WB, 25 Jan. 2004. Fan posting from "Feedback," online postings, 3 Feb. 2004, The WB Home Page, 4 Feb. 2004 www.thewb.com/Faces/CastBio/0,7930,146600,00.html.

10. "Ro-Day-O vs. Ro-Dee-O," *The Simple Life*, FOX, 2 Dec. 2003.

11. Interview with *USA Today*, quoted in Michael A. Lipton and Steve Barnes, "Girls Gone Hog Wild," *People*, 15 Dec. 2003: 66–68.

12. "Catching Up with the Osbournes," *The Osbournes*, MTV, 19 Nov. 2002.

13. "The Accidental Tourist," *The Osbournes*, MTV, 24 Feb. 2004.

14. *Primetime Thursday*, ABC, 19 Feb. 2004.

15. "Survivor," *VH1 Goes Inside*, VH1, 13 Sept. 2003.

16. "Vegas/Church," *The Surreal Life*, WB, 30 Jan. 2003.

17. Sut Jhally, "Image-Based Culture: Advertising and Popular Culture," *Gender, Race, and Class in Media: A Text-Reader*, ed. Gail Dines and Jean M. Humez, 2nd ed. (Thousand Oaks, C.A.: Sage Publications, 2003) 249–257.

18. *Reality TV Secrets Revealed*, VH1, 2 Jan. 2004.

19. "Return of the One-Eyed Monster."

20. Laura Mulvey, "Visual Pleasure and Narrative Cinema," *Feminism and Film Theory*, ed. Constance Penley (New York: Routledge, 1988) 57–79.

21. "Return of the One-Eyed Monster."

22. "Dirty Laundry," *The Surreal Life*, WB, 22 Feb. 2004.

23. The Christian Broadcasting Network (CBN, with Pat Robertson), The Trinity Broadcasting Network (TBN, with Paul Crouch), and PTL with Bakker, which included a theme park, Heritage USA. "Cast Bio: Tammy Faye Messner," The WB Home Page, 4 Feb. 2004 www.thewb.com/Faces/CastBio/0,7930, 146600,00.html.

24. "Back in the Saddle," *The Surreal Life*, NBC, 4 November 2004. The program notes her television show with Jim Bakker had, at its peak, 14.5 million viewers.

25. *The Eyes of Tammy Faye*, dir. Fenton Bailey and Randy Barbato, Lions Gate Films, 2000.

26. "Feedback."

27. Mimi White, "Television, Therapy, and the Social Subject; or, The TV Therapy Machine," *Reality Squared: Televisual Discourse on the Real*, ed. James Friedman (New Brunswick: Rutgers UP, 2002) 313–322. See also White, *Tele-Advising: Therapeutic Discourse in American Television* (Chapel Hill: UNC Press, 1992).

28. "Dirty Laundry."

29. "Feedback."

30. John Pettegrew, "A Post-Modernist Moment: 1980s Commercial Culture and the Founding of MTV," *Gender, Race, and Class in Media: A Text-Reader*, ed. Gail Dines and Jean M. Humez, 1st ed. (Thousand Oaks, C.A.: Sage Publications, 1995) 490.

31. Amy Keyishian and Sarah Malarkey, eds., *MTV's The Real World Diaries* (New York: MTV Books/Pocket Books/Melcher Media, 1996): 5.

32. Pettegrew, p. 489.

33. Lisa Lowe, "Imagining Los Angeles in the Production of Multiculturalism," *Mapping Multiculturalism*, ed. Avery F. Gordon and Christopher Newfield (Minneapolis: University of Minnesota Press, 1996): 415.

34. Robert Stam, "Multiculturalism and the Neoconservatives," *Dangerous Liaisons: Gender, Nation, and Postcolonial Perspectives*, ed. Anne McClintock, Aamir Mufti, and Ella Shohat (Minneapolis: University of Minneapolis Press, 1997): 188–203.

35. "Human Race," *The Real World: San Diego*, MTV, 13 Jan. 2004.

36. "Racism is Bad," *The Real World: New Orleans*, MTV, 1 Aug. 2000.

37. Alison Pollet, *The Real World New Orleans Unmasked* (New York: MTV Books/Pocket Books, 2000): 18.

38. *Reality TV Secrets Revealed*, VH1, 2 Jan. 2004.

18

The Future of Documentary?
"Conditional Tense" Documentary
and the Historical Record

by Paul Ward

This essay will examine the ways in which a particular type of documentary can be said to be part of the "mockumentary" category. The documentaries under scrutiny here are notable for the ways in which they orient the viewer to a *possible* world, via a representation of events that have *not yet* happened, or did not really happen in the way they are depicted. Obviously, all mockumentaries show a possible world in the sense that they show a fictional world that is plausible enough to make the viewer ask, "Is this a *real* documentary?" (though, as we shall see, the viewer's relationship with documentary in general and mockumentary in particular, is far from straightforward). For the films I am looking at, however, my contention is that their positioning of the viewer is a most peculiar one in relation to history and narrative. They represent particular historical events with chilling accuracy and plausibility, and the "mock" aspect of the texts opens up a space where the viewer's relationship to those events needs to be interrogated.

So, in this chapter I will be looking at how some documentaries, particularly *Smallpox 2002: Silent Weapon* and *The Day Britain Stopped* (UK, Wall to Wall Productions, 2002 and 2003 respectively) use what might be termed "conditional tense" strategies in order to address their audience. I will explore some of the formal strategies used in these specific films, and discuss the way they address their audience in a moment; first of all we need to recognize some of the difficulties of this term conditional tense, and how it is inflected when talking about audio-visual representations (as opposed to just speech or written discourse). There are also some issues relating to these films' use of specific tropes — their representation of the future, basically — that will require me to refer to some other documentary films that attempt to represent things that have not actually happened, not happened *yet*, or did not happen in *quite the way* that they are shown to us. All of these issues are potentially very fertile and as yet under-explored areas within the study of documentary. As we shall see, there is some debate over the appropriateness of the term conditional tense in relation to certain films; my use of the term therefore requires some qualification. The discursive and rhetorical strategies used by specific mockumentaries of this type are also in need of some description and explanation. I shall conclude the essay with a consideration of how narrative (re)construction looms large in any debates about mockumentary, but is often implicit, and how making such discussion more explicit can help us reach a more informed understanding of the sub-genre. The spectatorial activity involved in reading a mockumentary opens up a space where the phenomenological and the political come to the fore.

Conditional Tense Documentary: Some Problems with Definitions

In simple terms, conditional tense is being used here to refer to the mode of address that shows "this is what *might yet* happen"; it outlines a *possible* (or, some would say, in relation to the specific films I am analyzing, *highly probable*) course of events rather than simply showing us what *did* happen.[1] We should remember that the term "tense" derives from the Latin *tempus*, meaning time; a discussion of use of *tenses* in documentary signification therefore means we are engaging directly with the representation of *time*, and of *history*. However, as Mark J.P. Wolf points out in his discussion of how computer imaging and simulation impacts upon documentary signification, there is a group of films that

> are concerned with what *could be, would be,* or *might have been*; they form a subgenre of documentary we might call *subjunctive* documentary, following the use of the term *subjunctive* as a grammatical tense.[2]

The difficulty lies in the different ways that both conditional and subjunctive are used, along with the fact that they are variously described as tenses, moods, and modes. It is also apparent that both terms can be used to describe the same thing, no doubt to the horror of grammarians everywhere. Of course, the main problem here is that we are attempting to apply specifically linguistic (written and spoken) rules to the audio-visual language of documentary, and there is never going to be an ideal fit in cases such as this. However, I'd maintain that thinking through how such rules might apply to documentary will help us to further understand not just documentary but any form of audio-visual representation.

In purely linguistic terms, the subjunctive mood has been described as "one of the great shifting sands of English grammar ... [it] is a verbal form or mood expressing hypothesis, usually denoting what is imagined, wished, demanded, proposed, exhorted etc."[3] The implication is, of course, that any conditional or subjunctive statement will be *yet to happen*; but, as *It Happened Here* (1966) shows, it is entirely possible for events to be shown in what Glenn Erickson describes as the negative subjunctive:

> [*It Happened Here* is] a story of WW2 in the "negative subjunctive" ... that
> is, a tale of events which could have happened but did not happen, but if
> they did happen they might have happened like this. It's actually an alter-
> nate reality story, a time-splinter concept commonplace in films now but
> unheard of then. *It Happened Here* takes as its springboard the simple idea
> that Hitler launched an invasion during the Battle of Britain and quickly
> subdued England. Everything else follows with complete credibility.[4]

For the purposes of this essay then, I shall use the term conditional tense to cover
the *range* of strategies seen in films like *Smallpox 2002*, *The Day Britain Stopped*, *The
War Game* (1965), and *It Happened Here*. In all of these films there is an engagement
with and attempt to represent historical events in such a way as to draw attention to
their provisional or conditional nature. Yet not all of these films function in the same
way, as we shall see. *Smallpox 2002* and *The Day Britain Stopped* have a specific narrative frame that some would argue means their mode of address is not conditional
at all, in that they recount events *as if* they are *from the past*, and the tone is one of
"this *did* happen." Similarly, *It Happened Here* constructs an alternative past, where
the Nazis succeeded in their invasion of Britain, and extrapolates from there, to see
what would have happened if....[5] In many respects then, this film's address of the
viewer is similar to the other two films, even though it is exploring a possible past.
The War Game, in a slightly different fashion, examines a *possible future*. Yet, I believe
that the positioning of the viewer in relation to all of these films foregrounds the conditional nature of the events depicted. It is for this reason that I think these films
should be discussed under the banner of mockumentary, rather than drama-
documentary: their mode of address is one that "mocks" (in a serious way) the conventions of certain types of documentary, and makes the viewer interrogate their
relationship to the so-called history they are viewing.[6] It is for this reason, too, that
I shall argue that we need to pay careful attention to documentary spectatorship, as
this is ultimately where documentary conventions — and their mocking — are understood: in the space where viewers actually interact with and interpret these films.

Matters are further complicated when Bill Nichols states, "Images, as we know,
are always present tense."[7] Yet this simple statement tends to mask a range of paradoxes — not least the paradox that John Ellis posits as being central to the cinematic
experience itself: that of "present-absence."[8] Accepting that images are always in
present tense does not mean that we are not engaging in very complex ways with
audio-visual texts, nor does it preclude their ability to show us the future (or, indeed,
the past). As Nichols continues:

> Historical consciousness requires the spectator's recognition of the dou-
> ble, or paradoxical, status of moving images that are present referring to
> events which are past.[9]

As we shall see, the films I am looking at problematize this definition, but it does
point to one of the key problems for those thinking about how history is represented
in audio-visual media. The complexity of the way that *Smallpox 2002* and *The Day
Britain Stopped* address their audience is key: they tell a story of events that in reality

Smallpox 2002 (2002): The direct address of the "video diary" format is used to personalize the conditional narrative. (Pictured here: Sam Stockman as the character Sean Cooper.)

have not happened *at all*, but tell it as if those events have *already* happened — in the case of *Smallpox 2002*, the events unfold as if from a vantage point of a conventional documentary made in 2005. The plausible detail of the production — not to mention that of the events depicted — adds another level of complexity: these are events that have not happened at all, told as if they have already happened, with the resultant implication to the audience that this *could yet* happen. It is this "might-have-been" or "might-still-yet-be" contingency that characterizes these two films. There is a pro-visionality to the discourse that some might argue tips the films over into the realm of fiction; my response would be that these films are most certainly documentary in *intention* and in their *reception*, and the most useful way to discuss them is within the still-emerging critical category of mockumentary. I shall return to the way that these films might be perceived as fictions in due course, when discussing Vivian Sobchack's phenomenology of documentary viewing; for the moment, I'd like to elaborate on the temporal and conditional aspects of the texts themselves.

As suggested above, there is also some debate over the category of conditional tense, in how it might apply to documentary. Nichols for example, refers to Peter Watkins' *Culloden* (1964) and *The War Game* as conditional tense documentaries but Richard Kilborn and John Izod take issue with this. Nichols suggests that although such films offer an informed speculation, or "imaginary extrapolation from the present world, based on factual evidence," they "necessarily present ... *a* world rather than *the* world to us."[10] Kilborn and Izod object to this on the grounds that, although his is a useful analysis, Nichols is wrong because such films offer "not a conditional view of an *imaginary* world but a conditional view of *the* world."[11] What sounds like splitting hairs is a key distinction. I tend to side with Kilborn and Izod on this point: the very idea of conditional tense documentaries is that they refer to the *actual* world of the viewer but the crucial characteristic is that certain aspects of the text are *provisional*, or are *dependent* on such-and-such happening.

For example, in *The Day Britain Stopped* the story that unfolds is one that is reconstructed as if from the future, by participants looking back to a fateful day, 19 December 2003, when a series of entirely plausible occurrences—a rail strike, a traffic jam, problems with a shift-change for air-traffic control staff—all coincided to cause disaster on a grand scale. The forensic detail and retrospective framing of these events adds to the persuasiveness of the film, but it has to be stressed that all of the films under discussion here are so effective precisely because the events depicted are persuasive and plausible. Anyone who lives in early 21st century Britain and uses the transport systems represented in *The Day Britain Stopped* realizes that such events are not only possible, but probable.[12] The incremental build-up of detail means that

Tom Walker MP
Transport Minister, Sept 2003 - March 2004

The Day Britain Stopped (2003): Official titles of fictional characters adds to the documentary verisimilitude. (Pictured here: Eric Carte as the character Tom Walker, MP.)

the film unfolds as a grim causal chain. The conditionality of the events is obviated by the retrospective told-from-the-future framing; and yet, the fact that viewers *know* these events have not actually happened restores some of the conditional power of what we see and hear. That is, the modality of address is not the same as in *The War Game*, where we can say that the address of the viewer is "this is what will happen, if...." The way the viewer is addressed in *The Day Britain Stopped* is, on the face of it, a more straightforward "this is what happened when..." or "this is what happened because....": the simple explanatory discourse that we know from conventional documentary. And yet, the ultimately fictional status of the events depicted means that the actual way that the viewer takes up (to use Sobchack's phenomenological phrase) those events, the way that s/he interprets them is very much "this is what *will* happen, *unless*...." In this respect, *The Day Britain Stopped* and *Smallpox 2002* are important films from a political perspective because they make the viewer interrogate the representational strategies of the films, but also the viewers' own role in interpreting and anchoring meaning. Although the films are based around what might be seen as a highly contingent causal chain — a traffic jam *just happens* to contain an air-traffic controller, someone infected with smallpox *just happens* to walk past another certain person — what these films are stressing are the social connections between things and people, the material relations. To bring the point specifically to how any of these films can (or rather should) be discussed as mockumentary, my argument would be that mockumentaries are celebrated for their ability to make audiences ask, "Is this a real documentary?" (or alternatively, "Are the events depicted real?"), and this is what these films are doing, albeit inflected differently from most mockumentaries. For, the mode of address is not "Is this real?" or "Did this really happen?" but "*Could* this actually happen?" Framing the events in such a way as to suggest that they have *already* happened is the filmmakers' way of emphasizing how plausible they think these events are.[13] It is clear that these films must be viewed as part of a wider context: if the mode of address is "this is what will happen, unless...," then the crucial term there is "unless." It is a call to (social) action: despite these films' ostensibly conventional (i.e. mainstream) appearance, they have a potentially innovative political edge, due to the way they frame the historical discourses they represent to their viewers.

In his discussion of *JFK* (1991), Nichols draws out what he sees as the distinction between the different modes of discourse used in that film and the kinds of histories mobilized as a consequence of this. He states:

> [*JFK*] highlights ... alternative tenses and modes to those we normally associate with expository, nonfictive, and historical discourse. Instead of straightforward past tense ["Oswald shot Kennedy"] we encounter subjunctive tenses ["Kennedy would have jeopardized the military-industrial complex if..."] and conditional tenses ["Oswald might have been exactly what he said he was, a patsy"] ... historical representation falls under the sign of performative documentary.[14]

In the case of *Smallpox 2002* and *The Day Britain Stopped* we have something different again however: films that address us from a *supposed future*, talking about a set of events in the *past* (i.e. past in relation to the future from which the story is told), while those events are still in our future.[15] While *The War Game* can more accurately be described as being in the conditional tense — more so than the two main examples I am discussing here (which tell their story *as if* from the future, in what therefore amounts to the *past* tense) — it is actually the case that we need to further complicate our typology of modes or tenses in order to fully understand the complexities of how these films address us as viewers. *The War Game*, it seems to me, is an example of the future subjunctive — a case of "what will happen *if*" such-and-such turns out to be the case. For instance, at one point in *The War Game* we are informed by radio-broadcast voiceover that Russian and East German troops have entered West Berlin ("one hour ago"). The non-diegetic voiceover of the film then states:

> Faced with this situation, it is possible [cut to a still of Johnson] that the American President would have no choice but to threaten to release tactical nuclear warheads to the forces of NATO, in order to show collective determination in the event of a possible Russian attack. Faced with this situation [cut to a still of Kosygin] the Soviet Premier would possibly be left with no alternative but to call this bluff and attack.

There are many other examples of such conditional moments — "there *would probably* be found the necessary flashpoint," "*Should* Britain ever thus attempt," "This *could be* the way the last two minutes of peace in Britain would look" — that imply that the film is hedging its bets somewhat in its assertions. Yet what we have in the film is not simply these highly modalized (which is to say, *conditional*) statements alone. The statements are accompanied by shocking and highly plausible images and sounds, and it is these that help to anchor the meaning. It is worth stressing the concept of modality, as this is the level of certainty that is attached to a statement or assertion, and it is therefore vitally important when we are discussing things that may not have happened (yet). A statement's modality can be inflected differently according to the levels of certainty implied. For instance, saying "This is *definitely* what would happen if..." has a different modality to saying "This is *possibly* what would happen if...." *The War Game* uses a range of modalities in this respect — a spectrum of *could*, *would*, and *almost certainly* — but it is the way that these statements are allied to sounds and images that makes the difference. Also, there are moments when the shift to present tense makes Watkins' intention even clearer — during sequences that contain what Derek Paget refers to as the citing of precedents[16] — "Everything that you *are now seeing* happened in Germany after the heavy bombing in the last war." And, most startlingly, during the scenes of people dying from gassing as a consequence of the fire storm: "This *is* nuclear war."

In contrast, a film like *Smallpox 2002* is straightforward in the way it is constructed — in many respects it is a standard contemporary history documentary. But, as Dan Percival, the director of *Smallpox 2002* puts it:

> [we aimed to recreate] the classic contemporary history documentary ... in [which] momentous events are forensically pieced together through the

hindsight testimony of those who lived through them. The difference with
ours being that the events haven't happened.[17]

The key thing with these films is that they therefore rely on us, as viewers, interrogating our position *as* viewers, the disputed (to say the least) historical status of the
events depicted, meaning that we have to reflect on what we are viewing (and *when*
we are viewing it). Therefore, I'd now like to move on to explore the mode of address
and point(s) of view mobilized in these texts. The role and position of the viewer in
relation to mockumentary is crucial for various reasons, as tentatively suggested by
Roscoe and Hight.[18]

Dystopian Visions, Point of View, and the Discourse of Sobriety

I'd like to return to a discussion of the mode of address of these films, as what
makes them chillingly effective is their plausibility. This means we have to think
about how spectators are *reading* the films. There are a number of paradoxes at work
here. Not least of these is the fact that plausibility is not normally something one
would point to in a documentary of any kind (as documentaries, being about *the*
world are by definition plausible?) So, what is important is *how* these films construct
a plausible version of future events (or, as noted earlier, how they construct a plausible version of people looking back and reflecting on past events which are still in
our future), how they address us as spectators, and how we interpret them in the
course of the viewing process.

Dai Vaughan has usefully referred to what he calls the "documentary response"—
by this he means that documentary should not be defined by any stylistic or generic
criteria, but rather by how we, as viewers, *respond* to specific texts.[19] Instead of analyses that concentrate on formal aspects of documentary texts, this would take us down
a more phenomenologically-inclined route, where we concentrate on the spectator's
viewing of a documentary and, in these cases, their active engagement with historical
discourse. This is something that Vivian Sobchack has explored in her work on the activities of the spectator, not just in relation to documentary but, interestingly, in relation
to the whole spectrum of film experience. Adapting the ideas of Jean-Pierre Meunier,
Sobchack states that there are three "positions" on an "experiential spectrum" that are
relevant to our viewing of any particular film (or any visually-based media text for that
matter). It is interesting to think about mockumentary in the light of these positions.
First of all, there is what can broadly be termed home movies (though as Sobchack
points out, the French term *film-souvenir* is both more accurate and more evocative):

> We take these images up as existentially and specifically known to us
> already — as referring to beings and things and events that exist now or
> once existed "elsewhere" than solely on the screen.[20]

Secondly, there is the documentary modality, "which entails not only our existential
and cultural knowledge, but also our partial *lack* of it — a lack that modifies the nature

of our identification with the image."[21] Finally, there is the *fiction* film and our identification with it. Here, "we take up the cinematic object as unknown to us in its specificity."[22] So, the argument is that while watching films of these different modalities, the viewer is positioned differently according to the images that are on the screen. In the *film souvenir* they are "known to us already"; we have *direct* experience of the things we are now seeing. In documentary, we may not have *direct* experience of what we are now seeing, but we have some cultural knowledge of it (e.g. a documentary about Hitler) and we *know* that the people and events depicted did (or still do) exist. In fiction, however, we are aware that we only know the characters and events unfolding before us *in* and *as* a fiction — they do not exist anywhere 'outside of' the text itself.

The interesting thing for the purposes of this discussion is how such a model relates to mockumentary, with its contentious fusing or overlapping of what might be thought of as separate modalities—that of fiction and nonfiction. Roscoe and Hight make a clear distinction between mock-documentaries and drama-documentaries, saying, "What distinguishes [them] is especially the former's potential critique of factual discourse ... mock-documentary contains a 'latent reflexivity.'"[23] They further argue that this reflexivity is latent precisely because it is "difficult to predict exactly how audiences will interpret these texts."[24] This is true enough, but I would suggest that it is the reception or interpretation of mockumentaries that is of most use as a way to understanding how they function. Noël Carroll has usefully proposed a model whereby films can be divided into two broad categories, the fictional and the nonfictional. Within this (admittedly very broad) latter category are what Carroll terms "films of presumptive assertion." This is a term he coins to cover certain types of documentary, having found the term documentary itself too imprecise.[25] Central to his typology is an acknowledgement that the viewer will, in the process of watching certain films, *recognize* the filmmaker's intention to address them in a certain way and will respond to the film accordingly. Hence, *presumptive* assertion: the viewer presumes, in the course of watching certain films, that films of this kind are asserting particular things about the real world, making truth claims about this or that aspect of the real, material world of actuality, and that they as viewers are meant to respond to these assertions as true or factual (in a way that one wouldn't respond when watching a film one knew to be fictional, for instance). In the case of mockumentaries, and especially those that use conditional tense strategies as I have outlined them here, the process of assertion is foregrounded precisely because viewers recognize the *provisional* nature of the events depicted.

One of the things that *Smallpox 2002* and *The Day Britain Stopped* have in common is a high level of co-operation from the news media, to the extent that authenticity is added by having actual current newsreaders in amongst the fiction. It is of course possible that someone could turn on their television and see newsreader X saying, "A smallpox attack today...," and possibly believe it.[26] However, it is much more likely that people will be watching *knowing* that the programme is what it is. (This is something that Noël Carroll refers to as "indexing"[27]; that is, we do not have to *guess* whether a programme is fiction or nonfiction, because it comes "indexed" as such beforehand). So, the tropes of news broadcasts are there to add to the verisimilitude.[28] The discourse of sobriety of news and current affairs broadcasting is invoked in order to make plausible this vision of the future. At the same time, the detailed invoking of such a discourse means that attention is drawn to it — the spectator both looks *at* and looks *through* the highly mediated presentation. By this I mean, following Sobchack, that there is a sense that some representations exist only there, on the screen, as we are looking *at* them; but there are also those representations that have an existence outside, in the real world, in the sense that they refer to actual people and actual events. The way these films use the conventions offers a fusion of these two positions, an oscillation between merely looking *at* what is unfolding (what might be termed a fictive stance), and looking *through* what is being shown to us, as a route to thinking about its real-world existence (what might be termed a nonfictive stance). It is this oscillation that characterizes the spectator's position when viewing these films — an oscillation between believing in the images as they unfold before us and simultaneously reflecting on their status as things that have not-actually-happened. It is this characteristic, to my mind, that also makes the films examples of mockumentary: they position the spectator in such a way as to make the veracity of the events depicted (and also, importantly, the very discourse of sobriety as figured by the news media) the center of attention; the reflexivity referred to by Roscoe and Hight is therefore far from latent, but is an integral part of these films.

The other major documentary trope used in these films is the amateur camcorder video footage. On one level, such footage is present to allow the audience to see events that they would not otherwise see, as the filmmakers cannot in these films (ironically) use standard reconstructions like some documentaries would, because the investment is in "you are right there" immediacy, or hindsight witness testimony. The other thing that the camcorder footage adds is the human story. In *Smallpox 2002* it is the poignancy of the young man dying from smallpox; in *The Day Britain Stopped* it is the young boy off to his doom in a plane. In the former example, we therefore get to see scenes where the character videos houses being quarantined, the process of people being taken away for isolation, and so on. This footage — either of him talking direct to camera, video-diary style, or candid footage of his sister and mother — is interspersed with interview material with his mother, quite clearly coded as being proper interview material (i.e. done by the film crew within the film), where the mother is offering hindsight testimony after her son's tragic death. In the case of *The Day Britain Stopped* the video footage is shot by a young boy. A similar technique is used, this time inflected by the specific subject matter of the film. For instance, the video footage is initially introduced via a "satellite" shot that cuts closer to a more precise location, mimicking a surveillance camera of a road network, before a caption designates the location as "Basingstoke, Hampshire." Cut to traffic moving on a motorway. The non-diegetic voiceover states:

> A unique record of the day's events would be captured on video by 12 year-old Thomas Galt [at this point the camerawork has shifted to noticeably grainy, hand-held video footage from the interior of a moving car, where a small boy is pulling faces into the camera he is holding]. That morning his family set out for their Christmas holiday in Spain.

Again, the effective dramatic device of juxtaposing these snippets of candid home video with the sober, reflective hindsight testimony of the father, Julian Galt—who survives the day while his wife and two children do not—invests both video footage and interview footage with considerable power. This power derives from the different ways in which the viewer relates to each type of footage: they are indexed distinctly. Following Sobchack/Meunier, we can suggest that the range of devices used in *Smallpox 2002* and *The Day Britain Stopped* draw attention to their relative mockdocumentariness by invoking different positions on a signifying continuum. The plausibly home-video sections, the formal hindsight interviews, the harrowing footage from various other sources, the painstakingly accurate news reports—all of these are created or mocked up by the filmmakers, and they are clearly believable in the ways noted above, that is, as part of a plausible record of early 21st-century disaster.

By way of conclusion, I'd like to offer a few thoughts on the use of narrative strategies in these films, as it strikes me that the overall narrative frame is what holds these other techniques and strategies (such as the video diary) in place. The main thing I want to consider here is some of the issues relating to the use of reconstruction. This sort of thing has been written about in relation to documentary before, with varying degrees of sophistication and opprobrium. When, for example, it was revealed that Robert Flaherty had reconstructed certain elements of the Eskimo's life for *Nanook of the North* (1922), it caused a fair amount of controversy. There have been countless other examples, some of which are mundane and forgettable, some of which are scandalous and unethical.[29] In the case of the films under consideration here, it is less a case of commentators becoming upset by the inaccuracies and/or poetic license taken with *reconstructing* past events. Rather, the issue becomes one of how well the filmmakers have *constructed* a plausible vision of certain future events. This is not only addressing the audience in a different way, but it is also asking us to rethink what we expect from a documentary. Clearly, these films are not mere idle speculation, but they are informed, credible (hence the frightening nature of what they are doing) possible versions of a specific future. The focus is therefore on the *potential* causes of events, and a discursive pathway is opened up for people to *reflect* on the future, in a way that is not usually the case with documentary. Certainly, there are many other related discourses circulating around these programmes—critical dissections in the newspapers, online discussions with viewers, filmmakers and experts, etc.—that suggest that there is a space and need for such reflection.[30]

The difficulty for many documentaries is imposing a narrative framework. As documentaries are about *the world* of actuality, it is sometimes difficult, if not impossible to achieve a sense of *closure*, precisely because the world of actuality continues beyond the realm of the text. It also has to be said that making documentary material subject to the logic of narrative can, arguably, distort what one is viewing. In many respects of course, it is precisely the *opposite* of what a documentarist should be aiming for, looking to tie up loose ends and close off potential links to the real world of actuality. Because of their retrospective frame, however, *Smallpox 2002* and *The Day Britain Stopped* easily achieve an extremely powerful narrative thread, and an equally effective sense of closure. The logic of the narrative—looking back, in the case of *Smallpox 2002*, from the vantage point of documentary-makers in 2005, making a doc about the 2002 pandemic — imposes a strong sense of hindsight. And yet, the conditional or yet-to-have-happened status of the events makes the narrative, and particularly the closure, distinctly more chilling. It is this marshalling of the sober, detailed discourse of current affairs programming, in tandem with such a conditional or subjunctive narrative stance that makes these films a powerful type of history and, perhaps, the future of documentary.

1. Any historian worth his or her salt will know that "just" showing us what *did* happen is very far from simple, and the mode of address, the position from which the story is told and so forth can problematize this apparently very straightforward procedure. A useful anthology exploring issues of representations of historical events and historiography is Vivian Sobchack (ed.), *The Persistence of History: Cinema, Television, and the Modern Event,* (New York: Routledge, 1996).

2. Mark J.P. Wolf, "Subjunctive Documentary: Computer Imaging and Simulation" in Jane M. Gaines and Michael Renov (eds.) *Collecting Visible Evidence,* (Minneapolis: University of Minnesota Press, 1999): 274. Original emphases.

3. R.W. Burchfield, *The New Fowler's Modern English Usage,* (Oxford: Oxford University Press, 1998), 746.

4. Glenn Erickson, *DVD Savant* review of *It Happened Here,* at www.dvdtalk.com/dvdsavant/s100here.html#return 1.

5. It is worth noting the "certainty" of the title: an emphatic statement that "it" not only actually "happened," but it happened here.

6. All mockumentaries arguably fall into the "drama-documentary" category, in that they use dramatic construction of fictional scenes in a recognizably documentary style, but with mockumentary the emphasis is on a critical reflection on the form itself. (Though as Roscoe and Hight make clear, there are degrees of "mockdocness" and levels of critical reflection). In all the films I am examining, the reflection is triggered by the positioning of the viewer in relation to the historical events depicted. These films *could* be examined as drama-documentaries, but it is my contention that we will reach a fuller understanding of them if we discuss them as mockumentaries, as this compels us to work through some of the complex ways that the films address their audiences.

7. Bill Nichols, *Blurred Boundaries: Questions of Meaning in Contemporary Culture,* (Bloomington and Indianapolis: Indiana University Press, 1994): 117.

8. John Ellis, *Visible Fictions: Cinema, Television, Video,* (London: Routledge, 1982), 58.

9. Nichols, *Blurred Boundaries,* p. 117.

10. Bill Nichols, *Representing Reality,* (Bloomington and Indianapolis: Indiana University Press, 1991), 112. Italics in original.

11. Richard Kilborn and John Izod, *An Introduction to Television Documentary,* (Manchester: Manchester University Press, 1997): 133. Italics added.

12. The same can be said of the events depicted in *Smallpox 2002* (in an era where threats of bio-terrorism are very real), *The War Game* (which at the height of the Cold War was so grimly plausible that it was effectively banned for fear it would panic — or anger — the public), and *It Happened Here* (we now know that the Nazis came very close to successfully invading Britain in 1941).

13. In the case of *It Happened Here,* the mode of address is of course one that constructs the previously noted "negative subjunctive" world where the Nazis succeeded in invading Britain immediately after Dunkirk. This is very far from a fanciful notion: as noted above, the Nazis almost succeeded in defeating Britain during the Battle of Britain.

14. Nichols, *Blurred Boundaries,* p. 122.

15. At the time of the first (British) broadcast for both *Smallpox 2002* (5 February 2002) and *The Day Britain Stopped* (13 May 2003), an extra frisson was added because "D-Day" as discussed in each film was still in the *viewers'* future. So, although these documentaries were constructed as if being pieced together and narrated from the (diegetic) future, part of their address of the audience relied on this highly specific temporal relationship. This has dissipated somewhat, due to the fact that anyone watching these films now would be doing so *after* the respective "D-Day" of each film. Having said this, the films remain something more than an exercise in temporal trickiness, and they certainly come across as far more than mistaken prophecy.

16. Derek Paget, *True Stories? Documentary drama on radio, screen and stage*, (Manchester: Manchester University Press, 1990): 103. The "precedents" seen in *Smallpox 2002* and *The Day Britain Stopped* are the ways that these films refer to previous similar disasters, and the measures that were taken to deal with them. For example, in *The Day Britain Stopped*, there is frequent mention of a major train crash at Waverley, near Edinburgh. The Transport Minister, Tom Walker is seen visiting the site of this crash on 19 December 2003, and is interviewed at a later date in the film about this crash and the events of the fateful day itself. Both the Waverley crash and Tom Walker are fictional. However, the film also makes frequent mention of train crashes at Potters Bar (in Hertfordshire) and Ladbroke Grove (in West London). These crashes did actually happen. It is this mixing of fictional events and characters with actual events that "anchors" the meanings of the film, and gives them a strange power that combines mockumentary and drama-documentary. The viewer cannot help but view the conditional/fictional events in the stark light cast by those events that are a matter of historical record. Having said this, this point raises interesting issues for cross-cultural readings of such a film as *The Day Britain Stopped*: because it relies on specific cultural and topical knowledge of Britain, its power may be diminished for viewers without the requisite knowledge, and they may view the film simply as a very effective piece of drama-documentary.

17. Quoted on the BBC website relating to the production of *Smallpox 2002*, at: www.bbc.co.uk/drama/smallpox2002/making_dan.shtml.

18. Jane Roscoe and Craig Hight, *Faking It: Mock-documentary and the Subversion of Factuality*, (Manchester: Manchester University Press, 2001): 21–2, 64–7.

19. Dai Vaughan, *For Documentary: Twelve Essays*, (Berkeley and Los Angeles: University of California Press, 1999), p. 58.

20. Vivian Sobchack, "Toward a phenomenology of nonfictional film experience" in Gaines and Renov (eds.), *Collecting Visible Evidence*, p. 243.

21. *Ibid.*

22. *Ibid.*

23. Roscoe and Hight, *Faking It*, p. 53.

24. *Ibid*

25. Carroll's main point in proposing the category "films of presumptive assertion" is to counter what he sees as a lack of precision in the terms "documentary" and "nonfiction." As he correctly states, not all nonfiction films are necessarily "documentaries" (although they do, of course, "document" something): he gives the example of *Arnulf Rainer*—a flicker film—and the videotape of the Rodney King beating as examples. He also notes that Grierson's original coining of the term "the creative treatment of actuality" was to distinguish what Grierson saw as "proper" documentary practice from "lower" forms such as simple recordings of events, or lecture films. By the same token, then, Carroll looks to demarcate "films of presumptive assertion" as a subcategory within nonfictional film practice, suggesting that it is a more useful nomination than "documentary." See Noël Carroll, "Fiction, Nonfiction, and the Film of Presumptive Assertion: Conceptual Analyses" in his *Engaging the Moving Image*, (New Haven: Yale University Press, 2003), p. 193–224.

26. Indeed, there was until very recently, in Britain at least, a directive that barred *current* newsreaders from being involved in these sorts of programmes, so those from a different era would be drafted in. As Mark Lawson notes: "From the 1980s, for at least a decade, actual BBC television news anchors were banned from appearing in dramas because of fears of what management called 'brand contamination.' This meant that fictional wars, catastrophes and government sex scandals were read by former newsreaders such as Jan Leeming, Pamela Armstrong and Richard Whitmore." See "A pox on all your houses," *The Guardian*, 4 February 2002.

27. Carroll, "Nonfiction Film and Postmodernist Skepticism" in *Engaging the Moving Image*, 169.

28. It is therefore no real surprise to find that *Smallpox 2002* was produced by the BBC News and Current Affairs Unit.

29. See Brian Winston, *Lies, Damn Lies and Documentaries*, (London: BFI, 2000), for a discussion of some of these controversies.

30. See for example the online links to discussions of *Smallpox 2002* at: www.bbc.co.uk/science/hottopics/smallpox/advice.shtml (online record of a "live chat" between viewers of *Smallpox 2002* and the producer, director, and a medical expert). There were also countless examples of reviews of both *Smallpox 2002* and *The Day Britain Stopped* that reflected on the "real world" impli-

cations of these mockumentaries (much of which revolved around the "could it happen?" type questions). This sort of dialogue and debate, extending as it does beyond the viewing of the texts themselves, can only be a good thing. It should be seen as a vital part of the process, if we are to take seriously documentary's claim to make meaningful comments about the world of actuality. It is worth noting that Peter Watkins' politically-committed stance saw education, information, dialogue and debate as a crucial aspect of a mature society, and his films were meant to play a role in this. The reaction of the British Establishment to *The War Game* effectively closed down debate and dialogue, showing at one and the same time how plausible his mockumentary vision was thought to be and how interested the Establishment was in truly engaging with what the people might think.

About the Contributors

Gerd Bayer is assistant professor of languages and literatures at the University of Wisconsin–Whitewater. He is also the author of *"Greener, more mysterious processes of mind": Natur als Dichtungsprinzip bei John Fowles* (2004), as well as articles on popular culture, postcolonial literature, and contemporary fiction.

Doug Bentin works in marketing for the Metropolitan Library System in Oklahoma City during the week, but by weekend is senior film reviewer for the *Oklahoma Gazette*. He has been married for 35 years and his wife, Alice, thinks that his DVD collection has gotten dangerously out of hand. His son, Nicholas, insists that it isn't large enough — although he could do with less Lucio Fulci. Bentin is a native of San Antonio, Texas, and prefers *Man from the Alamo* to every other film that addresses the pivotal event in world history.

Mark Bould is senior lecturer in film studies at the University of the West of England. He is a co-editor of *Historical Materialism: Research in Critical Marxist Theory* and an editorial consultant for *Science Fiction Studies*. He is the author of *Film Noir: From Fritz Lang to Femme Fatale* (2005) and the co-editor of *Parietal Games* (2005), the collected essays and reviews of M. John Harrison. He is currently completing *The Cinema of John Sayles: A Lone Star* (2007).

Ian Conrich is senior lecturer in film studies at the University of Surrey Roehampton. The chair of the New Zealand Studies Association, he has contributed to *Sight and Sound, p.o.v., Cultures of the Commonwealth,* and *Anglofiles*; he is an editor of *Journal of Popular British Cinema*, and a guest editor of *Post Script,* for a special issue on Australian and New Zealand cinema. He is the co-editor of *New Zealand — A Pastoral Paradise?* (2000), *New Zealand Fictions: Literature and Film* (2004), and four books forthcoming: *The Cinema of John Carpenter: The Technique of Terror; Musical Moments: Film and the Performance of Song and Dance; Horror Zone: The Cultural Experience of Contemporary Horror Cinema,* and *Contemporary New Zealand Cinema.*

Leigh H. Edwards is assistant professor of English at Florida State University. Her current book in progress is *Reality TV's Family Values: Narrative, Ideology, and the American Family.* Her research focuses on U.S. literature and popular culture. Recent projects include an article on gender and reality TV in *Feminist Media Studies,* an article on multiculturalism and film in *Narrative,* and an upcoming book on Johnny Cash and popular music.

Jared F. Green completed his doctorate in comparative literature at Brown University in 2002 and is assistant professor of modern literature and culture at Stonehill College in Easton, Massachusetts. Recent and forthcoming publications include work on Bram Stoker, Virginia Woolf, Toni Morrison, and William Faulkner. He is currently at work on a book-length study of the role of racial science in the construction of class identity in fin-de-siècle England, entitled *White Primitives: Urban Ethnography and the Empire of the Image, 1890–1926.*

Fincina Hopgood teaches in the cinema studies program at the University of Melbourne, where she is completing her doctoral thesis on the portrayal of mental illness in contemporary Australian and New Zealand films. Fincina has contributed to a range of publications including the edited collection *Australian Film 1978–1994, Cinema Papers, Metro, Screening the Past, Ormond Papers* and *Senses of Cinema,* for which she wrote a critical essay on the films of Jane Campion.

Reynold Humphries is professor of film studies at the University of Lille and author of two books on the American films of Fritz Lang. He has recently published *The American Horror Film: An Introduction* and is the author of the forthcoming *Madness in a Social Landscape: The Hollywood Horror Film, 1931–1945.* He has contributed to the special issues of *Post Script* and *Paradoxa* devoted to the horror film and to the collective volume *Horror Zone.* His contribution to *Film Noir Reader 4* addresses the issue of the role of the Left in postwar noir, especially in the light of blacklisting. He is currently working on two books devoted to the history of Hollywood's blacklists and the films written and directed by future blacklistees.

Michael Lee is associate professor of musicology and film studies at the University of Oklahoma. His work includes research on American experimental music and genre cinema. He has written a book on film music specialist Georges Auric and is currently preparing a monograph on film composer Roy Webb's work with the Lewton Unit at RKO Pictures. He remains somewhat afraid of sea anemones.

Donald Levin is associate professor of English at Marygrove College in Detroit, where he directs the graduate English program and edits *The Maxis Review,* a literary journal. He is the author of a novel, *The House of Grins* (1992), and is widely published as a poet. Before joining academia, he was a professional writer for 25 years, including a stint with the industrial film production company that evolved from the Jam Handy Organization. He lives in Ferndale, Michigan.

Steven N. Lipkin, professor of communication, joined the faculty of Western Michigan University's School of Communication in 1981. He received the doctoral degree from the University of Iowa. Professor Lipkin's area of expertise is film studies. He has taught courses on film history, the film industry, documentary film, methods of film analysis, film and video production, and scriptwriting. His current research focuses on film and television docudrama. He has presented his research at the Society of Cinema Studies, the University Film and Video Association, and Visible Evidence conferences. His work is published in *Quarterly Review of Film and Video, Cinema Journal,* and the *Journal of Film and Video.* His book *Real Emotional Logic: Film and Television Docudrama as Persuasive Practice* was published in January 2002.

Harvey O'Brien is director of research and curriculum development at the O'Kane Centre for Film Studies, University College Dublin. He is the author of *The Real Ireland: The Evolution of Ireland in Documentary Film* (2004), and co-editor of *Keeping it Real: Irish Film and Television* (2004). He has written for such publications as *Dox, Cinéaste, Historical Journal of Film, Radio and Television, Film Ireland, Irish Studies Review, Eire-Ireland,* and *Film and Film Culture.*

Derek Paget is visiting research fellow in the department of film, theatre and television at the University of Reading, UK. Formerly a theatre worker, he is the author of two books on docudrama—*True Stories?: Documentary Drama on Radio, Screen and Stage* (1990) and *No Other Way to Tell It: Dramadoc/docudrama on Television* (1998)—and has written extensively on this subject in collections and in periodicals. He also researches and writes on documentary theatre. He is currently working on a second edition of *No Other Way to Tell It* for publication in 2005 and researching the docu-opera and docu-musical.

Gary D. Rhodes is a documentary film-maker who has directed *Solo Flight* (1992), *Fiddlin' Man* (1994), *Lugosi: Hollywood's Dracula* (1997), and *Banned in Oklahoma* (2004). He has also directed such fictional films as *Wit's End* (2004) and the mockumentary *Chair* (2000). Rhodes is also the author of over 200 film essays and articles since 1986, as well as books like *Lugosi* (1997) and *White Zombie: Anatomy of a Horror Film* (2000). His upcoming works include a book on silent film star Alma Rubens. He is an assistant professor at the University of Oklahoma film and video studies program.

Jane Roscoe is the founding head of the Centre for Screen Studies and Research at the Australian Film, Television and Radio School, Sydney, Australia. She has been a senior screen and media academic in the UK, New Zealand and Australia. She is the author of *Documentary in New Zealand: An Immigrant Nation* (1999), and co-author (with Craig Hight) of *Faking It: Mock-Documentary and the Subversion of Factuality* (2001).

Robert Sickels earned his Ph.D. in English at the University of Nevada, Reno. He is currently associate professor of American film and popular culture at Whitman College in Walla Walla, Washington, where he teaches courses on film genres, major figures in cinema, and digital production. In addition to writing *Popular Culture Through History: The 1940s* (2004), he has published numerous articles in a variety of journals, including *The Journal of Popular Culture*, *Journal of Popular Film & Television*, and *Critique: Studies in Contemporary Fiction*.

Roy Smith is principal lecturer in international studies and co-director of the Centre for Asia-Pacific Studies at Nottingham Trent University. He has written for *World Today* and *Security Dialogue* and is the author of *The Nuclear-Free and Independent Pacific Movement: After Moruroa* (1997); the co-author of *Diseases of Globalisation: Socio-Economic Transition and Health* (2001); and a contributor to *Globalisation: Theory and Practice* (1996) and *Contemporary New Zealand Cinema* (forthcoming).

John Parris Springer is the director of film studies at the University of Central Oklahoma, where he is also an assistant professor in the department of English. Working from a cultural studies perspective, his research focuses upon the multiple intersections between print and visual media in twentieth century American culture. He is the author of *Hollywood Fictions: The Dream Factory in American Popular Literature* (2000) as well as essays and reviews for such journals as *Genre*, *Iris*, and *Literature/Film Quarterly*.

Wayne Stein teaches at the University of Central Oklahoma on such topics as kung fu films, cyberpunk film and literature, and anime and manga. His areas of interest are Asian cinema, Asian pop culture, and Asian American literature. While working on a book about hybridity in martial arts films involving eastern and western films, he is also sponsor of the Budo and Buddhist Societies at his campus.

Paul Ward is lecturer in film and television studies at Brunel University, UK. His main teaching and research interests are animation and documentary, particularly the relationship between animated and live action media, and new and hybrid modes of documentary practice. His work has appeared in *Animation Journal*, *Scope: An Online Journal of Film Studies* and various anthologies. He is currently completing a book on documentary films and editing a special animation-related edition of the online journal EnterText (http://www.brunel.ac.uk/faculty/arts/EnterText/). He can be contacted at paul.ward@brunel.ac.uk

Index

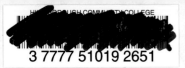